THE FUTURE OF SOCIAL DEMOCRACY

THE
FUTURE
OF
SOCIAL
DEMOCRACY

*Problems and Prospects of Social Democratic Parties
in Western Europe*

edited by

WILLIAM E. PATERSON

and

ALASTAIR H. THOMAS

CLARENDON PRESS · OXFORD
1986

Oxford University Press, Walton Street, Oxford OX2 6DP
Oxford New York Toronto
Delhi Bombay Calcutta Madras Karachi
Kuala Lumpur Singapore Hong Kong Tokyo
Nairobi Dar es Salaam Cape Town
Melbourne Auckland
and associated companies in
Beirut Berlin Ibadan Nicosia

Oxford is a trade mark of Oxford University Press

Published in the United States
by Oxford University Press, New York

British Library Cataloguing in Publication Data
The Future of local democracy: problems
and prospects of social democratic
parties in Western Europe.
1. Socialist parties—Europe
I. Paterson, William E. II. Thomas, Alastair H.
324.24'072 JN94.A979
ISBN 0–19–876169–4
ISBN 0–19–876168–6 Pbk

Set by The Castlefield Press, Wellingborough
Printed in Great Britain
at the University Printing House, Oxford
by David Stanford
Printer to the University

PREFACE

IN 1976, impressed by the absence of a serious study of Social Democratic Parties in Western Europe, we edited a volume of original essays under this title which was published the following year (Paterson and Thomas, 1977). We included much material on the history of the parties and their political and institutional settings, together with a collection of statistical data on party membership, since our intention then was to produce a source of reference and a basis from which comparative inferences might be drawn. That intention has been justified by the reference made to it by authors such as Merkl (1980), Daalder and Mair (1983), and von Beyme (1985). It also proved to be a model for Zig Layton-Henry in his production of his work on Conservative Parties (1983), and to Emil Kirchner for his forthcoming book on Liberal Parties.

Recent times have seen dramatic changes in the internal and external circumstances of the major parties covered by the 1977 volume. In France the Parti Socialiste has been swept into presidential and governmental office, but has also begun to show signs of ennui as the cares of office have mounted. In Sweden the social democrats returned to power in 1982, but wielded it without the assurance displayed in their heyday. In Norway, Denmark, and West Germany, however, social democractic parties are no longer in office after the long periods in the middle of the twentieth century when they were able to set their stamp on social conditions in their respective countries. In Britain the Labour Party lost office and the break-away by the Social Democratic Party, and its alliance with the Liberals, threatens to break the two-party mould into which British party politics was cast some sixty years ago.

As a political force social democracy has been under challenge since its inception, from its conservative and liberal opponents on the right and from its socialist and communist rivals on the left. By the late 1960s, the view was widespread that social democracy had outlived these challenges. The social democratic paradigm of commitment to political liberalism, the welfare state, the mixed economy managed on Keynesian principles, and the gradual transformation of society in an egalitarian direction seemed more likely than its rivals to provide the basis for a widely shared consensus. Social Democratic parties benefited from the trend towards secularization which hit the right and the continued prosperity and social peace over much of Western Europe which undermined the appeal of the communist left. The growth in public expenditure fostered by social democratic governments created a new public sector bureaucracy which, unlike the traditional bourgeoisie, was prepared to support social democratic parties.

The apparent inevitability of a social democratic future met new and serious challenges in the 1970s. Conceptions of economic policy-making which assume that each national economy is susceptible to domestic management have had to be revised in the face of volatile oil prices, recession in international trade, a record US balance of payments deficit, and alarming pressures on the policies of full employment which were central to the social democratic consensus. Electors became increasingly resistant to financing the high levels of taxation which are an essential concomitant of social democratic welfare and employment policies. Social democratic parties were also challenged by a new focus on environmental questions in the 1970s which appeared to undermine some of the growth assumptions of social democracy. The US 'twin-track' strategy of installing medium-range nuclear weapons in Western Europe, intended as a means of encouraging the USSR to negotiate the reduction of their own such forces, gave rise to rapidly expanding peace movements which bore witness to a widely shared concern that such a strategy was far more likely to have the contrary effect. The difficulty of developing a coherent response to these challenges led to a tension between 'the politics of support' and 'the politics of power', between policies acceptable to party members and policies required to sustain social democratic parties in power.

All these considerations indicate that the time is ripe for a second look at social democracy. The present volume therefore focuses attention on the issues just outlined, offering a more interpretive review than before of the problems associated with the social democratic paradigm and the prospects of the political parties, whether socialist, social democratic, or labour, which seek to attain governmental power in order to implement social democratic policies.

Initial discussion of many of the themes included here was greatly assisted by a conference held in the Centre for European

Governmental Studies at the University of Edinburgh in September 1982. We are grateful to Professor Malcolm Anderson of the Department of Politics, Edinburgh University, for making this possible, to the University Association for Contemporary European Studies, and to Eva Evans, the tirelessly helpful secretary of UACES.

As editors, we are grateful to those who have contributed chapters, as well as to Ivon Asquith, Andrew Schuller, Nina Curtis and their OUP colleagues, for their knowledge, care, and patience. We also thank the anonymous readers for OUP for suggestions which contributed to the final shape of the volume.

Our wives, Phyllis Paterson and Janet Thomas, gave us the encouragement, support, and much else besides, without which the completion of this project would have been far less easily attained. Alastair Thomas also remembers Hugh O. Thomas (1899–1984) with gratitude for his continuing support, interest, and encouragement over a lifetime.

CONTENTS

LIST OF TABLES AND FIGURES

Tables

Figures

LIST OF CONTRIBUTORS

DR PETER BYRD is a Lecturer in Politics at the University of Warwick. He has written articles on the British Labour Party, the peace movement, and British defence policy. He is a co-author of *The Making of Foreign Policy: A Comparative Perspective* (1985).

BYRON CRIDDLE is Senior Lecturer in Politics at the University of Aberdeen. During 1984–5 he was visiting Professor in the Department of Political Science at the University of Massachusetts. His many publications on French electoral politics include *Socialists and European Integration: A Study of the French Socialist Party* (1969), and *The French Socialist Party: Resurgence and Victory* (1984).

DR HENRY DRUCKER is Senior Lecturer in Politics at the University of Edinburgh. His publications include *The Scottish Labour Party* (1977), *Doctrine and Ethos in the Labour Party* (1978), *Multi-Party Britain* (editor, 1979), *J. P. Mackintosh on Scotland* (1982) and *Developments in British Politics* (co-editor, 1983).

DR KEVIN FEATHERSTONE is a Lecturer in Political Studies at the University of Stirling. He is preparing a study entitled *Socialist Parties and European Integration: A Comparative History* (Manchester University Press, forthcoming) and has published articles on West European politics, Greece, and the European Community.

DR DAVID HINE is Tutorial Fellow and Lecturer in Politics, Christ Church, Oxford. Until 1985 he was a Lecturer in Politics at the University of Newcastle-upon-Tyne. He has published numerous articles on Italian party politics and electoral behaviour, European social democracy, party organization, and comparative party systems. His books on the Italian Socialist Party and on the Italian Political System are about to be published.

DR WILLIAM E. PATERSON is Reader in Politics at the University of Warwick. His numerous publications include *Social Democracy in Post-War Europe*, with Ian Campbell (1974), *The SPD and*

European Integration (1974), *Social and Political Movements in Western Europe* (co-edited with Martin Kolinsky, 1976), *Social Democratic Parties in Western Europe* (co-edited with Alastair Thomas, 1977), *Foreign Policy-Making in Western Europe* (co-edited with William Wallace, 1978), *The German Model: Perspectives on a Stable State* (co-editor with Gordon Smith, 1981), and a number of books and contributions in German. His book with Simon Bulmer on *West German Interests and the Community* will be published in 1986.

DR MELANIE A. SULLY is a Senior Lecturer at North Staffordshire Polytechnic, where she has taught History since 1972. Her publications include *Political Parties and Elections in Austria* (Hurst, 1981), and *Continuity and Change in Austrian Socialism* (Columbia, 1982).

ALASTAIR H. THOMAS is Head of the Division of Political Science in Lancashire Polytechnic at Preston. With William E. Paterson he edited *Social Democratic Parties in Western Europe* (1977). He is also the author, with Neil Elder and David Arter, of *The Consensual Democracies? The Government and Politics of the Scandinavian States* (1982) and of articles on political parties and coalition politics in Scandinavia.

DR DOUGLAS WEBBER is a Research Fellow studying government–industry relations in the School of Social Sciences at the University of Sussex. He has published articles on West German, West European, British, and New Zealand politics and is the co-author, with J. J. Richardson, Jeremy Moon, and Martin Rhodes, of *Information Technology and the State*: a comparative analysis of public policies in Britain, France, the Federal Republic of Germany, and Sweden (forthcoming).

ABBREVIATIONS

AC	Akademikernes Centralorganisation, Danish confederation of professional associations
ACUS	Austrian church–socialist organization
ADF	Aktion Demokratischer Fortschritt, Action for Democratic Progress (West Germany)
AES	Alternative Economic Strategy (proposed by the British Labour Party)
AFA	Arbeitsgemeinschaft für Arbeitnehmerfragen, Working Group for Employees Affairs (West Germany)
AFP	the Swedish national basic pension scheme
AL	Alternative List
ALÖ	Alternative List Österreich, alternative list (of election candidates) in Austria
APO	Ausserparliamentarische Opposition, extra-parliamentary opposition (West Germany)
ASTMS	Association of Scientific, Technical and Managerial Staffs (Great Britain)
ATP	the national supplementary pension scheme in Denmark and Sweden
AUEW	Amalgamated Union of Engineering Workers (Great Britain)
CDU	Christlich-Demokratische Union, Christian Democratic Union (West Germany)
CERES	Centre d'études, de recherches et d'éducation socialiste, Centre for Socialist Studies, Research, and Education, a group on the left wing of the French Socialist Party
CFDT	Confédération Française et Démocratique du Travail, the French socialist confederation of trade unions
CGT	Confédération Générale du Travail, the French communist confederation of trade unions
CLP	Constituency Labour Party (Great Britain)
CLPD	Campaign for Labour Party Democracy (Great Britain)
CLV	Campaign for Labour Victory (Great Britain)
CND	Campaign for Nuclear Disarmament (United

Kingdom)

CO:I Statstjenestemændenes Centralorganisation I, the central organization of senior civil servants in Denmark

CSU Christlich-Soziale Union, Christian Social Union (Bavaria, West Germany)

DGB Deutscher Gewerkschaftsbund, (West) German Trade Union Federation

DKP Deutsche Kommunistische Partei, the (West) German Communist Party, reformed in 1968

EC European Community

ECSC European Coal and Steel Community

EDC European Defence Community

EEC European Economic Community

EEPTU Electrical Electronic Telecommunication Union, Plumbing Trades Union (Great Britain)

EFTA European Free Trade Area

EMS European Monetary System

FDP Freie Demokratische Partei, the West German Free Democratic (liberal) Party

FEN (French schoolteachers' union)

FPÖ Freiheitliche Partei Österreichs, the Freedom ('liberal') Party of Austria

FR Hovedorganisation for Arbejdsleder- og Tekniske Funktionærforeninger i Danmark, the federation of foremen's and technicians' unions

FTF Fællesråd for danske Tjenestemands- og Funktion-ærorganisationer, Federation of Danish Civil Servants' and Salaried Employees' Organizations

GDR German Democratic Republic (East Germany)

GLC Greater London Council

IMF International Monetary Fund

INF Intermediate Nuclear Force talks

ITP salaried employees' complementary pension plan in Sweden

KPD Kommunistische Partei Deutschlands, the Communist Party of Germany (1920–53)

KPÖ Kommunistische Partei Österreichs, the Austrian Communist Party

LCC Labour Co-ordinating Committee (Great Britain)

LO	Landsorganisationen, the trade union federation in, respectively, Denmark and Sweden
NATO	North Atlantic Treaty Organization
NEB	National Enterprise Board (United Kingdom)
NEC	National Executive Committee (of the British Labour Party)
NNFZ	Nordic Nuclear-weapon-free Zone
NUM	National Union of Mineworkers (Great Britain)
NUPE	National Union of Public Employees (Great Britain)
NUR	National Union of Railwaymen (Great Britain)
OECD	Organization for Economic Co-operation and Development
ÖGB	Österreichischer Gewerkschaftsbund, the Austrian Trade Union Federation
ÖVP	Österreichische Volkspartei, the Austrian People's Party (conservative with Christian Social origins)
PASOK	the Pan-Hellenic Socialist Movement
PCF	Parti communiste française, the French communist party
PS	Parti Socialiste, the Socialist Party in France
PSB/BSP	Parti Socialiste Belge/Belgische Socialistische Partij, the Belgian Socialist Party
PSI	Partita Socialista Italiano, the Italian Socialist Party
PSOE	Partido Socialista Obrero Español, the Spanish Socialist Workers' Party
PSP	Partido Socialista Português, the Portuguese Socialist Party
PvdA	Partij van der Arbeid, the Labour Party of the Netherlands
RPR	Rassamblement pour la République, the French Gaullist movement
SAF	Svenska Arbetsgivareföreningen, the Swedish Employers' Confederation
SAP	Socialistisk Arbeiderparti, the Socialist Labour Party (Sweden)
SD	Socialdemokratiet, the Danish Social Democratic Party
SDP	Social Democratic Party (Great Britain)
SDS	Sozialistischer Deutscher Studentenbund, the Socialist German Student Federation, the SPD student organization expelled from the party in 1960

SED	Sozialistische Einheitspartei Deutschlands, Socialist Unity Party (East Germany)
SFIO	Section Française de l'Internationale Ouvrière, the French Socialist Party, 1905–69
SIF	the Swedish union of general workers
SLP	Scottish Labour Party
SNP	Scottish National Party
SPD	Sozialdemokratische Partei Deutschlands, the Social Democratic Party of (West) Germany
SPÖ	Sozialistische Partei Österreichs, the Socialist Party of Austria
START	Strategic Arms Reduction Talks
STP	manual workers' complementary pensions plan in Sweden
T & G TGWU	Transport and General Workers' Union (Great Britain)
TUC	Trades Union Congress (Great Britain)
TULV	Trade Unions for a Labour Victory (Great Britain)
UDF	Union pour la démocratie Française, a French party of the centre
USDAW	Union of Shop, Distributive and Allied Workers (Great Britain)
VGÖ	Vereinte Grünen Österreichs, United Greens of Austria

1

Introduction

William E. Paterson and Alastair H. Thomas

The Historical Development of Social Democracy

MOST political concepts change their meaning over time, and social democracy is no exception. In the struggle to replace autocracy by democracy in the nineteenth century, 'social democratic' was the label used to describe those who were in favour of socialism and democracy. It was essentially a way of distinguishing between the minority of democrats who were also socialists and the majority of democrats who were not. Marx and Lassalle were united in this usage of the term, if in little else.

The essentials of social democracy at this time have been encapsulated by Anton Pelinka (1983: 3):

Social democracy was . . . geared to a relatively common goal: consummation of political democracy, fundamental restructuring of the economy, and the establishment of international solidarity. Social democracy was the antithesis of the remnants of political absolutism, of the principles of mature capitalism, and of the egoism of nation states.

The outbreak of war in 1914 destroyed this 'heile Welt' (perfect world) for ever, since the fragility of the commitment to these ideas was demonstrated by the way in which social democrats in all the belligerent countries ignored international solidarity in favour of the claims of patriotism and national solidarity (including solidarity with the hitherto reviled capitalists). It also brought about the collapse of the Tzarist autocracy and the triumph of the Bolshevist revolution in Russia. This led to a split of the socialist movement between those who were prepared to accept Leninist principles and the discipline of the Comintern, and those who insisted on the democratic character of socialism. Henceforward 'social democracy' was used to identify socialists who were committed to democracy in the liberal representative sense. One group of socialists, the communists, were organized in the Communist International, and the social democrats were organized in the Second International. An attempt by the Austrians to found an International which would steer a middle way was short-lived.

The 1930s were a very difficult decade for social democracy. The onset of the world depression after 1929 undermined the strength of the trade unions, and the Nazi take-over in Germany meant the virtual destruction of social democracy there. The rise of fascism led to a playing-down of the distinctive identity of social democracy, as social democrats worked together with other groups in anti-fascist alliances to try and prevent the spread of fascism in Spain and elsewhere.

The major, and ultimately very significant, exception to this picture of unrelieved gloom was in Scandinavia, where the foundations of a period of social democratic hegemony were established on the basis of agreements with non-socialist parties: in Denmark with the Radical Liberals, in a coalition which, in a decade of co-operation, laid the foundation for the welfare state; and in Sweden with the Agrarians, in a red–green alliance which began their unbroken 44-year period of office. In Norway the Labour Party never shared power in cabinet, although since the start of its period of predominance in 1935 it has had to rely on parliamentary support from other parties from time to time. Following the demand-management policies of Wicksell and the Stockholm School, the Scandinavian social democrats were successful in combating the worst ravages of unemployment. It had been the failure of the British and German social democrats, wedded as their leaders were to classical economic doctrines, to deal with unemployment in the face of the world recession which had undermined both their support and their self-image. The Scandinavian experience of the 1930s and 1940s was crucial to the modern conception of social democracy. It involved a reduction in class conflict and an accommodation between capital and labour on the basis of a profound extension of social citizenship and welfare rights and, perhaps most importantly of all, a shared commitment to full employment.

In the immediate aftermath of the Second World War, in a climate of deepening tension between East and West, social democracy was again generally identified with a commitment to western representative parliamentary institutions. This commitment was very forcibly expressed in the founding declaration of the

Socialist International in Frankfurt in 1951. It was also expressed in the readiness of parties which were committed to social democracy to support the collective defence of the West. A major cleavage emerged at this time between social democrats who were prepared to accept the protection and the obligations entailed in membership of the North Atlantic Treaty Organization and other socialists who were not.

This bedrock conception of social democracy, which stressed what social democrats had in common with other liberal democrats, ran parallel to and was eventually incorporated in a view of social democracy initially identified with Scandinavia, but which later came to dominate the concept of social democracy more widely. The latter view has been brilliantly summarized by Mark Kesselman (1982; 402) as follows:

First, an acceptance of a capitalist economy is coupled with extensive state intervention to counteract uneven development. Second, Keynesian steering mechanisms are used to achieve economic growth, high wages, price stability and full employment. Third, state policies redistribute the economic surplus in progressive ways, through welfare programs, social insurance and tax laws. And, finally, the working class is organised in a majority-bent social democratic party closely linked to a powerful centralised, disciplined trade union movement.

This new concept of social democracy which, because of its stress on the accommodation between capital and labour was often called 'revisionism', found its most popular and influential expression in the writings of Anthony Crosland, especially in *The Future of Socialism* (1956). The basic tenets which Crosland subscribed to were five. They were: political liberalism, the mixed economy, the welfare state, Keynesian economics, and a belief in equality. The widespread adoption of this conception of social democracy was made possible by a number of converging historical developments. The developing Cold War and the extinction of parliamentary socialism in Czechoslovakia reinforced the existing commitment to political liberalism.

The influence of Keynesian economics and the mixed economy as defining characteristics of post-war social democracy was a more complicated process. Keynesianism was oriented towards the solution of the unemployment problem which had plagued the 1930s. It envisaged a role both for the market and the state, with the state's function being to intervene where lack of demand threatened to cause unemployment. It was essentially a strategy designed to cope with the inherent tendency of capitalism to go through a cycle of boom and slump. Its attraction for social democrats was its promise of full employment. In return for this, social democratic parties accepted the essentials of capitalism and continued private control of the economy. For its part, capital had to accept a degree of state intervention, both in the overall management of the economy and in the control of the process of the distribution of wealth. Not surprisingly, capital was most willing to do this where it was faced by a strong and united labour movement, as in Scandinavia and Britain.

The adoption of the mixed economy as desirable objective rather than as regrettable necessity was based on the assumption that demand-management techniques had removed mass unemployment, the most unacceptable feature of capitalism. It is in its adoption of the mixed economy that social democracy can most plausibly be viewed as 'reform or managed capitalism'. The more distinctively socialist components of the Croslandite conception of social democracy were contained in the commitment to the extension of the welfare state and the belief in equality. The extension of welfare rights was a function of the belief in equality and was designed to be part of a transformation from which the less privileged sections of society would benefit disproportionately. The belief in equality was more than a belief in equality-of-opportunity or of citizenship rights. There was a commitment to redistribution of income, even if this proved very difficult to operationalize.

Underlying this complex of policies was a set of assumptions about the desirability and practicality of economic growth. It was the assumption of growth that made the accommodation between capital and labour possible. With growth it was possible to envisage a continuous increase in welfare spending and the incomes of working class people without either having to raise income tax to punitive levels or to reduce the real living standards of the middle and property-owning class. It thus promised to be a successful electoral strategy, if only growth could be achieved and sustained.

There were three significant trends across European societies in the 1950s and 1960s which served to bolster the chances of social democracy. The first and most striking was the long and sustained period of economic growth, a period without parallel in European history in its scale of expansion. This long period of boom appeared to undermine the Marxist and strengthen the Croslandite conception of the proper strategy for socialists.

This period of economic boom was associated with a long period of reduced class conflict. This again served to weaken the attraction for European socialists of the Marxist analysis. The prevailing temper is very well summarized in the famous passage from Seymour Martin Lipset's *Political Man* (1959: 406):

The fundamental political problems of the industrial revolution have been solved: the workers have achieved industrial and political citizenship; the conservatives have accepted the welfare state, and the democratic left has recognised that an increase in overall state power carries with it more dangers to freedom than solutions for economic problems.

The third main trend of the 1950s and 1960s was the steady reduction in the size of the manual working class, the traditional core clientele of the social democratic parties. This decline was balanced by a steady growth in the service sector. In particular, there were new jobs for the sons and daughters of working-class homes, who found careers opening up in education, the new technologies, and the caring professions in the expanding public service sector. These developments encouraged West European social democratic parties to move away from a more or less exclusive orientation towards the industrial worker and turn instead to a 'people's party model': a catch-all party which sought to attract voters not adherents, and which attempted to make some appeal to all strata of society. This concept was most successful in Austria and West Germany, but it affected all the parties to some degree. In the British Labour Party, for example, Anthony Crosland suggested that the manual worker's 'cloth-cap' image of the British Labour Party was socially inappropriate and that the party should seek to build a new identity as a 'people's party'.

These three trends acted to undermine strategies of class conflict and encouraged accommodation with capitalism. This initially helped the conservative adversaries of the social democrats, but these developments were compatible with the assumptions of social democracy and reinforced its ascendancy among the European left. The changes in class structure, the spread of prosperity, and the decline in class conflict led social democrats to further weaken the class nature of their approval and to play down the role of ideology. This development, which reached its apogee in the Bad Godesberg Programme of the SPD in 1959, was paralleled by similar developments in other European social democratic parties.

Intellectually social democracy was dominant in these years. Marxism was apparently discredited by its identification with the Soviet Union and by the developments in Western Europe outlined above. Liberalism was widely believed to be outmoded. Conservatism found fewer intellectual adherents in a period of very rapid social and demographic change—change which appeared to be moving in the social democratic direction of managed capitalism. Social democracy appeared to be a doctrine which was in tune with modern realities in its acceptance of capitalism, while yet retaining a powerful undercurrent of idealistic appeal in its commitment to redistribution and equality.

Electorally the success of social democracy was more uneven, reflecting the differing stages of economic and political development in Western Europe. By the late 1960s, however, there seemed to be a fairly steady trend in favour of social democrats, referred to in the Federal Republic as the *Genosse* (comrade) trend. Politics was not as polarized as at some points in the past, but class continued to play a dominant role in structuring voting preferences in the advanced industrial societies of Western Europe. Indeed, there appeared to be some force in the argument that as other cleavages such as the urban/rural and religious became less important, class become more salient than in the past. This is the paradox to which Butler and Stokes (1969: 116) drew attention: 'the intensity of the class tie may have declined at the same time as its extent became more universal.' The process in which people in Western Europe moved from rural agricultural jobs to places in industrial and unionized factories was one which appeared to promise continual gains for social democracy. This picture of electoral advance was apparently well founded. By the early 1970s social democratic participation in the governments of Western Europe was very high. But this high level of governmental participation at that time proved to have fateful consequences for social democracy later.

The collapse of the social democratic paradigm: from 'wave of the future' to 'the future that does not work'

> The end of the historical strength of this (the social democratic) consensus is in sight. The social democratic syndrome of values has not only ceased to promote change and new developments, but it has begun to produce its own contradictions, and it can no longer deal with them effectively. . . . The right-wing social democrats who administer power are sad creatures because it is so obvious that they represent yesterday's world (Dahrendorf, 1980: 106–7).

There is general agreement that social democracy, in the Croslandite sense in which we have been using it, lost its intellectual coherence and force sometime in the 1970s. Indeed, Crosland himself commented that 'the party is over'. Arguments abound as to the exact date and cause of death, but there is little argument about the demise of the particular version of social democracy that had dominated the previous two decades; even when social democratic parties themselves had not been in power, social democratic ideas and policies had often been put into practice by their political opponents, and in the end this contributed to their discredit.

The intellectual problems associated with the social democratic paradigm led to a loss of ascendency over other ideologies as social democracy came increasingly under critical fire from both left and right. Initially this was not reflected in poor electoral performances by social democratic parties, but rather in the increasing difficulty the parties experienced in attempting to put their ideas into practice.

The difficulties they encountered in government are sometimes explained solely in terms of the oil-price rise of 1973–4 and its effect on world trade and government budgets. The 1973 oil crisis, in its check on economic growth, significantly impaired the ability of governments to put Keynesian policies into effect; but problems and difficulties with the Keynesian perspective had been building up even before 1973.

The most obvious problem with Keynesianism was its apparently inherent impetus towards the growth of government expenditure and inflation. The ineluctable growth in state expenditure had various roots. Keynesianism assumed that demand could be controlled rationally. Given the commitment to full employment, however, there was no obvious constraint on wage demands by unions, whether or not they had an inflationary effect.

Keynesian politics assume two things: that governments have enough autonomy to be able to act rationally, and that there is enough of a market for market manipulation to work. They can break down if either of these assumptions is false. Either powerful interests can distort the making of policy, or they can have enough independence from market forces to disregard policy which does not suit them. In practice both occur, to produce a malign interaction. Powerful trade unions can price products and labour out of competitive international markets. Business and unions can then force governments afraid of industrial collapse to subsidise unemployment. Thus a trade union induced inflation can trigger off a demand inflation as governments try to save industries and jobs (Skidelsky 1979: 67–8).

Social democratic governments tried to get round this problem by attempting to make unions responsible. This was usually done by offering them some wider bargain in return for wage restraint. By the 1970s, as increasing numbers of workers had come to enjoy an affluent consumer-centred existence and were also increasingly subject to higher marginal rates of taxation, it proved more and more difficult to get trade unions to accept income restraint.

The rational basis of Keynesian income policy had been further eroded by the imperatives of electoral competition. Governments had found it easier to stimulate demand and to increase welfare entitlements than to raise the level of tax. This could be sustained in a period of continuous growth but caused enormous problems once there was any check to growth (Brittan, 1975).

Finally there was the problem of what Rose and Peters (1977: 647) called 'the inertia claims of public spending'.

The costs of public policy do not reflect the current claims of the day, but past decisions. They are commitments embodied in laws authorising and requiring government to spend annually for stated purposes. . . . Any newly elected government is immediately committed to them, unless it wishes to risk the political odium of replacing measures providing benefits that millions of citizens have come to expect.

The strains apparent in the Keynesian solution to the management of the economy were of themselves very damaging to the concept of social democracy. Damage to this central conception coincided with a wide range of attacks on nearly all its other central assumptions and concepts. This represented a significant reverse because the most striking feature of social democracy in the 1960s had been its intellectual ascendancy over rival doctrines of the left and right.

The attack on growth

Growth was and remains a central assumption of the social democratic approach. Thus the check to growth due to the recession that followed the oil price rise seriously threatened the social democratic consensus. Moreover the very idea of growth started to come under sustained intellectual attack. A whole stream of books and articles, the most influential of which was The Club of Rome's *The Limits of Growth* (Meadows *et al.*, 1972), focused attention on the finite nature of the earth's resources and the implications that continued growth would have for their exhaustion.

The criticisms of the Club of Rome were very widely read and even more widely diffused. A slightly later attack by Fred Hirsch (1977) in his *Social Limits to Growth* reached a much smaller audience but nevertheless made a significant dent in what had been up to then the imposing intellectual edifice of Croslandite social democracy. Hirsch argued that the limits to growth were not just physical but also social. The social limits to growth . . . are bound up with the idea of positional goods. 'Positional goods are those which cannot be distributed more widely or more equally by the echelon advance or trickle-down effect without altering their value as goods. The paradigm case of a positional good is standing on tiptoe in order to see something better.' (Plant in Ellis and Kumar 1983: 47–8.) This argument had a number of direct implications for the Croslandite view. If we take a central policy area like education, we find that it loses its value as a commodity to the extent that more people possess it. This means that conflict between groups can never be eliminated even in a period of growth because there are inherent conflicts about distribution, what Hirsch called 'the distributional compulsion'. In a period without growth the conflict is, of course, very much heightened and questions arise as to the realizability of the Crosland type of democracy.

The attack on bureaucracy

The realization of social democractic goals in the economy,

education, and social welfare involved the creation of large bureaucracies. As we have seen earlier, one effect of this was the creation of reservoirs of potential support for social democratic parties among the personnel thus employed. In the 1970s the bureaucratic element of social democratic policies began to be widely perceived as a major drawback. Much of the criticism came from the left. From the late 1960s onwards this was expressed in a renewed emphasis on devolving power to 'the grass roots', on giving people control of their own industrial and political environment. This pressure was immeasurably strengthened by the enthusiasm for participatory democracy engendered by the 'movement of 1968' which grew out of 'the events' of that year in France but spread in one form or another to almost all West European countries.

The large state bureaucracies were also a target for attack from the right, whose solution was to restore the authority of the market. While the left proposed democratizing the bureaucracies, the right advocated breaking them up altogether, and letting the market allocate resources. The relevance of this threat to social democracy was dramatically illustrated by the success of Mogens Glistrup's Progress Party, which came from nowhere to gain 16 per cent of the vote (so becoming the second largest party) in the Danish election of 1973.

The attack on the welfare state

Once questions were raised about taxation and bureaucracy it was not long before the welfare state itself came under attack. Since Bismarck in Germany and Lloyd George in Britain there had been a steady extension of social insurance, replacing the limited security offered by trade unions or friendly societies with universal and uniform coverage backed by the state. Indeed, Crosland had argued persuasively that the socialist objective of greater social equality and a more compassionate and just society could be achieved through the managed economy and social welfare.

From the viewpoint of the new right, social welfare blocked the way to economic recovery and a prosperous market economy. The welfare principle of universality was therefore replaced by a principle of selectivity which conveniently also provided a justification for reducing the proportion of the populations covered and the rates of benefit paid, while requiring those citizens who could afford to do so to supplement state provision by resorting to the financial services provided by the private sector.

Principled arguments in favour of the welfare state were sometimes accompanied by the adversarial arguments of those who were simply opposed to any government of which they were not a part, and sometimes by the arguments of those whose jobs were to deliver the benefits and services which it was proposed to cut. There were also problems in opposing the rationalization of a structure which had grown by a process of accretion and had failed to adapt as rapidly as necessary to changes in the normal structure. Esping-Andersen (1978), in an interesting comparison of party policy and party decomposition in Denmark and Sweden, has even argued that the much heavier losses to left and right suffered during the 1970s by the Danish social democrats by comparison with their Swedish counterparts may be the consequence of his finding that the Danish welfare state model lies much closer to Crosland's than does the Swedish. He concludes that 'for the Danish Social Democratic party the realization of the modern welfare state appears to have decomposed the party rather than class inequalities' (p. 56).

To Marxists and other radicals the idea of bringing about structural change through the agency of the liberal state was unrealistic: mass unemployment, cuts in social expenditure, and tax concessions to the rich, they argued, were a reminder that 'welfare' was only tolerable as long as it did not interfere with the logic of production. Whether viewed from right or left, in short, the legitimacy of the welfare state, like that of Keynesianism, has been weakened intellectually and morally.

A defence of the welfare state, in Mishra's view, can be mounted on several grounds. First, public support for state-provided services remains high in capitalist democracies, and governments are seen as responsible for maintaining full employment and general conditions of equity. Second, the recession, the fiscal crisis, and other problems of the welfare state have also shown the importance of economic and social security and prosperity to the mass of voters. So a basis remains on which to rebuild the legitimacy of the welfare state, and his preference is to structure it on a corporatist base, since this would extend the notion of collective responsibility for system maintenance by involving those with most economic power in collective decision-making. The chances of success are likely to be improved when it is recognized, from the experience accumulated

over 30 years, that expectations of changing the nature of income
distribution through a sharply progressive system of taxation and
free social services have not been realized. In Austria, for example,
there was a tacit understanding that the respective shares of capital
and labour were not a subject of bargaining and that the social
consensus was based on a recognition of this point.

The corporatist welfare state . . . is not much concerned with equality.
Rather it is concerned with enhancing economic and social welfare
simultaneously . . . and ensuring that national minima are maintained and
improved. This is not to say that the pursuit of equality (in its various
aspects) cannot be carried on in conjunction with the structures and
institutions of welfare. But it must be borne in mind that that objective is
extraneous to the corporate welfare state (Mishra, 1984: 172).

The Revival of Marxism

In the two decades after the war social democracy was faced by an
intellectually moribund Marxism. A striking feature of the period
since the mid-1960s has been the recovery of the intellectual vitality
of the Marxist tradition. This revival led to the renewed critique by
Marxists of social democracy. Many of the criticisms repeated the
old clichés, that social democracy is simply a snare and delusion
calculated to encourage false consciousness and to undermine the
propensity of the working class to smash capitalism. There was also
a great deal written on the alleged failure of redistribution under
social-democratic governments. The most interesting and
influential attack, however, was contained in James O'Connor's
The Fiscal Crisis of the State (1973). O'Connor's central argument is
summarized by Skidelsky (1979: 78) as follows:

The growth of monopoly capitalism intensifies the tendency to over-
production, leading to unemployment and crisis. To legitimise capitalist
relations the state has to plug this growing gap by increasing state
expenditure, hence the 'warfare-welfare' state. Since this spending is
unproductive of further revenues, the budget deficit tends to grow.

The fiscal crisis thus arises as a result of the irreconcilable demands
of monopoly capital and of the surplus population on the state.
Clearly, if O'Connor is correct, then the social democratic formula
of accommodation with capitalism is illusory. Although a great deal
of scepticism is in order in relation to his prognosis about the

establishment of socialism, there is little doubt that his diagnosis of the narrowing margins available to the state has been very influential and has weakened intellectual support for social democracy.

In the preceding sections we have argued that during the 1970s the intellectual ascendancy of social democracy came to an end. As we have already noted, the intellectual reach of social democracy far outdistanced its electoral appeal—a phenomenon encapsulated in the term Butskellism, the phrase used to describe the social democratic consensus in Britain, which for a time reached from the Labour Party across to many Conservatives. Social democrats had always hoped that the gap between intellectual appeal and electoral performance would close as changes in West European societies swept away some of the social props which sustained the electoral support of their rivals. The defeats they suffered on the intellectual plane led them to fear, and their opponents of left and right to hope, that they would be accompanied by severe electoral reverses for the social democrats. This view was strengthened by the difficulties that social democratic governments were having in putting these ideas into practice.

The central preoccupation of the present volume is not with the perennial debate about the general applicability and validity of social democratic ideas and policies, but with the analysis of the present dilemmas and the likely future of the major social democratic parties of Western Europe.

The Response of the Social Democratic Parties

The 1970s did indeed turn out to be a difficult decade for the social democratic parties. The recession, on a scale unprecedented since the 1930s, cruelly exposed the limitations of Keynesian policy. Participation in government during this period put a sometimes well-nigh intolerable strain on the relations of social democratic parties with their allies in the labour movement, as was certainly the case in Britain. As the decade passed, three different strategies became evident in the attitudes of the parties (Wolf, 1978).

One strategy was to pretend that the intellectual and practical difficulties encountered had not happened, or even if they had, they were only of short-term significance. In this the parties relied on the unpopularity of their opponents, against which their own policies and personalities might appear attractive by contrast. Popular at the beginning of the recession, this strategy has never been wholly abandoned by any of the major parties.

The second strategy was for a party to emphasize the elements of social democracy which stressed discipline and control.

We used to think that you could just spend your way out of a recession and increase employment by cutting taxes and boosting government spending. I tell you in all candour that that option no longer exists, and that in so far as it ever did exist, it worked by injecting inflation into the economy. And each time that happened the average level of unemployment has risen. Higher inflation, followed by higher unemployment. That is the history of the last twenty years (James Callaghan, cited by A. Gamble, 1983: 91).

This was the strategy adopted by the government of Helmut Schmidt (1974–82) and James Callaghan (1976–9). It stressed incomes policy and corporatist relationships, formally in the case of the Callaghan government and informally in Schmidt's. This option necessarily involved playing down completely the transformative dimension of social democracy. The result was considerable tension between members of the government, and even more strikingly between governmental members and party members outside parliament, who responded adversely to having their expectations so rudely dashed.

The third option was to move leftwards. This strategy was adopted by parties in opposition, such as the Labour Party in Britain after 1979, the *Parti Socialiste* in France in the years before it came to power, or the Danish Social Democrats after leaving office in 1982. Although generally very popular with party members, it was electorally unsuccessful where the social democratic parties had recently been in power.

The choice between these strategies was often a very painful one which encouraged factionalism and dissent within the parties and which made them much harder to manage than in the past, as David Hine shows in Chapter 10. It was also a process accompanied by fission. In Britain the self-proclaimed heirs to the social democratic tradition left to form a party to the right of the Labour Party, in a move the implications of which are discussed in Chapters 3 and 4. The policies pursued by the Schmidt government were a major factor in persuading many German social democrats to leave the

SPD and play a key role in founding the Greens, a development discussed in Chapter 5.

The scale and depth of the recession, and the pressures this exerted on the unions, also made it more difficult than in the past to keep the industrial and political wings of social democracy in harmony. As the recession deepened, unemployment rose very swiftly. This posed a severe problem for social democratic parties, since full employment was a core value of modern social democracy and at the heart of the bargain with their industrial allies in the unions. The significance of the unemployment issue and the variety, and varied success, of policy responses to it by social democratic governments are analysed by Douglas Webber in Chapter 2.

In addition to those already mentioned, three further factors weakened the unity of social democratic parties. The advent of Ronald Reagan as President of the USA and the move away from détente during his presidency seriously depressed the hitherto high level of support for the North Atlantic Alliance among social democratic parties. In nearly all the major parties this has become an issue of intra-party conflict. This is one of the themes pursued in Chapters 3, 5, and 7.

We have already noted how central the idea of growth was in the intellectual patrimony of modern social democracy, and also the appearance in the 1970s of some important critiques of growth. The debate between its advocates and its opponents, although initially largely intellectual, had far-reaching consequences for a large number of social democratic parties. In Sweden, Austria, and West Germany in particular, 'post-materialist' anti-growth values proved very attractive to many members of the younger generation, but such ideas were generally unattractive to those who were more closely involved in the productive process. Balancing these conflicting claims added further to the difficulties of party leaderships.

In all the major parties there were shifts in the occupational background and expectations of party members: in general, the new members were more middle-class and more highly educated. Some of the implications of these shifts are brought out in Chapter 10. The way in which the expansion of higher education in the 1960s determined these changing expectations remains insufficiently explored, but that it made a major contribution to these changes is universally accepted. The increased expectations and participatory ethos of the new members imported strains both on the existing members and the party leadership.

Conclusion

The general conclusion is an obvious one. Social democracy has not one but several different futures. The coherence of the social democratic paradigm has been dissolved under the sustained pressure of events and intellectual criticisms.

Ideologically social democracy is in a period of disarray. This disarray is reflected in a renewed concern with party programmes. Perhaps most importantly, the SPD is in the process of carrying out a major revision of the Godesberg Programme—the programme which was universally seen as the most comprehensive realization of the Croslandite conception of social democracy. Similar revisions are also being undertaken by other parties. The Croslandite version is apparently no longer viable. On the right of the tradition there is a preoccupation with market socialism and with weakening the elements of bureaucratization and centralization which were previously thought to be essential to the achievement of its goals. In the centre of the tradition there is a concentration on the workplace, on industrial democracy. In Germany there has been a desire to democratize the work situation through co-determination and in Scandinavia there has been a sustained attempt to change the conditions of capitalism through pension fund schemes, and an extension of the influence of workers over production and investment decisions. In the German-speaking countries, and in Scandinavia, heavy emphasis has been placed on redistribution of work through shorter working hours. The left regrets much of the social democratic tradition, but the overwhelming majority still accept the need to find a solution which includes both democratic and socialist values.

The demise of the Croslandite definition of social democracy has left the bedrock conception of democratic socialism intact, however. In recent years even this distinction was somewhat blurred by the emergence and growth of the idea of Euro-communism, with communist parties appearing to accept the fundamentals of representative democracy. But after more than a decade the repercussions of this change appear to be largely confined to Italy.

The external and security policy orientation of the social democratic parties is again a pluralist one. The long post-war period in which support for social democracy was coextensive with support for NATO is now over and there are divisions both between and within parties about the degree of support to be accorded. The parties are also divided in their conceptions of the correct policy to be adopted towards the European Community, as Kevin Featherstone illustrates in Chapter 9.

Nor are the prospects for power for the social democratic parties uniformly promising. As traditional structures change, there has been a general trend towards increased electoral volatility. This in turn has increased the importance of short-term political variables as determinants of electoral victory. Election results are much harder to predict over the longer term, and they appear to be increasingly open and dependent upon such factors as the performance of the governing party or parties, the appeal of party policies and the attractions of candidates and party leaders: the 'Kreisky effect' is discussed in Chapter 6, for example. There has also been an interesting reversal of the political geography of the 1950s and 1960s, in that social democratic parties are now in office in the countries of Latin Europe and largely out of office in Northern Europe.

What social democratic parties will do when they achieve power is again not susceptible of a single answer. In defence policy the constraints on some governments are narrower than on others. For example, whatever programme the SPD adopted in opposition, its options in government would be very seriously restricted by West Germany's geographical position, its place in the alliance structure, and the presence of considerable numbers of allied troops on German soil.

In economic policy, the central concern of social democrats, there is no prospect of uniformity. Economic interdependence and the internationalization of the European economy imposes varying degrees of limitation on the freedom of action of individual governments—a point clearly illustrated by the relative success of Austrian and Swedish policies of full employment and the failure of the French experiment. Although easier to apply in smaller countries with very disciplined labour movements, where the chances of imposing wage discipline and avoiding inflation are correspondingly higher, the success of labour-market policy in

Austria and Sweden, and the disastrous failure of the economic policy pursued in Britain by the Thatcher Conservative government, indicates that there is still some vitality in social democratic policy.

2

Social Democracy and the Re-emergence of Mass Unemployment in Western Europe

Douglas Webber

THERE is possibly no single political aspiration with which social democratic parties in the advanced industrial democratic states have identified themselves more closely than the achievement or maintenance of full employment. However, it is unlikely that a volume of essays on the future of social democracy published twenty, or even perhaps ten, years ago would have contained a contribution on social democracy and the issue of unemployment, except perhaps to say that this was a problem which social democracy and Keynesian economics had solved. In so far as a 'welfare' or 'social democratic' consensus can be said to have existed in this period in the advanced industrial democracies, an economic policy oriented towards economic growth and full employment was certainly one of its distinguishing characteristics.[1] Probably not too many social democrats would have dissented from Crosland's view, expressed in *The Future of Socialism*, that, in the unlikely event of the endogenous economic pressures towards high levels of employment growing too weak, political pressures—above all, the fear of electoral defeat—would compel governments to intervene to prevent unemployment rising (Crosland, 1964: 289–90). As such traditional social democratic objectives were gradually being fulfilled, argued Crosland, social democrats would turn their attention increasingly to the pursuit of other, less material concerns (Crosland, 1964: 353).

Since Crosland wrote *The Future of Socialism*, the framework of social democratic political practice has, of course, been transformed. The principal agent of this transformation has been the economic recession which since 1974, with varying degrees of intensity, has enveloped all the advanced industrial democratic states. Together with progressive cuts in working-time, steady economic growth constituted a prerequisite for the maintenance of full employment. With the deceleration of growth and its periodic cessation and even reversal *and* with the simultaneous growth in the potential labour force in many of the advanced industrial democracies, unemployment has in most of them risen to levels which Crosland and other social democrats then would have considered unthinkable. Questions of unemployment and employment policy have returned—inevitably—to the agenda of social democratic politics.

The ways, however, in which social democratic parties have reacted, programmatically and in their political practice, to the re-emergence of high levels of unemployment have varied widely. This chapter deals firstly, therefore, with the differences and similarities in the responses of social democratic governments to rising unemployment, or the threat of rising unemployment, comparing and contrasting the principal policy instruments which they have mobilized to try to combat unemployment and making a preliminary attempt to identify some of the factors which might explain why some governments' records in this field have been more successful than others'. The second part of the chapter discusses the impact, especially the electoral impact, of high levels of unemployment on social democratic parties. Our analysis focuses on five states, of which three—Austria, West Germany, and Britain—have had exclusively social democratic or labour administrations, or coalition governments led by social democratic or labour parties, right through, or for a great part of, the economic crisis. We also look at Sweden, where, until the Social Democratic party returned to office in 1982, a series of bourgeois governments pursued employment policies which were in most respects identical with those followed earlier by the Social Democrats, and at France, where the socialist-led and dominated coalition government elected in 1981 promised to give overriding priority to combating unemployment.

The Impact of 'Social Democratic' Governments on Unemployment

The considerable variations in levels of registered unemployment, even between states where social democratic or labour governments have been in office during the economic crisis, are depicted by the data in Table 2.1. Evidently, even if social democratic governments tend to attach higher priority to combating unemployment than others, social democratic governments in some states are 'better' at curbing unemployment than governments of a like ideological hue in others. Cross-national differences in unemployment levels have also become much more pronounced. Open unemployment has been held at its approximate 'pre-crisis' level only in Sweden and Austria.

Table 2.1: *Registered unemployment in Austria, Sweden, West Germany, France, and Britain, 1974–82 (% of working population)*

	1974	1975	1976	1977	1978	1979	1980	1981	1982
Austria	1.5	2.0	2.0	1.8	2.1	2.0	1.9	2.4	3.7
Sweden	2.0	1.6	1.6	1.8	2.2	2.1	2.0	2.5	3.2
Germany	2.2	4.2	4.1	4.0	3.9	3.4	3.4	4.8	6.9
France	2.3	3.9	4.3	4.9	5.2	6.0	6.4	7.8	8.9
Britain	2.4	3.7	5.0	5.4	5.3	4.9	6.3	9.6	11.1

Source: Institut der Deutschen Wirtschaft, 1984: Table 5.

The Social Democratic government in *Sweden* up until 1976 responded to the 1974–5 recession with a policy of deficit-spending aimed at 'bridging' the crisis. This policy, which represented a departure from the Swedish Social Democrats' traditional fiscal conservatism, assumed, or at least hoped, that the crisis would be short-lived and the Swedish economy would be geared to take advantage of the following international economic upswing. The upswing, when it came however, was weaker and more fleeting than the bridging policy required and the sharp rise in production costs in Sweden between 1974 and 1976 meant that Swedish export industry was not in a position to take advantage of it. In 1977 and 1978, Sweden felt the full weight of the international slump. The newly-elected bourgeois coalition government (of the Centre, Liberal, and Conservative parties) continued, however, to pursue an expansionary budgetary policy (see Table 2.2). It took over in their entirety, and even broadened the scope of, the labour-market programmes which the Social Democrats had built up, initially as an adjunct to the trade-unions' 'solidarity' wages policy, since the late 1950s (see Table 2.3). Not until 1981, motivated by the mushrooming of the public-sector budget deficit, did the bourgeois parties begin to change course in labour-market policy. Increased

Table 2.2:	*Government indebtedness in Austria, Sweden, West Germany, France, and Britain, 1974–81*

	% rise		% GNP
	1974–9	1976–81	1981
Austria	203	235	37
Sweden	136	198	61
Germany	117	82	34
France	142	104	16
Britain	82	80	59

Sources: Bundesministerium der Finanzen, 1980 and 1982.

emphasis was given to the placement of unemployed persons in jobs on the open market, as opposed to government labour-market programmes, the budgetary requests of the labour-market administration were (for the first time) not met in full, government subsidies to the unemployment insurance funds were cut, and the government's employment policy objectives became more modest (cf. Webber, 1983: *passim*). Nevertheless, the scope of labour-market programmes in Sweden (retraining and work-creation schemes and recruitment subsidies) still far exceeded that in any other Western European state.

Table 2.3:	*Scope of labour market policies in Austria, Sweden, and West Germany, 1974–80*

*(a)	Reduction of registered unemployment by labour-market policy measures (%)*

	1974	1975	1976	1977	1978	1979	1980
Austria	0.2	0.3	0.3	0.3	0.3	n.a.	n.a.
Sweden	2.9	2.5	3.0	3.3	3.9	4.0	2.9
Germany	1.0	1.6	1.3	1.2	1.3	1.3	1.4

*(b)	Expenditure on labour-market policy measures (% GNP)*

	1974	1975	1976	1977	1978	1979	1980
Austria	0.12	0.13	0.10	0.10	0.11	n.a.	n.a.
Sweden	1.26	1.18	1.45	2.04	2.13	1.99	1.75
Germany	0.48	0.67	0.49	0.45	0.47	0.58	0.65

Note: 'Labour-market policy measures' include state retraining programmes, job-creation schemes, recruitment subsidies, sheltered employment, etc.

Sources: Gruppe Politikinformationen, 1981c: 3; Wösendörfer, 1980: 104 and 121.

Table 2.4: *Public-sector employment in Austria, Sweden, West Germany, France, and Britain, 1974–9 (employees in general government in thousands)*

	1974	1975	1976	1977	1978	1979	% rise 1974–9
Austria	516	541	560	582	595	605	17.2
Sweden	992	1,043	1,093	1,138	1,196	1,250	26.0
Germany	3,441	3,512	3,558	3,572	3,646	3,755	9.1
France	2,861	2,917	2,969	3,031	3,078	n.a.	7.6
Britain	4,930	5,225	5,330	5,289	5,304	5,379	9.1

Source: OECD, 1982: 70–1.

The comparatively low level of open unemployment in Sweden has not been secured by the implementation of vast labour-market programmes alone. A second contributory factor has been personnel policies in the public sector. Employment in the Swedish public sector increased between 1974 and 1979 by more than a quarter (cf. Table 2.4). This expansion compensated for a sharp decline in employment in manufacturing industry. There has also been a major reduction in annual average working-time, primarily as a consequence of a rapid growth in part-time work (Gruppe Politikinformationen, 1981c: 7 and 8). After a three-fold increase in the number of part-time workers between 1970 and 1980, a quarter of all employees in Sweden at the end of the decade worked part-time. The Swedish trade unions, however, have maintained a more sceptical attitude than their counterparts in other Western European states to cuts in working-time for 'existing' employees as an instrument of employment policy. The principal, and most incongruous, innovation made by the bourgeois governments in Swedish employment policy was their nationalization and massive subsidization of numerous firms in those branches of industry (for example, steel and ship-building) worst hit by the economic crisis. The volume of government financial support for these industries, which has always been justified in terms of employment considerations, even exceeded spending on labour-market programmes (Henning, 1981: *passim*).

The bourgeois governments maintained comparatively low open unemployment in Sweden, despite a continued *growth* in the foreign labour force (cf. Table 2.5) and despite the fact that the

Table 2.5:   *Changes in the employment of foreign workers in Austria, Sweden, West Germany, and France, 1973–8 (%)*

	(1)	(2)	(3)	(4)	(5)
Austria	+8.8	+10.0	−19.9	9.8	2.0
Sweden	+7.4	+ 7.1	★	n.a.	n.a.
Germany	−4.4	− 1.1	−22.7	10.9	2.7
France	+1.4	+ 5.9	−11.4	8.5	1.0

(1) Change in total number of jobs.
(2) Change in total labour supply (employees and unemployed).
(3) Change in supply of foreign workers.
(4) Proportion of foreign workers in total labour supply 1973.
(5) Reduction in supply of foreign workers 1973–8 as proportion of total labour supply 1973.

★ Considerable increase. Exact data not available.

Source: Gruppe Politikinformationen, 1981a: 4.

Table 2.6:   *Unit labour costs in Austria, Sweden, West Germany, France, and Britain, 1974–80 (% changes over previous year)*

	1974	1975	1976	1977	1978	1979	1980
Austria	+11.4	+13.4	+ 4.4	+ 5.9	+ 7.7	+ 1.3	+ 4.5
Sweden	+11.0	+16.9	+16.3	+15.6	+ 9.8	+ 5.5	+12.0
Germany	+ 9.5	+ 6.0	+ 2.1	+ 3.8	+ 3.3	+ 3.0	+ 5.9
France	+15.6	+17.5	+10.4	+10.3	+ 9.0	+ 9.7	+13.5
Britain	+22.7	+29.4	+ 9.3	+ 9.2	+10.1	+15.5	+20.0

Source: Institut der Deutschen Wirtschaft, 1982: table 32.

explosion of wage costs in Sweden from 1974 to 1977 (cf. Table 2.6) led to a sharp decline in the international competitiveness of Swedish export industry. The cost of their defence of employment, however, was high. The Swedish economy ran a current accounts deficit every year from 1974 to 1981. Government indebtedness (much of it abroad) has soared since the late 1970s, so that the constraints on the further pursuit of an expansionary budgetary policy have become much tighter. None the less, the Social Democratic administration elected in autumn 1982 resolved to pursue an ambitious economic policy giving priority to economic growth and safeguarding employment. Various cuts in welfare benefits (including the unemployment benefit) carried out by the bourgeois government were restored, a major public investments programme was launched, and the Social Democrats undertook to implement labour market programmes 'in full force' (Swedish International Press Bureau, 1982: 2). The government hoped to win greater scope for the pursuit of a full-employment-oriented economic policy through a drastic (16 per cent) devaluation of the Swedish krona. How successful this measure proved in increasing the international competitiveness of Swedish industry would depend very heavily on the trade unions' acquiescence in real wage cuts. This was in fact secured in the 1982–3 wage-bargaining round, but its continuation may be contingent upon the Social Democrats proceeding to implement, in some form, union-inspired plans for collective wage-earners' investment funds, which the unions and Social Democratic Party hope would assist capital formation and stimulate investment in industry. (See Chapter 7.) However, these plans are strongly opposed by Swedish capital, whose co-operation the government knew it must also secure if the declining rate of investment in Sweden was to be reversed—as the Social Democratic Prime Minister Palme himself recognized in announcing that the government would pursue a policy of the 'outstretched hand' towards the business community (Palme, 1983: 13). The sharp devaluation in 1982 paved the way for an export-led recovery, in the course of which the already low level of open unemployment was reduced further, but there were signs early in the election year of 1985 that this upswing was starting to peter out.

The institutional constraints upon the pursuit of a full-employment-oriented economic policy in West Germany are greater than in Sweden. First, the Federal Government's lee-way in economic policy-making is limited by the role of the *Bundesbank* (federal bank), whose independence from the government is protected by law and which has always attached priority, where economic policy goals conflict, to the preservation of price stability. Secondly, the federal government, in a wide range of policy areas affecting its ability to manage the economy, requires the co-operation of the state and local governments, whose combined expenditure far exceeds that of the federation. During the life-time of the Social–Liberal coalition, the majority of the states were governed by the Christian Democratic (and Bavarian Christian Social) opposition. Indeed, in the *Bundesrat* (upper house of the Federal Parliament), which has extensive powers of veto (for example, on questions of taxation), the opposition parties were able, in some issue-areas, to form a parallel government.

These constraints cannot account wholly, however, for the failure of the Social–Liberal coalition to pursue a more ambitious policy to combat unemployment than it in fact did (cf. Webber and Nass, 1984: *passim*). Not only the philosophy of the SPD's Free Democratic coalition partner, but also the attitudes of the Social Democratic Chancellor and Finance Ministers militated against the pursuit of such a policy (cf. also Webber, 1982: *passim*). Certainly, in comparison with the Swedish bourgeois governments and the Austrian Social Democrats, the Social–Liberal coalition adhered to a restrictive budgetary policy (see Table 2.2). Chancellor Schmidt referred to his government's style of economic management as a 'middle way' between the expansionary, demand-oriented policy followed by the French Socialists in their first year in office and the restrictive, monetarist policies pursued by the British Conservative government (Schmidt, 1983: 21). Motivated by the wish to curb a growing current accounts deficit and also to uncouple West German interest rates from the high interest rates in the United States, and to try to defuse opposition claims that it was leading West Germany down the road to financial chaos and a new currency reform, the coalition tightened its fiscal policy following the 1980 federal election. In the two-year period before the coalition collapsed in September 1982, partly on account of differences in the sphere of employment policy, registered unemployment in West Germany doubled.

Similarly, the Social–Liberal coalition did not resort to labour market policy measures as a means of combating unemployment on the same scale as did the Swedish Social Democratic and bourgeois administrations. Even in the SPD, the usefulness of labour market programmes on the Swedish scale was doubted. The scope for a contra-cyclical implementation of labour-market programmes tends to be limited in West Germany by the fact that such measures are financed by the labour-market administration, whose primary obligation, in practice, is to pay unemployment benefits. As a consequence of this method of financing, the resources for labour market policy are squeezed at the same time as their contra-cyclical expansion is demanded. The trade unions and the SPD tried at least to broaden the financial basis of the labour-market administration, but such efforts failed on the opposition of the Free (and Christian) Democrats and on considerations of constitutional law (cf. Webber, 1982: 271). In principle, the cost of expanded labour-market policy measures could have been met by the federal government granting additional subsidies to the labour-market administration. But, precisely because the latter represented the chief liability to the coalition's budgetary policy (inevitably, given rising unemployment), such measures were the principal victims of the major spending cuts decided in 1975 and in 1981.

Compared with Sweden, the increase in public-sector employment in West Germany was also moderate under the Social–Liberal coalition. Indeed, from 1975 onwards, employment in the federal government, in contrast to that in the state and local governments, actually declined (Bundesministerium der Finanzen, 1981: 2). Also the reduction of working-time, which West German employers have opposed vigorously, and the expansion of part-time work have not been as substantial as in Sweden, although, paradoxically, the German unions have supported cuts in weekly working-time as a means of curbing unemployment more strongly than the unions in Sweden (see Table 2.7).[2] The employment policies of the Social–Liberal coalition were biased especially, and more strongly than those in Sweden, towards reducing the labour supply by encouraging early retirement and 'exporting' foreign workers. Between 1970 and 1979, especially following the introduction of optional early retirement in 1973, the proportion of persons aged between 60 and 65 still working fell sharply (see Table 2.8). Whereas in Sweden the labour-force participation rate for women has continued to rise during the economic crisis (probably because of the increase in part-time job opportunities), in Germany it has stagnated, and at a much lower level.[3] Under the impact of a general ban on the further recruitment of non-EEC foreign workers

Table 2.7:   *Weekly working-time in manufacturing industry in Austria, Sweden, West Germany, France, and Britain, 1974–9 (in hours)*

	1974	1975	1976	1977	1978	1979	+/−
Austria	36.0	33.9	34.4	33.9	33.4	33.6	−2.4
Sweden	36.8	36.6	36.3	35.9	35.7	35.7	−1.1
Germany	41.9	40.4	41.4	41.7	41.6	41.8	−0.1
France	42.9	41.7	41.6	41.3	41.0	40.8	−2.1
Britain	44.0	42.7	43.5	43.6	43.5	43.2	−0.8

Source: Institut der Deutschen Wirtschaft, 1982: table 6.

28   *Douglas Webber*

Table 2.8:   *Labour force participation rates for workers aged between 60 and 64 in Sweden, West Germany, France, and Britain, 1970 and 1979*

	Men		Women	
	1970	1979	1970	1979
Sweden	79.5	69.0	35.8	39.4
Germany	74.7	39.5	22.5	11.4
France	65.2	38.2	33.7	22.4
Britain	86.6	75.8	51.9	54.9

Source: Gruppe Politikinformationen, 1981b: 1.

imposed at the beginning of the economic crisis and the restrictive implementation of existing legislation relating to the employment of foreigners, the number of foreign workers in West Germany fell between 1973 and 1978 by about 730,000, equivalent to almost a quarter of the entire foreign work force and 2.7 per cent of the labour force as a whole (cf. Table 2.5).[4] To a far greater extent than the Swedish bourgeois governments, the Social–Liberal coalition delegated responsibility for the creation of employment to the private sector of the economy. The considerable success enjoyed by this policy between 1976 and 1980, when overall employment rose in West Germany in net terms by about one million, may be attributed in large part to the moderation exercised in wage bargaining by the trade unions.[5] Thanks to this restraint, which was partly voluntary and partly enforced by the bargaining strength of the employers' organizations and the tight monetary policies of the Bundesbank, West German export industry remained exceptionally competitive on international markets during the 1970s, despite a massive revaluation of the German mark against almost all other major currencies (cf. Table 2.6). Without the contribution made to German export competitiveness by wage restraint, it is also inconceivable that, even following the second oil-price explosion, foreign demand for German production would have remained so strong as to constitute the major expansionary influence on the domestic economy.

The Social Democrats in *Austria* have not had to face such formidable constraints on the pursuit of a full-employment policy as did the SPD while it was in federal government in West Germany. From 1970 until 1983, the SPÖ was able to govern alone. The

Austrian central bank is not autonomous of the government and the political structure of Austria is not as decentralized as the West German. As in West Germany, however, trade-union wage moderation has made a decisive contribution to the maintenance of a high level of employment. Austria has had a very impressive export record during the economic crisis, although, apart from the Swiss franc, its currency is the only one which has appreciated in the period of the crisis against the German mark (see Table 2.9). The Austrian trade unions' rejection of a redistributive wages policy, along with the absence in Austria of a strong indigenous capitalist class, has undoubtedly also contributed to the stability of the system of 'social partnership' between labour and capital.[6] The unions' wage moderation, a highly-developed system of government investment promotion, and the major role played by the nationalized banks in providing investment capital may explain why the level of investment in Austria during the economic crisis has been the highest in Western Europe.

Table 2.9: *Volume of exports from Austria, Sweden, West Germany, France, and Britain, 1974–80 (% changes over previous year)*

	1974	1975	1976	1977	1978	1979	1980
Austria	+8.0	+12.5	+16.0	+2.5	+10.0	+13.0	+5.5
Sweden	+5.5	−10.0	+5.0	+1.0	+6.5	+8.0	−8.2
Germany	+11.4	−11.5	+11.4	+5.4	+4.2	+7.1	+4.1
France	+9.6	−4.1	+9.1	+6.6	+6.0	+10.1	+2.1
Britain	+4.8	−2.6	+8.9	+9.0	+3.5	+2.4	+2.0

Source: Institut der Deutschen Wirtschaft, 1982: table 50.

Also as in West Germany, the Austrian Social Democrats have pursued a very restrictive policy towards foreign workers (cf. Table 2.5). In other respects, however, the Austrian and West German employment policies have differed considerably. On the one hand, the scale of Austrian labour market policy measures has been comparatively small (see Table 2.3). On the other hand, the reduction in weekly working-hours in Austrian manufacturing industry has been greater than in West Germany, Sweden, France, or Britain (cf. Table 2.7). In public administration, the Austrian Social Democrats have also pursued a comparatively expansionary

personnel policy (cf. Table 2.4), while the industrial enterprises in
the public sector, which is the largest in Western Europe, have tried
as far as possible to avoid lay-offs and redundancies (cf. Chaloupek,
1979: 230; Wösendörfer, 1980: 98–9; Müller, 1981: 400). In order to
finance these policies, the Social Democrats have been forced to
follow an extremely expansionary budgetary policy, which the
former Chancellor Kreisky justified with the argument that it was
better to have another billion schilling in government debts than to
have a hundred more workers unemployed (cf. Table 2.2).

Over the period from 1974 to 1979 as a whole, the Labour
governments in *Britain* pursued a more restrictive budgetary
policy—measured by the growth of state indebtedness—than any of
their Social Democratic counterparts in continental Western
Europe (cf. Table 2.2). Certainly, however, their scope for
combating unemployment by means of an expansionary demand-
management policy was more limited than that of their 'sister'
administrations, given the economic situation inherited from the
Conservatives in February 1974. None the less, in its first year in
office, the Wilson government followed a contra-cyclical economic-
management policy which held the growth of unemployment within
limits. This policy could not be sustained however, especially as,
fuelled by high nominal wage increases, inflation began to
accelerate out of control.[7] By the middle of 1975, when it secured
the unions' acquiescence in an informal wages policy and long
before it was forced, after the sterling crisis in 1976, to borrow on
strict terms from the International Monetary Fund, the government
had already embarked on a restrictive public expenditure course
(Ormerod, 1980: 50–1). In so far as the wage-induced rates of
inflation which were reached in Britain in 1975 might rapidly have
destroyed the competitiveness of British industry and therefore
undermined employment, the results of the wage-bargaining
process in this period might be considered to have been
incompatible with the pursuit of a full-employment-oriented
economic policy. The government seemed to hope that wage
restraint would lay the foundations for a process of export-led
employment growth when international trade revived. Certainly,
the government's industrial 'strategy' reflected the philosophy that
the primary source of new jobs should be investment in
manufacturing industry.

As a quid pro quo for the unions' acquiescence in wage restraint, the Labour governments initiated a major expansion of labour-market policy measures through the Manpower Services Commission. However, as these measures, where they were not entirely new, began from a very low base, their impact on the level of open employment remained fairly limited—certainly more so than in West Germany and, in particular, in Sweden.[8] A significant role in efforts to safeguard employment was also played by measures of industrial policy and subsidies, through which financial support was granted to failing firms in both the public and private sectors. In comparison at least with Sweden and Austria, the contribution made to the curbing of unemployment by reductions in weekly working-time was modest (see Table 2.7). In practice, the chief economic policy priority of the Labour governments was the reduction of the level of inflation, which Wilson described as the 'father and mother' of unemployment. In this sphere, from 1975 onwards, their policies were very effective. Despite a considerable redistribution of wealth to the business sector after 1975, however, manufacturing investment did not revive sufficiently to prevent a continued decline in employment in manufacturing industry. While public-sector employment expanded over the period from 1974 to 1979 as a whole, it did so at a much slower rate than, for example, in Austria and Sweden (cf. Table 2.4). The *growth* in unemployment was brought under control, but the level of registered unemployment remained almost stagnant during the last years of Labour government at well over one million.

The Socialist-led coalition government of the Left in *France* assumed office in 1981 dedicated primarily to the combating of unemployment. Certainly, its employment policy programme corresponded well with the Socialist Party's image of itself as an agent not merely of 'Social Democratic' reform, but of radical Socialist change—it amounted to the boldest package of measures for curbing unemployment launched by a Western European government during the economic crisis. The major extension of the public sector in industry and banking carried out in the government's first months in office was legitimized in terms of the role the enlarged public sector would play in regenerating French industry and stimulating economic growth and employment (*The Times*, 1981; *Frankfurter Rundschau*, 1981). An extremely expansionary demand-management policy was also adopted. The Labour Ministry's 1982 budget was raised over that for 1981 by 110 per cent, numerous social-welfare benefits were raised, and expenditure allocations for a wide range of labour-market policy measures were increased in total by 46 per cent (Gruppe Politikinformationen, 1982: 4).[9] A substantial increase in public-sector jobs was initiated. In addition, various, and taken together, major reductions in working-time (earlier retirement, longer annual holidays, and a thirty-five hour working week) were proposed.

This programme was not entirely unsuccessful in the government's first eighteen months in office. After carrying on rising in 1981, unemployment stabilized in France in 1982, while it was increasing rapidly in almost all other Western industrial states (Mitterand, 1983). However, the recovery in the international economic conjuncture on which the government, when elected, had banked, did not materialize (Delors, 1982; Mauroy, 1982). The comparatively low level of state indebtedness in France (cf. Table 2.2) might have permitted a considerable expansion of the public-sector budget deficit, but inflation began to rise and, and in particular, the French current account deficit increased sharply, diminishing international confidence in the French franc. The government's economic policy had triggered off a consumption-dominated import boom rather than a wave of new investment and production growth in French industry.[10]

The Socialists' employment policy thus turned out to be inappropriate to the 'long distance', at least in the context of an international economic recession in which France's major trading partners were all more concerned with maintaining price stability than with curbing growing unemployment. In the middle of 1982, after it had been forced twice to devalue the franc within the European Monetary System, the government switched its economic policy tack. Wages, prices, and the social security contributions levied on companies were temporarily frozen, proposed reductions in the working week were suspended, and measures were announced to curb the growth in the budget deficit. These steps proved insufficient, however, to halt the continued deterioration in the French trading position and further cuts in public expenditure (including a range of unemployment benefits) and tax and social-security contribution increases were decided in November 1982 and again, after a renewed run on the franc and another devaluation, in March 1983. Despite the increased concern demonstrated by the government for the problems of the business community, the latter's attitude to the Left administration remained one of great suspicion and, in part, as shown by the demonstrations in May 1983, of open hostility. The investment continued to decline: in the analogy painted by the former Socialist Economics Minister Delors, it was impossible to get a horse to drink so long as it was not thirsty (Bremer, 1981 and 1982). Any more far-reaching concessions made by the government to the business lobby—apart from their uncertain impact on investment and employment—might have alienated still further the trade unions, which had been becoming increasingly dissatisfied with the change of orientation in government economic policy. With the clear demotion of the combating of unemployment in the hierarchy of economic policy goals, unemployment rose much more rapidly after the middle of 1983 than it had done during the Socialists' first two years in office.[11]

Just as each Western European state, to appropriate Schumpeter's description, has its 'own' social democracy, so has each social democratic government in Western Europe responded in its own fashion to the actual or imminent growth of unemployment since 1973. Whereas British Labour governments and (temporarily, at least) the French Socialists have resorted to informal or statutory wages policies to manage the economy, the West German Social Democrats, the Austrian Social Democrats, and the Swedish bourgeois and Social Democratic administrations have refrained, or been able to refrain, from intervening directly in private-sector wage bargaining. Whilst the French Socialists (motivated more perhaps by ideological conviction than by employment considerations) and the Swedish bourgeois administrations have carried out major programmes of nationalization, the West German Social Democrats and their counterparts in Austria (who, in any case preside over a large public sector) have placed their faith predominantly in established instruments for the 'global' management of the economy. Whereas labour-market policy measures have been allocated a central role in the combating of unemployment in Sweden, their significance in Austria, West Germany, and Britain has been more limited.

Similarly, in respect of policies towards foreign workers, public-sector employment, and working-time, the range of policy stances among Western European 'social democratic' governments has been wide. In part, these differences may be attributable to the

widely contrasting ideological complexions of the parties with
which the different Social Democratic, Labour, or Socialist parties
have formed coalitions or, as in Britain temporarily, a pact: the
ideological gulf between, for example, the French Communists and
the West German Free Democrats is enormous. But there is, of
course, no necessary correlation between the presence of Social
Democratic parties in government and the pursuit of what might be
considered 'social democratic' policies. Hence, if internationalism
is taken to be a central value of social democracy, the Swedish
bourgeois governments pursued a much more 'social democratic'
policy towards foreign workers than did the West German and
Austrian Social Democrats.

This analysis of employment policies and employment policy
performance in five Western European states during the economic
crisis hints that, apart from inherited economic circumstances and
employment levels, two variables exercise a particularly strong
influence on the capacity of 'social democratic' governments
effectively to combat unemployment. The first of these is the
closeness of the social democratic parties' relationships with the
respective national trade union movements *and* the character of
these unions. Where these relationships are close and the unions are
highly centralized and 'co-operative' (in the sense that their wage-
bargaining behaviour is congruent with the social democratic
governments' overall strategy for managing the economy), the
conditions for the maintenance of a comparatively low level of
unemployment are favourable. This was, or has been, the case in
West Germany and Austria. In Britain, where, despite a close
organic union-party relationship, authority in the unions is
relatively decentralized and the unions have not been as 'co-
operative', in terms of wage bargaining, as their counterparts in
Austria and West Germany, the constraints of inflation and the
feared or actual loss of industrial competitiveness have made the
containment of unemployment much more difficult. Moreover,
capital in Britain, particularly *banking* capital, which has attached
low priority to investment in domestic industry, has not been as 'co-
operative' as capital in Austria, Sweden or, indeed, West Germany
(cf. Lever and Edwards, 1980). The stronger the 'social partnership'
between trade unions, industrial *and* banking capital, and the social
democratic state, the lower is likely to be the level of
unemployment.[12]

'Co-operative' trade unions and close relationships between the unions and social democratic governments are not, however, sufficient, or even necessary, conditions of the maintenance of low unemployment. The second variable which seems to exercise a powerful influence on the capacity, or *will*, of such governments to maintain low unemployment levels is the strength of the social democratic *culture* in society: it is this which shapes what levels of unemployment are, or are perceived to be, electorally acceptable or undamaging. The electoral strength of the social democratic parties, or the political Left as a whole, may not always be a reliable measure of the strength of the social democratic culture, since where the latter is very strong, centre or right-of-centre parties may be compelled, in practice, to embrace social democratic values to remain electorally competitive.[13] In Sweden, although union–government relations were extremely cool and the trade unions were rather 'uncooperative' between 1976 and 1982, the bourgeois governments felt compelled to go to quite extraordinary lengths and to pursue policies quite at odds with their ideological tenets (large-scale nationalizations and massive deficit-spending) in order to curb the growth of unemployment. In West Germany, where, in any event, the institutional constraints on the pursuit of a full-employment-oriented economic policy are strong, the Social–Liberal coalition adjudged the curbing of the growth of the federal budget deficit to be politically (and economically) more important after the 1980 election than the combating of unemployment. The existence of close links between the co-operative West German unions and the social democratic-led government did not guarantee that unemployment would be kept low. The most favourable conditions for the combating of unemployment have prevailed in Austria. Not only are there co-operative trade unions and a strong system of 'social partnership' between labour and capital, but the threshold of popular tolerance of unemployment is perceived to be low, as illustrated by the fact that all the political parties appear to view full employment as the primary objective of government economic policy. Moreover, the costs of maintaining low unemployment have been lower in Austria, in terms of the realization of *other* economic policy objectives, than in Sweden.

The general economic and political conjuncture in Britain was most unfavourable to the curbing of unemployment. In comparative perspective, Britain has had uncooperative trade unions and uncooperative industrial and banking capitals and the Labour governments' reading of the mood of the electorate did not prompt them, in practice, to give employment the highest priority among conflicting economic policy objectives. Moreover, as Britain does not have a large pool of foreign workers with limited and revocable residence and employment rights, it could not resort to the 'export' of unemployment as a means of tackling its domestic labour market problems on the same scale as did, for example, Austria, and West Germany. Even before the Thatcher Conservative government assumed office in 1979, unemployment was higher in Britain than in Sweden, Austria, or West Germany. As well as having inherited a comparatively high level of unemployment from the Giscard–Barre government, the Socialist-led coalition of the Left in France confronts an antagonistic capitalist lobby and cannot count on support or acquiescence from the (divided) trade union movement to the same extent as could the social democratic parties in Sweden, Austria, and West Germany, not least because the largest union organization is controlled by the Communist Party, whose departure from the government in 1984 possibly presaged more militant union opposition to the now exclusively Socialist administration's industrial and economic policies. One of the chief preoccupations of Delors was, significantly, an improvement in the relationship between French labour and capital (Delors, 1981: 88, and 1982: 63).[14]

The Impact of Unemployment on Social Democratic Parties

The high levels of unemployment in Western Europe since 1974 have not led to as much political instability and unrest as was feared when the economic crisis first made itself felt. The prediction of politicians, especially those influenced by the experiences of the 1930s' depression, that levels of unemployment as high as two per cent (!) would give rise to political radicalism have not been fulfilled. A number of factors may *help* to explain why this has not occurred. Firstly, despite high overall levels of unemployment in most Western European states, the length of time for which *most* unemployed persons are out of work has remained limited. In West Germany, for example, two-thirds of the persons who became (officially) unemployed between 1976 and 1979 found work again within a period of three months (Scharpf, 1982: 60). Thus, for most unemployed persons in most states up until 1982, unemployment was a quite transitory phenomenon—and certainly not an experience which was likely to serve as a basis for political radicalism and extremism. Secondly, in *most* Western European states, the level of social security provision for the unemployed is— by international standards—very high. For north-western Europe (excluding Britain), the West German benefit levels of 63 per cent of the former net income for the first year of unemployment and 56 per cent (means-tested) thereafter were below the average. Given that (at least in the second half of the 1970s), two out of every three unemployed persons in West Germany remained jobless for less than three months, the loss in *annual* net income incurred through unemployment was, for most unemployed, less than ten per cent.[15] Thirdly, labour force participation rates were so high in most states that most unemployed persons may live in households where someone else is working—about 60 per cent, according to one survey finding, in West Germany in 1978 (Bundesministerium für Arbeit und Sozialordnung, 1978: 2). This may also help ease the material deprivation incurred through unemployment.

The potential political repercussions of high unemployment levels may be checked, fourthly, by the way in which the burden of unemployment is distributed. Most of the groups which are disproportionately likely to be affected by unemployment tend to be either policitically inarticulate or defenceless (for example, foreign workers and school-leavers) or to have alternative roles which enable them to come more easily to terms with their unemployment than might otherwise be the case (for example, married women and older workers who may be able to opt for early retirement) (cf. von Rosenbladt, 1981: 42, 43, and 85). Conversely, key groups in the trade-union and labour movements in most Western European states, such as skilled workers, have generally retained a comparatively strong position on the labour market. In West Germany, for example, the number of vacant jobs for skilled manual workers exceeded the number of such workers unemployed in September 1979, although the overall level of unemployment was still over 730,000. The possibility that, at least up until the renewed slump in 1981–2, core groups of unionized workers remained relatively well insulated against the danger of unemployment may account, to some extent, for the apparent acquiescence of some trade-union movements in high levels of unemployment. However,

where *social democratic* or *labour* parties have been in government
and presided over high unemployment levels, such acquiescence
may also have been motivated by the unions' consideration of the
interests of their political allies. There are some grounds for
suspecting this to have been the case in Britain and (until the final
months of the Social–Liberal coalition) in West Germany, where
union criticism of the employment policies of their 'allies' in
government was rather muted. Where such motivations did indeed
prompt the unions to curb the strength of their protest against high
levels of unemployment, however, historical bonds and
overlapping union-party personnel and personal relationships must
not necessarily be invoked as explanatory factors. Trade-union
strategy may have been influenced equally by the (highly rational)
belief that a social democratic or labour government still
represented the 'lesser evil'.

Obviously the five above-mentioned factors could together form
no more than one element in the construction of an explanation of
why high unemployment has not had a more destabilizing and
radicalizing impact on Western European politics. With these
variables alone, it would be difficult to explain why, up to 1983,
unemployment had not induced more manifest political discontent
and unrest in Britain, where, by Western European standards, the
level of unemployment was not only extremely high, but the
average duration of unemployment was also extremely long and
getting longer, the level of unemployment benefits was low, the
Conservative Party had been in office for four years, and
unemployment had long since ceased to be an experience affecting
only, or even mainly, the 'marginal' groups of the labour market.

If high unemployment has not led to any significant political
instability or unrest in Western Europe, then has it had any
discernible effect at all on the *electoral* fortunes of governing social
democratic, or, indeed, other parties or on the development of
Western European party systems in general? Paradoxically, the
most striking phenomenon in the party systems during the
economic crisis has been the emergence of numerous 'Green' or
environmentalist parties, which are uniformly hostile towards the
promotion of economic growth or the creation of jobs 'for their own
sake'. It would be too precipitate, however, to interpret the growing
appeal of 'post-material' values as meaning that electorates are
growing indifferent to high levels of unemployment. Attitudes to

work may have become more instrumental—but, in order to be able to pursue post-material ends, people may still need—and want—a job.[16] Moreover, despite their rapid growth, the 'Green' parties are still, of course, very small.

The 'clientelist' theory of voting behaviour suggests that, irrespective of whether they are in government, social democratic or labour parties should *benefit* from the existence of high unemployment—voters incline in such a situation towards the party which attaches the greatest emphasis to combating unemployment (cf. Rattinger, 1979: 53). Certainly, the *unemployed* themselves vote preponderantly for social democratic parties or the political Left, probably irrespective of which party or parties are in office (The Economist Intelligence Unit, 1982: 19; von Manikowsky, 1983: 177; Sales, 1981: 33; Crewe, 1983).[17] Whether this is influenced at all by their unemployment, rather than by such variables as occupation or class location, is not wholly clear.[18]

When one turns to consider the effects of high unemployment at the 'macro-electoral' level, the picture is a good deal more complex. It may be correct that the social democratic parties were, or have been, traditionally viewed as the 'party of full employment' in their respective national states—this is one possible interpretation of the high level of employment policy 'competence' attributed to the parties in West Germany, Britain, and Sweden before, or soon after the beginning of the economic crisis (see Tables 2.10, 2.11, and 2.12). Equally, they may have earned this image of employment policy competence on the basis of their performance, or that of their rival parties. During their period in office from 1966 to 1972, the West German Social Democrats had proved very successful in first reducing unemployment and then holding it at a very low level. This applied, too, over a very much longer period, to the Swedish Social Democrats—except for a short period in the early 1970s, when their image as the 'party of full employment' correspondingly suffered (cf. Table 2.12).

An examination of the development of the employment policy competence attributed to social democratic parties and their electoral support *during* the economic crisis yields at best patchy evidence in support of the 'clientelist' theory. In Britain, the Labour Party quickly lost its employment policy advantage over the Conservatives, but this had no perceptible impact on its electoral support, even when unemployment was rising very rapidly in 1975–6

Table 2.10: *Unemployment as a political issue and public opinion on the competence of the political parties in employment policy in Britain, 1974–9*

(a) *Percentage of survey respondents saying that unemployment is the 'most urgent problem facing the country at the present time'*

1974 Dec.	1975 Apr.	1975 Dec.	1976 Apr.	1976 Dec.	1977 Apr.	1977 Dec.	1978 Apr.	1978 Dec.	1979 May
1	5	18	19	14	13	23	36	24	22

(b) *Rank of unemployment as political issue*

1974 Dec.	1975 Apr.	1975 Dec.	1976 Apr.	1976 Dec.	1977 Apr.	1977 Dec.	1978 Apr.	1978 Dec.	1979 May
8=	5	n.a.	2	3	2	2	1	2	2

(c) *Answers of survey respondents to questions 'which party do you think can best handle the problem of unemployment' or 'which parties do you think are particularly good at reducing unemployment?'*

	1974 Nov.	1975 May	1975 Oct.	1978 Mar.	1978 June	1978 Sep.	1979 Feb.	1979 Apr.
Labour	45	35	36	32	33	33	28	32
Conservative	26	33	35	38	35	38	39	35
Liberal	5	3	6	2	3	2	4	5
Don't know	23	29	22	26	26	25	31	30

Source: Gallup 1975–9, various issues.

—its popularity first plummetted during the sterling crisis at the end of 1976 and then recovered before collapsing again in the 'winter of discontent' in 1978–9.[19] Although the electorate displayed greater sensitivity to inflation, sterling crises, and strikes than to unemployment, this should not be construed as indicating that it was indifferent, except in a very relative sense, to the existence of high unemployment levels. From 1975 onwards, unemployment was consistently one of the two or three greatest issues of popular political concern (see Table 2.10). An overwhelming majority of voters believed that the Labour government was not doing enough to stop unemployment rising.

Table 2.11:   *Unemployment as a political issue and public opinion on the competence of the political parties in employment policy in West Germany, 1972–83*

(a)   Percentage of survey respondents saying that they 'personally' hold the overcoming of unemployment to be 'very important'

1978 Mar.	1979 Dec.	1980 June	1980 Sep.	1980 Nov.	1981 May	1981 Oct.	1982 May
91	83	75	77	79	84	89	88

(b)   Rank of unemployment as political issue

1978 Mar.	1979 Dec.	1980 June	1980 Sep.	1980 Nov.	1981 May	1981 Oct.	1982 May
1	3	4	2=	3=	2	1	1

(c)   Answers of survey respondents to the question: 'Who best guarantees job security?' (%) ⋆

	1972 Sep.	1974 Oct.	1975 Apr.	1976 Sep.	1980 Sep.	1982 Oct.	1983 Jan.
SPD/SPD–FDP	38	35	39	37	43	17	21
CDU–CSU/ CDU–CSU–FDP	25	36	38	45	32	45	43

⋆ Question 1972 'Which of the two main parties is better at safeguarding jobs'; question 1974: 'The problem of job security is best solved by . . .'; question 1982: 'Will the new (CDU–CSU–FDP) government have more or less success than the old (SPD FDP) government in combating unemployment?'; question 1983: 'Which government is better able to solve the problem of (combating) unemployment—the present (CDU–CSU–FDP) government or an SPD-led government?'. Respondents who did not answer or thought that the respective parties or governments were equally good or bad at safeguarding employment are excluded.

Sources: Institut für Demoskopie, 1978–82; Webber, 1982: 275; Emnid–Institut, 1982: 11; *Der Spiegel*, 1983a: 36.

The 'winter of discontent' evidently also served to undermine its credibility in the sphere of employment policy. At the general election in May 1979, voters who expected unemployment to fall under a new Labour government were outnumbered about three to two by those who regarded this as more likely to happen under the Conservatives.[20] In so far as unemployment affected the outcome of the 1979 election, it is thus likely that it benefited the Conservative rather than the Labour Party.

Table 2.12:   *Unemployment as a political issue and public opinion on the competence of the political parties in employment policy in Sweden, 1968–82*

(a)   Percentage of survey respondents citing 'work or full employment' as the most important present political issue

1979 Autumn	1980 Winter	1980 Spring	1980 Autumn	1981 Winter	1981 Spring	1982 Spring
41	33	30	34	41	38	61

(b)   Rank of unemployment as political issue

1979 Autumn	1980 Winter	1980 Spring	1980 Autumn	1981 Winter	1981 Spring	1982 Spring
2	2	2	2	2	2	1

(c)   Answers of survey respondents to the question 'what sort of government would be best suited to ensure employment in the country—a Social Democratic or bourgeois government?'

	1968	1970	1973	1976	1979	1982
Social Democratic government	48	29	30	38	42	50
Bourgeois government	28	35	40	27	32	20

Sources: Dagens Nyheter, 1982; Korpi, 1983: 205.

Similarly, the Social Democrats were not the political beneficiaries of high, or at least high *and rising*, unemployment during the economic crisis in West Germany. Although popular confidence in the SPD's competence in safeguarding employment remained stable during the period of rapidly growing unemployment from 1974 to 1976, it nevertheless lost considerable ground in this policy sphere to the Christian Democratic opposition (see Table 2.11). This trend had no perceptible effect, however, on the SPD's popularity, which showed an upward trend after the party's internal conflicts had subsided and its leadership crisis had been resolved by Schmidt's accession to the Chancellorship in May 1974.[21] Even so, the Social–Liberal coalition would very likely have been defeated in a federal election in later 1975 or early 1976. Popular expectations regarding the development of the economy and the SPD's electoral standing improved as an economic upswing got under way during the year.[22] The fact that the Christian Democrats enjoyed greater popular confidence in respect of safeguarding employment indicates, however, that unemployment, which was by far the leading election issue, did not work to the benefit of the SPD.[23] Rather, the economic recovery of 1976 probably contained the political damage done by the high level of unemployment sufficiently for the Social–Liberal coalition, despite some losses, to be re-elected.

The subsequent fluctuations in the SPD's popular support suggest also that the *development* of the labour market and general economic situation may exert an important influence on governing parties' electoral fortunes: that is, the latter may be shaped as much (or more) by whether unemployment is rising or falling, and at what rate, as by the *absolute* level of unemployment. In 1980, after a four-year period in which the Social–Liberal coalition had had considerable success in combating unemployment, the SPD regained its superiority over the Christian Democrats on the terrain of employment policy and the coalition was returned to office with an increased majority. Then, as unemployment increased extremely steeply (and re-emerged as the political issue arousing greatest public concern) in the renewed slump of 1981–2, the electorate's confidence in the employment policy competence of the SPD—and the SPD's overall popularity—fell equally precipitously.[24] The Social Democrats could not repair the damage done to their employment policy credibility in the short period between the collapse of the Social–Liberal coalition and the March 1983 election.

Thus the case for the clientelist theory, that the presence or threat of high unemployment should benefit social democratic or labour parties, does not stand up at all well to scrutiny. Is there, then, any evidence to sustain the reverse contention that economic crisis and high unemployment *necessarily* strengthen the parties of the Right or centre-Right? In both Britain and West Germany, the appeal of Conservative explanations of unemployment seems to have grown during the second half of the 1970s. The number of persons in Britain believing that the unemployment-benefit level was 'too high' rose between October 1975 and October 1977 from about 34 to about 41 per cent (Gallup, 1975–7). Between March 1976 and October 1977, the proportion of voters blaming unemployment at least partly on the unwillingness of the unemployed to work grew from 21 to 33 per cent (ibid.). In West Germany, the proportion of voters thinking that many of the unemployed were 'work-shy' rose between 1975 and 1981 from about 49 to about 58 per cent (Institut für Demoskopie, *passim.*). Rather than being firmly-rooted, however, public opinion on such questions may follow the economic conjuncture or be a function of disaffection with the social democratic government of the day. In any event, as unemployment rose in West Germany after the 1980 election, the proportion of the electorate maintaining that many of the unemployed did not want to work sank within eighteen months by 18 per cent (ibid.), while in Britain the number of voters wanting (further) cuts in unemployment benefits was, by 1982, minimal (Gallup, January 1982).[25] There has been a marked growth of support in some states for conservative or right-wing liberal parties, but this has usually been at the expense of other non-leftist parties (as in Scandinavia, Belgium, and Holland). Moreover these parties are, or were, distinguished by the fact that they have or had spent the economic crisis period in the opposition.[26] Where unemployment has been high and also rising under governments of the Right or centre-Right, these, too, have been regularly punished at the polls. The primacy of the issue of unemployment in Sweden in 1982 and the lead over the bourgeois parties which the Social Democrats enjoyed in this policy sphere indicate that even a modest rise in unemployment from a comparatively low level had disastrous electoral consequences for the bourgeois government (cf. Table 2.12). Similarly, rising unemployment may have played a critical role in the defeat of Giscard d'Estaing in the 1981 French Presidential election: in the seven-month period preceding the election, the growth rate of unemployment accelerated rapidly, the political salience of unemployment increased at a corresponding pace, and the comfortable lead which Giscard had occupied in opinion polls in late 1980 collapsed (Lafay, 1982: 698–700; Reif, 1981: 41; Machin and Wright, 1982: 14 and 22–4).[27] While retaining office, the Belgian, Dutch and Italian Christian Democratic parties have also suffered considerable electoral reverses during the economic crisis and, in *pre*-Falklands Britain, the British Conservatives, too, lay in the electoral doldrums.

Inferences concerning the relationship between unemployment and the popularity of governing political parties must be drawn with a high degree of caution. Public confidence in the employment-policy competence of the parties may be affected by voters' general assessment or image of them or by economic forecasts or projections, as well as, or instead of, by actual developments on the labour market. Although, to varying extents, unemployment has been a major political issue in all the states looked at in this analysis, it is but one of a large number of issues which have pre-occupied, and structured, public political opinion. Moreover, as argued above, there are different national sensitivities to unemployment, conditioned by the different strengths of the social democratic culture in the respective states: the growth in unemployment which helped unseat the bourgeois government in Sweden, for example, would barely have caused a political ripple in most other Western European states. Lastly, and most importantly, voting behaviour, despite having become more volatile and more sensitive to short-term influences, including political leadership and candidates as well as political performance and issues, is still largely shaped by more stable and enduring variables such as social class, religion, and organizational affiliation. Taking due regard of these qualifications, one thus arrives at the somewhat mundane conclusion that high, and especially high *and rising*, levels of unemployment are politically disadvantageous for governing parties irrespective of their ideological complexions. What counts above all is *performance*. As the defeat of the Swedish party in 1976 and the setback for the Austrian party in the 1983 election illustrate, a successful full, or nearly full-employment policy is not a sufficient condition of electoral success for social democratic parties.[28] But, as testified by the electoral record of the Austrian Social Democrats over the period of economic crisis as a whole and, negatively, by the electoral decline of the SPD between 1980 and 1982, it is an immense political asset. The SPÖ largely managed to preserve its image as the 'party of employment' in Austria up to 1983 and suffered a far less drastic decline in its electoral appeal between 1979 and 1983 than did the SPD in West Germany between 1980 and 1982 (see Table 2.13).[29]

The international and domestic obstacles to the successful pursuit of a full-employment policy are, however, becoming more formidable. From different base levels and at very different rates, unemployment has been growing *everywhere* in Western Europe since the early 1970s. Social democracy has been able in some states to slow down or moderate this trend, as Kreisky has rightly maintained, but not to halt or reverse it (Kreisky, 1983: 132). The degree of economic interdependence between the Western European states and between Western Europe, on the one hand,

Table 2.13: *Public opinion on the competence of the major political parties in employment policy in Austria, 1980–3: proportion of survey respondents rating SPÖ or ÖVP as the party best able to safeguard jobs*

	1980	1981	1982	1983
SPÖ (Socialist Party)	60	58	54	51
ÖVP (People's Conservative Party)	12	15	15	18

Source: Plasser and Ulram, 1983: 278.

and the rest of the trading world, especially the United States, on the other, increasingly forecloses 'national' roads back to full employment. This applies especially to those states, such as Britain, whose currencies occupy an important role in international trade and financial transactions and are exposed to speculative attack if confidence in the government's economic policies is lost. The SPD's proposal for an 'international employment pact' to launch a concerted international economic reflation represents a logical response to this fact (SPD 1983). But, despite numerous international 'economic summits' between the leaders of the major Western industrial states since the beginning of the crisis, a co-ordinated economic strategy for an international reflation appeared further away than ever in 1983.

The *range* of economic policies being pursued in the Western industrial states was extremely wide, reflecting in part major differences in the political conjuncture among them. An especially contractionary impact was exerted on the Western European economies in the period from 1980 to 1983 by the high interest rates prevailing in the United States. These were conditioned by the high federal budget deficit, which was in turn a consequence of the Reagan administration's enormous re-armament programme and initial tax cuts. The high American interest rates stimulated proposals, especially in the French Socialist Party, for the creation of a Western European interest-rate zone to uncouple interest rates in Western Europe from those in the United States. To be effective, however, such a zone would very likely need to be supported by the imposition of controls on capital movements between the United States and Western Europe—with the attendant risks of increased economic and political conflict between the two 'blocs'. The deepening of the slump in the period between 1981 and 1983 and the failure hitherto of all plans for an internationally-concerted reflation also strengthened demands within the labour movements of the worst-hit states for the imposition of import controls and a general retreat towards economic protectionism. This was evident not only in Britain, but also, increasingly, in France.

The domestic, like the international, constraints on the pursuit of a full-employment policy are political and ideological, as well as economic in nature. Where the *political* conditions for their effective functioning are present (as, for example, in Austria), broadly Keynesian methods of economic management are by no means obsolete. The scope for governments to try to combat unemployment by raising public expenditure may be increasingly constrained by existing levels of taxation or state indebtedness, but what constitutes a 'tolerable' or 'acceptable' level of taxation or state indebtedness is defined as much by political as by economic considerations. The tolerable burden of taxation in Sweden, for example, seems to be a great deal higher than in most other Western European states, and the acceptable level of state indebtedness is much higher in Austria, for example, than in West Germany (cf. pp. 26 and 29–30 above).

The clearer it has become that the high rates of economic growth achieved in the post-war 'boom' are unlikely to be re-attainable, the more intense has become the debate within Western European social democracy over the possibilities for curbing unemployment by reducing working-time. In West Germany and in Britain, the *principle* of reducing working-time as a means of combating unemployment appears to command quite widespread popular support.[30] There is also some evidence that in West Germany (depending, however, on their existing incomes) employees may prefer cuts in working-time to further increases in income.[31] However, precisely in a period of economic stagnation or recession, in which cuts in working-time imply reductions in either real wages and salaries or in real profits, the scope for compromise in collective bargaining over cuts in working-time tends to become narrower. This was illustrated by the *de*celeration in the rate of reduction in weekly working-time in West Germany during the economic crisis and in France by the conflict over the Left coalition's plans for the introduction of a 35-hour working-week and its outcome. Moreover, this is a sphere in which the success of any social democratic initiatives will depend very heavily on the attitudes of the trade unions, which vary considerably from state to state.

A further area in which more vigorous action to combat unemployment is conceivable is the re-allocation of public expenditure, within its existing volume, to maximize its positive effects on employment. Although public investment has a strong impact on employment, especially in particular industries such as construction, it was cut disproportionately heavily in periods of spending restraint in West Germany and fell both in real terms and in proportion to public spending as a whole under the 1974–9 Labour governments in Britain (Nass & Webber, 1984; Hughes, 1979: 106–7). The discretionary nature of public investment makes it especially vulnerable to being cut. Whilst public investment might be expanded, there might be scope, at least in a number of Western European states, for cuts in defence spending (which is relatively capital-intensive), in agricultural policy spending, in no longer justifiable subsidies to sections of industry, and in some regions of the public service and social-security systems.

However, some such measures might be expected to encounter strong resistance from within the social democratic parties and from their customary allies, the trade unions. From industrial, financial, and professional groups' lobbies, the opposition to many such cuts would be, or is, intense. Conflicting philosophies over how to combat unemployment and how to distribute the burdens of the economic crisis have in fact steadily diminished the scope for compromise between social democratic parties and centre and bourgeois parties in those states where the former can govern only in coalitions. The tensions for these social democratic parties between, on the one hand, the demands of coalition politics and, on the other, the expectations of their members and voters and the trade unions grew gradually more and more irreconcilable in the early 1980s. This, more than a slump in support for social democratic parties, or, at least, social democratic *policies*, accounted for the displacement from government of the social democratic parties in West Germany, Belgium, Holland, and Denmark in 1981 and 1982. Faced with the prospect of being forced by coalition partners not only to acquiesce in high and rising unemployment, but also to load the burden of the economic crisis on to their own electoral clientele, social democratic parties may find going into opposition the easiest—and *best*—political option, *provided* they do not then dissipate their energies in opposition in intra-party conflict and warfare.

Unemployment and the Future(s) of Social Democracy

The problem of unemployment grew more acute in Western Europe in the early 1980s, while the problem-solving capacity of social democratic parties declined. Given prevailing and likely rates of productivity and production growth, the growth in the labour supply in most Western European states, and increasing labour-saving investment, unemployment may be expected to remain at very high levels in Western Europe until the end of the 1980s at least. The differences in the employment-policy performance of 'social democratic' governments in Western Europe during the economic crisis, however, have been quite vast—and those which have performed worst have been punished electorally, in varying extents, for their failure.

There is no overlooking the fact that the passing of the post-war 'boom' has caused much ideological disarray among Western European social democratic parties. It has become much more difficult than it once was to pursue 'gross national product socialism' (Nenning, 1981: 1074). But, equally, there is little evidence of a *general* 'withering away' of social democracy. For broad segments of Western European electorates, 'muddling through' with social democracy remains, and is likely to remain, a lesser political evil than life under conservative monetarist austerity. Neither is *mass* unemployment inevitable, as the differences in the employment policy performance of various social democratic governments in Western Europe during the economic crisis illustrate. However, if, as argued here, these differences are not simply the consequences of wrong policies or negligence or ineptitude on the part of social democratic politicians (although such factors may have played a rôle), but are more strongly related to more durable variables such as trade-union character, the outlook for the unemployed—and for social democracy—is not nearly as rosy in some Western European states as in others.

In respect of social democracy in Austria and Sweden, there were grounds for considerable optimism in 1983. In both of these states, the level of open unemployment was comparatively low. Although it lacked an overall Parliamentary majority, the Swedish party had more seats in the *Riksdag* than the three bourgeois parties together until the 1985 election and, together with the Left–Communist Party, was still stronger than the bourgeois parties in the new Parliament. The Austrian party had lost its absolute Parliamentary majority, but the coalition agreement reached after the 1983 election indicated that its new coalition partner, the Freedom (Liberal) Party, was unlikely to carry as much weight in the coalition as did the Free Democrats in the Social–Liberal coalition in West Germany. Neither party was therefore in a position where it was likely to be forced to enter into damaging compromises in questions of economic management. Both parties also maintained close and amicable relations with (normally) co-operative trade union movements and were not riven to the same extent as many of their sister parties by intra-party conflict and strife. In Austria in particular, the 'social partnership' was still stable, the scope for the expansion of some employment-supporting measures, such as those of labour-market policy, was still considerable, and—something which had a possible electoral significance—the domestic labour force could still be partially protected against the effects of the crisis by sending foreign workers 'home'.

The outlook for social democracy in West Germany was rather less encouraging than in Austria or Sweden. There remained in West Germany, despite the SPD's defeat in the March 1983 election, a solid bed-rock of popular support for a 'socially equitable' crisis-management policy of the kind which, programmatically, the SPD supports (Webber, 1982: 271–2). As the SPD leadership was now determined to lead the party from the centre (rather than from the right in the style of Schmidt), so there was a very good chance that it would present a more cohesive image to the electorate than it had done in the last years of Schmidt's Chancellorship. Despite the friction which developed between the SPD and the trade unions, especially during the final months of the Social–Liberal coalition, the German unions remained essentially co-operative. There was still considerable *economic* scope for the pursuit of a full-employment-oriented economic policy. However, a future social democratic government would still be confronted with the institutional obstacles to such a policy imposed, for example, by the Bundesbank and the federal organization of the West German state. More importantly, it was not foreseeable just how the SPD could, or hoped to, regain control of the federal government. To its right, a coalition with a now preponderantly right-wing Liberal party was out of the question and, as the party leadership recognized, a new 'Grand Coalition' with the CDU/CSU would provoke massive intra-party protest and opposition and give further impetus to the Greens—quite apart from the fact that the programmatic differences between the two parties were much less reconcilable than in the 1960s. To its left, the chances of any kind of coalition or predictable co-operation with the Greens were hardly any less remote. Such an arrangement would be resisted by strong groupings within both the SPD and the Greens and opposed by large numbers of SPD supporters and a majority of the trade unions.[32] The SPD would therefore probably aim to win Green *voters* (back) to the SPD and bank on the Green *parties* proving an ephemeral phenomenon in the West German political landscape. Even if it were to succeed in doing so, however, short-term electoral influences would have to work exceptionally strongly in its favour for it to be able to defeat the Christian Democratic parties, which have far more stable partisans than the SPD (Güllner, 1983: 22 and 29).

Within two years of the change of power in France, there were few traces left of the euphoria which had accompanied the massive election victory of the Left in 1981. Popular support for the new government held up very well during its first year in office, but then started to weaken after its 'U-turn' towards a more austere style of economic management in the middle of 1982.[33] The effectiveness of its general strategy for managing the economy and its employment policies were viewed with widespread, and growing scepticism.[34] The results of the 1983 local elections supported the hypothesis that disillusioned Left voters were lapsing into political abstention rather than switching their allegiance to the Right.[35] The continuation of such a trend, however, would be sufficient to destroy the Parliamentary majority of the Left parties at a 1986 election, especially as the parties of the Right would in any case need only to mobilize their 'hibernating' electorate in order to regain their former ascendancy over the Left.[36] Within the trade-union movements and the Socialist Party itself, growing disenchantment with the direction of the government's economic policy, especially with its probable impact on employment, was visible.[37] Moreover, with the Communists' withdrawal from the government in 1984, the 'Union of the Left' was effectively defunct.

Although the shift in the balance of forces within the French Left in favour of the Socialists was perhaps the most remarkable aspect of the results of the 1981 election, there could still be no stable government of the Left which did not incorporate the Communists. Plans implemented by Mitterrand and the Prime Minister, Fabius, to change the electoral system obviously aimed at creating the possibility of an 'opening of the centre'. This was a very high-risk project, whose success required at the very least that the traditional parties of the Right bloc fail to win an absolute majority of the vote by themselves in 1986.

Following the 1983 election the future of social democracy in Britain looked decidedly bleaker than in Austria, Sweden, West Germany, or France. With the formation of the new Social Democratic Party by the Labour right-wingers in 1981, the left vote in Britain was split. Although the SDP polled better than had at first been expected in the 1983 election, the wave of support it enjoyed immediately after its establishment had in fact ebbed very substantially. Even in partnership with the Liberals, it could not overcome the obstacles to significant Parliamentary representation posed for smaller parties by the British electoral system. The mutual animosity between the SDP and the Labour Party was such as to exclude any co-operation between them for the foreseeable future. There thus existed a danger that their competition could facilitate a prolonged period of government in Britain by the Conservative Party, even if the Conservative vote were to fall considerably below its 1983 level. *No* social democratic pa y in post-war Europe—let alone one which had spent the previous four-year period in opposition—had suffered as profound an electoral defeat as the Labour Party at the 1983 election. Labour suffered from still deep internal divisions, a crumbling party organization, a severe lack of credibility of its leadership, and declining public identification with many of its fundamental values (cf. Crewe, 1982: 26–39). If it had won the election, a Labour government would have inherited a real level of unemployment of well over three million.

Nevertheless, the party had reached no agreement with the trade unions before the election over a wages or incomes policy (statutory, voluntary or informal) which the government could have pursued with the unions' collaboration. Yet, without such an agreement and its effective implementation, a programme for an economic reflation in Britain would have been almost bound to founder, like its predecessors, on the recurrent problems of rising inflation and trade deficits. The likelihood of a Labour government having been able to 'reduce unemployment to below one million within five years of taking office' (Labour Party, 1982: 17) is not obvious. Labour experienced a modest revival under its new leader, Kinnock, but the party's deeper structural problems remained unresolved, and this could not disguise the fact that its standing in opinion polls was still much lower than it had been at a comparable stage in the previous parliament.

The success or failure of social democratic, or other, parties in combating unemployment is but one of very many variables which will influence the future development of social democracy in Western Europe. But, in so far as unemployment trends and the future of social democracy *are* intertwined, then social democracy in Western Europe is likely to have a wide variety of futures.

Notes

1. For the concept of the 'social democratic consensus', see Dahrendorf, 1980: 106–9.
2. Whilst having made little progress against the resistance of the employers with regard to weekly working-time, the unions have succeeded, however, in winning longer annual holidays for most German employees.
3. Between 1974 and 1980, the labour force participation rate for women rose from 57% to 65% in Sweden, but from 38.7% to only 39.3% in West Germany, See Webber, 1983b: 29.
4. According to the author's own calculations, if these foreign workers had stayed, or had been able to stay, in West Germany, and had been enrolled as unemployed, the level of registered unemployment would have been higher in West Germany in 1978 than in Britain.
5. A major contribution to this rise in employment was also made, however, by a major medium-term programme of public investment during this period. Cf. Nass and Webber, 1984.
6. According to the former Chancellor, 'there were no longer any

Austrian capitalists' when the SPÖ came to power in the Grand Coalition in Austria after the Second World War (Kreisky, 1983: 129).

7. Regarding the inevitability of a change in the Labour government's economic policy, the author concurs with Bosanquet, 1980: 35.

8. *E*xcluding subsidies for the retention of existing jobs (such as the temporary employment subsidy), these programmes 'employed' about 1.1 per cent of the dependent British work force, according to the author's calculations, in 1978–9. For comparative figures for West Germany and Sweden, see Table 2.3.

9. For detailed analyses of the Left government's initial employment policy, see the Gruppe Politikinformationen, 1982: 1–4; Kühlewind, 1982: 292–311; and Alf, 1982: 68–76.

10. The principal beneficiary of the French government's programme for stimulating the economy was the West German export industry. From 1981 to 1982, West Germany's trade surplus with France rose from just under DM 12 billion to over DM 17 billion (*Der Spiegel*, 1983b: 136).

11. In President Mitterand's television speech announcing the government's intention to introduce a further package of savings measures in March 1983, the emphasis lay clearly on curbing inflation, reducing the trade deficit, encouraging export industry and containing social security spending, rather than on combating unemployment (Mitterand, 1983).

12. The author's argument here follows fairly closely that of Schmidt, 1981: *passim*.

13. For some of the determinants of the strength of 'social democratic cultures', gleaned from a comparative analysis of Sweden and West Germany, see Webber, 1983b: 35–8.

14. According to Delors, 'the relations between our social partners, measured against that which is customary in other European countries, are not very satisfactory. I have always been concerned by this state of affairs. . . . We must be able today to bring about a change of climate in industry by enabling the workers to participate more strongly in the affairs of the company and in the problems of productivity and work organization. The dialogue between entrepreneurs and trade unions will develop and serve as a basis for a policy of combating inflation through more moderate movements of nominal prices and wages' (Delors, 1982: 63).

15. Not all unemployed people, of course, are registered as such or receive benefits. In West Germany in 1979, for example, less than two-thirds of the *registered* unemployed received one or other of the two kinds of unemployment benefits. See also, on West Germany, Webber and Nass, 1984: table one.

16. Güllner, 1983: 25, cites data for West Germany, according to which the

proportion of persons regarding work as a 'heavy burden', 'necessary evil', or 'possibility to earn money' rose between 1965 and 1976 from 41% to 60%.

17. The surveys of the party preferences and/or voting intentions of the unemployed in Britain, West Germany, and France cited in the text produced the following findings (preferences for the electorate as a whole are recorded in brackets). West Germany: SPD 53% (40.2%); CDU/CSU 31.6% (46.7%); Free Democrats 1.7% (6.4%); and Greens 11.1% (6.2%). Britain: Labour 54.5% (30.5%); Conservatives 23% (44%); SDP 10.5% (8.5%); and Liberals 7.5% (12%). France (Presidential election, voting intentions for second round): Mitterand 64% (46%); Giscard 36% (54%). The data exclude in all cases those persons who had not decided how to vote or had decided not to vote. In Germany, the propensity of the unemployed not to vote or to be 'undecided' was no higher than for the electorate as a whole (von Manikowsky, p. 177). However, the British unemployed displayed a disproportionately high degree of political alienation, apathy, or indecisiveness. About one-third said that they would not vote, or that they did not know how they would vote, at an imminent general election. Of the unemployed electorate *as a whole*, therefore, Labour's share was 36%, the Conservatives' 15%, the SDP's 7%, and the Liberals' 5% (The Economist Intelligence Unit, 1982: 19). According to an election-day BBC/Gallup poll, which produced a very accurate forecast of the actual election result, some 45% of unemployed persons voted for the Labour Party in June 1983, 30% for the Conservatives and 26% for the SDP/Liberal alliance (Crewe, 1983).

18. The voting patterns for the unemployed reported above did not differ notably from those in the respective states for the manual working classes, from which the majority of the unemployed is drawn. There are no available survey data, however, which would permit this question to be answered conclusively. Of the French unemployed, 18% said they would not have planned to vote as they did if they had not been out of work—the majority of these people presumably planned to switch *to* Mitterand *from* Giscard (Sales, 1981: 33).

19. The development of the electoral popularity of the Labour Party during this period was read from the monthly Gallup polls, whose findings are documented in Webb and Wybrow, 1981: 168–71.

20. Of the respondents asked by Gallup at the time of the election, 27% said that there would be less unemployment if the Conservatives won the election (and 26% that there would be more), while 19% thought that there would be fewer unemployed under a new Labour government (and 28% that there would be more) (Gallup, May 1979).

21. Trends in the popularity of the SPD during the economic crisis have

been gauged from the surveys carried out by the Emnid polling agency and published in *Der Spiegel*, 1982: 45.

22. Survey data show clearly that voters' expectations regarding the general development of the economy were much more optimistic in 1976 than in 1975 (Tschirner, 1978: 115). The SPD captured 42.6% of the vote in the October 1976 election—its support in February and March 1976, for example, had been measured at 38% (Kaase, 1978: 217).

23. All surveys on election issues carried out in 1976 found that unemployment was viewed as 'the most important problem in politics' by far more voters than any other issue (Kaltefleiter, 1977: 176).

24. The last poll taken before the collapse of the Social–Liberal coalition in September 1982 indicated that support for the SPD had dropped to under 30% (compared with its 1980 election poll of 42.6%).

25. This trend, however, could have been at least partly attributable to the fact that the Conservative government had meanwhile made a number of severe cuts in the unemployment benefit, reducing the average 'replacement rate' of net income for a 13-week spell of unemployment from 83% (in 1978) to 63% (in 1982) (Morris, 1982: 10). However, almost half of the electorate confessed to not knowing whether benefit levels were 'too high', 'too low', or 'about right'.

26. The exception to this generalization was the Swedish Conservative Party. However, after having joined the bourgeois coalition governments after the elections of 1976 and 1979, it later withdrew from them, on the first occasion over the issue of nuclear power and on the second over the question of tax reform. Thus, it had to contest neither the 1976, nor the 1979, nor the 1982 election as a 'party of government'.

27. Between October 1980 and May 1981, unemployment rose by 353,000, compared with an increase in the preceding ten-month period of only 51,000. In the same period, the number of voters who thought that the government's first political priority should be combating unemployment grew from 46% to 63% (Lafay: 700). The IFOP polls showed a decline in Giscard d'Estaing's 'vote' between November 1980 and May 1981 from 60% to 48.5% (Reif: 41).

28. The issue which tipped the balance against the Social Democrats in the 1976 Swedish election may have been that of nuclear power (cf. Särlvik, 1977: 125). A half of the votes lost by the SPÖ in the 1983 election in Austria went to the Green and 'alternative' parties (which suggests that the fall in the SPÖ's vote had little to do, at least, with the slight rise in unemployment in Austria in 1982–3) (Neuwirth, 1983: 269).

29. One cannot, of course, overlook the rôle of Kreisky and his personal

popularity in the electoral successes of the SPÖ. However, it is notable that the comparable stature of Schmidt in West Germany did not halt the precipitate downward electoral slide of the SPD after the 1980 election. For an analysis of some of the factors influencing the SPÖ's victory in the 1979 Austrian election, see Blecha, 1979: *passim*.

30. Asked whether the best way of safeguarding jobs was by promoting economic growth or by ensuring a 'better' distribution of the available work, 45% of the trade union members in a West German survey opted for each of the two alternatives (Infas, 1981: table 5.4b). In Britain, 76% of the respondents in a survey on unemployment agreed to the proposition that 'those in work should be prepared to accept changes, for example, no over-time or work a four-day week, in order to share work' (Gallup, January 1982).

31. Among trade unionists surveyed in West Germany in 1981, 33% thought that shortening working-time should have priority in future collective bargaining and only 20% that priority should be attached to obtaining increases in income. Shortening working-time was not mentioned as often, however, as 'more humane working conditions' and 'protection against rationalization' (Infas, 1981: table 2.2b).

32. While the vast majority of Green voters favoured some kind of co-operation between the Greens and the SPD, opinion among SPD supporters was much more evenly divided: 55% in March 1982 thought the SPD should co-operate with the Greens where there was a possibility for it to do so; 38% opposed any such co-operation (Harenberg, 1982: 49).

33. The IPSOS polls measured a decline in support for the Left parties from 49% to 37% between May and November 1982 (Charlot, 1982a: 64; and 1982b: 66).

34. Throughout 1982, even before the Left's popularity started to decline, three-quarters of the electorate viewed the government's policies for combating unemployment as 'not very effective' or 'not effective at all' (*Le Figaro-Magazine*, 1982). The proportion of the electorate which thought it was doing a 'rather bad' or 'very bad' job of tackling France's economic problems rose between February and November 1982 from 41% to 60% (Charlot 1982a: 63; and 1982b: 67).

35. Despite a 12% fall in the Left's surveyed electoral support between May and November 1982 (see above), the Right's estimated share of the vote rose by only 4%, while those who declined to state a preference rose as a proportion of the total from 21% to 27%.

36. The total *number* of votes cast for the Left as a whole was almost exactly the same at the 1981 Parliamentary election as at the election in 1978. Electoral turn-out plunged, however, from 81.7% in 1978 to 69.9% in 1981—which suggests that there was massive abstention on

the part of the 'normal' voters of the Right.
37. For the statements made by the executive of the Socialist Party and the leaders of the various trade-union organizations on the government's austerity package of March 1983—which reflected this dissatisfaction —see *Le Monde*, 1983.

3

The Labour Party in Britain

Peter Byrd

Defeat in 1983

THE Labour party suffered an unprecedented defeat in the general election of 9 June 1983. The party's share of the vote slumped to the lowest level since 1918 and confirmed a marked, and accelerating, secular decline in support since 1951. Failure to adjust to the post-war developments of general prosperity followed by depression contrasts with the relative successes of social democracy in Western and Mediterranean Europe.

The dimensions of the defeat of June 1983 can be stated quite briefly. Share of the popular vote fell from 36.9 per cent in 1979 to 28.3 per cent in 1983, enabling the Liberal and Social Democratic Party Alliance to establish itself as a credible third party (26 per cent of the vote). In parliamentary terms Labour was reduced to a party of the inner-city and the periphery. The party's strength was consolidated in Scotland, largely retained in the north-east, north-west, West Midlands and, though to a declining extent, in Wales, but outside of central London (where the party lost further support and was reduced to only 25 of the 84 seats in the Greater London Council area) it held only 3 out of 176 in the whole of the south and east, and came second in only 24. Deposits lost were 119 compared with 82 in the 11 general elections 1945–79. Labour held 209 seats and in the 397 seats held by the Conservatives came second in only 125 with the Alliance second in 265. Of the 24 seats held until June by SDP defectors from Labour, Labour regained only 10, the Conservatives took 9 and the SDP 5.

In its regional fortresses the Labour position appears, in the short-term, fairly secure. The Alliance challenge to Labour here is muted: of Labour's 209 seats the Conservatives were second in 160. Moreover in the south and east the Alliance squeezed the Labour vote almost to insignificance *without* achieving a major breakthrough in seats. Hence Labour's position as second party to the Conservatives is safe but the recapturing of enough seats to regain a governing majority is altogether more problematical. Labour had to recapture 117 seats to gain a majority, but the party was second in only 132 seats and third in 284.

In social-class terms Labour's position has weakened and altered. The middle-class share of the vote (A, B, C1) continued to expand through the Wilson era, reaching a peak of 24 per cent in 1979. Labour benefited both from first-generation middle-class voting and from public-sector employees who were likely to favour high levels of public expenditure. In 1983 Labour's share of this growing sector of the electorate (41 per cent) fell back to 16 per cent, almost entirely to the benefit of the Alliance. Labour thus reverted to being a working-class party electorally, but it could not claim to be *the* working-class party. Trade union members (25 per cent of the electorate) voted only 39 per cent for Labour (51 per cent in 1979). Collapse of support was particularly marked amongst skilled workers (C2) where Labour fell from 49 per cent in 1974 to 41 per cent in 1979, and only 32 per cent in 1983—with the Conservatives at 40 per cent. Labour was the largest party amongst unskilled and semi-skilled workers but only amongst unskilled trade unionists did it actually achieve a majority (Crewe, 1983; Kellner, 1983).[1] Labour did particularly badly amongst home-owning workers where opposition to council-house sales was a major liability.

Labour in 1983 appeared therefore to be a party partially marooned in the past—tied to the declining working-class of the old industrial era. It had little appeal to the skilled working-class and to the workers in new industries in the south-east who lacked the traditional social and cultural reinforcements of Labour voting (Radice, 1983; Selbourne, 1983). Electoral recovery required, therefore, a re-consolidation of the middle-class vote and a major reconstruction of the working-class vote which, more than ever before, cannot be reached by Labour in simple class terms.

The electoral failure of 1983 is to be explained not only in terms of long-run social change but also by the difficulties confronting the Labour Government of 1974–9 and the inability of Labour after 1979 to offer a credible alternative government to the Conservatives.

Social Democracy in Power?

The 1974–9 government, like its predecessor of 1964–70, failed to secure fully its goals of economic growth, expansion of social welfare, and greater equality.

After the two elections of 1974 the Labour Party entered government with parliamentary support which was only barely adequate to sustain it in power. Its share of the vote was lower than in 1970, in Wales and particularly Scotland it faced a major challenge from nationalism, and a decline in working-class support was not fully compensated by a larger middle-class vote. Between 1970 and 1974 the party had endured virtually an internal civil war, precipitated by differences over EEC membership but reflecting more fundamental differences over Harold Wilson's conception of social democracy. A truce had been arranged on the basis of *Labour's Programme for Britain 1973*, a strikingly radical document which heralded a more interventionist economic strategy centred around an enlarged public sector consisting not only of public corporations but also of a new state holding company (the National Enterprise Board). By 1974 classical Keynesianism was in retreat. In foreign policy also Labour's programme was radical: both 1974 election manifestos committed the government to removal of American nuclear bases and the phasing out of the independent nuclear deterrent. The key element of Labour's governing strategy was an understanding with the trade unions (the 'social contract') consisting of the government's non-intervention in collective bargaining, restoration of legal immunities, and support for the 'social wage' (i.e. social welfare provision financed by progressive taxation) in return for moderate wage claims.[2]

This governing strategy worked surprisingly well, at least until 1978, despite accusations that all the concessions flowed from the government and that the social contract merely institutionalized excessive trade-union power. Nevertheless, the economic strategy was at best only partially successful. Why was this? Firstly, the government inherited a weak economic situation. Internally, inflation was high and rising. Externally, the pound was depreciating in the unstable monetary arrangements instituted in 1971. The international economy was reeling from the shocks and subsequent depression triggered by the Yom Kippur war. Secondly, Wilson's commitment to Labour's economic strategy was less than complete. The essential legislative foundation was an Industry Act to give the government and the NEB wide-ranging powers. The chief authors of the industrial strategy, Tony Benn, Eric Heffer,

and Michael Meacher, had been appointed to the Industry
Department in 1974. Following their defeat, and the defeat of the
whole left, in the European Referendum in June 1975, Wilson
effectively dismantled the department by removing its ministers to
other posts (Byrd, 1978: 146). The Industry Act which emerged was
weaker than that promised and its implementation severely
emasculated. The NEB's role was limited and planning agreements
with private firms completely ineffective.[3] Thirdly, in 1975 and 1976
the pound suffered further bouts of intensive external pressure
culminating in a crisis at the end of September 1976, during the
party conference, when 'the British Government formally
surrendered control of policy' (Keegan and Pennant-Rae, 1979:
165; Coates, 1980; Fay and Young, 1978). An earlier panic in June/
July 1975 had already forced the government to reconsider its public
expenditure programme and hence the social wage. A White Paper
in February 1976 announced a freeze in expenditure and following
the September crisis a major programme of expenditure cut-backs
was forced through as part of an IMF package to save the pound.
Government expenditure shifted emphasis in the summer of 1975
away from social expenditure towards assistance to industry to
maintain employment. Although Callaghan pronounced Keynesian
reflation dead during the IMF crisis, the government in fact from
1975 onwards was spending vast sums on various temporary
employment subsidies. The character of these measures was
classically Keynesian (i.e. *indirect*) and in the worsening economic
climate the government abandoned the 1974 programme of *direct*
government control of the industrial economy.

    The failure to realize the ambitious aspirations of 1974 led to a
major realignment of forces within the Labour party. In 1974 the
Cabinet was dominated by moderates and the Tribunite left weakly
represented by only Barbara Castle and Michael Foot, plus Tony
Benn who had already set out on his journey towards capturing the
non-Tribunite (i.e. non-parliamentary) left in the party. In contrast
the left had consolidated its hold on the Party Conference. In the
NEC constituency and women's sections only Denis Healey and
Shirley Williams remained from the right. In the trade unions,
leaderships had moved to the left in the late 1960s with Jack Jones of
the Transport and General Workers and Hugh Scanlon of the
Engineering Workers constituting a dominant left axis. Wilson's
position was thus constrained, especially as until June 1975 he had

to tread a delicate path through the complexities of EEC renegotiation and referendum. Here he was confronted not merely by the left but by important figures on the right and centre of the party in Scotland, Wales and the periphery of England and by the committed 'Atlanticists' led by Peter Shore.

In 1975 two major realignments of power within the party occurred. The massive referendum majority in favour of continued membership strengthened Wilson's hand *vis-à-vis* the anti-Community majority within the Party Conference, the NEC, and the trade unions. Almost immediately Wilson used his new-found authority to deal decisively with the problem of wage inflation. Inflation had reached almost 30 per cent, was rising, and the pound suffered in June and July a major shock. The trade-union leadership concluded that governmental intervention to stop inflation was necessary. In August the government and the TUC jointly announced wage limitations, although with a strong re-distributionist element. Jack Jones emerged as a dominant figure in Labour's governing circle. Whereas until June the left of the party had been allied with the unions in opposition to the EEC, the referendum had destroyed the effectiveness of this alliance and the incomes policy then separated the left from the TUC. The left was isolated and humiliated.[4]

This new balance of power favourable to Wilson did not survive the IMF crisis of 1976. Although a second year of incomes policy was successfully inaugurated and implemented in August 1976, and supported at Conference, the government's retrenchment policies to save sterling were soundly defeated at Conference.[5] In 1977 the government suffered a further battering at Conference and the left–union alliance was re-established. The TUC opposed in 1977 a third round of incomes policy but, with unemployment rising, did not press their opposition and the government's incomes policy was implemented.

The real weakness of the left in opposing the government was its lack of a credible alternative. In March 1976 a Tribune revolt by 37 MPs defeated a government proposal on expenditure cuts but the government won its vote of confidence, pressed on with its policy, and the only Tribunite minister who resigned, Joan Lestor, was replaced by another Tribunite, Margaret Jackson (now Margaret Beckett). The only serious defeat inflicted on the government was another Tribunite revolt in June 1977 which, with Conservative support, forced the government to concede indexation of tax allowances (the 'Rooker–Wise amendment').

By the summer of 1978 the government was confronted with a choice. Either it could seek a renewed popular mandate on the basis of its successes in reducing inflation and halting the rise in unemployment caused by the world depression, or it could consolidate these successes through a fourth year of incomes policy. The government's record in by-elections and local elections in 1976 and 1977 was bad, its relationships with the left and with the unions were difficult. Prime Minister Callaghan postponed the election and launched a fourth incomes policy. At Conference the government's economic strategy and incomes policy were again defeated so that the government entered its final year without the usual 'rallying to the flag' in the pre-election period.[6] The government's incomes policy in the public sector led to a war of attrition with the unions and a 'winter of discontent'. By the election in May 1979 Labour's claim to be a party of national consensus possessing a special relationship with the unions appeared hollow.

The leadership which lost in 1979 had changed considerably since 1974. In 1976 Callaghan succeeded Wilson as leader in an election which revealed the considerable strength still deployed by the right within the parliamentary party.

Table 3.1: *The election for the leadership in the British Labour Party, 1976*

	First Ballot	Second Ballot	Third Ballot
Foot	90	133	137
Callaghan	84	141	176
Jenkins	56 (withdrew)		
Benn	37 (withdrew)		
Healey	30	38 (eliminated)	
Crosland	17		

Foot became Callaghan's key lieutenant. Under Wilson he had handled relations with the unions and delivered their support for incomes policy. In October he succeeded formally to the deputy-leadership (beating Shirley Williams 166–128). Callaghan charged Foot with responsibility for devolution. Foot had never supported devolution but he eventually succeeded in getting a bill through parliament with Liberal support and against considerable Labour opposition. From March 1977 he conducted the Lib–Lab pact, an informal coalition which kept Labour in office despite loss of its parliamentary majority (Michie and Hoggart, 1978). This was a curious culmination to Foot's governmental career after years of inveighing against the centre-orientation of his front bench from his position as unofficial leader of the Tribunites—especially as he also kept the Ulster Unionists in the government's pocket. The third member of Labour's ruling triumvirate was Denis Healey, who carried the burden of the IMF negotiations, introduced the deflationary budgets of 1976 and 1977, and thus earned himself the undying hostility of the left.

Although in 1978/9 the right was firmly entrenched in Cabinet, its position was anomalous in two ways. Firstly, the Conference and NEC were in open revolt against its policy. Healey was brusquely removed from the NEC in 1975 and thereafter did not even seek election. Shirley Williams remained comfortably elected to the NEC by the union block vote in the women's section but the government's only other support in the NEC came from a few loyalists in the union section. The last loyalist in the constituency section was Jack Ashley who, enjoying great personal affection, survived until 1978. Secondly, Callaghan's government displayed no clear social democratic strategy. Tony Crosland, the architect of modern British social democracy, had remained convinced but in 1976 he failed completely to persuade the government against the IMF deflation and in February 1977 he died.

The other leading figure on the right was Roy Jenkins, but following his poor performance in the leadership election he left the government for the EEC in September 1976. By that time Jenkins stressed only the libertarian side of social democracy and no longer its redistributive and egalitarian aspects. Since resigning as deputy-leader in 1972 over the EEC referendum, Europe had become the dominant issue in Jenkins's politics; Europe linked him with David Owen who also resigned a (junior) front bench post in 1972, and with Shirley Williams who threatened to resign over the referendum in 1974. Jenkins, by 1976, had ceased to espouse the social democratic tradition and after Crosland's death the leading social democrats, such as Roy Hattersley, John Smith, and Gerald Kaufman, were younger and less prominent.

Callaghan and Healey were pragmatists rather than committed

social democrats of the Crosland variety. In short, the right-wing which controlled government until May 1979 had ceased to represent a positive socialist approach to government. A major readjustment of party policy was inevitable after the election.

The Trials of Labour

The election of 1979 was the worst for Labour since 1935. The party received only 36.9 per cent of the vote and the recovery of the Conservatives, at the expense largely of the Liberals, reduced Labour from 319 seats in October 1974 (314 at the dissolution) to 269. While the middle-class vote increased, working-class, especially skilled working-class support fell disastrously.

Ivor Crewe attributed Labour's decline to three main sets of factors.[7] Firstly, identification with Labour was declining. A process of *dealignment* was under way which also affected, though less severely, the Conservatives. Secondly, Labour's social basis of support was shifting. Although it was becoming more middle-class, the bulk of Labour support was still overwhelmingly working-class but both the size of the working-class and self-identification with being working-class were declining rapidly as employment patterns changed.

Demographic change was also adverse to Labour. In contrast to the 1960s, Labour voters were dying at a higher rate than Conservatives and fewer Labour identifiers were now entering the voting registers. Thirdly, on examining issues and policies, Crewe found that in eight of the major issues of the day Conservative policies were more popular than Labour's. Labour won on only two issues: the retention of welfare benefits as against tax cuts; secondly, hostility to the EEC (an issue Labour exploited neither in 1979 nor 1983 because of major differences amongst the parliamentary leadership). Of course, the unpopularity of Labour policies amongst Labour voters was not new in 1979, but the process of dealignment gave the factor greater salience. Furthermore, the analysis suggests that the differences between Labour voters and Labour policies had increased. Crewe detected increased electoral volatility compared with the 1950s and 1960s. Relatively stable patterns of firm party identification had declined in favour of more pragmatic electoral responses to political issues and party programmes.

This analysis offered little comfort to the Party's social democratic wing since its emphasis on egalitarianism, social reform, and social welfare appeared, according to Crewe, almost as unpopular as the left's more fundamentalist socialist prescriptions. Moreover both social democrats and, in practice, the left had seen economic growth as a necessary condition for egalitarian reform. But the mixed economy and Keynesianism could no longer be seen as guaranteeing economic growth. Externally Britain was confronted by economic instability, uncontrolled multinational capitalism, and threats to national autonomy. Domestically neither capital nor labour had been constrained into a satisfactory relationship with government.

Electoral support for the classical components of social democracy offered by the Labour Party appeared to be declining. Academic speculation tended to confirm this view and to suggest that social democracy had run its course.[8] According to the new intellectual realism of the later 1970s there were two alternative policies to replace social democracy. The right wing of politics argued for a return to vigorous market capitalism, to be achieved by means of monetarist strategies. The left's alternative was a much more state-interventionist and nationalistic socialism in which the economy would be insulated from international constraints to a greater degree than since the 1930s. This in turn demanded that British socialism develop, for the first time, a theory not only of government but also of the state. According to both revelations, from the new right and the new left, the old central ground occupied by Labour's social democracy was simply obsolete.

Those in the Labour party who did not embrace the left's new vision were thrown onto the defensive: unable satisfactorily to reconstitute the old social democracy, they were forced to make concessions to the left's policies while disagreeing, at times fundamentally, with the left's analysis.

Within the Labour party there was a major debate after May 1979 which involved both the development of new policies and the redistribution of power within the party. The latter, to be achieved by constitutional reform, was seen as necessary by the left to ensure that the parliamentary leadership was 'accountable' to party conference and would pursue party policy in government rather than, as it was alleged had happened after 1974, policy dictated by the exigencies of civil servants, the IMF, multinational companies, or unaccountable party leaders. The debate within the party thus involved shifting power from one set of policies to another. The weakness of the party's right from a policy perspective inevitably forced it to concentrate its attack on the left's constitutional proposals. The left also saw the constitutional changes as a necessary precondition for future policy changes. The result was that the party turned in on itself and failed to offer any effective opposition to the Thatcher government.

The Policy Response to the Wilson–Callaghan Government

After 1979 the left successfully challenged the policy of the past government in three key areas—European policy, economic policy, and defence policy. In each case it built on left-wing critiques developed *before* 1979. Inevitably therefore the policy debates after 1979 implicitly and explicitly confronted the right-wing leadership which had controlled that government. Various pressure groups within the party articulated the alternative policies. The most important was the Labour Co-ordinating Committee, founded in 1978, which developed an impressive list of supporters and publications. The LCC can be regarded as the source of Bennite policy within the party: its first chairman, Michael Meacher, was a close associate of Benn. Other leading members were Frances Morrell, Benn's political adviser, Francis Cripps, a member of the Cambridge Economic Policy Group, and Stuart Holland, who developed the LCC's policy on Europe. On economic policy another important group was the Conference of Socialist Economists, an older group whose membership extended beyond the left of the Labour party.

European policy

After 1945 the international environment, characterized by military interdependence within NATO and economic interdependence with the industrialized economies (each arena being led by the United States) was seen as favourable to social democracy. During the 1970s the international environment became much more hostile to the United Kingdom. The left of the party reacted by developing a new set of policy responses which challenged social democratic orthodoxy, while the right failed to produce clear new policies.

In the 1960s membership of the EEC was seen by most of the right and a few on the left of the party as offering a new institutional structure to replace both the declining Commonwealth and American special relationships. The majority of the left favoured a more unilateral stance whilst the Atlanticist right favoured a revitalization of the American connection. As late as the referendum in June 1975 a majority of both the party conference and the parliamentary party, together with a one-third minority of Cabinet, favoured withdrawal.[9] The referendum enabled Wilson to take the final decision outwith his divided party but it failed to resolve the issue. Wilson favoured a nationalist, almost Gaullist, attitude to the EEC but neither he nor Callaghan seriously contemplated withdrawal. While some social democrats such as Crosland and Hattersley supported Europe as a necessary international support for Britain, they were not prepared ultimately to challenge party unity on the issue, whereas others—including the eventual SDP defectors—saw Europe as a defining element of their position.

Until 1977, NEC and Conference opposed participation in the direct elections to the European Assembly. For the 1977 Conference the NEC policy statement argued that unless a formidable (and unrealistic) range of reforms could be secured then withdrawal was necessary.[10] In 1979 the NEC manifesto for the European elections was openly hostile to Callaghan's policy of continued membership and later the Party Conference carried 'unanimously' a resolution demanding withdrawal unless the structural changes were produced.[11] In 1980, 1981, and 1982 resolutions in favour of withdrawal were overwhelmingly passed, on each occasion after very short debates in which the obstacles to withdrawal were simply ignored. The alternative policy was vacuous, consisting of co-operation with social democratic parties and Eurocommunist parties, the revitalization of the long-forgotten United Nations Economic Commission for Europe and even a 'European Nuclear Free Zone'.[12] Did party leaders take this seriously? Probably not.

This lurch into the unknown produced a rather ineffective backlash in the form of the Red Rose Group, a successor to the old Labour Movement for Europe and still bearing all the hallmarks of heavy subsidy from Brussels.

The TUC beat a similar path but with a shade more realism. Its decision to support withdrawal, taken in 1981, led to the economic secretariat producing an analysis of the economic costs which seriously challenged the view that withdrawal could be other than difficult.[13] Nevertheless at Congress in 1982 this assessment was given scant attention and the policy of withdrawal was confirmed.[14]

The general election manifesto of the party made an unequivocal commitment to withdraw 'well within the lifetime of the parliament', the only concession to pro-marketeers and sceptics being a reference to withdrawal being 'amicable and orderly'.[15] Yet, as if in recognition of the unrealism of the policy, the party made virtually nothing of the issue during the election campaign and, when Roy Hattersley argued that in fact the issue had yet to be decided, his intervention was met with an embarrassed silence.[16]

After the election, Foot's successor as leader, Neil Kinnock moved quickly to abandon tacitly the policy of withdrawal in favour of the more credible policy of defence of British interests within the Community for as long as Britain was a member. Unlike Foot, he was prepared to engage in dialogue with the Socialist Group in the European Parliament and to participate more fully with the Confederation of Socialist Parties. He stressed the importance of the June 1984 European elections not only as a major *national* test of the Thatcher government and in particular of Labour's claim to be the major opposition party to the Conservatives, but also as a necessary component of a *European* socialist response to conservatism. Two policy arenas are worth noting where a measure of European socialist agreement was possible. On defence and disarmament, strong opposition was expressed to NATO's policy on cruise and Pershing missile deployment in alliance with the West German and north European socialist parties. On employment, the party urged the case for a Community-wide reflation to maximize the benefits and to avoid the adverse consequences of purely national uncoordinated reflations. This new-found commitment to internationalism represents a staggering reverse from Labour's attachment to the nationalist/autarchic economic policies which had dominated after 1979 and which are discussed in more detail in the following section.

In the election the party partially recovered the ground lost since 1979. In terms of seats it doubled representation to 32 out of 78. Its share of the vote, on a low turnout of only 32 per cent was 36.5 per cent, 9 per cent up from the preceding general election, while the

Alliance vote fell back to only 19.5 per cent. The north–south polarization of the electorate which had been so marked in the general election was overlaid by an urban–rural divide. Labour's recovery was strongest in urban areas including towns in the south where the party had done badly the previous June and was particularly strong in London where it had exploited the unpopularity of the government's proposals for abolition of the Greater London Council. Nevertheless, it is important to emphasize the partial nature of the recovery. The Conservatives' share of the vote fell only marginally to 40.8 per cent. The elections did not confirm the hypothesis that Labour was in a state of terminal decline, but neither could the party interpret the results as indicating that victory in the next general election was other than a very remote possibility.

Economic policy

Alongside the rejection of the EEC after 1979, the party developed a nationalist economic strategy to sustain a more isolationist Britain. This came to be known as the Alternative Economic Strategy. The *internal* component of the AES was essentially a restatement and expression of *Labour's Programme 1973*: a national plan to co-ordinate expansion and public spending; planning agreements within individual companies to regulate their investment strategies; expansion of state holdings in companies through the National Enterprise Board and its regional variants; nationalization in certain key sectors; and controls on multinational companies. The *external* component can be traced back to early left dissatisfaction with the 1974 government and the 1975/6 monetary crisis.

   Labour's Programme for Britain 1976 was critical of the government's failure to implement fully the 1973 programme and, in addition to restating that, the programme added an external element involving restrictions on imports.[17] The intellectual basis for this marked switch from the Party's traditional commitment to free trade was the work of the Cambridge Economic Policy Group. The Group argued that reflation required management of foreign trade in order that the economy could grow without sucking in imports at the expense of home production and the balance of payments. Trade management became the key-note of the AES. It was developed in party statements in 1977, even found a muted entry in the 1979 manifesto and was endorsed by the Party–TUC liaison committee in two major policy documents in 1978 and 1981.

The AES became in fact part of the broader struggle for power within the party. Until 1979 the AES was part of the left's armoury in attacking the Callaghan government; after 1979 it was part of the drive to cement the left-orientation of the party. The AES in its full form failed to convince much of the traditional social democratic wing and even on the left there remained fears about the consequences of autarchic measures for international stability and the development of the third world.[18] The common element in the AES, linking left and right, was support for a major reflation as an alternative to monetarism. Reflation was emphasized by Denis Healey in the 1981 deputy-leadership contest while Tony Benn articulated the full AES package. Peter Shore, the shadow Chancellor, emphasized reflation in his alternative budgets and plans for recovery, and also tried to nudge party policy closer towards an incomes policy.[19] Shore remained hostile to protectionism. Social democrats still favoured Keynesian reflation plus the classical social democratic policies of income redistribution and social welfare within a mixed economy. The left in contrast espoused more radical economic reforms as necessary for the social changes it sought. This conflict is fundamental to modern socialism. Notwithstanding almost thirty years' debate since Crosland's *Future of Socialism* (1956) the party remains divided about the route towards a socialist society. The left argues that Keynesian and social reform is neither realistic given the power of capitalist institutions, nor conducive to real socialism, while the right doubts both the feasibility of the left's version of socialism given Britain's international position, and its compatibility with a free society. Labour's 1983 manifesto certainly reflected the left's view more clearly than any manifesto since 1959 or earlier, but the debate had not been conclusively resolved and the agreed emphasis on reflation was only a partial emollient. Moreover, there was a further, and rather paradoxical, element of disagreement. Whilst it is fair to depict left and right within the party as favouring greater and lesser *direct* state intervention in the economy, on incomes policy the situation is reversed.

The 1975–8 incomes policy was sustained longer than any of its many predecessors. In some ways it was successful from a socialist perspective—its early phases were redistributionist and it directly contributed to easing inflation. But by 1978/9 the policy could not be successfully implemented and the major conflict with the unions was extremely debilitating to the party. In the immediate aftermath of 1979, therefore, the response was 'never again'—a view echoed even by the policy's erstwhile staunchest advocate, Denis Healey. Yet the problem of incomes policy remained. In arguing for a major and partially deficit-financed inflation the question immediately arose of how to control wage inflation and ensure that reflation could be sustained and lead to more jobs as well as higher wages for those with jobs. As late as the July 1981 liaison committee statement, *Economic Issues Facing the Next Labour Government*, the problem was largely set aside:

There is a need for a national economic assessment of the prospects for the growth of the economy, involving such key issues as the use of resources between personal consumption, public and private investment, public services, and the balance of trade. Such an assessment, to be comprehensive, has to embrace such issues as the share of the national income going to profits, to earnings from employment, to rents, to social benefit, and to other incomes.[20]

In the manifesto the reference to agreement on earnings was almost squeezed out completely. The absence of a credible incomes policy was a major weakness in the election campaign. The commitment to reduce unemployment to a million within a parliament was probably damaging in its ambitiousness.

The debate on economic policy after 1979 suffered, perhaps fatally, from its inevitable political context—a post-mortem on the failures of the 1974–9 government. The AES, including withdrawal from the EEC, protectionism, abolition of wage controls, and major nationalizations, was, quite simply, directly contrary to that government's policy. Not surprisingly, therefore, those who sought to defend the achievements of that government and to resist the onslaught of the left embraced the AES in only a highly qualified sense.

Defence policy

In defence policy the left's victory after 1979 was much more complete and, at least until the 1983 campaign itself, when the facade of unity was shattered, the rearguard action of the right much less effective. Defence is one of the oldest arenas of Labour's internal debate, having sharply divided the party in 1914, in the 1930s, in the Cold War, and in the late 1950s/early 1960s. After 1962 the temperature of the debate fell and new issues arose. In 1973 resolutions at Conference were passed opposing American nuclear bases in Britain and reliance on British nuclear weapons, against the advice of Callaghan speaking for both the NEC and the shadow cabinet.[21] The 1974 manifesto had favoured these policies to a surprising degree in view of the committed Atlanticist and pro-nuclear policies of the parliamentary leadership which then, however, ignored the manifesto commitments, consolidated even further the American role in Britain and, without informing parliament, spent a billion pounds on updating Polaris. By the time the government left office it was almost certainly involved in preliminary internal discussions over two issues which dominated the defence debate throughout the early 1980s, namely Polaris replacement and deployment by the United States of new theatre nuclear weapons in Britain. In December 1979 the theatre nuclear weapons decisions were taken by NATO. In January the Conservative government revealed its predecessor's successful updating of Polaris (Chevaline). In July 1980 the government concluded an agreement with the Americans to purchase Trident as a replacement for Polaris.

Defence assumed again the highest salience within the Labour party. Already in 1978, Conference had passed a resolution opposing any possible deployment of cruise missiles in Britain and the party's defence study group had been completely captured by unilateralists.[22] In 1980 a special party conference approved the NEC statement *Peace, Jobs, Freedom* which, while critical of NATO's cruise strategy, nevertheless called for multilateral negotiations on cruise and Soviet SS-20 missiles.[23] At the 1980 Annual Conference defence was the major policy issue. The CND and the movement for European Nuclear Disarmament had captured the hearts and minds of most constituency parties and some trade unions (the largest of which, the Transport and General, had long pursued a unilateralist course). Resolutions were passed rejecting American nuclear bases in Britain and opposing any defence policy based on the threat of nuclear weapons.[24] In 1981 further resolutions were approved including a demand for an unambiguous commitment to unilateral nuclear disarmament. Party propaganda emphasized the party's leading rôle in the peace movement which had swept much of Western Europe.[25]

The parliamentary leadership was embarrassed by the prominence given to defence. Admittedly Michael Foot, who succeeded Callaghan in November 1980, succeeded in shaking off his previous allegiance to government policy (including of course Chevaline) and in taking up again his old mantle of leading unilateralist—though Foot's nationalist brand of unilateralism, emphasizing Britain's duty to lead the struggle for disarmament, coexisted uneasily with the European character of the new peace movement. Other members of the shadow cabinet pursued a more ambiguous policy. During the deputy-leadership election throughout 1980, and in fact from the moment of Healey's unopposed election by the parliamentary party as deputy leader in 1980, defence was a major issue. Tony Benn supported party policy on this as over the AES. Healey's position was more equivocal. He strongly opposed both cruise and Trident, but from the multilateralist perspective that they were strategically unnecessary for NATO, membership of which, he was constantly at pains to express, remained party policy. The defence spokesman, Brynmor John, was equally uncomfortable. At Conference 1981 he was even prevented from presenting his case. John was replaced by John Silkin whose views were more flexible.

At Conference 1982 a unilateralist policy of unequivocal opposition to nuclear weapons obtained a two-thirds majority (4,927,000 to 1,975,000) and hence became part of the party's programme from which the election manifesto would be drawn. Most of the multilateralist vote came from just two unions, the 928,000 votes of the engineers and the 650,000 votes of the General and Municipal. The left preferred not to make an issue of membership of NATO and throughout the period 1978–82 motions calling for withdrawal from NATO received only negligible support. The left wished to develop a policy of minimal participation in NATO, along the lines of Norway or Greece. Multilateralists/Atlanticists within the leadership, in contrast, emphasized continuing support for NATO membership. The manifesto gave the unilateralists most of their demands but contained just enough ambiguity to appease the right, except for Peter Shore, at the manifesto-drafting conference of the NEC and shadow cabinet.

The manifesto stated that 'unilateralism and multilateralism must go hand in hand'. There should be: an immediate nuclear freeze; a shift in strategy towards conventional weapons; the rejection of fresh nuclear bases (i.e. cruise); and the cancellation of Trident.[26] On these four commitments there was unity. Two decisive issues remained. The first was Polaris. The manifesto stated: 'Britain's Polaris force be included in the nuclear disarmament negotiations.' The unilateralists, including Foot, argued that this meant unconditional renunciation. Callaghan, Shore, Healey, and Hattersley argued that this meant Polaris would be offered in negotiations but if no counter-concessions were offered then Polaris should remain. A major row on Polaris dominated the whole of the second week of the election campaign and the party's cause was damaged. Neither Foot, Silkin, nor general secretary Jim Mortimer could resolve the difference of interpretation. The ambiguity had been deliberate, of course, papering over a major crack. Agreement that within a decade or so Polaris would have to be withdrawn in any case did not heal the breach, which reflected a basic difference of approach to national defence.

The second divisive issue was more fundamental, though it received less attention in the campaign. The manifesto called for a 'non-nuclear defence policy' within the lifetime of the next parliament. But the relationship between this commitment and continued membership of the alliance was ambiguous. The manifesto called for the removal of 'all existing nuclear bases and weapons' but conceded that this could not be achieved 'at once' and 'the way we do it must be designed to assist in the task to which we are all committed—securing nuclear disarmament agreements with other countries and maintaining co-operation with our allies.' The qualifications left policy hardly clearer than in 1974. Moreover the manifesto could not define a nuclear base. Healey energetically argued for removal of both F1-11 bombers and Poseidon bases, on the grounds that America no longer needed these bases with longer-range weapons, but did not agree with the left that all of America's 100-plus installations in Britain should be closed. He realized that, whilst remaining allied to a nuclear power, a completely non-nuclear defence policy was impossible. For him therefore the manifesto merely represented a shift of emphasis towards a more conventionally-oriented strategy within NATO.

So far as the electorate was concerned the fine print was less important than Foot's insistence that the party was part of the 'peace movement'. Despite public opposition to cruise and doubts about Trident the peace movement was in fact very unpopular with public opinion.[27] The party suffered twice over, from support for an unpopular policy and from its most popular figures—Healey and Callaghan—opposing their leader's interpretation of policy.

In doctrinal terms the defence debate had been of great importance. Since modern social democracy was reconstructed in Europe after 1945, anti-communism and support for NATO had been two of its distinguishing characteristics. In France and Italy the socialist/social democratic parties had defined themselves in 1947 in relation to collaboration with the communists. By 1983 Labour's support for NATO was considerably less than whole-hearted. Some of the left were also attracted towards dialogue with communist parties—both old-style and Eurocommunist. 'Unilateralism within NATO', the policy favoured by the new leader, Neil Kinnock, may not satisfactorily resolve this major ambiguity within Labour's programme.

Reform of the Party's Constitution

While all sections of the party accepted the need to re-evaluate policy after 1979, the constitutional debate challenged the very legitimacy of Labour's leaders. Three major constitutional reforms were debated. Although these are discussed separately below, it was the *cumulative* effect of the three reforms at each conference that proved so internally divisive and externally weakening. The result of Labour's constitutional changes has been to give much greater emphasis to a 'party democracy model' of party organization. While Labour remains firmly committed to parliamentary means to gain power, the internal power structure of the party emphasizes party democracy at the expense of the elected representative.

Reselection of MPs

In the 1950s the right-wing-controlled NEC had regularly intervened to protect right-wing MPs in difficulties with Bevanite-oriented constituency parties (see Robert J. Jackson, 1968: Ch. 10).

After relative tranquillity in the 1960s the NEC in the 1970s pursued a different line and intervened in selection matters only to safeguard the party's procedures rather than the security of MPs. In 1972 Dick Taverne was successfully deselected by his local party (Lincoln), leading to Taverne taking on his party and defeating it in a by-election. In 1973 Eddie Griffiths was deselected in Sheffield Brightside. In the same year the Campaign for Labour Party Democracy was established, inspired originally by the refusal of Wilson to accept Conference's demand that Labour's election manifesto reflect party policy in favour of the nationalization of the twenty-five largest companies. CLPD took up the issue of reselection of MPs by local parties to ensure that MPs were accountable to local activists, with a clear threat of deselection for those who lost activist support.

Reselection at first divided the 'parliamentary left' of Tribune from the 'new left' who did not share Tribune's predilection for parliamentary politics. Reselection failed at Conference in 1974 (by 3,260,000 to 2,044,000). It was taken up in 1975 and 1976 by 12 and 45 constituency parties, but was not debated because of the 'three-year rule' which prevented the same (constitutional) issues being debated year after year (Kogan, D. and Kogan M., 1983: 27). After 1974 more parties ran into major difficulties with their MPs—the most publicized being Frank Tomney in Hammersmith (deselected 1976), Neville Sandelson (Hayes and Harlington), and Reg Prentice in Newham North-East (1976).[28] Prentice was a Cabinet Minister and the opposition to him was clearly Trotskyist-orchestrated. Leading right-wingers spoke on his behalf in Newham, his case appeared quite strong and he inevitably received favourable press publicity. However, after resigning from the Cabinet, he crossed the floor to join the Conservatives in October 1977.

In 1977, 79 constituencies submitted resolutions on reselection and constitutional reform dominated Conference. The NEC by a vote of 15–13 agreed to sponsor reselection in 1978.[29] CLPD accepted and Conference agreed by 4,858,000 to 1,565,000, most of the opposition coming from right-wing unions opposed to reselection. However the NEC working-party charged with examining the change then settled for a compromise procedure whereby constituency parties would be required to pass a formal vote to initiate reselection. A reselection procedure would not automatically be laid down.[30] The compromise antagonized many constituency parties, 67 of which again submitted motions on reselection and they voted off the NEC Ian Mikardo, the person most closely associated with the compromise formula. Nevertheless Conference narrowly rejected automatic reselection (by 3,066,000 to 2,670,000) after Scanlon failed to cast the 877,000 votes of the AUEW in accordance with union support for reselection.

In 1979 the NEC, itself moving to the left, agreed to waive the three-year rule to allow discussion again and by 4,008,000 to 3,039,000 reselection was agreed. In 1980 the NEC submitted the necessary constitutional changes to conference and these were approved, though by a smaller majority of 3,798,000 to 3,341,000— the AUEW having moved decisively (though by a precarious majority of only one in the national committee) to the right with the election of Terry Duffy as President in succession to Scanlon. The AUEW delegation played a crucial role at Conference in this period and at times Duffy had to use his casting vote in order to throw his block vote behind the right.

The right might easily have salvaged something from this issue on which union leaders felt considerable disquiet. In 1980, right-wingers in the Campaign for Labour Victory changed policy and argued for reselection of MPs by a ballot of all members. However their opposition to the principle of reselection throughout the 1970s damaged their proposal and what might in 1978, or even 1979, have been a successful tactic was, by 1980, badly received. Moreover, the late conversion of the right on this issue damned its later proposals on electing the leadership by universal balloting.[31]

Even in 1980 the issue was not quite dead. Some parties reselected from a short-list of one, that is the sitting MP. The NEC was unsympathetic but did not forbid it. In 1981 CLPD sponsored a resolution to make unconstitutional the short-list of one. The resolution was remitted by Conference to the NEC, and the newly-elected NEC, which reflected a successful right-wing coup, decided to take no action.

Control of the Manifesto

Election manifestos are agreed at a joint meeting of the NEC and the parliamentary leadership which selects items from Labour's programme (i.e. party policy which has been approved by a two-thirds majority). This procedure (clause V(2) of the Constitution) allows a Labour leader to exercise a veto. In 1974 Wilson used this power decisively, and control of the manifesto formed part of the emerging constitutional debate within the party as the left sought to make the parliamentary leadership more 'accountable' to Conference. In 1979 Callaghan used clause V(2) to exclude policies, in particular abolition of the House of Lords. This added fuel to the debate.[32]

The left had already secured one gain on this front. In 1979 NEC alone drew up (in the absence of any corresponding clause V(2) procedure) the manifesto for the European Assembly elections. At Conference in 1979 the NEC, against Callaghan's wishes, supported a resolution instructing it to produce for 1980 Conference a constitutional change transferring power to the NEC alone (3,936,000 to 3,088,000). This proposal did not meet fully the wishes of CLPD which wanted a decisive vote in 1979 before the right could regroup. In 1980 at Blackpool, Tony Benn argued the NEC case, attacking his former leader Callaghan's handling of the 1979 manifesto. However the NEC lost by 3,508,000 to 3,625,000, as enough of the big unions voted against to frustrate the majority of constituency parties. The issue was debated again the following year, notwithstanding a decision in 1980, at the insistence of the unions and against the wishes of the NEC, to reintroduce the three-year rule. In 1981 the NEC argued for its own sole control of the manifesto, though only by the chair's casting vote (Alex Kitson), forcing the new leader, Michael Foot, to argue from the platform against his NEC colleagues—a situation with which Wilson and Callaghan had, of course, grown familiar.

Foot, surprisingly, lost the vote by 3,609,000 to 3,400,000 but immediately one union, USDAW, switched its vote on a substantive proposal to implement the change and Foot won by 3,791,000 to 3,254,000.

Party Leadership

The first effort by the CLPD in 1978 to replace the election of the leader by MPs in favour of an 'electoral college' of MPs, trade unions, and constituency parties was rejected by 4,158,000 to 2,407,000. However by an even larger margin Conference approved an NEC proposal to alter the constitutional position of the leader.

Hitherto the party leader had been leader only of the parliamentary party, the party as a whole having no leader but only a chairman, an honorary post which rotated annually by seniority within the NEC.

Of course the logic of this change was that the party as a whole should participate in the choice of leader. At Brighton in 1979, 34 constituency parties proposed an electoral college and the NEC, yielding to the pressure for change, waived the three-year rule to enable a further debate to take place.[33] The Transport and General's opposition helped decisively to defeat the proposal by 4,010,000 to 3,076,000.

The constitutional debates had necessarily created intense interest about the consultation procedures within unions, particularly in the case of the leadership, of course, where the unions might be given a direct say in the election. In 1979 Joe Gormley cast the miners' vote against an electoral college in direct contradiction to union policy and, from 1980, in the finely-balanced AUEW delegation Duffy regularly used his casting vote against change.

In 1980 the constitutional debates reached a climax. The abolition of the three-year rule in 1979 invited continuous constitutional debate: the NEC was at the extreme in its drift to the left and indeed opposed the unions' wishes to reintroduce the three-year rule. The revelation of the Wilson/Callaghan government's Chevaline programme had infuriated the constituency parties. Conference in 1979 had established a commission of enquiry into the party at the behest of the trade unions, particularly David Basnett of the General and Municipal Workers. Constituency parties and unions were thus obliged to debate constitutional proposals in order to give evidence to the commission. This ensured that constitutional changes were prominent in the mind of Conference. In fact, the report of the commission on 25 July 1980 avoided all the major constitutional debates, because of internal disagreement, except for recommending re-establishment of the three-year rule.

In July 1980 the NEC, against Callaghan's protest, decided to support the electoral college, which was agreed in principle by 3,609,000 to 3,511,000, the virtually unanimous constituency vote tilting the balance with the unions remaining predominantly hostile. However the votes on specific forms of the electoral college were rejected. A proposal to give MPs, unions, and constituency parties weightings of 50:25:25 respectively was narrowly lost (3,495,000 to

3,557,000) and a proposal to divide the college 33:33:33 was more heavily defeated. The party was in fact becoming unmanageable. The Callaghan leadership and the policies of the previous government had been totally disowned by Conference but no clear alternative leadership or strategy had yet secured itself. In the NEC the left was clearly in control, and a right-wing union coup in the women's section badly misfired with all three candidates defeated.

Callaghan resigned after the Conference. The procedure for electing the leader remained to be decided at a special conference at Wembley in January 1981. The NEC (by 16–7 votes) appealed to the parliamentary party to postpone its election of leader until the new procedure could be used. The parliamentary party declined, by 119 votes to 66. The election went ahead. Tony Benn declined to stand; his now unchallenged leadership of the extra-parliamentary left of the party had alienated much of the parliamentary party.[34] The three potential challengers were Foot, Healey, and Peter Shore. Foot had become much more acceptable to the parliamentary party after his years of solid support for Callaghan. Healey was the obvious right-wing contender. Shore's claim, as a candidate broadly acceptable to the parliamentary party but at the same time not identified factionally with the right, depended on an agreement with Foot. In 1979 Shore had been favourite to succeed Callaghan, on the assumption that he had Foot's support. Moreover Foot was older than Callaghan (just as Callaghan was older than Wilson). In the event Foot ran against Shore, condemning Shore to defeat although both he and Silkin, the other candidate, endorsed Foot in the eliminating ballot.

Table 3.2:   *The election for the leadership in the British Labour Party, 1980 (numbers of votes)*

	First Ballot	Second Ballot
Foot	83	139
Healey	112	129
Silkin	38 (eliminated)	
Shore	32 (eliminated)	

Foot's election indicated the desire of the parliamentary party to avoid further rows with Conference which a victory for Healey undoubtedly would have produced. Healey was elected unopposed as deputy-leader but the left immediately indicated that it would challenge him, though not Foot, under the new arrangements of the electoral college.

Within the party four main variants of the electoral college were favoured. The left split in the NEC 33:33:33 (favoured by the Transport and General Workers) and 30:40:30 in favour of the unions (favoured by Benn), with small minorities supporting 40:30:30 in favour of MPs (sponsored by Neil Kinnock), and 50:25:25 in favour of MPs (supported by Michael Foot and John Golding). The NEC finally endorsed 33:33:33. The majority of the parliamentary party supported Michael Foot. After the NEC vote the non-Bennite left in the parliamentary party continued to seek a compromise between the NEC and the parliamentary party based on Kinnock's 40:30:30 proposal.[35]

David Owen, Bill Rodgers, and Shirley Williams argued in favour of a ballot of all individual party members, which would exclude both the union block vote and the parliamentary party but, equally, it would transform the constituency parties, with decisions taken by mandated delegates to a decision of all party members. The campaign for a universal ballot proved as ineffective as the previous campaign for balloting on reselection: in the eyes of many activists the conversion to constitutional change had come too late in the day. Already Owen, Rodgers, and Williams had written to the *Guardian* and the *Daily Mirror* on 1st August arguing that the Labour party was becoming an unacceptable and inappropriate instrument for the pursuit of moderate democratic socialism.

By the time of the special conference the 'gang of three' were clearly on their way out of the party. The universal ballot of members received a derisory vote, half made up of the Electricians' block vote. Foot's preference for a 50:25:25 split ran into serious difficulty in the second ballot, and failed to gain a clear majority at Conference with just under 43 per cent of votes cast. The NEC option and the USDAW resolution which reiterated Benn's proposal for 30:40:30 in favour of the unions each received 28 per cent. USDAW itself was committed, illogically, to supporting Foot's preference if its own scheme failed. To prevent this the Transport and General Workers and a number of constituency parties, co-ordinated by the CLPD, switched votes on the third ballot to the USDAW scheme as second best to the NEC's scheme which clearly had no hope of success.[36] This tactical coup succeeded brilliantly and the USDAW motion won comfortably by 54 per cent to 46 per cent.

The conference proved a fiasco for Foot, offered a plausible pretext for the 'gang of three' to form the Council for Social Democracy, and revealed the problems implicit in any scheme of voting which gave power to the block votes cast by union delegations. Two further factors facilitated the left's victory: firstly, a late switch by NUPE to the USDAW plan; secondly, the refusal of the Engineers to vote after the first ballot when their proposal to give the parliamentary party 75 per cent of the votes had been defeated. The tactics of Duffy, the president of the union, misfired. At Annual Conference he had voted against any electoral college but his refusal to vote, after the first ballot, for the General and Municipal Workers' proposal, which would at least give the parliamentary party 50 per cent of the votes, led to the parliamentary party receiving only 30 per cent. The Engineers' vote would have been enough to have altered the outcome in the last ballot.

Benn challenged Healey for the deputy-leadership in a contest which ran, damagingly, for eight months. Benn's campaign opened up the gulf which had already developed between the parliamentary Tribunite-left (now termed the 'soft left') and the new left in the constituencies. Both Benn's conduct at Annual Conference in 1979 and 1980 in denouncing the previous government and the cult of the personality which surrounded his campaign, a cult which Benn neither welcomed nor disowned, antagonized many on the left. On 3 June the conflict culminated in a bitter exchange at the shadow cabinet, when Foot challenged Benn to run against him for the party leadership.[37] At Conference Benn narrowly lost to Healey after the elimination of Silkin, who had secured reasonable support as a compromise unity candidate. Healey dominated the parliamentary party and to a lesser extent the unions, Benn the constituencies (see Table 3.3).

The split within the left was revealed by the failure of some leading left-wingers on the NEC to vote for Benn. Kinnock and Joan Lestor from the NEC led the abstainers in the second ballot. The electoral college revealed in full all the problems implicit in casting the block vote. Unions varied widely in their methods of consulting members. The Transport and General, with 7.8 per cent

Table 3.3: *Electoral College vote for Deputy-Leader of the Labour Party, 1981*

	Benn		Healey		Silkin	
	%	votes	%	votes	%	votes
FIRST BALLOT						
Unions (40%)	6.41	(1,030,000)	24.696	(3,968,000)	8.894	(1,429,000)
MPs (30%)	6.734	(55)	15.306	(125)	7.959	(65)
CLPs (30%)	23.483	(490)	5.367	(112)	1.150	(24)
TOTALS	36.627		45.369		18.004	
SECOND BALLOT	%	votes	%	votes		
Unions (40%)	15.006	(2,383,000)	24.994	(3,969,000)		
MPs (30%)	10.241	(71)	19.759	(137)		
CLPs (30%)	24.327	(506)	5.673	(118)		
TOTALS	49.574		50.426			

See *Labour Weekly*, 2 October 1981.

The Table shows clearly the overwhelming constituency preference for Benn, the strength of Healey's union vote, the importance of the Transport Unions' switch from Silkin to Benn and the considerable support amongst left MPs for Silkin. Although Healey picked up 12 MPs' votes from Silkin in the second ballot, and Benn 16, 37 MPs abstained—an indication of soft-left antagonism towards Benn which was, of course, decisive to Benn's defeat—a clear shift of votes to Benn by MPs in the second round would have given him a comfortable victory by over 4 per cent in contrast with Healey's actual margin of under 1 per cent.

of all votes, consulted members through branches and found a clear preference for Healey. The executive of the union (composed largely of lay members, including a few communists but excluding the chief officers) ignored the members and favoured Benn. At Brighton the delegation to Conference voted for Silkin and, after Silkin had been eliminated, for Benn. Healey thus reasonably claimed that he would have won comfortably in the first ballot if the union had voted in accordance with the wishes of the membership.[38]

The chronology of the constitutional changes is summarized in Table 3.4. When they were complete, power had shifted decisively in the party. Until 1979 the party may be thought of as two hierarchies of power and accountability. One hierarchy was the party activists and the trade unions who elected the NEC and made party policy. Another hierarchy was the parliamentary party which elected the leadership. The formal links between the two hierarchies before 1979 were twofold: first, selection of MPs by local parties, with particular emphasis on selection of new candidates, given the difficulties of deselection; second, the drawing up of the election manifesto, which in terms of content reflects party policy but over which the leader could exercise massive negative power. After 1981 the two hierarchies were linked formally by reselection of MPs and the electoral college, though the leader continued to have a negative power, if he chose to exercise it, in drawing up the manifesto (see Figure 3.1). Of course, the informal links before 1979 were manifest: shared membership of the party, give-and-take, anticipated reaction to the punishments to be inflicted by the electorate in case of failure to produce credible policies.

After 1981 the independence of the parliamentary party was severely shaken. The informal links between the two hierarchies were altered in two respects. Firstly, the party now placed greater emphasis on extra-parliamentary activity, though Labour remained fundamentally a parliamentary party. Secondly, activists were now much more critical of MPs and the reselection process gave influence over MPs' general behaviour—for instance, over MPs' voting in leadership elections.

By 1981 Labour had moved significantly away from its traditional character as a mass party dominated by a strong parliamentary leadership and towards the classical European social democratic model of 'party democracy'. Within party democracy, great emphasis is placed on the direct influence exercised by the member-

Table 3.4: *The three major constitutional reforms in the Labour Party*

Conference	Reselection of MPs	NEC Control of Manifesto	Electoral College for Leadership	
1974 London	Lost 3260–2044			
1975 Blackpool	Proposed by 12 CLPs			
1976 Blackpool	Proposed by 45 CLPs	ruled out of order		'Three-year rule' in force
1977 Brighton	Accepted in principle by NEC, 4858–1565			
1978 Blackpool	'Mikardo Compromise' approved 4081–2519		Lost 4158–2407	
1979 Brighton	Approved in principle 4008–3088	Approved in principle 3969–3088	Lost 4010–3076	Three-year rule ineffective and abandoned
1980 Blackpool	Change confirmed 3798–3341	Lost 3508–3125	Approved in principle 3609–3511 (Details confirmed at Wembley Jan. 1981)	Three-year rule approved 5882–1160
1981 Brighton	Abolition of short-list of one remitted to NEC which later rejected abolition	Approved in principle 3609–3400 then immediately lost 3791–3254		Three-year rule confirmed 5196–1507

All voted in thousands.

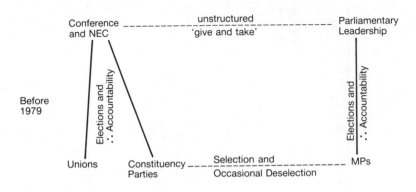

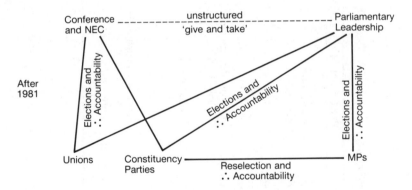

Fig. 3.1:   *Power and accountability in the Labour Party before 1979 and after 1981*

ship over the party's programme and strategy with the parliamentary rôle reduced to that of implementing party policy (Duverger, 1964: Ch. 2; William E. Wright, 1971).

There is of course a potential conflict between representative parliamentary democracy, in which the Burkean concept of the elected representative dominates, and the party democracy model in which the elected representative assumes the role of a party delegate. Until the late 1970s the Labour party successfully avoided that conflict. The leadership operated within a parliamentary system which naturally emphasized its legitimacy at the expense of the extra-parliamentary party. The leadership, moreover, was constantly at pains to emphasize that it alone was responsible for determining the implementation of party policy and when in government was inspired by the national interest rather than a mere partisan interest. In any case, within the party the leadership could usually rely on the trade unions' block vote for support in conflicts with the demands for greater direct control from the activists in the constituency parties.

All social democratic parties have had to face up to these problems of parliamentary democracy and party democracy. The management of the problem is complicated in Labour's case for two reasons. First, the gulf between the views of activists and of leaders is greater than in, say, Germany or Austria. Put another way, the distance between party doctrine and ideological aspiration on the one hand and, on the other, operational performance in government and parliament is greater and has increased. Second, Labour's structure does not fit neatly into the party democracy model of direct control by members because the structure builds in a dominant role for the trade unions. Trade unions do not merely support the party financially and view themselves as the industrial wing of a broader Labour movement—phenomena common of course to all social democratic parties; they also cast about 90 per cent of all votes at party conference on behalf of their 'affiliated membership'. This federal or 'indirect party' (to use Duverger's term) prevents Labour from assuming a pure form of party democracy, although it was in this direction that the reformers aimed to push the party after 1974. Until about that time the trade unions had, with the single important exception of the 1960 vote on nuclear disarmament, managed power within the party on behalf of the leadership. By the 1970s not only had the unions moved towards the left but, more importantly, they had generally lost interest in their historic role as party managers. The displacement of the unions gave the party reformers their opportunity. By 1981, when the unions moved decisively to end the instability within the party, the period of constitutional reform came to a halt.

Labour remained a parliamentary party in the sense that its objectives were to be achieved primarily by parliamentary means, nationally and also locally. However, the prestige and influence of the parliamentary party *vis-à-vis* Conference and constituency parties had been seriously eroded and its freedom of manoeuvre constrained. Exponents of the extra-parliamentary route to socialism made little impact on the party.

The Militant Issue

Relations with the ultra-left are a perennial problem for the Labour party. The problem is more acute for Labour than for European social democratic parties. There is no electorally important party to the left of Labour and hence the ultra-left is bound to be interested in Labour as the only credible vehicle for pursuit of their socialist goals. In Europe, parties exist to the left of the social democratic parties, communist and/or Trotskyist, sustained by Marxist tradition or proportional voting systems. In these circumstances social democracy has clearly to define a position on the left which is distinct from other left-wing parties. In Britain the need has not arisen seriously since the immediate aftermath of 1917, and the Labour party has continuously to face issues of co-operation with the ultra-left.

One sort of issue concerns political co-operation (for instance, co-operation in the 1970s with the Anti-Nazi League which was Socialist Workers' Party-led). A more serious issue concerns party membership. Individuals disillusioned with the politics or ineffectiveness of small left parties have regularly decided that the Labour party offers a more credible route to socialism—an attractiveness which increases when the Labour party moves to the left. Considerable numbers of communists joined Labour after Hungary 1956 and Czechoslovakia 1968. Communists and members of the International Socialists/Socialist Workers' Party joined Labour as the party moved to the left in the late 1970s. Politically more important, and perhaps potentially more damaging to the party, is organized 'entryism' in which a group decides to enter the party, maintain its group cohesiveness and transform the party. Various Trotskyist groups have pursued entryism, the Chartists in the early 1970s and, in the late 1970s, the International Marxist Group/Socialist League. Tariq Ali, the best known IMG activist, applied to join Labour in 1981 though his application was rejected by the NEC. Socialist League publishes its own paper *Socialist Action* (previously *Socialist Challenge*). Other Trotskyist factions within the party include the Socialist Campaign for Labour Victory which publishes *Socialist Organizer*; *London Labour Briefing* which brought together various groupings in London and prepared the way for Ken Livingstone's take-over of the Greater London Council Labour Group in 1981; and the Institute for Workers' Control. The Institute's chief spokesman is Ken Coates, expelled from the party in the late 1960s but by 1983 a parliamentary candidate and successful in bringing Tony Benn and other left-wing MPs regularly to the Institute's conferences. During the constitutional debates in the party Trotskyist factions and non-Trotskyist CLPD were uneasily united in the Rank and File Mobilizing Committee.

The most contentious recent issue arising from entryism and Trotskyism has concerned Militant Tendency, which has pursued a policy of 'deep entryism' since the early 1950s. Militant was for a time the British section of the Fourth International and for a long period in the 1950s and early 1960s pursued entryism when other Trotskyist groupings were either uninterested in the Labour party, abandoned the Labour party (International Socialists in 1966), or were proscribed (Socialist Labour League in 1964). Militant's strength is concentrated in certain areas—Liverpool, Bradford, and London in particular; Coventry and Swansea in a more localized way. Sales of *Militant* and members of the Tendency are probably only a few thousand.[39]

In 1977 the NEC established a committee on entryism and concluded, on the basis of a report produced by the Chief Agent, Reg Underhill, that Militant was a separate and secret organization within the party with 'secret methods to subvert the party'.[40] No action was taken and the affair rumbled on until 1981 when the right at last staged a successful coup in the NEC elections at Conference. In December 1981 the Militant enquiry was reopened and a new report commissioned. This report, by the general secretary and chief agent, came to similar conclusions to the Underhill report. It recommended that the party establish a register of all organizations within the party and a code of conduct. The NEC endorsed the report, which pointed out that Militant would not be able to meet the requirements of the register.[41]

. Conference approved the register by 5,173,000 to 1,565,000—a striking demonstration of union power and union frustration with the leftward drift of the constituency parties. The NEC elections reflected a second right-wing coup and the hard-left lost control of the NEC and its committees, hard-line right-wingers assuming the key committee chairmanships. The NEC expelled in February 1983 the five members of the *Militant* editorial board, a decision confirmed by Conference. This action was surprisingly decisive but nevertheless limited—the purge did not extend to Militant's nine parliamentary candidates, two of whom were elected, and during the election Foot was repeatedly embarrassed by having to share a platform with Militant candidates.

Since the 1930s the Labour Party has suffered from organized penetration by Trotskyist groupings, and the Militant issue should be set in that context. However, it seems reasonable to conclude that penetration has increased in recent years and that Militant has, despite its slight numerical strength, captured not only the Young Socialists but also constituency parties (Forester, 1980). Why has this occurred? Firstly, the abolition of the 'proscribed list' in 1973 facilitated organized groupings within the party. Secondly, the NEC itself became the focus of organized caucuses and leading NEC members championed far-left groupings within the party. Thirdly, as the party moved to the left from the early 1970s it became more attractive as a vehicle for the ultra-left. The constitutional instability since 1977 and proliferation of groups involved in the constitutional debates provided an ideal context for Trotskyist groups. Fourthly, the strategy of Trotskyist groups appears to have switched away from industry towards the political struggle. Full employment in the 1950s and 1960s, the growth of the shop-stewards movement, union power—all made industrial agitation the obvious target for Trotskyists and the ultra-left. Depression in the 1970s, set-backs to union power after 1974, and the fall in industrial militancy clearly encouraged these groups to switch focus primarily towards political institutions and in particular towards the Labour Party, exploiting the concern felt about mass unemployment which, perhaps paradoxically, the unions themselves could not effectively demonstrate in the work-place. Perhaps most important of all, the collapse of party membership facilitated entryism. Underhill himself put Militant's strength in 1980 at no more than 2,000 (excluding the Young Socialists), but, in inner-city areas particularly, the decay of constituency parties has made take-overs easy.

Two further points need to be made about the party's relations with the ultra-left. The first is that the CLPD, which initiated the whole constitutional debate in 1973, has remained resolutely parliamentary and hostile to Trotskyism. Its aim was to secure the accountability of the parliamentary party to Party Conference within a parliamentary road to power. CLPD conflicted not only with the Trotskyist groups within the Rank and File Mobilizing Committee but also criticized aspects of the Labour Co-ordinating Committee. The LCC is not Trotskyist-controlled but its policy objectives go beyond Party Conference's policy and hence were opposed by CLPD.[42] CLPD moreover decided to abide by the decision to establish a register of groups within the party, albeit by a narrow majority and after acrimonious debate, as part of its acceptance of the sovereignty of Conference.[43]

The second point is the organized response by the party's right. Three stages of response can be noted. Firstly, in 1974 MPs formed the Manifesto Group with the objective of ensuring that government policy did not advance *beyond* that outlined in the 1974 manifesto. Of course, in this the group was entirely successful but the group was completely ineffective in combating the growth of the left outside parliament. The Manifesto Group survived until 1982, protesting at the deselection of Ben Ford in Bradford in favour of the Militant Pat Wall, but throughout 1981 was losing strength as some of its members defected to the Social Democrats. In 1977 an attempt was made to establish a constituency organization with Campaign for Labour Victory. In practice CLV was largely dominated by its parliamentary members and never succeeded in establishing a mass organization. CLV's leaders were David Owen, Bill Rodgers, and Shirley Williams and other prominent supporters included Roy Mason, Roy Hattersley, Giles Radice, and union leaders such as Roy Grantham of Apex and Frank Chapple of the electricians' union. In 1981 CLV disbanded when a majority of its committee adhered to the Limehouse Declaration and then to the

Social Democratic Party. Its organizer, Alec McGivan, remained in post but on behalf of the SDP, and with access to CLV's membership lists.[44] Those who chose not to defect rallied to a new organization, Labour Solidarity, under joint chairmen Peter Shore and Roy Hattersley. Shore had previously not identified himself with Labour's right factions. Moreover, in addition to the usual figures (Healey, Kaufman, Austin Mitchell, Merlyn Rees, etc.), Solidarity attracted some members of the traditional left, notably Frank Field, and was careful in not taking up CLV's right-wing policies. Solidarity supported Healey's deputy-leadership bid, established a regional organization and, with the exception of John Grant, avoided defections to the SDP.

On the other hand, Solidarity had few clear objectives beyond opposing the influence of Tony Benn, denouncing the ultra-left in the party and modifying some of the constitutional changes. Amendment of the electoral college to give MPs 50 per cent of the vote was pursued but was clearly not practical. Thereafter in 1982 and 1983 the chief constitutional objective was to replace mandated delegate voting in selection meetings and leadership elections with ballots of all members. In this it enjoyed some success in the 1983 leadership elections, though the organization endorsed no candidates as its joint chairmen ran against each other.[45]

Alongside Solidarity was another organization sympathetic to the right. This was Trade Unions for a Labour Victory, organized primarily by David Basnett. TULV was important in mobilizing trade union organizational skills and finance for the party. Behind TULV stood another, more shadowy, informal grouping of right-wing union leaders, the so-called St. Ermin Group. This group, marshalled by one of Basnett's officials, was responsible for the right-wing coups in the NEC elections of 1981 and 1982. However by 1983 the group was in some difficulty. It had lost Sidney Weighell, the NUR leader, who was forced to resign after casting his vote at 1982 Conference for a right-wing slate against union policy. Further right, Frank Chapple of the electricians was displaying increasing impatience with the Labour party as a whole. Basnett and the maverick Duffy remained the only leaders of major unions firmly committed to working within the party for right-wing leadership.

The decline of membership

The pressure for greater 'democracy' and 'accountability' vis-à-vis

the parliamentary party coincided with a declining party membership. Although greater democracy might eventually attract more
members in large numbers, until recently the stridency and
intolerance of the new left, which demands that democracy, has
probably contributed to decline.

For the period before 1980 the party's membership figures are
unreliable. Nevertheless, the trend they reveal is of an increase
from 1945 to 1952 and then a steady decline. In 1979 *Labour Weekly*
estimated membership at about 284,000 and by 1981, with more
accurate figures, 277,000. Membership then recovered modestly
and reached 297,000 in 1983 and (provisional figures) 320,000 by
1984.[46] The affiliated trade unions membership is practically
meaningless except in the sense that, through affiliation, unions
contribute about 90 per cent of the party's funds. Unions affiliate
members by buying votes at 50p each with their political funds.
Some unions affiliate practically all their members (for instance the
miners), the NUR has regularly affiliated more members than
belonged to the union, while other unions such as the ASTMS or
TGWU show considerable self-restraint, either from deference to
their members' views or from political prudence. The affiliated
membership exists simply as a block of votes; it does not relate to
particular individual affiliated members. Unions vary widely in
their systems of decision-making. In no unions are decision-making
procedures for party business confined to Labour party members,
although union delegations to Party Conference and constituency
parties consist of party members. At Party Conference the unions'
block votes are never split to reflect divisions within unions but
always cast as a block.

Affiliated membership depends to a considerable extent on the
legal requirement that, within unions affiliated to the Labour party,
members must 'contract out' of paying the political levy into the
unions' political fund. The 1927 Trades Disputes Act, which
established 'contracting-in', led unions to reduce affiliation to the
party by over a third and the abolition of the act in 1946 allowed
unions to increase affiliation by over two-thirds. Current
Conservative ideas for union reform, including a reintroduction of
contracting-in and periodic union ballots on affiliation to the party,
could again reduce affiliation, especially in some white-collar
unions. Some unions, notably ASTMS, might disaffiliate.

The real membership of the party is thus small and declining. It now constitutes only about 3 per cent of the party's electoral support. Even allowing for different party systems and national values, this is small compared with European social democratic parties (Paterson and Thomas, 1977: 435).

Does declining party membership matter, other than for financial reasons? First, although television is a more effective transmitter of political ideas than are local activists, in marginal seats organization can be decisive. Declining membership has caused a decline in full-time agents. At its peak in the 1950s the system provided an agent in about half of all constituencies—and all the constituencies the party had to win or hold on to. Now only about 65 agents remain.

Second, the party's rush into party democracy at the expense of the party's elected representatives in parliament would have carried greater conviction if Labour had remained a mass party. The fall in membership necessarily made some of the claims to party democracy rather hollow, particularly as the increased powers were given not to all party members via balloting but to a much smaller cadre of activists on management committees of constituency parties.

Third, declining membership reveals a declining penetration of social institutions and a declining impact on British values. Whereas in Scandinavia or in Austria the social democratic image of society is maintained by large (even if largely inactive) party memberships, in Britain the reverse is the case. The party's hold on the nation declined, mutually reinforcing the decline in social democratic values in society noted by Crewe and others. This may help explain why, after 1979, the party's response to Thatcherism was ineffective politically, turning in on itself in bitter and morale-sapping conflict, rather than turning outwards to rebuild electoral support.

Fourth, declining membership reflects the changing social structure of the party. The debate here can be summarized quite briefly. Hindess argued that the party was ceasing to be an essentially working-class institution and was becoming dominated by the middle-class.[47] The obvious response was that party activists had always been middle-class (the Attlee model rather than the Bevin model) (Forester, 1975 and 1976). A recent study of Sheffield supports the thesis that party members are drawn disproportionately from the middle-class and specifically from the public-sector, especially teachers, lecturers and, to a lesser extent, social workers (Chandler, Morris and Barker, 1982). This middle-class/public-sector bias had increased. It reflected a high upward mobility amongst party members, many of whom were 'first generation' middle-class. Middle-class articulate membership probably contributed to the decline of deference within the party towards MPs and to demands for party democracy and accountability. Greater middle-class membership naturally reflects the expansion of public-sector white collar employment (the 'caring professions'), dependent on high public expenditure and hence inclined towards Labour. Labour's increasing hold on the middle-class vote in 1974 and 1979 thus reflects this trend in party membership. The other face of the party, of course, is declining working-class participation and electoral support.

Labour still obtains most of its vote from the working-class and any credible scenario for Labour recovery must include a recovery of Labour's former hold on the working-class, in particular on the 'new' working-class employed in new industries and, increasingly, living in owner-occupied homes.

A particularly striking manifestation of the embourgeoisement of membership is the character of the parliamentary party and candidates. Middle-class professionals dominate the parliamentary party. However, this embourgeoisement of the parliamentary party is an old-established trend and amongst candidates and MPs the upward mobility from working-class to middle-class is strong (Morris, 1983). Among recent leaderships, Callaghan represented the continuing working-class presence and both Kinnock and Hattersley are representatives of the 'respectable' working-classes in contrast to their middle-class predecessors, Foot and Healey.

Conclusion

In 1980 the familiar pattern of government unpopularity developed. Labour moved ahead in the opinion polls, in March 1980 it nearly captured the safe Conservative seat of Southend (though admittedly against a maverick Scot), and the bitterness of Party Conferences in 1979 and 1980 did not disturb Labour's lead. The Wembley Conference and the formation of the Social Democratic Party (and later the Alliance) transformed the situation. From July 1981 Labour lost votes to the new third force and in several by-elections found its vote seriously squeezed.

By the begining of 1982 Labour's internal wrangles had

contributed to the party's decline and Michael Foot was proving an unpopular leader. The Conservatives were recovering. The Falklands War completed the transformation of Conservative fortunes and left Labour fighting with the Alliance for second place in the polls. The Falklands War damaged Labour. It enormously increased Mrs Thatcher's popularity, to such an extent that in the 1983 election the 'Falklands factor' did not have to be emphasized by the Conservatives; it had entered the national consciousness. Foot, Healey, and the parliamentary party, with very few exceptions, supported the government, as (more surprisingly) did the NEC, but Labour's emphasis during and after the war on the continuing importance of negotiation with Argentina was inevitably interpreted by the popular press and public opinion as indicating opposition to the war. With many Labour activists, on the other hand, the attitudes of the parliamentary leadership merely confirmed distrust and outright antagonism.

The nadir of Labour's electoral fortunes was the Bermondsey by-election in February 1983. Bermondsey epitomized Labour's difficulties—a local party hopelessly divided between the old guard and a young, and dominant, new left; an old and popular MP, Bob Mellish, who was completely out of sympathy with his new party and his chosen successor, Peter Tatchell; a candidate in Peter Tatchell who espoused extra-parliamentary action and libertarian reforms and was an obvious target for press attacks. Foot conducted a public rear-guard action against Tatchell, and then completely altered tack and supported him.[48] The by-election was fought in circumstances which could hardly have been worse for Labour. The Alliance scored a smashing success and Labour's share of the vote fell from 63.6 per cent in 1979 to 26.1 per cent.

Foot's ineptitude led to rumours of a coup against him. He survived unbloodied, saved possibly by the difficulties of timing and securing an alternative, possibly by the recovery of the Labour vote in the Darlington by-election in March 1983.

After March the party staged a pre-election recovery of unity, though in comparison with the strongly-defined phenomena of the 1950s and 1960s, Labour was now unable to rally to the flag with great conviction. Indeed, an earlier attempt to re-establish unity, organized by Trade Unions for a Labour Victory at Bishops Stortford in January 1982, had flopped. The party agreed in March on its election programme, *Labour's Plan: the New Hope for*

Britain, without the acrimony of 1979. In May this statement became the manifesto. The unity behind the manifesto was, as we have seen, wafer-thin in places. In defence policy unity was not maintained. Over Europe disagreement was successfully papered-over although even on the left some opposition had developed to the policy of withdrawal.[49] The recovery of the right in the NEC elections 1981 and 1982 did not affect the policies of the party. The majority for Foot in favour of halting further constitutional change and of expelling Militant consisted of an alliance between the right and the soft-left led by Kinnock. On policy questions over Europe, disarmament, and the economy, the soft-left sided with the hard-left led by Benn. Foot naturally led the parliamentary leadership into rapid agreement with the NEC in formulating the election programme, with the right merely ensuring that there were enough ambiguities to safeguard its own preferences.

The differences over policy were exposed during the election campaign and contributed to Labour's defeat. But beyond differences of policy, which were probably no more severe than had been contained in previous election manifestos, Labour had lost credibility as a party of government. How does one explain the turmoil which had beset the party since the 1970s and accelerated an already existing electoral decline? One popular explanation of Labour's internal politics is the 'government–opposition dichotomy'.[50] In government, the parliamentary leadership and party tend to dominate the extra-parliamentary Party Conference and local parties. The parliamentary leadership is sustained by popular electoral support and its policy reflects the many constraints which surround implementation of party politics. In opposition, the extra-parliamentary party pushes policy back to the left and the Conference tends partially to displace the parliamentary leadership which is shorn of the aura of government and saddled with responsibility for electoral failure. Party doctrine pushes out pragmatic considerations in the formulation of policy. The shift to the left occurred after 1951, more intensively after 1970, and after 1979 in an extreme form.

In the 1950s a loyalist trade union block-vote had stabilized the Attlee/Gaitskell leaderships. By the 1970s the unions had themselves drifted to the left and, more importantly, no longer saw their role as that of sustaining the leadership. The constitutional reforms were, of course, an attempt to control the shift of power implicit in the government–opposition dichotomy by placing the leadership as firmly accountable to the extra-parliamentary party in government as in opposition.

Opposition itself has contributed to Labour's long-term decline by exposing to the electorate the less acceptable face of Labour. Thus in government the decline in support from 1964 to 1970 was 4.9 per cent; in opposition from 1970 to 1974 it was 5.9 per cent; in government from 1974 to 1979 it was only 0.2 per cent; in opposition from 1979 to 1983 it was a massive 9.3 per cent.[51]

However the government–opposition dichotomy alone does not explain Labour's turmoils. The leadership was in difficulty from 1976 and, even in victory in 1974, Wilson had not succeeded fully in carrying along the extra-parliamentary party as he had done in 1964. Changes in the social composition of the party, discussed above, may help to explain the leadership's difficulty while still in government. Ideology also played a role. The conviction had developed in the party by 1976 that Keynesian and social democratic reforms were inadequate responses to economic crisis. *Labour's Programme 1976* explicitly attacked the strategy of the Wilson/Callaghan government. The sterling crisis of 1976 confirmed, for the left, its analysis. The onset of the second phase of depression in 1980 exacerbated doctrinal dispute. It is natural for the party to move left in economic crisis, as had happened in 1931: against Thatcherism the left developed a response which was equally critical of the monetarism of Callaghan and Healey. The external difficulty the left confronted was the indifference of the electorate. Depression does not turn the electorate leftwards and from 1980 onwards the left's attempts to arouse extra-parliamentary protest against the government—the 'Day of Action' in 1980, the 'People's March for Jobs' in 1981 and 1983—were conspicuous failures.

The party system itself, of course, partially explains Labour's troubles. As Thatcherism took the Conservative party strongly to the right, Labour reacted by moving to the left. But Conference moved further and further to the left than the parliamentary party where the right remained the dominant force, able for instance to control elections to the shadow cabinet and to exclude Benn in 1981 and 1982. Parliamentary party and Conference were thus increasingly out of step. The establishment of the SDP and the 24 defections to it tended to move the centre of gravity of the party to the left. It also, paradoxically, galvanized the remaining right into action in order both to prevent further gains by the left, and also to establish the credibility of Labour's right *vis-à-vis* the Social Democrats. Reselection did not prove damaging to the right. Most of the potential victims of deselection had defected and, of those who remained, only Ben Ford and John Sever lost their places. In the reselection process that began for a second time at the end of 1984 the record, in the early stages, was more mixed. The right recorded a number of notable successes at the expense of the hard-left, but on the other hand there were also a number of MPs who stood down rather than face a bruising reselection.

In facing up to the reality of defeat in 1983 the party could rebuild from four solid platforms. The first was the electoral support it received in 1983, greatly diminished and highly concentrated but still constituting, in contrast to the Alliance's more evenly scattered vote, a basis for consolidation and recovery. The 1984 European elections indicated a partial recovery and by early 1985 the party was enjoying modest leads in the opinion polls. At the same time, the government appeared to become noticeably less popular, so that the reversion to traditional 'pendulum swings' offered some hope of a Labour victory at the next election. The second was the alliance with the trade unions. This alliance presents difficulties: unions are unpopular even with their own members and the 1974–9 government had foundered essentially over union opposition. Nevertheless, any credible Labour programme for the future would depend on union support and the unions themselves favoured the return of a Labour government. The union ballots over maintenance of political funds (and hence affiliation to the party) required under the 1984 Trade Union legislation threatened the possibility of some disaffiliations. On the other hand, the ballots promised the possibility of re-cementing links. The party's launch of a major campaign on jobs and the economy in spring 1985 was clearly designed partly to win back trade union support for the party by demonstrating a commitment to traditional union concerns, and a return to traditional party priorities. However, the party also had to take into consideration the changing nature of trade unionism, particularly the greater displacement within the TUC of middle-class and white collar unions suspicious of the Labour party. In addition, for the twelve months beginning in March 1984, politics within the TUC and within the party were thrown into confusion by the miners' strike. For several months the National Union of Mineworkers made little effort to develop close links with either the TUC or the party. However, as its position weakened in the autumn it made increasingly desperate appeals for support to other unions and to the party. The parliamentary leadership responded coolly, emphasizing the problems created by the absence of a national ballot in the union and by continuing picket-line violence, though offering general support (which really amounted to very little) for the cause of a stable coal industry. The dispute undoubtedly placed great strains on the party leadership, which sought to emphasize its independence of manoeuvre, and led to tensions with party activists who favoured more overt support for the miners. Finally the strike collapsed, and the party leadership was able to salvage something from the government's unyielding policy which had become less acceptable to public opinion. With the strike out of the way, the party's standing in the opinion polls rapidly increased and the party moved to improve its relations with the trade-union movement.

The third was the party's control of important local authorities, particularly the large urban authorities at county and district level. During the late 1970s these bastions of traditional Labour strength had been partially transformed by the advent to power of the new left within the party, culminating in the election of Ken Livingstone as leader of the controlling Labour group on the Greater London Council in 1981. After the 1979 election, these large authorities served as a natural institutional focus of Labour opposition to the government—in much the same way as Labour control of the London County Council from 1934 helped focus opposition to the National Government. The authorities also displayed the policy ideas of the new left with great emphasis being placed on gender and ethnic employment practices, refusal to collaborate in government contingency planning for civil defence in time of nuclear war, and in general mobilizing political opposition to the government. In 1983 the government's election manifesto pledged abolition of the Greater London Council and the metropolitan counties. These authorities, supported by the party nationally, mounted major campaigns against abolition. At the same time, the government pursued a variety of strategies to limit 'excessive' spending by local authorities, which led to major confrontations with Liverpool city authority in 1984 and, in 1985, with a number of Labour councils which had been 'rate-capped', that is had legal limits placed on the rate they could levy.

The fourth, and last, platform for recovery was a new parliamentary leadership. The Foot–Healey partnership dissolved itself immediately after the 1983 election and a strong consensus for a Kinnock–Hattersley leadership quickly emerged—a 'dream ticket' combining the anti-Bennite soft-left and the most vigorous exponent of the old revisionist tradition. Kinnock conceded during his leadership election campaign the need for modification of Labour policies on Europe, defence, and council house sales. Hattersley went further and called for abandonment of the commitment to withdraw from the European Community, an unequivocal membership of NATO (though with continued opposition to cruise bases and to acquisition of Trident), a radical revision of policy on council house sales and, perhaps above all, an incomes policy to give credibility to the pursuit of economic growth without renewed inflation. Despite policy differences, each was overwhelmingly elected with strong support from all three divisions of the electoral college.[52] The new leadership thus enjoyed much greater legitimacy throughout the party than its unfortunate predecessor and showed renewed determination to mobilize support for Labour in the electorate rather than continue the introspective debate within the party. By 1984 considerable progress had been made in healing the damaging rift over defence. A new policy statement more successfully compromised differing views by emphasizing both continued opposition to nuclear weapons together with an increased emphasis on conventional defence within the NATO framework.[53]

Whether these foundations, together with the overtly pragmatic and electoral emphasis which had developed in the party by 1985, are adequate to halt a process of thirty-plus years of electoral decline, or indeed are cohesive enough to maintain a consensus within the party, remains uncertain.

Notes

1. Crewe, 1983; Kellner, 1983; also the analysis of the polls by Peter Shore's political adviser, *The Times*, 4 August 1983.
2. The Liaison Committee was formed to unite Labour and the TUC against the Conservative government's industrial relations bill. The key social contract document is *Economic Policy and the Cost of*

Living, Labour Party and TUC, February 1973. For a discussion of the social contract in its historical context see Warde, 1981.

3. For a critical view from the far-left see Coates, 1980: chapter 3.

4. Jack Jones publicly denounced Ian Mikardo, the doyen of the left, at the Tribune rally and the incomes policy was approved by Conference 'overwhelmingly': *Report of the Annual Conference 1975*, p. 166. On Labour and Europe see Byrd, 1978 and Robins, 1979.

5. Incomes policy was reaffirmed in 1976 without a card-vote, *Report of the Annual Conference 1976*, p. 155.

6. Incomes policy was defeated by 4,017,000 to 1,924,000, with only two large unions supporting the government. The general economic strategy of the government was defeated by 3,626,000 to 2,806,000. *Report of the Annual Conference*, p. 230.

7. Crewe *et al.*, 1977; Crewe, 1982; Särlvik and Crewe, 1983; Crewe, 1983.

8. Howell, 1979. See also Mackintosh, 1978; Arblaster, 1977; Whiteley, 1983; Gamble, 1981. There were many attacks on social democracy from a right-wing perspective, invoking images of 'ungovernability' or 'overload' of government. The best, explicitly monetarist, is Brittan, 1975. For a more dispassionate view see Rose, 1979.

9. Byrd, 1978: 142, and *Labour and the Common Market*, report of the special conference of the party held on 26 April 1975.

10. 'The EEC and Britain: A Socialist Perspective' published in *Statements to the Annual Conference by the NEC*, 1977.

11. *Report of the Annual Conference 1979*, p. 332. On the European election campaign and the results, in which Labour gained only 33% of the (Great Britain) vote and 17 of the 78 seats, see Butler and Marquand, 1981.

12. *Report of the Annual Conference 1980*, p. 297; *Withdrawal from the EEC: Statement by the NEC to the 1981 Conference* and *Report of the Annual Conference 1981*, p. 236. See also *A Socialist Foreign Policy*, The Labour Party, 1981 and Heffer, 1982.

13. Paper produced for the TUC Economic Committee, 5 February 1982. The paper was marked 'Private and Confidential', but see the 'leak' in *The Times*, 10 February 1982.

14. *TUC Report 1982*, pp. 260 and 564.

15. *The New Hope for Britain*, p. 33.

16. *The Times*, 17 May 1983.

17. *Labour's Programme for Britain 1976*, p. 12. This statement generally can be seen as an alternative strategy, implicitly critical of the government-endorsed strategy produced also in 1976 by the Labour Party–TUC Liaison Committee, *The Next Three Years and the Problem of Priorities*. Conference endorsed both documents, though

the debate revealed the contradictions: *Report of the Annual Conference 1976*, pp. 137–55.

18. TUC–Labour Party Liaison Committee: *Economic Issues Facing the Next Labour Government*, July 1981, p. 5; *The Socialist Alternative: Statement by the NEC to the 1981 Conference*, p. 15. See also the joint Conference of Socialist Economists–Labour Co-ordinating Committee: *The Alternative Economic Strategy: A Labour Movement Response to the Economic Crisis*, 1980, (London, CSE and LCC) and Cripps *et al.*, 1981.

19. *Programme for Recovery*, produced by Peter Shore and the team of Treasury spokesmen, November 1982, and Shore, 1983. For a vigorous right-wing argument for reflation without the direct state intervention in the economy and the trade controls demanded by the AES see Mitchell, 1983a and 1983b.

20. *Economic Issues Facing the Next Labour Government*, para. 33. See the analysis of the liaison committee's operation and in particular the incomes policy issue in the *New Statesman*, 22 July 1983.

21. *Report of the Annual Conference 1973*, p. 301. The vote was 3,166,000 to 2,462,000.

22. *Report of the Annual Conference 1978*, p. 323. See also the report of the Labour Party Defence Study Group, 1977; Kaldor *et al.*, 1980; and Smith, 1980.

23. *Peace, Jobs, Freedom: Labour's Call to the People*, presented to the special party conference, 31 May 1980. Conference report is in *Report of the Annual Conference 1980*.

24. *Report of the Annual Conference 1980*, pp. 156–73. A motion opposing membership of NATO was lost by 6,279,000 to 826,000.

25. *Nuclear Weapons and the Arms Race: Statement by the NEC to the 1981 Conference* was approved overwhelmingly, *Report of the Annual Conference 1981*, p. 157. A motion unconditionally opposing all nuclear bases in Britain was approved by 4,596,000 to 2,315,000. Opposition to NATO was defeated by 5,206,000 to 1,619,000. On propaganda see, for instance, *No Cruise, No Trident, No Nuclear Weapons*, 1981.

26. *The New Hope for Britain*, p. 36.

27. For a summary of the opinion poll data and the argument that defence was decisive in Labour's defeat see George and Pawlisch, 1983. Crewe, 1983 concluded similarly. On defence, Conservatives had a staggering 54% lead over Labour, according to MORI.

28. See Kogan and Kogan, 1983: 33. Turner, 1981 gives a figure of 29 reselection problems 1974–9. This is a useful article on parliamentary–activist relationships within the party. The other two MPs deselected in this period were Maureen Colquhoun (Northampton North) and Sir

Arthur Irvine (Liverpool Edge Hill).

29. *Labour Weekly*, 7 October 1977.

30. *Report of the Annual Conference 1978*, p. 443.

31. Contrast the case against reselection in *Labour Victory* 13, published by the CLV, October 1979, with support for reselection by all party members in *Campaign for Labour Victory: Briefing Paper no. 1*, 1980.

32. The politically significant publication was the account by the secretary of the research department of the way Callaghan drew up the manifesto: Bish, 1979. This episode is discussed briefly in Whiteley, 1983: 129.

33. *Report of the NEC 1978–9*, p. 26.

34. On the NEC and the parliamentary party see *Labour Weekly*, 24 and 31 October 1980. See Kogan and Kogan, 1983: 98 for an account of Benn's decision not to challenge Foot.

35. *Labour Weekly*, 5 December 1980.

36. *Labour Weekly*, 30 January 1981. Kogan and Kogan, 1983: 102.

37. *Labour Solidarity*, June 1981, published Foot's speech in full as part of its campaign for Healey and against Benn.

38. Interesting analyses of the tactics of the TGWU's delegation are given in *Labour Weekly*, 2 October 1981 and much more fully in the *Guardian*, 1 September 1982.

39. For Underhill's estimates see *The Times*, 21 March 1980, which summarizes his report. There are many accounts of the far-left in Britain. For an amusing one see Kaur, 1983.

40. *Report of the NEC 1976–7*, p. 160. The report itself by Underhill was never published by the party. He finally published it himself.

41. *Report of the NEC 1981–2*, pp. 4 and 123.

42. See Vladimir Derer the secretary of the CLPD's review of the LCC's statement: 'Labour and Mass Politics', *Labour Weekly*, 16 July 1982.

43. The *Guardian*, 31 January 1983. The vote was 297 to 280.

44. Alec McGivan wrote to all CLV supporters on CLV-headed paper but with a request for support for the Council for Social Democracy, 11 March 1981.

45. Balloting of members was carried out by perhaps half of all local parties and confirmed both Kinnock's overwhelming support but also a preference for Hattersley over Meacher as deputy. See the *Guardian*, 6 and 30 September 1983 and for a fuller analysis the *New Statesman*, 7 October 1983 (which also discusses the balloting within unions which assisted Hattersley over Meacher).

46. *Labour Weekly*, 28 September 1979 and 12 April 1985. On the decline in membership see Whiteley, 1982 and 1983: chapter 3. The only analysis contradicting this view and arguing for an increase in membership after a slump in the late 1960s is Seyd and Minkin, 1979.

47. Hindess, 1971. By looking at the same city (Liverpool), Baxter, 1972, drew the diametrically opposite conclusion of increasing working-class dominance. Whiteley's analysis (see note 46) supports Hindess. For a shorter analysis see Whiteley, 1981.
48. The key denounciation of Tatchell, whom some journalists thought Foot had confused with Tariq Ali, came in the House of Commons on 3 December 1981. See *Hansard* 1981–2, vol. 14, col. 389. Foot endorsed Tatchell after Tatchell made a statement which appeared to retract, at least partially, his support for extra-parliamentary activity.
49. *Labour Weekly*, 6 and 16 July 1982. The leader of Labour MEPs, Barbara Castle, finally abandoned her own long-held opposition to membership in favour of defending British interests from within the EP. See *The Times*, 16 September 1982 and *New Statesman*, 17 September 1982. See also Holland, 1983; Palmer, 1982.
50. The 'government–opposition dichotomy' refers to the different pressures and constraints acting on parties in government and in opposition, the balance of power between institutions within parties, and hence the behaviour of parties in government and opposition.
51. These figures are from Webber, 1983a.
52. Kinnock overwhelmingly took the trade union and constituency party divisions and a comfortable majority in the parliamentary division (with a 2:1 lead over Hattersley). Hattersley even more completely took the trade union and parliamentary divisions in the deputy-leadership, and, less predictably, a majority of the constituency division. *Labour Weekly*, 7 October 1983.
53. *Defence and Security for Britain*, statement to Annual Conference by the NEC, 1984.

4

'All the King's horses and all the King's men': The Social Democratic Party in Britain

*Henry Drucker**

CRUELTY can be unfair; it can also be memorable. The most memorable characterization of the Social Democratic Party (SDP) came twenty years before the party's founding. It is contained in 'a message from Brian Bright, the popular, socio-economist, television personality' on behalf of the 'Modern Living Party, the new centre party founded with the go-ahead people of today in mind'.

Most of us are young. Most of us are ordinary—that's to say, middle-class—people . . . But . . . the quality we all share (and I say this in all modesty) is successfulness. By that I mean that we are the sort of people who are good at passing exams . . . and, in general, doing well for ourselves in a highly competitive world . . .

In short, the sort of people who join the Modern Living Party are men and women who enjoy certain natural advantages which they've inherited from their parents, and which they confidently expect to hand on to their children. . . .

Turn your back on the vested interests—whether it be the Tory Party's vested interests in the status quo, or the Labour Party's vested interests in dragging us all down to the same level. Forget sectional advantage. Let us unit and devote ourselves seriously to a noble principle—Equality of Opportunity (Barry, 1982).

Brian Bright epitomizes what many of its critics—and some of its friends—think of the SDP. It is utterly dominated by and attractive to readers of the *Guardian*; well-educated, highly-paid, young (under 45), people who care about the great social and moral issues which they see with a clarity unavailable to those engaged in life's heavier struggle—as from the sidelines.

* Thanks are due to the Nuffield Foundation for a grant to aid my research into the Social Democratic Party.

The SDP was born in March 1981. It was created by a breakaway from Labour of four prominent and a dozen other MPs. Roy Jenkins—shortly to be the new Party's first Leader—was an ex-Home Secretary, ex-Chancellor of the Exchequer, ex-Deputy Leader of the Labour Party, and ex-President of the European Commission. David Owen was an ex-Foreign Minister; Shirley Williams and Bill Rodgers had also been members of Labour's Cabinet from 1974–9. The Party they began could not be accused of lacking weight or the experience of office; on the contrary, it was to be a Baron's party—not a mass party built from the grass roots.

In this respect, the SDP resembled the Conservative and Liberal Parties more than Labour: and to this extent formation of the Party was a further nail in the once authoritative belief that in a mass democracy (a country with adult suffrage) new parties required a mass base before they could acquire an élite leadership. This is apt, for the SDP leaders had become restive in their final years in Labour, with the notion that local party activists counted for much. In the contemporary world, parties were no longer important channels of communication between citizens and politicians. This role had been taken over by radio and—much more important—television (neither of which could exhibit party bias openly in Britain) and—to a lesser extent—by the press. One of the things about the Labour Party which annoyed and worried the SDP leaders, even before they thought to leave it, was the outdated reliance that Party placed on local workers. The fact that these activists had recently begun to co-ordinate their efforts to circumscribe the autonomy of Labour's MPs only compounded the future SDP leaders' frustrations.

The faction within the Labour Party from which the SDP leaders came called itself Social Democratic before it broke away to form the SDP. At its best this group associated itself with the ideas and principles expressed by Anthony Crosland in his *The Future of Socialism* (1956). This did not always extend to personal association. Most of the future Social Democrats voted for Jenkins when the two were candidates for the Labour Party leadership in 1976. One reason why the future SDP leaders had such difficulties getting their idea across to Labour Party constituency workers was that these ideas—as even Crosland admitted—had been undercut by events unforeseen in 1956.

In essence, the social democracy of *The Future of Socialism* which still inspires SDP thinking, derives from an analysis of how the changes in British government and society of the 1940s and 1950s changed the socialist task. With most Labour leaders of the late 1940s Crosland argued that the Labour Government of 1945–50 had shown that:

(a) the machinery of state was sufficiently independent of capitalism to be captured by a determined Labour Government with a sizeable parliamentary majority;

(b) the Labour Governments of 1945–51 had sufficiently transformed Britain so that further wholesale change was unnecessary, and specifically:

    (i) the government had the control of the economy it needed;

    (ii) the machinery of state support for the poor was largely in place and in no danger of being tampered with by the Conservatives;

    (iii) mass poverty had been eradicated;

(c) further changes were needed to erase the psychological residue of previous class conflicts but these could be accommodated by the status quo. Increased welfare payments and improved state services, particularly state schooling, could be paid for out of taxation of economic growth. Further redistribution was not needed (Warde, 1981).

Crosland's social democracy was reformist not transformative. It took for granted the withering away of class and of institutions based on class solidarity. It relied for its realization on an electorally popular Labour Party appealing to citizens of all stations on the basis of enlightened self-interest. It was based on a consensus—which included the leadership of the Conservative Party—and the institutions created by a Labour government inspired by the ideas of two Liberals—John Maynard Keynes (about demand management) and William Beveridge (about the role of state-provided welfare).

Crosland's vision was the sole British socialist text since the Second World War to achieve an international audience. It was also one of the few works of stature produced by a Labour politician. It has been undercut by subsequent events. Paying for increased social services out of growth is impossible when there is no growth: mass poverty has not disappeared: state schools do little to eradicate inequality (or improve the economy); actions of the European Community and the IMF deprive British governments of much of their former autonomy. Both Labour and Conservative Parties have abandoned consensus politics so that the Keynes/Beveridge institutions are under attack.

Collectively, these factors pulled the rug out from underneath social democracy. When the Labour Government of 1976 was faced with a monetary crisis it bowed to IMF conditions for a loan which were incompatible with Keynesianism. Controlling inflation became a more important priority than controlling unemployment and the size of the public sector borrowing requirement was admitted to be a key factor in inflation. Labour cut public expenditure. Crosland, with support from some left-wingers, resisted the IMF conditions. He lost. Subsequently, prominent social democratic thinkers like John Mackintosh wondered about the consequences of the death of social democracy. But such wonder was an élite phenomenon. It affected the position of the social democrats within the Labour Cabinet because they were thus deprived of a vision, but their problems in the Labour Party had other and more immediately influential causes. Their real difficulties were traceable to the leftward move of key trade unions; a similar course taken by many constituency activists; the failures of Labour in power, and the consequent loss of status for MPs within the Labour Party.

During the Attlee Governments of 1945–51, the parliamentary leadership had been supported whenever it was challenged by a solid front of the largest unions. The biggest union, the Transport and General Workers (T & G), was itself dominated in this period by the man who had created it, Ernest Bevin, and he was second only to Attlee in the Cabinet. When Attlee handed over his Party in 1955 to Gaitskell, reliable support from the major unions was part of the heritage.

Gaitskell and the people around him were, all the same, uncomfortable with the proximity to power which the Party Constitution granted to the unions. When the Party (unexpectedly) lost the 1959 General Election, Douglas Jay even proposed breaking this tie. The social democrats, as the Gaitskellites called themselves, thought the tie unpopular with the electorate and didn't like being beholden to the somewhat boorish, often poorly educated, trade-union leaders.

The Gaitskellites made no move to separate party from unions, for all that they may have wished it done, but the unions did begin a series of slow, often cumbersome moves away from the social democrats and their heirs toward the left. These moves were hastened under the first Wilson Governments (1964–70). The T & G, the AUEW (Engineers) temporarily, the NUM (Miners), and some of the newly-enlarged white collar unions, like NUPE (public employees), moved left. After the defeat of the Labour Government in 1979 the social democrats could no longer count on support at Annual Conference, or in the National Executive Committee (NEC), from union delegates.

This problem was exacerbated by the move further left of constituency parties, already anti-Gaitskellite in the early 1960s. Though even rough figures are unavailable, the impression of a loss of membership, especially working-class membership, from local Labour parties is strong. The middle-class (often ex-working-class) members who inherited the constituency parties were—against all expectation—more, often much more, doctrinaire than those they replaced. In some areas, London and the south-east particularly, the divorce of the ideas of party workers from those of Labour's voters, as well as the social democrats, became intense. The failures of the Wilson and the Callaghan (1964–70 and 1974–9) Governments were better remembered in the Party than their successes and the social democrats—well placed in both governments—suffered accordingly.

One issue divided the social democrats from the Party most painfully: British membership of the European Communities. Gaitskell's demand for safeguards before Britain could join not-withstanding, the social democrats were avid 'pro-Europeans' when the balance of opinion in the party was against. When (in 1975) the division in the Labour leadership could not be contained and a referendum was agreed, Roy Jenkins resigned as Deputy Leader. All the prominent figures who later formed the SDP (though not, intriguingly, Tony Crosland) shared Jenkins's view, even if they did not resign with him.

In the 1979 general election, forced on an exhausted government after a dreadful winter of political strikes against its pay policy, Labour performed astonishingly poorly. It was the worst defeat since 1931. Labour won only 36.9 per cent of the vote (28 per cent of the electorate). The Party was deserted particularly by manual workers (10 per cent). 52 per cent of manual workers who voted, voted against the Labour Party. Moreover, overwhelmingly the most important reason why Labour lost was that people, especially workers, preferred Conservative Party policies. Moreover, the 1979 result was the culmination, not of transient factors, but of long term factors which had been building for over twenty-five years (Crewe, 1982).

For the social democrats, outmanoeuvred in a party which ignored their ideas, while moving further and further from electoral popularity, the final blows came in the aftermath of the election. So far from reforming itself, the Party gave way to a spasm of witch-hunting directed at the MPs. Election of the Leader and Deputy Leader by the Parliamentary Labour Party was replaced by a complicated system which gave weight to MPs (30 per cent), constituency parties (30 per cent), and trade unions (40 per cent). MPs were also to be (relatively) easily removed by their local parties from renomination. The intense factional fighting which produced these changes was accompanied by unpopularity for Labour, and at the same time, polls (sponsored by newspapers friendly to the SDP) showed more than 40 per cent of electors in favour of a new political party of the centre. In March 1981, the four leaders—Jenkins, Williams, Owen, and Rodgers—could contain themselves no more. The new Party was formed.

Performance

The thinking underlying the new Party was set out two months before its foundation in the Limehouse Declaration of January 1981. Though Rodgers, Owen, and Williams shortly published theoretical treatises and the new Party was soon to publish a raft of policy documents, the January 1981 declaration remains the best statement of the SDP's ideology. The declaration reads:

. . . Our intention is to rally all those who are committed to the values, principles and policies of social democracy. We seek to reverse Britain's economic decline. We want to create an open, classless and more equal society, one which rejects ugly prejudices based on sex, race or religion. . . . We do not believe in the politics of an inert centre merely representing the lowest common denominator between two extremes. We want more not less change in our society, but with a greater stability of direction.

The initial attractiveness and ultimate weakness of this declaration is that no one could possibly disagree with it. Being all things to all men, it is no guide to anyone. Unless you favour ugly prejudices, wish for Britain's continued economic decline, cleave to the inert centre and want both no change and continued instability, the declaration is for you. It was this indefiniteness, which contrasted so sharply with Labour's increasingly programmatic ideology and the Conservatives' increasingly strident Victorianism, which struck observers. It led to the charge that the social democrats had no policies and to contemptuous dismissals: 'mere fluff' (James Callaghan), and 'offering you a better yesterday' (Ralf Dahrendorf).

But a substantial number of voters and party members were attracted. Within a year of its foundation the Party had 70,000 paid-up members (£8 minimum subscription suggested). No systematic analysis of this membership exists, but work in Newcastle, the south of England, and Scotland broadly confirms the general impression of a *Guardian*-reading, Volvo-driving, claret-drinking member-ship. (The party became so sensitive about this last that at one point a directive went out from headquarters asking members not to allow themselves to be photographed eating or drinking) (Bochel and Denver, 1984; Goodman and Hine, 1982). A survey of members who attended the Party's first Scottish conference in January 1983, gave the social composition summarized in Table 4.1.

This profile is probably not so radically different from the membership of the Conservative and Labour parties. There is a (small) political stratum in Britain. The SDP draw on it, or rather, the SDP added further recruits to it. Amongst those who had a previous political affiliation, the disproportionate strength of ex-Labour recruits matches the characteristics of MPs and, at the same time, suggests that the new party is in a strong position to hurt Labour further.

The new Party's achievement in drawing in 70,000 members in its first year is considerable. With similar encouragement from the press the (also ex-Labour) breakaway Scottish Labour Party (SLP) only won 883 members—on a proportionate basis one would expect the SDP to get about 8,830 members, a ninth of their actual achievement. For a heady four months the SDP and its Liberal allies were the most popular political group in Britain.

Before the SDP was created, the Liberals were winning 15 per cent or so of popular support (not bad for a British 'third' party but

Table 4.1: *Social composition of SDP conference delegates, January 1983*

Occupational group	%	1979 vote	%	Previous membership	%	Housing tenure	%	Sex	%	Age	%
Professional and Managerial	57	Cons.	17	Cons.	3.0	Owner-occupiers	86	Male	60	Up to 29	18
		Labour	45	Labour	27.5	Council tenants	6	Female	40	30–49	51
Other white collar	27	Liberal	25	Liberal	9.9	Other	9			50+	31
Manual workers	5	SNP	13	SNP	3.0						
Student/ housewife/other	10			None	57.0						

Source: J. M. Bochel and D. T. Denver (1983).

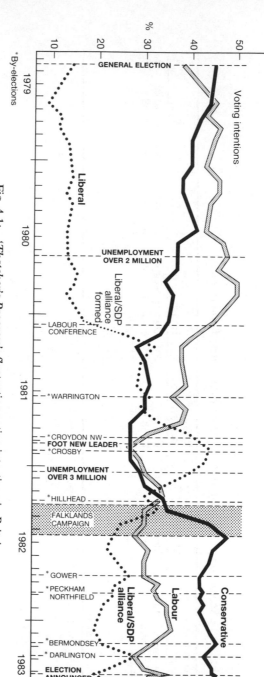

Fig. 4.1: *'Thatcher's Progress': fluctuating voting intentions in Britain between the 1979 and 1983 General Elections*

far behind Conservative and Labour). The popularity of the governing party was eclipsed and not really regained until the Falklands campaign in the summer of 1982. After Labour replaced the then still popular James Callaghan with Michael Foot, the SDP became—briefly—tops.

The other parties' errors made the achievement possible: a failed economic policy on the one hand, a bitterly divided Party on the other. By-elections provided the occasion. The first by-election since the SDP's creation occurred in July 1981, in the previously safe Labour seat of Warrington. Where the Liberals had won only 9 per cent in the previous General Election, Jenkins won 42 per cent in the July by-election. Labour retained the seat, but the encouragement for the SDP was considerable. In October the Liberals, with SDP support, won Croydon North-west with a previously unknown candidate Mr Bill Pitt. Pitt won 40 per cent of the vote, the Conservatives won 31 per cent and Labour 26 per cent. The Liberal vote was up by 29 per cent. At Crosby in November, Shirley Williams took the previously safe Conservative seat with 49 per cent of the vote.

Table 4.2: *Liberal and Lib/SDP performance at by-elections between 1979 and 1983*

Seat	date of by-election	Lib, Lib/SDP %	Lib % in 1979
Manchester Central	27 Sept. 79	14.10	5.30
Hertfordshire S/W	13 Dec. 79	23.60	17.90
Southend, East	13 Mar. 80	25.10	13.10
Glasgow Central	26 June 80	no candidate	
(Social Democratic Party formed)			
Warrington	16 July 81	42.40	9.10
Croydon, N/W	22 Oct. 81	39.95	10.51
Crosby	26 Nov. 81	49.10	15.20
Glasgow Hillhead	25 Mar. 82	33.36	14.63
Beaconsfield	27 May 82	26.79	17.10
Merton, Mitcham	3 June 82	29.45	8.88
Coatbridge	24 June 82	3.45	no candidate
Gower	16 Sept. 82	25.11	9.05
Birmingham Northfield	28 Oct. 82	26.21	8.15
Peckham	28 Oct. 82	32.91	7.66
Glasgow Queen's Park	2 Dec. 82	9.41	no candidate
Bermondsey	24 Feb. 83	57.71	6.81
Darlington	24 Mar. 83	24.49	10.19

While the SDP, unlike the Liberals, showed little ability actually to win seats unless their candidates were already well-known (even in the 1983 election only one completely new SDP candidate, Charles Kennedy [Ross, Cromarty and Skye] won a seat), both they and the Liberals markedly improved their performances immediately after the inauguration of the SDP.

Yet even at this euphoric stage there were warning signs for the SDP that their vote was simply negative, that they had succeeded in winning votes from people disaffected by the other parties by convincing these people that the new Party could do well so that a vote for them was not wasted. A poll of SDP voters (by MORI) at Warrington (which was prophetic of SDP 1983 General Election voters) showed why SDP voters had chosen their party: nearly 70 per cent of SDP voters were protest voters (see Table 4.3).

Table 4.3:   *SDP voters' reasons for choosing their party, Warrington, July 1981*

	All SDP	ex-Con/SDP	ex-Lab/SDP
Extremism of others	35	18	29
Fed up/want change/ fresh ideas of SDP	26	27	26
Liberal alliance	10	9	7
Dislike of Labour's split	9	5	5
Agree with SDP policies	9	0	12
Like Roy Jenkins	8	14	14
Impressed with SDP campaign	8	14	5
Keep out Labour	6	8	0
Dislike Labour candidate	5	4	12

Source: Worcester, 1981.

A frequent complaint from the SDP's opponents was that the Party's popularity, or rather its credibility as a vehicle for protest voting, owed much to a flattering press. One opponent calculated that in the week of its launch, the Party won £20 million worth of free (largely favourable) publicity. Politicians are notoriously jealous of the favourable publicity accorded to their competitors and there was some evidence that the improvement of Liberal performance during the 1979 General Election owed something to the more nearly equal (to the main parties) share of publicity the

Liberals enjoyed in the campaign itself. Research on foreign experience suggests that publicity tends to exaggerate, not create, trends.

The interest, then, of sympathetic journalists in making the new Party *the* story was real. And, certainly there was no initial lack of general sympathy in the serious newspapers for a centre party, but Colin Seymour-Ure has argued:

When checking a list of news values derived from content analysis, it is easy to see why the SDP does so well. It is orientated to personalities more than policies. Its leaders are already élite politicians, focusing on parliament, an élite institution. The party is 'negative' in the sense that it reacts or deviates from the old parties—and 'bad news is good news'. It is 'culturally proximate', readily comprehensible to the media audience (unlike many 'extremists') and located firmly in that middle ground towards which national news media—especially the broadcasters—tend to gravitate. It involves the unexpected and unpredictable (Who'll be the next to join?) within a familiar and predictable frame of reference. It is a good running story, with a progressive dribble of MPs defecting to it, of by-election challenges and so on (Seymour-Ure, 1982).

But once the peak of popularity faded in early 1982 so did press interest. Then SDP members could be heard bemoaning that nothing they did was taken seriously by the press.

One immediate difficulty the Party faced was writing a Constitution. In principle, this comprised two difficulties—interim arrangements, and permanent structures. In practice everyone knew that first steps would set a path difficult to change.

Given the SDP leaders' experiences in the Labour Party and the fact that the effective cause of their departure was a dispute about the organization of the Labour Party— who chooses the Leader?— the new Party's leaders were very conscious of the need to get the structure right. They created a structure in which the leaders (all of whom would be MPs) had considerable incentive to be attentive to the interests and wishes of ordinary party members, but in which both initiative and final decision rested ultimately with the leaders.

The Party Constitution contains six provisions which ensure that local parties cannot mount a challenge to the SDP leadership, as happened in the Labour Party:

1. money raised from subscriptions of members is paid directly to

party central headquarters. Initially, before there was a local party structure, nothing else would have been even possible. Latterly, the provision is still necessary if the central party is to maintain a machine anything like its competitors. Nevertheless, one consequence of the way subscriptions are paid is to deprive local parties of one important source of income allowed to their equivalents in other parties. Power follows money. The provision also deprives local parties of any direct incentive to collect the subscriptions.

2. the local basis of the party is the Area Party—not constituency parties. The Constitution's authors were determined to create a basis of local organization larger than a single constituency in order to forestall attempts by local parties to control 'their' MPs. In an Area the authority of an MP's own members is diluted. Areas are defined as 'two to seven' constituencies. When the Constitution was adopted in the summer of 1982, the SDP had already concluded an Alliance with the Liberal Party which led to a share-out of seats. Proponents of Area parties could argue that this sharing would be advanced by this loose organization. Opponents argued less successfully at the constitutional conference but with increasing conviction since, that the Areas were just too large. People just would not travel far for a political meeting: the problem is greatest, of course, in the largest seats.

3. Area parties' objects are defined vaguely, as 'to promote and support the policies and interests of the Party in the Area'. They also organize local elections and select candidates. 'Promoting' and 'supporting' are quite different from making or initiating policy. It is indicative of the lack of importance accorded to the local Area parties that the responsibilities outlined here are culled from the Constitution. They are not listed in one place. Emphatically, Area Parties in the SDP could not play the rôle which constituency Labour Parties had, for example, in forcing an anti-EEC policy on the parliamentary group.

4. the Party's annual conference (called a Consultative Assembly—the name portends little) is a 'forum for discussion'. It too is not a policy-making body. Policy is initiated by any one of twenty-five policy groups whose membership and remit are decided by the Policy Sub-committee. The Policy Committee consists of twenty members; ten MPs (until the 1983 election

when only six were elected, thereafter ex-MPs were co-opted), and ten others. All twenty are members of the National Committee to which the Policy Committee reports. The ideas of the Policy Committee are published in Green Papers and circulated for comment to Area Parties and outside interested bodies. In light of comments received the Green Papers are rewritten as White Papers. The White Papers are then sent for ratification (*not* amendment) to the 400-member Council for Social Democracy. The Council meets three or four times a year. It has succeeded in forcing the Policy Committee to change tack on the, not trivial, issue of incomes policy, but, in general, the procedure keeps power in the hands of those in the centre. United the MPs should be able to use it to silence and diffuse any objections to their policies.

5. the Constitution keeps the decision about who is to be Leader in the MPs' hands provided they can agree on their choice. In 1982 there was an election in which Roy Jenkins beat David Owen. All party members vote by postal ballot (an expensive procedure). The postal ballot reduces the possibility of Area Party cabal. It ensures that the main channels of communication from candidate to party member are the public media and that (unlike the situation at party meetings) the communication is all one way. No questions can be asked. The draft Constitution had proposed the election of the leader by MPs alone. Party members, inspired perhaps by the fight within the Labour Party, rejected this particular provision. The Constitutional procedure was in any case circumvented in the lee of the June 1983 election. Roy Jenkins, the elected Leader, resigned. David Owen, his previously defeated rival, declared for the post and none of the other five SDP MPs joined him. With only one candidate there could be no election.

6. the weakness of local parties in the SDP can be glimpsed in the way the Constitution can be simply ignored by the leaders when they see fit. Nowhere does the Constitution mention an Alliance with the Liberal Party, nor joint Commissions with that Party on key policies, still less does it imply a division of seats with the allies in local, parliamentary, or European Community elections. Yet Joint Commissions on Constitutional issues (proportional representation, most importantly) and industrial strategy were established. There was a division of seats for the

1983 election. To be sure, neither of these innovations has given rise to any serious local opposition, but they do serve to illustrate where power in the Party lies.

Power in the Party is not complicated by a special relationship with the trade unions. Most of the larger British unions are affiliated to the Labour Party. One or two, such as the EEPTU (electricians) might leave that party, but it is most unlikely that it would join any other party. In any case the possibility is foreclosed by the SDP constitution. The party has individual members only. Poised rhetorically half way between labour and capital the SDP was not about to compromise this stance by admitting the unions to formal membership. In one respect this does make the new party a more formidable challenge to the Conservatives than Labour could have been in recent years: the Conservatives have always been able to charge that Labour's leaders were beholden to the trade-union leaders. No such accusation can be levelled at the SDP. The SDP's constitution was drafted by a Scots lawyer, Robert MacLennan, MP. One complaint most commonly made against it from within the Party is that it is overprecise and overcomplicated, even legalistic. But perhaps a more important objection is that it is too easily ignored, or circumvented, by the Party leaders. We have already mentioned the Joint Commissions. They are an aspect of the most important organizational feature of the SDP—its alliance with the Liberal Party.

Competition between two parties, both disputing the ideological centre, would have been joint-suicide, given the British 'plurality' electoral system. Some arrangement, at very least, about the allocation of seats was a condition of survival. But the alliance, as yet still informal, between the parties was, and is, more than that. David Steel, the Liberal Party leader, encouraged the creation of an organizationally distinct new party when Roy Jenkins, then still, so far as the world knew, a Labour Party member, spoke to Steel about his determination to leave Labour. Steel suggested that joining the Liberals would have less impact than forming a new party.

The suggestion was something of a gamble. Steel, for all his prominence, has never had full control of his Party. He might not have been able to keep it true to the spirit of his relationship with Jenkins. In the event, Jenkins and Steel did all they could to smooth the parties' harmonious co-operation and awkward remarks from inside both parties did not amount to much. Only in Liverpool, where the Liberal Party has particularly robust local organization, were there serious difficulties. In only three British seats did both parties have candidates during the 1983 General Election. They fought under a jointly-drafted manifesto in which the SDP influence is clearer than the Liberal influence. Jenkins was Prime Minister designate. Steel (the more popular of the two) was to lead the new group in the House of Commons.

The alliance between the two parties was agreed between the party leaders, then sold and implemented as best possible. Active members of both parties reckoned that the Liberals got the better of the winnable parliamentary seats. Studies in several areas of the country bear this out. Goodman and Hine in Newcastle, and James in Bristol, have come to similar conclusions. James argues that the main relevant difference between the parties rested in their organizational principle: and the locally-based Liberals, knowing through experience where the green pastures were, having more and more experienced workers—and knowing they had less to lose if the scheme failed—beat the centrally-organized, thinly-spread, newly-gathered SDP (James, 1983).

Negotiations in Edinburgh were, perhaps, typical. The SDP in Scotland focused on Edinburgh as promising territory and demanded the larger number of seats (four of the six). The Liberals agreed only if they could have their first choice, Edinburgh West. SDP negotiators thought they had the better of the deal. They were certainly right to see the city as promising, but Edinburgh West was the only seat in the city near to capture by the Alliance.

Strategy and relationships with other parties

James notes that the Alliance in Bristol had all to do with convenience and perceived advantage: it owed little to principle. Seat allocations are not the obvious places to look for principle, to be sure, but the nagging thought is that the promising places yield little more. Liberalism and Social Democracy are not identical. They differ, historically, over the not trivial question of the role of the state. Should the state intervene actively in society and economy? For all that the large extensions of state intervention in Britain have followed the prescriptions of individual Liberal thinkers, especially Keynes and Beveridge, the ideology and party remain suspicious of the state. Social Democrats take a more relaxed view. The two parties also proceed from opposed perceptions of the way forward. The Liberals have a long history of wishing to reject two-party politics and move to something new. The SDP's opposition to the 'extremism' of Labour and Conservative parties is quite different. There is a strong current of opinion within the SDP, led by David Owen, which wishes to restore the old post-war two party consensus with themselves replacing Labour. In this way a moderate responsible alternation of two parties each competing earnestly for the central ground could be restored (hence Dahrendorf's jibe 'a better yesterday').

Crosland's emphasis on 'equality' as the key note of social democracy is missing from SDP literature. This is hardly surprising: 'equality' is associated with the Labour Party. Putting it too firmly on the masthead might frighten off some of the Conservative voters the new party hopes to woo. 'Equality' has also frequently been counterposed to 'freedom' and the SDP leaders have been at pains to champion 'freedom' and to paint the Labour Party as the champion of Eastern European-style unfree equality. But the SDP's ill ease at the egalitarian banner is hardly surprising. They lack the electoral incentive to support that virtue. They do not represent the poor—Labour retains their support. The Party has also turned its back on the institutions—the trade unions—which have traditionally represented the poor and had an interest in a more egalitarian society. In its attitude to equality the SDP is much like its Liberal allies.

The effect of the alliance between SDP and Liberals is to produce pressing tactical arguments for not dwelling on these differences lest the Conservative and Labour parties benefit from the allies' squabbles. Undwelt on, they are unresolved. Rapidly a marriage of Liberals and Social Democrats becomes an Alliance of convenience. The difficulties of putting the social democratic Humpty together again are ignored.

Unlike the Conservative Party which stands for a principle— freedom—and the institutions and groups which have an interest in the implementation of some aspects of freedom, or the Labour Party which stands for a principle—equality—and the institutions and groups which have an interest in the implementation of some aspects of equality, the Social Democrats in their alliance stand not so much for social democracy (somehow understood) as for no principle whatever. And the reason that they stand for no principle is that they stand for no precise or definite group or interest. The most telling aspect of the Limehouse Declaration, and of subsequent SDP and Alliance publications, is not so much their vagueness on the matter of principle but their disavowal of the politics of interest. Without interests, political principles are merely fashionable rhetoric.

In the one General Election, June 1983, since the formation of the SDP that was the electorate's verdict too. The election is best understood as an unpopularity contest. Of all voters, 59 per cent disliked the other parties more than they liked their own. 65 per cent of Alliance voters, the largest proportion, were so moved. A MORI poll, taken as voters left the polling booths, showed only 15 per cent of voters (10 per cent Liberal; 4 per cent SDP; 1 per cent Alliance) generally thought of themselves as Alliance (as against 40 per cent Conservative; 34 per cent Labour). On *no* issue did the voters think the Alliance best. David Steel at 35 per cent was the second most popular choice as Prime Minister (Thatcher 46 per cent; Foot 13 per cent; Jenkins 6 per cent) (Crewe, 1983).

The Alliance was the least unpopular party with more than 7 million voters (see Table 4.4).

Table 4.4: *Results of the United Kingdom General Election, 1983*

	total vote	% of votes		% of electorate	seats
		1983	1979		
Conservative	12,991,377	43.5	43.9	31.9	397
Labour	8,437,120	28.3	36.9	20.6	209
Alliance	7,775,048	26.0	13.8	18.9	23
SNP	331,975				2
Plaid Cymru	125,309				2
Others (Ulster)					17

Even on this negative basis their achievement was substantial. They had considerably improved on the Liberals, 13.8 per cent of the previous election. By reducing the two-party share to 72 per cent they had done much to shatter the two-party system.

The electoral system had performed its predictable alchemy and awarded the Conservative and Labour parties higher percentages of seats than votes. For the Alliance the mere twenty-three seats constituted a set-back which harmed it during the ensuing parliament. Even another twenty-three seats would have enabled them to make a much better show in the House and in the Commons' committees. It would also have brought the possibility that some new stars would be found amongst the new intake.

But it is unreasonable to dwell on these failings. The Alliance was well placed, following the 1983 election, to overtake Labour as one of the two major British parties. Across whole swathes of the south of England the Alliance are the second party. When voters fall out with the Government they will move to the Alliance; when socialists become desperate with the continued feuding in the Labour Party they will vote Alliance. Labour, barely 1.5 per cent ahead of the Alliance in England, are in trouble. Not so much the positive attractions of social democracy, but the failures of its opponents, have provided the new party with its opportunity.

5

The German Social Democratic Party

William E. Paterson

IN any attempt to assess the future of social democracy no party is more important than the SPD. It is Europe's oldest and, through its position, size, and international connections, most influential social democratic party. Its party programme of 1959, the *Bad Godesberg Programme*, has served as an encapsulation of social democratic ideals for other West European parties. A period of continual success for the party as measured in terms of increasing influence and electoral support came to an end in the early 1980s. It has been succeeded by a period of doubt and questioning about the party's policies and strategies. This chapter will focus primarily on present and future dilemmas for the SPD but some analysis of the party's development is necessary to put them in context.

The Post-War History of the SPD

The SPD was founded in 1875 by the amalgamation of two rival socialist parties. In the period up to the outbreak of the First World War, it was marked both by enormous growth in membership and electoral support and deep-seated factional conflict over the direction the party should take. A radical left wing led by Karl Liebknecht and Rosa Luxemburg advocated revolutionary action; the party establishment represented by August Bebel and Karl Kautsky supported a judicious mixture of reformist practice and revolutionary theory; and a reformist wing led by Eduard Bernstein argued for reformist theory and practice.

The left wing of the SPD quit the party at the end of the First World War to form the German Communist Party (KPD) and thenceforward the party was less marked by factional conflict. The SPD played a leading rôle in a number of Weimar governments but it faltered in the face of the world depression. The arrival of the Nazis in power meant banning for the SPD and imprisonment and exile for its leaders.

The re-established SPD after 1945 was dominated by Kurt Schumacher, the first post-war leader. In these years the accent was on continuity and the SPD was rebuilt on the foundations of Weimar. Although by 1952 the SPD was well on the way to becoming an electoral party, in that its orientation was almost exclusively towards electoral success, the Party had largely failed to extend its appeal much beyond the industrial working-class districts, whilst the Christian Democrats had consolidated their hold on the middle-class electorate. The apparent strength of its organization and the uncompromising nature of its programme were becoming an embarrassment, making the SPD unable to escape from the image of a class party. It was also handicapped by the identification of Socialism with the GDR.

After the second electoral defeat in 1953, and after the banning of the Communist Party in 1956 had removed all competition on the left, the efforts to change the party accelerated, culminating in the adoption of a new Party programme against very little opposition at the special conference in Bad Godesberg in 1959. This programme totally ignored Marx and accepted the principle of private ownership, in so far as it did not hinder the creation of a just social order. Economic and social change, it was argued, had outstripped the old party doctrines. The SPD would now concentrate on improving and reforming rather than abolishing the system of free competition. At the same time, in a famous speech in the Bundestag on 30 June 1960, Herbert Wehner indicated, on behalf of the SPD, its willingness to join with other German parties in defence of the Federal Republic against Communist threats, by fully accepting NATO and its foreign policy postulates. These programmatic alterations were accompanied by the dropping of many of the old symbols associated with the party. The colour of Party membership books was changed from red to blue and Party members were expected to stop addressing each other as 'comrade' and to use the term 'party friend'. The flag of the Federal Republic was now flown alongside the traditional red flag above party headquarters.

Taken together, these changes represented a conscious choice by the Party leadership wholeheartedly to embrace the concept of a *Volkspartei*, to turn their back on 'the mass integration party model' of the past in favour of what Otto Kirchheimer (1966) has called 'the catch-all party model'.

The overriding aim of the Party leadership in the years after Bad Godesberg was to participate in government. 'That the party exists not to sustain the organization but that the organization is there to attain and determine governmental power—to have made this clear is what is historically correct about the series of reforms associated with Bad Godesberg' (Narr, Scheer, and Spori, 1976: 91).

The attempts by the party leadership, especially associated with Herbert Wehner, to create a coalition with the CDU finally succeeded in November 1966 when the so-called 'Grand Coalition' of CDU/CSU and SPD was formed. Although broadly accepted by the Party membership, it did lead to a crisis of legitimacy for what remained of the young-left in the SPD after the expulsion of the SDS in July 1960. These members of the extreme-left of the SPD coalesced with extreme-left groups outside the party in what came to be known as 'the extra-parliamentary opposition' (APO). Although this movement gained a lot of support among the critical young intelligentsia its social base remained very narrow. An attempt to form a new party to the left of the SPD known as the Action Community for Democratic Progress (ADF), which relied heavily on the newly legalized Deutsche Kommunistische Partei, was a complete failure.

The SPD in Government, 1969–82

After the federal election of 1969 the SPD and FDP were able to form a governing coalition, and Willy Brandt became Federal Chancellor. This seemed to many observers both inside and outside the Federal Republic to be a triumphant vindication of the 'embracement strategy', of the SPD as a 'catch-all' party which had brought it such striking electoral gains in the 1960s. Contrary to these expectations, however, the period since 1969 has been one of intense programmatic concern and one in which both the values embedded in the Bad Godesberg Programme and the whole notion of a *Volkspartei* have been fiercely debated. The main catalyst for this change was firstly the changing membership of the Party and latterly the emergence of a viable rival, the 'Greens' on the SPD's left flank. The failure of the ADF and the break-up of the SDS, combined with the SPD victory and the promises of reform identified with Willy Brandt, led to a vast influx of young members in the period following 1969. There were 93,827 new members in

1969 and 155,992 new members in 1972. (These and other membership figures in this chapter are from *Jahrbücher der SPD*, 1968–9, 1970–2 and 1972–4.) In 1973 the number had dropped to 68,772 and fell further to 55,036 in 1974. The percentage of those who can class themselves as Young Socialists (*Jusos*, party members under thirty-five years) rose from 54.6 per cent of new members in 1969 to 65.6 per cent in 1971. The most marked increase was in new members under twenty-one. They doubled in number from 10.4 per cent of new members in 1969 to 21.1. per cent in 1971. Similarly the percentage of new working-class members which had been 55 per cent in the period 1956–61 had fallen from 39.6 per cent in 1969 to 35 per cent in 1971. By 1974 it had fallen to 26 per cent. In the same year the percentage of new members under twenty-one had fallen to 14 per cent. The demands of these new members were articulated by the Young Socialists.

The response of the Party leadership to the challenge from the *Jusos* was not to expel them, as they had done with the SDS, the SPD student organization in 1960, but to attempt to integrate the *Jusos* into the Party. This was done in two ways. Firstly, many *Juso* activists were encouraged to become Party functionaries, since the post-war veterans were nearing retirement. This often led them to align their views more closely to the mainstream of party opinion. More ambitiously an attempt was made to involve the whole Party in programmatic endeavour and to project the discussion about the Godesberg programme into the future. At the Saarbrücken Conference of the Party in 1970, a long-term programme commission was established to draw up an *Entwurf eines ökonomisch politischen Orientierungsrahmens für die Jahre 1973–85*. Although this commission was safely under the chairmanship of Helmut Schmidt, several *Jusos* and leftists were given places on the commission.

Willy Brandt resigned as Chancellor in May 1974 but remained chairman of the SPD (Paterson, 1975). Helmut Schmidt became Federal Chancellor while Herbert Wehner remained leader of the *Bundestagsfraktion*. Initially this arrangement worked well and the late 70s saw a marked diminution in the factional conflict which had plagued the Brandt years and some revival of SPD fortunes after the trough of 1974.

The Chancellor meets the public's need to be governed efficiently and, indeed, perfectly; the party chairman absorbs and channels everything that goes beyond matters of state; he preserves the identity of the party and keeps the Chancellor free for his task, and finally the parliamentary party leader reconciles the necessities of government and conflicting trends within the party. Despite internal conflicts and tensions, this trio, which can be taken as representative of the party as a whole, has functioned splendidly (*Die Zeit*, 22 December 1978).

By the early 1980s profound difficulties were emerging. The Party contained supporters and opponents of economic growth, supporters and opponents of deficit spending, supporters and opponents of maintaining the welfare state at all costs, supporters and opponents of NATO's twin-track decision. In January 1982 an SPD member of the Bundestag, Karl Heinz Hansen, resigned on the grounds that the Party was no longer true to its ideology, and in February Manfred Coppik was expelled for constant criticism of the party leadership. Both men were mavericks, but their departure from the SPD symbolized the growing unease within the Party. Neither the government reshuffle of April 1982 nor the Munich Congress in May resolved the Party's problems. The former was seen as a case of too little and too late: the new Finance Minister, Manfred Lahnstein, a conservative economist close to Schmidt, may have helped the unity of the coalition, but he did nothing to reassure SPD left-wingers. Heinz Westphal, the new Labour Minister, was more sympathetic to the Left, but it soon became apparent that his influence in the government was limited, as the budget agreement of July 1982 was distinctly conservative and led to major trade-union demonstrations. Pensioners were to pay higher health service contributions; a 5DM per day hospitalization charge was introduced; and public borrowing was to be kept below 30 thousand million DM. In other words, workers, pensioners, and the jobless were going to have to bear the brunt of the austerity measures. As far as the Munich Congress was concerned, Schmidt and Brandt achieved a measure of unity. The Congress agreed to postpone until a special conference in 1983 the final decisions on the stationing of new missiles and defeated proposals for an outright moratorium on the building of nuclear power stations. But the party leadership was defeated on economic strategy. In particular, the delegates supported a resolution providing for a special tax on the better-off to finance job creation schemes. This resolution increased significantly the strains inside the coalition.

Even at the time of the 1976 and 1980 general elections many

Socialists believed that the SPD should have been concerning itself not simply with financial orthodoxy and traditional foreign policy, but with nuclear issues (both weapons and power-stations), with education, with fiscal reform, and with the problems of *Gastarbeiter* within Germany, and of the poor and disadvantaged throughout the world. When domestic unemployment began to rise dramatically (900,000 in 1980; 1.3 million in 1981; 1.8 million in 1982; 2.4 million by spring 1983), and at the same time the national debt rose from 328 billion DM in 1977 to 620 billion DM in 1982, the underlying malaise within the SPD finally erupted. Relations between Schmidt and the SPD Left came close to breaking point, with Schmidt determined to control the public debt while the left-wingers, supported for the first time by some trade unions, were determined to maintain all the benefits of the welfare state and embark on a Keynesian programme of deficit spending. In 1981, when the first public expenditure cuts were announced by the Economics Minister, Count Lambsdorff (FDP), it was only with difficulty that Schmidt held his party together over the budget. Then in February 1982 Schmidt had to resort to the unprecedented step of calling for a vote of confidence in order to bind not only the FDP, but also the SPD Left, to the continuance of the coalition. With constant and open quarrelling going on between Schmidt and the SPD Left, it was not surprising that by the spring of 1982 the SPD had reached its lowest opinion poll rating for thirty years (under 30 per cent).

Meanwhile, the SPD's position was further weakened by the steady rise of the Greens. Consisting of 'green Greens' (mainly environmentalists) and 'red Greens' (former radical students, disillusioned SPD left-wingers, and others), the conglomerate known as *die Grünen* emerged as a national electoral force in the late 1970s. They won 4.5 per cent and 3.9 per cent respectively at the Hamburg and Lower Saxony state elections in 1978, and at the Bremen and Bade-Württemburg elections of 1979 and 1980 they polled 5.1 per cent and 5.3 per cent, thus winning representation in the state parliaments of these two *Länder*. At their various national congresses from January 1979 onwards it was apparent that the Greens were both a divided, factional grouping and at the same time a serious threat to both the SPD and FDP. As far as the SPD was concerned, many people—especially the radical young, the so-called 'post-materialists'(Inglehart, 1977)—believed that, whatever the failings of the Greens, they were at least debating the sort of issues which the SPD should have been tackling: the problems of nuclear power (in all its forms), of the environment, of modern technology, of social and economic inequality, of the third world. These issues had in fact been ignored by the SPD at the 1980 general election, and it was only thanks to the Strauss (CDU/CSU) candidature that the SPD was able to mobilize almost its full electorate and squeeze the Greens on that occasion.

The FDP leadership, conscious of the SPD's unpopularity and worried by the increasing difficulty Helmut Schmidt was experiencing in getting the SPD as a party to swallow governmental proposals, gave clear indications in the summer of 1982 that they were contemplating an end to the coalition with the SPD. Their problem lay in the extraordinary popularity of Helmut Schmidt and the odium that would attach to a party which toppled him as Chancellor. The solution of the FDP leader Hans Dietrich Genscher seems to have been to signal the FDP's future intentions by changing running mates from SPD to CDU in the Hesse state election in September 1982. Genscher's intention was to let the CDU and FDP win a decisive victory in Hesse and then make the break at national level in late 1982. Schmidt pre-empted this by forcing the four FDP ministers in the Cabinet to resign on 17 September 1982. Two weeks later the FDP combined with the CDU/CSU to defeat Helmut Schmidt in a 'constructive vote of no-confidence' and the SPD's period in government ended.

The Future of the SPD

The breakup of the SPD/FDP coalition in the autumn of 1982 left the SPD divided and demoralized. There was a temporary rally, even a feeling of elation at being released from the burden of government, but this mood passed very quickly and a picture of real underlying weakness was revealed in the Federal Election of March 1983. In the following sections an attempt will be made to evaluate the future of the SPD by seeking to answer a number of interrelated questions. What is the state of the organization of the Party and is the pattern of factional conflict likely to persist? Given the nature of its membership, can the Party indeed cohere at all? How will it manage its relations with organized labour? What is the nature of the electoral support for the Party and what prospects has the SPD of winning a coalition partner in the future?

The Internal Life of the Party

The SPD has a long historical tradition of organization; even of over-organization (see Michels, 1911). Conscious from its inception of the strength of the forces ranged against it in German society, the SPD has always favoured a mass organization and centralized decision-making structures as a counterweight. The historical advantage that this conferred on the SPD began to be eroded in the 1970s from a number of different directions. The main competitors to the SPD, the CDU/CSU, had by then greatly strengthened their respective organizational structures and in some areas were already more efficient than the SPD (see Paterson 1985: Mintzel, 1975). The expansion of membership in the late 1960s and early 1970s brought with it new difficulties. The new members were imbued with a participatory ethos which continually brought them into conflict with the centralized decision-making structures of the SPD (see above, pp. 129–30). Further difficulties were caused by the increasingly complex and diffuse social composition of the Party. Forms and structures appropriate to a party which considered itself traditionally to be of, as well as for, the working-class came under increasing strain.

After the membership expansion since the 'sixties and the new '*Volkspartei*' basis, the SPD no longer knew enough about its membership to appraise the party's place in society and the commitment of members to party aims (E. Kolinsky, 1984: 74).

The Changing Nature of Party Membership

The logical place to start an examination of the changing internal life of the SPD is to explore the changing nature of the membership of the Party. After reaching a peak in 1947, membership declined in the 1950s. As has already been noted, there was a very significant increase in membership at the end of the 1960s and the beginning of the 1970s (see above, p. 130). These new members tended to be much better educated than the SPD members had been in the past. Twenty-two per cent of new members in the 1970s had the ABITUR (A-level equivalent) as compared with the mid-1950s when over 91 per cent had received only the most basic school education (E. Kolinsky, 1984: 79). The social comparison of these new entrants indicated changes in West German society. Although a very clear majority were in middle-class occupations, an equally clear majority came from working-class backgrounds and had risen socially (E. Kolinsky, 1984: 77). Not surprisingly these new entrants were, as has already been noted, to cause considerable problems for the Party leadership. However, despite a period of *Sturm und Drang* and the almost complete failure of the generation of '68 (as we shall call them for convenience) to change the policy priorities of the SPD leadership, they were very successful in gaining office in the SPD itself. Fifty-eight per cent of the party office-holders in 1977 had joined the Party within the prevailing decade and only one in ten office-holders had been a member of the party since 1950 (E. Kolinsky, 1984: 81). Party office-holders were much more clearly middle-class than the membership of the party and an even larger gulf separated them from those who normally vote for the Party.

The changing nature of party membership and the social and educational gulf between the Party office-holders and the bulk of Party members has raised a number of difficulties for the SPD. The most obvious difficulty is in transforming the rather centralized decision-making structures to allow for greater participation than was desired by members in the past. This problem has presented itself in a number of different ways. In the Schmidt period of SPD-led governments there was a clash between members of the '68 generation, who had by then arrived in some numbers in the *Bundestagsfraktion*, and the Party and governmental leadership (Paterson, 1981). These new members were unwilling to accept the traditional SPD convention that a defeated minority in the *Fraktion* meeting should vote with the majority in any subsequent parliamentary vote. This same desire for participation is also demonstrated in the vastly increased number of critical resolutions to Party conferences in recent years.

The changing nature of Party membership has meant that the Party leadership has had to invest much more time than in the past in trying to find out about the motivations and interests of its membership, which is both more diffuse socially and more assertive than in the past. The leadership therefore commissioned a number of studies on the background and motivations of individual members (the major findings are available in Kolinsky, 1984), one or two of which have been published *Die SPD Von Innen* (1983) by Horst Becker and Bodo Hombach for example. More significantly, it has meant a change in emphasis in the use to which the traditional structures of the SPD are put and also a marked dissatisfaction with some of these traditional structures. Traditionally an important function of the SPD organization was to provide an avenue for working-class participation in politics. The markedly middle-class character of Party office-holders implies that this is much less the case than formerly. Office-holders with working-class occupations now typically occupy the less important positions such as *Beisitzer* (alternates) (E. Kolinksy, 1984: 82).

A recent investigation of two neighbouring Party branches in the Ruhr town of Mülheim sheds some interesting light on this. One branch was located near the Mannesmann steel plant. It was dominated by the right and had a high proportion of members with a working-class background. In this branch, office-holders were typically trade-union functionaries, an aristocracy of labour, rather than ordinary shop-floor workers. The city-centre branch was dominated by civil servants, students, and people not working in manufacturing industries. In both branches advancement for ordinary working people was blocked.

Those from the Metal Workers' Union or from the Miners' Union, those from large scale industries with their high degree of unionization and for those workers who still live on housing estates which belong to large firms— with their cohesive social fabric and climate, all those people experience difficulties of orientation and problems of asserting themselves in the mixed social environment inside the party. Municipal employees, teachers, civil servants have more time and perhaps more inclination to perform in public (E. Kolinsky, 1984: 82).

The changing social composition of the Party has given rise to a much less close fit between structures and the members' aspirations. The newer members are frustrated by what they see as the limited opportunities for participation and by the social functions performed by Party meetings. Working-class members on the other hand feel alienated by the academic and expert nature of much of the discussion at local branch meetings. An enormous amount of effort has gone into thinking about ways to revive Party life. This has been a continual preoccupation of Peter Glotz, the *Bundesgeschafts führer* or party manager of the SPD but so far no very satisfactory solution has been found.

The various difficulties, combined with left-wing dissatisfaction about the policies of the Schmidt government, led to membership losses in the early 1980s and fears of much greater losses (*Vorwärts*, 9 February 1982). Reports spoke of growing alienation but Germans, though enthusiastic joiners, are very reluctant to leave an organization. The overwhelming majority of West Germans, for instance, pay the so-called church tax, a not insignificant sum of money, while only a minority actually demonstrate by their attendance any further commitment to the churches. Membership of the SPD fell from 1978 onwards. In January 1982, 5,610 members left. Membership rose again in the wake of the collapse of the Schmidt/Genscher coalition and by January 1983 membership stood at 926,866.

There were some other signs of a revival of party life. *Vorwärts*, the party weekly which had been marked for closure, still survives and party meetings for a time at least regained their popularity. The underlying problems persist, however, and it remains to be seen whether these signs of revival were a flash in the pan or the beginning of a more sustained revival.

Factional Discord

The brief historical introduction to this chapter has indicated how persistent factionalism has been in the history of the SPD. The absence of factions in the 1950s is in retrospect a temporary phenomenon largely to be explained by the weakness of the left. Factionalism revived in the 1960s. The major faction in the party at large was, as we have seen, the Young Socialists (*Jusos*). They were unsuccessful in the goal of taking over the party at federal level. They were however very successful in displacing the established leadership of a large number of local Parties, for example Munich and Frankfurt (see Braunthal, 1984). Thus local Parties were deeply divided for a number of years as the right-wing members fought back.

Factionalism also emerged at a parliamentary level. The SPD *Bundestagsfraktion* has been dominated traditionally by a group of right-wing trade-unionist members known as the *Kanalarbeiter*, an expression which corresponds to their self-image as 'the parliamentary navvies' who do all the necessary dull but unglamorous work. The left in the *Fraktion*, organized initially in 1969 in the 16th Floor Group (of the parliamentary building) formed the so-called *Leverküsener Kreis* in 1972. There was no possibility of the left taking over the *Bundestagsfraktion* and the main objectives of the *Leverkusen* circle are to offer support to each other when defying the parliamentary whip, to try and move the *Fraktion* some distance to the left and to support left-wing candidates for *Fraktion* posts. The organization of a left-wing faction in the *Fraktion* led the *Kanalarbeiter* to regroup themselves somewhat more tightly in the *H.J. Vogel Kreis*. The secure dominance of the right which was never seriously imperilled has meant that although factions have been active in the *Bundestagsfraktion* there was little or none of the very bitter factional strife which characterized relations inside local SPD organizations.

Factional strife within the party as a whole receded for a period after 1973. For a period the left was, with some exceptions at the local level, on the defensive. They faced an electoral law which made secession apparently an unpromising alternative, since they would have to clear a five per cent threshold for representation. There was no evidence at that time that such a potential electorate existed in a country where suspicion of Socialism was rife. The slavish adherence of the DKP, the new German Communist Party, to the GDR rendered it an unattractive alternative. The narrow middle-class social basis and the overwhelmingly academic orientation of the Young Socialists had tended to cut them off from other members of the party. In contrast to the situation in Holland, the trade unionists in the Party have taken an explicitly hostile line and the *Jusos* have never established a successful industrial base. Lastly, and perhaps most importantly, the onset of the world economic recession in 1973 deprived them of much of their potential support in the left-centre of the Party and rendered much less attractive their pleas for zero growth.

Although West Germany was less affected directly by the 1973 recession, its psychological impact was threefold: it undermined the position of Willy Brandt's government, unable now to carry through the reforms which it had promised; Brandt was replaced by Helmut Schmidt, whose priorities were clearly management of the domestic economy rather than reform, and who was therefore unwilling to accord any priority to left-wing views. Secondly, with the change in the economy the job prospects of young people diminished and their radicalism, at least initially, tended to evaporate. Thirdly, the impact of economic recession correlated with a *Tendenzwende* to the right in the political system as a whole, evidenced by generally adverse *land* election results and a period of waning support for left-wing ideas within the SPD.

The emergence of new issues and the revival of conflict

In the early 1980s, and more particularly after the loss of governmental power in 1982, the SPD entered a new phase. In the post-war SPD the various left-wing factions and positions were clearly in a minority and the Party leadership was always able to carry the Party with it. In 1983 and 1984 the left of the Party scored a number of significant victories and the Party leadership had to make corresponding concessions. How did this come about?

A major explanation for these changes lay in the partial transformation of the agenda of German politics. Two issues assumed a new importance. One set of new issues arose from the debate on ecological and environmental questions and another was occasioned by the debate over NATO's 'dual-track' resolution on the stationing of modernized medium-range nuclear weapons. It is not surprising that environmental issues assumed such importance in the Federal Republic. The sustained and prolonged post-war prosperity made concern with 'post-materialist', quality-of-life issues more likely to take root in the Federal Republic than, say, in the United Kingdom where prosperity was both more shallowly-based and less prolonged.

Ecological and environmental issues

From the late 1970s environmental questions became a major source of division within the Party. The left and post-materialist wing of the Party, led by Erhard Eppler, demanded that less environmentally damaging energy alternatives be explored and that the government declare a moratorium on the construction of nuclear plants. Just before the Berlin Party Conference in 1970 Erhard Eppler had managed to get the regional Party Conference of the Baden-Württemberg SPD on 15 July 1979 to adopt a resolution calling for a moratorium on the building of further atomic power stations. Schmidt insisted that the government must retain the future expansion of nuclear power production as one of its options. Schmidt won a majority, but a substantial minority continued to oppose governmental policy (Paterson, 1981; see also *Die Zeit*, 7 December 1979).

Environmental issues became even more important after the 1980 election. Although the Greens failed to get into the Bundestag, they did get into a series of *Landtage* and there was a serious split in the SPD on how to respond. Willy Brandt, the Party Chairman, was in favour of some 'greening' of the Party in order to accommodate the Green voters. Helmut Schmidt saw no need to change Party or governmental policy since he held that such a strategy, as well as being impractical, would lead to a loss of votes in the centre.

In the last years of the Schmidt government there were a series of bitter battles between SPD Party branches and SPD governmental office-holders on the nuclear energy issue. In 1980 the South Hesse section of the SPD attacked the plans of Hesse's SPD Minister-President to build another nuclear plant at Biblis. In the following year the mayor of Hamburg, Hans-Ulrich Klose, resigned when his fellow SPD office-holders in the city government did not support him and the local SPD in their opposition to the further construction of the nuclear plant at Brokdorf.

Schmidt, supported by Adolf Schmidt of the miners' union, managed to defeat the call for a moratorium on the further building of nuclear plants at the Munich conference of 1982. There was, however, some movement towards the ecological position in the March 1983 election and subsequently in the summer of 1983 the SPD adopted a pretty thorough-going ecological position on nuclear power.

The Controversy over the twin-track decision

The controversy surrounding the twin-track decision proved for a time to be an equally difficult issue for the SPD. The problem here was that the progenitor of the decision was Helmut Schmidt himself, and he repeatedly made Party support for it a question of confidence in his government (Paterson, 1981). It was, however, equally clear that the bulk of Party members were very unhappy about the direction being taken.

The new debate of defence issues was connected with the massive growth of the Peace Movement attendant upon the NATO twin-track resolution of 1979 and the virtual collapse of *détente* under the

Reagan presidency. The resolution envisaged negotiation with the USSR to persuade them to remove their SS.20 missiles in Eastern Europe, but if this failed then NATO would deploy intermediate-range nuclear missiles in Western Europe, including 108 Pershing-2 and 96 cruise missiles in the Federal Republic. Both this and the environmental issues complex affected the SPD much more than the other established parties. The large influx of middle-class members into the SPD (already noted), often working in educational or governmental institutions, or at any rate removed in some way from the immediate productive process, constituted a natural reservoir of support for 'post-materialist values' and 'sunshine politics' (see Baker, Dalton, and Hildebrandt, 1981). Equally clearly, the trade-union core of the party and the Federal Chancellor Helmut Schmidt remained wedded to the priority of a growth economy, in turn dependent on the very high utilization of energy.

The approaching prospect of the deployment of the cruise and Pershing missiles gave impetus to the spectacular growth of the Peace Movement in the Federal Republic while, within the SPD, opposition to governmental policy mounted steadily after 1980. A demonstration in Bonn against the possible stationing of the missiles in October 1981 was the largest in the history of the Federal Republic, and was supported by the *Jusos* and by almost a quarter of the *Bundestagsfraktion* (*Suddeutsche Zeitung*, 12 October 1981).

A possible defeat for government policy at the Munich Conference of April 1982 was staved off by a compromise formula which left the final decision to an extraordinary congress of the Party in November 1983. The end of the Schmidt government put enormous pressure on the official Party policy of support for the 'twin-track' decision. Initially the move away was very cautious since the Party leadership were impressed by the need not to reverse the Schmidt policy so abruptly that he would make damaging statements during the 1983 election. The election over, events moved quickly. In June 1983 the SPD executive stated that the Party was in broad agreement with the themes and issues of the Peace Movement. At the Extraordinary Party Conference on 18–19 November 1983, the delegates voted overwhelmingly to reject the deployment of new NATO missiles on German soil. The isolation of Helmut Schmidt on this issue was brutally apparent. Despite what many considered to be his finest speech his viewpoint was defeated by 400 votes to 14 (*Der Spiegel*, 14 November 1983).

The Situation in 1985

The disagreement engendered in the debate over the stationing of the missiles continued to trouble the party. The left wing represented by Erhard Eppler and Oskar Lafontaine wished to push the Party in a more radical direction. In particular, they wanted a much closer identification with the Peace Movement and the adoption of more unequivocally 'green' policies. The right of the Party were deeply troubled. They continued to be in a very strong position in the *Bundestagsfraktion*. The collapse of the Schmidt government before the end of the legislative period meant that nomination processes were very compressed and nearly all the sitting MPs who wished to be were reselected to contest the election.

Despite their strength in the *Fraktion* the right felt themselves to be in a weak position. In the era of the SPD government the right was securely entrenched in the topmost leadership positions. Helmut Schmidt, the Federal Chancellor was unmistakably on the right of the SPD. Herbert Wehner, the Parliamentary Party Leader, saw his role as that of ensuring that the *Fraktion* supported the SPD government. At least until 1980 Willy Brandt defined his role as Party Chairman in terms of supporting the Social Democratic Chancellor and integrating the Party. After 1980 he gave more emphasis to the second function and as we have already noted something of a rift developed. Brandt had clearly adopted a left-of-centre position. Vogel, the former leader of the various right-wing factions in the Party took up a centre-left position, first as Chancellor candidate and then as Parliamentary Party leader. Johannes Rau, the Minister President of North Rhine Westphalia and Party Vice-Chairman, by early 1985 was the only member of the leadership troika clearly on the centre-right of the Party. Vogel's position as leader of the right-wing factions was taken by Hans Apel, the former SPD Finance and Defence Minister who took over the leadership of the SPD in West Berlin and then decisively lost the West Berlin election in March 1985.

The right-wing faction organized in the *Seeheimer* Circle were extremely active in the period after Schmidt's fall. They felt betrayed by Hans Jochen Vogel ever since he went to West Berlin in January 1981 where he struck a conciliatory note towards the Alternatives and Greens. They feared that a shift of the SPD towards the left-centre would eliminate the blue-collar workers in the traditional core clientele of the SPD. They believed that the counter-culture, as represented by the Peace Movement and the Greens, was very clearly a minority in West German society. They also articulated an instinct deeply rooted in the historical experience of the SPD against too close an identification with a movement, in this case the Peace Movement, that they could not control. (For the background to this see epecially Gaus, 1966; also Renger, 1981: 704–9.)

The prescription of those on the right was for the SPD to continue to be a pro-NATO party, to follow a middle-of-the-road policy generally and to rely on mistakes and omissions by the governing CDU/CSU/FDP coalition to enable the SPD to recapture the centre ground in German politics. This essentially reactive strategy looked unpromising in 1985, relying as it did on mistakes by the government. The difficulties become apparent if we take one key area, *Ost* and *Deutschland Politik*. This has been at least since the late 1960s a policy which unites the various wings of the SPD and allows the SPD to appeal to the moderate centre of West German politics. The hawkish line taken since 1969 by the CDU and even more the CSU raised SPD hopes that this would be one of their best cards in opposition and there was much talk of a second *Ostpolitik*. In government, however, the CDU/CSU opposition policy was dicarded and they fell over themselves to adopt a conciliatory policy towards East Germany. Even more damaging for the SPD's hopes was that East Germany's shortage of hard currency meant that they responded positively to the blandishments of the West German government. A further major difficulty in the views represented by the *Seeheimer* Circle was that it envisaged blue-collar workers as the core group to whom the SPD must appeal. There are two major problems with such a view. First, blue-collar workers, in West Germany as elsewhere in Western Europe, were in a clear and shrinking minority by 1985. Second, inflation and fiscal drift meant that it was becoming more and more difficult to mobilize the traditional skilled blue-collar worker for such social democratic policies as entailed high tax levels. Conversely, for the SPD to distance itself, as the *Seeheimer* Circle suggested, from the Peace Movement and the Greens, and therefore by implication from a large section of the younger generation in Western Germany, would greatly diminish its chances of attracting the electoral support which would be needed to return to power. (For a very influential view recommending concentration on the core clientele, see Lowenthal, 1981: 1085–90.) This difficulty was widely recognized even on the right of the Party, where it often led to feelings of depair and resignation. The task of the party leadership was to square the circle by articulating policies which would bring the SPD back to power by uniting the trade-unionist and post-materialist wings of the Party.

The Relationship with Organized Labour

The relationship between the SPD and the trade unions, crucial to the party's prospects, has often been an ambiguous one in the Federal Republic. When the united trade-union movement (the *Deutscher Gewerkschaftsbund*) was formed in 1949, it was officially neutral on party political questions. Despite extensive inter-penetration of membership with the SPD, its first Chairman, Hans Böckler, actually steered it in a direction where it could reasonably be seen as supporting the Christian Democratic Government, particularly over the issue of European Integration. The importance of the rearmament issue led in 1952 to the removal of Böckler's successor, Fette, and his replacement by Walter Freitag, an SPD deputy. During Freitag's period as Chairman in 1952–5, the DGB was very closely identified with the SPD.

Relations with the SPD were close after 1969, partly on account of their support for Brandt's *Ostpolitik*, but principally because the SPD was more sympathetic, if not much more successful, in practice than the CDU/CSU in responding to demands for an extension of industrial co-determination beyond the coal and steel industry. The German unions do not have the same institutionalized access to the SPD that their British counterparts enjoy to the Labour Party, nor are they an important source of finance. Yet they can, and often are, an important source of support to the SPD in various ways.

How valuable this support can be in electoral terms can be seen in the 1972 election. The DGB gave more decisive support to the SPD than in any previous campaign, including that of 1953. The DGB's action was the product of four main factors. There was first the tremendous sympathy for Brandt and his Government at the grass roots demonstrated in the spontaneous pro-Government strikes particularly in the Ruhr at the time of the no-confidence motion by the CDU/CSU opposition on 27 April 1972. There was also the hope that an SPD victory would increase the chance of co-determination (*Mitbestimmung*) on the basis of parity being extended to all industries. The visible decline in the influence of the Catholic Social wing in the CDU made it seem much less likely that the CDU would be accommodating in this respect. Finally, the clear identification of the business lobby with the CDU/CSU opposition helped to provoke the DGB support for the SPD. The backing by the DGB was very effective and was a major factor in the high degree of support that the SPD gained among working-class voters.

This backing was largely absent in the 1976, 1980, and 1982 elections. The then General Secretary of the CDU, Professor Kurt Biedenkopf, waged a campaign against *Filzokratie*, i.e. using trade-union positions to benefit the SPD in 1976. This campaign placed the DGB on the defensive and while many obviously worked as individuals for an SPD victory, there was very little of the public display of solidarity so characteristic of the 1972 election in subsequent elections.

The DGB support is important to the governmental wing of the SPD in two further ways. Firstly, some of the SPD Cabinet members had backgrounds as trade-union leaders. In the Schmidt Cabinet of 1974-6 there were five: Georg Leber (Defence), Walter Arendt (Labour), Helmut Röhde (Education), Kurt Gscheidle (Traffic and Post), and Hans Matthöfer (Research). Secondly, their support in not pressing for inflationary wage settlements was essential to the survival of the SPD in government. One of the factors in Brandt's resignation as Chancellor was his inability to get his view of the correct level of wage settlements accepted by an important union.

Although the DGB as such plays no recognized role in the factional balance inside the SPD, the role of trade unionists and trade-union functionaries is a crucial one. At the local level many of the party office-holders are trade-union functionaries. At the national level the major trade unions and the DGB are in a strategic position to influence the SPD leadership when the SPD is in government. Reflecting the generally conservative nature of the values held by the German trade unions, this weight is almost invariably exercised, as in the past, against the left of the Party. They are able to make their influence felt through the *Arbeitsgemeinschaft für Arbeitnehmerfragen* (AFA), the Working Group for Employees' Questions. This working circle was founded in 1972, partly as a counterweight to the *Jusos*.

After 1980 the relationship between the SPD and the DGB deteriorated. There were two main reasons for this. Firstly, the trade-union leadership pressed for a much more Keynesian response to mounting unemployment than the SPD/FDP government were prepared to contemplate. Secondly, there was increasing anger in the trade unions at the budgetary cuts suggested by the government. In November 1981, Franz Steinkühler, then I G Metall leader in Baden-Württemberg, had been able to mobilize over 70,000 workers against governmental budgetary cuts. Union anger grew considerably in the early months of 1982 and a 'hot autumn' was promised for the SDP/FDP government which, as we have noted, collapsed in September 1982. The growing strains between the SPD and the trade unions caused a great deal of alarm inside the SPD. Wolfgang Roth managed to get the party executive's proposals on the economy rejected at the Munich Conference and the resolutions which were finally passed were much friendlier to the unions. In the period between the end of the Munich Conference and the collapse of the Schmidt government there were frequent expressions of concern at the strains being imposed on SPD/trade-union relations by governmental policy. Subsequently relations were more harmonious, but were not without problems. At the time of the collapse of the Schmidt government many in the SPD calculated that the CDU/CSU would make sweeping budgetary cuts and thus drive the trade unions and the SPD closer together. The CDU/CSU/FDP did make some budgetary cuts but they were not nearly so draconian as some feared. This development seemed to reflect both shrewd political judgement on the part of the government and also the fact that Kohl's style was to allow his ministers free reign, a policy which worked to the benefit of Norbert Blum, a Catholic trade unionist who was Minister of Labour and Social Affairs. There were also very clear indications that some trade-union leaders were unhappy about the extent to which the SPD had adopted an ecological stance. In a controversy about emission filters, Adolf Schmidt, the powerful miners' leader and SPD Bundestag deputy, voted against his party and with the government. I G Chemie led those in the unions who were most critical of ecological concerns in the SPD, and I G Metall has been most concerned to build bridges—a concern best expressed in the slogan 'Work and Environment' of the Saar Election of March 1985. The success of the SPD in the Saar election has led to some concessions by I G Chemie and they are working with I G Metall leaders to produce a policy which will combine concern for the environment with preserving jobs.

A final area of potential conflict is on social policy. A number of SPD party strategists, notably the party's business manager Peter Glotz, worried by the impact of high taxes on the propensity of skilled workers to vote SPD, suggested changes in social policy and, by clear implication, a reduction in its cost. Such a policy would be anathema to the trade union leaders and, if it became party policy, would significantly reduce their readiness to play an active rôle in supporting the SPD.

Electoral Connections

The 1983 election was a disaster for the SPD, whose share of the poll plummetted to 38.8 per cent (1980, 42.9 per cent), its lowest level of support since 1961. It was without its massively popular standard bearer, Helmut Schmidt. It was also under intense pressure by the emergence of the Greens on its left flank. The presence of the Greens made the SPD leadership much more ready to make concessions to the 'post-materialists' than would otherwise have been the case. By making these concessions the SPD hoped to keep the 'post-materialists' in the party and attract a significant number of Greens. The problem with this strategy was that it repelled voters in the centre whilst attracting relatively few Greens. A further difficulty for the SPD was that it was clear that any likely governmental role for the SPD would have to depend on support from the Greens, together with failure by the FDP to return to the Bundestag. Either the Greens would form a coalition with the SPD, which was very improbable given the Greens' fondness for non-negotiable stances, or the Greens might have tolerated an SPD minority government. If neither solution was possible then a Grand Coalition was an obvious possibility. None of these options was attractive to floating voters in West Germany.

The final SPD strategy was one which envisaged drawing support from the Greens and the 'social liberal' (left-wing) elements of the FDP. In order to attract the social-liberals three prominent former left-wing members of the FDP stood as SPD candidates: Günter Verheugen, Ingrid Matthäus-Maier, and Andreas Von Schoeler. The SPD did make some gains from the FDP (approximately 700,000 votes), but they lost many more to the CDU/CSU and the Greens (1,600,000 to the former and 750,000 to the latter). Thus the 1983 election brought serious losses for the SPD in both directions.

The SPD reduced almost to a core clientele. Its greatest losses were in its middle-class electorate. Contrary to earlier speculation, it lost very little support among unskilled workers and its losses among the skilled working-class were not disproportionate. Its greatest losses were among low- and medium-level employees and civil servants, among voters with intermediate and advanced educational qualifications, and among voters with very loose ties to the SPD. Losses were greatest among young voters.

The 1983 elections left the SPD in a very difficult position. They had succeeded in mobilizing their traditional voters but the attempt to neutralize the Greens by some 'greening' of the SPD programme had been a failure. The indications were of the existence of a fairly solid post-materialist constituency in West Germany which would not be easily integrated into the SPD. In terms of social composition the Greens were the most homogeneous of the parties. Predominantly young and well educated, centred in large towns and university centres, they had few supporters over the age of 35 and were overwhelmingly middle-class in background. Further indication of the strength of the Greens was given by their very good performance in the Baden-Württemberg *Land* election of March 1983 when they gained 2.7 per cent on their 1980 result despite well publicized and real difficulties in the *Bundestagsfraktion*, a poorly organized campaign, and a totally new slate of candidates. The success of the Greens and the stagnation of the SPD vote which occurred in the Baden-Württemberg election were repeated in the European Election of June 1984 when the SPD dropped back 3.4 per cent and the Greens advanced 5 per cent on the preceding election in 1979. The Greens' prospects were enhanced by un-favourable publicity for all the established parties including the SPD, as a result of the Flick affair. The proceedings surrounding the Flick affair made it clear that the SPD, in common with the other parties, accepted money from the Flick concern in extremely dubious circumstances.

Coalition Possibilities

Power is normally attained at the federal level in West Germany, not by clear electoral victory, but by finding a coalition partner. This must be a vital ingredient in any strategy by the SPD to regain power. The idea that the SPD could ever win a majority on its own is not seriously entertained by any significant figure in the party. The circumstances surrounding the end of the coalition in 1982, the difficulties endured by the FDP in 1983–5 and the almost certain extinction that would befall the FDP if it changed partners again in the immediate future means that a possible coalition with the FDP can be excluded. It was a measure of the daunting difficulties faced by the SPD that a number of prominent SPD politicians, including Wolfgang Roth, called for a Grand Coalition with the CDU/CSU. This might emerge as a last resort in a 'hung' election where the FDP failed to get into the Bundestag and where the balance of power was held by the Greens who then faced unacceptable conditions for a coalition with the SPD, but would be a very unlikely possibility otherwise.

Coalition with the Greens

Although unlikely, this possibility is the only one on the political agenda in the short to medium term. Arithmetically, it had appeared an attractive option since the *Landtag* election in Hesse on 27 September, 1982, when the SPD polled 42.8 per cent and the Greens 8 per cent. It was this result which fired Willy Brandt's enthusiasm and moved him to speak of a new majority left of the centre (Boelling, 1982: 99–100). Where it appeared in practice, it proved very difficult to translate such a majority into a functioning government. Nearly all the leading figures and many of the ordinary members in the Greens and Alternatives have been members of the SPD, and they are extremely suspicious of any embracement strategy by the SPD, which they see not altogether incorrectly as an attempt to make the Greens superfluous. Repeated attempts, first in Hamburg by Klaus von Donhanyi and with less enthusiasm by Holger Börner in Hessen, to bind the Greens to supporting their

SPD governments foundered on the intransigence and suspicion of the Greens.

Things began to change somewhat in 1984. The SPD had moved leftwards on defence and ecology. Brandt now often presented the SPD as the Party of 'the new politics' and clearly encouraged the formation of a coalition with the Greens. The strategy seemed to be to test the possibilities of an alliance with the Greens at *Land* level. It is very significant that the first alliance was made in Hesse in June 1984. Hesse is a key area for the SPD. It is all the more significant because Holger Börner, the Minister President of Hesse, is a major figure on the right of the SPD. He was also something of a hate-figure to the Greens because of his support for the building of a second runway at Frankfurt airport, his advocacy of reliance on nuclear power, and his closeness to Helmut Schmidt. A second inconclusive election in 1983 had left both sides with reduced freedom of manœuvre. After a number of months of exploratory talks the alliance was concluded on 5 June 1984. The agreement provoked surprisingly little discussion in the local SPD. Only one minister, Herbert Reiz, resigned and delegates at an Extraordinary Congress of the SPD in Hesse approved the alliance by the overwhelming majority of 221 to 17.

But the proto-alliance or *Tolerierungsbündnis* collapsed in late November 1984. The Greens were opposed to the expansion of the nuclear plants Alkem and Nukem in Hanau. The granting or withholding of a licence to expand was the prerogative of the Interior Ministry in Bonn rather than of the Hessian government but the Greens argued that, notwithstanding the formal legal position, the Hessian government should contest the decision of the Interior Ministry to grant a licence. Holger Börner felt himself unable to back this admittedly hopeless tactic and the Greens withdrew their support (see Kerschgens, 1985: 117–28). The collapse of the Hessian experiment made it unlikely that any further proto-alliances would be entered into at state level at that time.[1] A federal alliance is much more unlikely given the probable attitude of West Germany's NATO partners.

The collapse of the proto-alliance in Hesse meant that the SPD had to try a different tactic. Oskar Lafontaine, the charismatic left-wing leader of the SPD in the Saarland, offered the Greens the option of a formal alliance with a number of ministerial pacts. As Lafontaine expected, the Greens refused this offer and he argued that the Greens' supporters should support the SPD in order to realize the Greens' ideas. This argument had some impact in the Saar, where the SPD led by Lafontaine and Jo Leinen is markedly on the left of the SPD generally, but seems less likely to work for the SPD as a whole.

Conclusion

The prospects for the SPD in the foreseeable future seem mixed. The emergence of a competitor on its left flank adds a fourth component to the party system and has significantly weakened the SPD. Even Peter Glotz, a professional optimist by virtue of his job as the party's federal business manager, assumes the SPD will lose the next election (Glotz, 1984). His optimism is demonstrated by his belief that the Greens will not clear the 5 per cent and the gap between the CDU/CSU and the SPD will thus narrow.

The indications available in 1985 point in contradictory directions. The support for the Greens declined, although the Flick Affair provided a favourable environment for them. If, nevertheless, the Greens survive, then presumably any SPD hope of attaining power lies in an accommodation with them. As already indicated, the difficulties of arriving at such an accommodation and making it stick are formidable. A long period in opposition is likely to be very testing for the SPD. One factor in its ability to deal with these challenges will be the performance of the new leadership troika: Hans-Jochen Vogel (Parliamentary Leader), Willy Brandt (Party Chairman), and Johannes Rau (Chancellor candidate). Notwithstanding Johannes Rau's very striking electoral success in the North Rhine Westphalia *Land* election of May 1985, it is difficult to imagine that this team is as strong as its immediate predecessor (Wehner, Brandt, Schmidt), and the challenges posed by Lafontaine and Eppler are probably stronger. These challenges have been increased by the effects of parliamentary competition on their left. They are magnified by continuing dissent about Party organization and the forms of Party life.

The SPD leadership has the immensely difficult task of putting together a package which will unite the partially conflicting interests and aspirations of the blue-collar workers and the environmentalists. Moreover they have to do this in a way that will increase rather than diminish the SPD's electoral appeal. Progress has, not surprisingly, been very slow. The Party is committed to a major programmatic revision of the Bad Godesberg Programme but the first ideas towards this, contained in the report of the Basic Values Commission of January 1984, look unlikely to achieve the objective of creating a consensus in the 'Party and attracting new support in society at large'.[2] They will however draw comfort from the victories in the *Land* elections of Spring 1985 where, at least in two local areas and with charismatic candidates, the SPD were able to combine ecological and work issues successfully and to drain support from the Greens.

Notes

1. The strengthening of the '*realos*' (the realists) in the Greens and the continued minority position of the Hessian government led to the conclusion of a coalition in December 1985. This coalition was bitterly opposed by Greens at federal level.
2. *Godesberg Heute*, 'Bericht der Grundwerte—Kommission zum Godesberger Grundstafl Programme', Bonn, January 1984. The quotation is a statement made by chairman Erhard Eppler at the press conference, 14 January 1984.

6

Austrian Social Democracy

Melanie Ann Sully*

Introduction

AFTER the Second World War, the Socialist Party of Austria (SPÖ) took an active part in constructing the Second Republic and was subsequently involved in building a new political system (Stadler, 1982). Aware of the catastrophes of the past (Rabinbach, 1983) and the dangers of class confrontation, the Party welcomed co-operation with former political opponents and joined the Conservatives (ÖVP) in a great coalition which was to last until 1966 (Sully, 1981). This was fundamental in shaping the political activities of Austrian socialists, who became steadily more committed to the Austrian state (Sully, 1982). Social and economic partnership further consolidated the new-style politics of the 'green table' based on discussions and amicable consultation between labour and capital on wages and prices (Shell, 1962). Both sides of industry could see the rationale behind this mood and its advantages over the pre-war violence and street battles. The Austrian approach to labour relations became identified with social harmony and the main political protagonists were proud of this image. Dissent came from minority groups who were dismayed at this smugness and regretted the inability to tolerate conflict, but for most labour leaders and conservatives this was the price to pay for social peace and stability.

The great coalition fell in 1966 and was replaced by an ÖVP single-party cabinet which lasted until 1970 when the SPÖ formed a minority government. In 1971 the SPÖ won an absolute majority and began its long period as a governmental party. The SPÖ consolidated its position in the elections of 1975 and 1979 but in 1983 lost its absolute majority (see Table 6.1). The break-up of the

* I should like to thank the Fonds zur Förderung der wissenschaftlichen Forschung, Vienna, for a grant enabling me to carry out this research.

Table 6.1: *Election results in the Austrian Second Republic*

Year of Election	SPÖ % of votes	SPÖ No. of seats	ÖVP % of votes	ÖVP No. of seats	FPÖ % of votes	FPÖ No. of seats	KPÖ (Communists) % of votes	KPÖ (Communists) No. of seats	Others % of votes	Others No. of seats
1945	44.60	76	49.80	85	—	—	5.42	4	0.19	—
1949	38.71	67	44.03	77	11.67	16	5.08	5	0.51	—
1953	42.11	73	41.26	74	10.95	14	5.28	4	0.40	—
1956	43.05	74	45.96	82	6.52	6	4.42	3	0.06	—
1959	44.79	78	44.19	79	7.70	8	3.27	—	0.05	—
1962	44.00	76	45.43	81	7.04	8	3.04	—	0.48	—
1966	42.56	74	48.35	85	5.35	6	0.41	—	3.32	—
1970	48.42	81	44.69	78	5.52	6	0.98	—	0.39	—
1971	50.04	93	43.11	80	5.45	10	1.36	—	0.04	—
1975	50.42	93	42.95	80	5.41	10	1.19	—	0.03	—
1979	51.03	95	41.90	77	6.06	11	0.96	—	0.05	—
1983	47.65	90	43.22	81	4.98	12	0.66	—	3.49	—

coalition in 1966 disturbed many who feared that the horrors of internal strife would return to sabotage the achievements of the Second Republic. They were relieved to discover that the new methods of negotiation had developed strong roots and, despite some rhetoric to the contrary, political life under the auspices of social partnership continued unruffled and with growing confidence.

The effective functioning of good labour relations laid the foundations for the later development of a prosperous economy. A dramatic increase in the standard of living and the growth of the 'affluent society' became associated by most Austrians with the decade beginning in 1970. In the minds of voters, happily for the Austrian socialists, prosperity became almost synonymous with the SPÖ government. The commitment to improving the welfare state, maintaining full employment and creating a 'modern' Austria appealed to the electorate throughout the 1970s. Fears of recession and threats to this new prosperity were considered to emanate from abroad and the SPÖ retained support even during troubled times. It seemed that the SPÖ, under the paternal leadership of Dr Bruno Kreisky, was the only party which could be relied upon to fight off international disasters and keep Austria safe and secure. The SPÖ had become a loyal bulwark of the Austrian republic and a faithful protector of the interests of its people. Little patience was shown to critics of the party line, given this success.

Potential dissenters were daunted by the fact that the SPÖ government was implementing a social welfare programme and safeguarding jobs. It was believed that internal disputes could lead to a loss of office and a reversal of these achievements. In this way the SPÖ retained the loyalty of those on the left who were uneasy at the lack of clearly defined 'socialist' policies. The Austrian socialists had always highly prized party unity and great pressure has traditionally existed to respect what some regard as a 'fetish' (Knapp, 1980). Factionalism has always been regarded as suicidal and insane although the party likes to feel that criticism can be voiced, providing it is not too public and follows the correct procedural rules (Sully, 1982). In contrast to many other European social democratic parties the SPÖ would seem to enjoy a high degree of internal cohesion.

The role of Kreisky as a father figure and his capacity for reconciling different groups has been important. The manageability of the SPÖ will become more acute in the post-Kreisky era. Questions which have been largely subdued are likely to come to the surface and worry the leadership at a time of mounting economic difficulties. The orientation crisis of the SPÖ has largely been ignored during the Kreisky era, while the party was reaping the harvest of electoral success. The future for the SPÖ is likely to present more of a challenge on the nature and meaning of social democratic values in the 1980s.

Party Reform

After the 1975 election all members were invited by the leadership to participate in a thorough reform of the party and to give their views on the reports of seven working groups. These were concerned with the 'open' party, women, youth, the tasks of the SPÖ in factories, leisure, organization, and propaganda. Non-members were to be included in future in internal discussions. In this way Kreisky hoped to fortify his progressive electoral alliance, based on the liberal floating voter, which provided the SPÖ with its absolute majority. Discussions on party reform also served to absorb the energies of party critics. The 'open' party featured prominently on the reform agenda and the idea was to appeal to catholics and liberals who sympathized with the goals of a humanitarian socialist party. Although this marked a welcome break from the former narrow, doctrinaire approach, the new 'openness' encouraged a dilution of principles which damaged the party's spiritual unity and sense of purpose. The educational machinery was unable to cope with the influx of a new type of member and some of the technocrats, little concerned with ideology, who subsequently flourished in the party became the *bêtes noires* of the left (Sully, 1981b).

Measures were introduced to democratize the structure of the SPÖ and improve communications between the leadership and the rank and file. A new statute was agreed in 1976 which stipulated that every member had the right to put questions or resolutions directly to the party executive and was entitled to a reply within eight weeks. The left remained sceptical of these efforts to democratize the party but a survey carried out by the *Sozialwissenschaftliche Studienges-ellschaft* in 1976 discovered that SPÖ supporters were more satisfied than their ÖVP counterparts with the opportunities for freedom of expression in their own Party. The Party, it seemed, like the society it was trying to change was in a state of permanent reform, for soon after organizational changes had been agreed, Kreisky announced that members should swiftly move on to re-examine the Party's programme. The initiative had come once again from the leadership: intellectuals engaged in debates with politicians to devise a set of principles, which received comment from members. Some queried the need for a new programme to supersede the one of 1958 and suspicions persisted that the entire exercise was designed to generate a dynamic Party and avoid atrophy creeping in after a long period in office. A new programme was finally adopted at a conference in 1978 and claimed to meet the challenges of a new epoch and the international crisis with the slogan of 'Ready for the 1980s'.

Some of the social welfare schemes outlined in the Party's previous programme of 1958 had been put on the statute books by the SPÖ government and there was a general feeling that a restatement of goals was necessary. Some on the left feared that too much revisionism would be adopted but at the end of the day most groupings in the Party were happy with the new programme. The final document stressed the importance to the Party of Freedom, Equality, Justice, and Solidarity. These principles had been mentioned briefly in the programme of 1958 but were amplified twenty years later. No alteration was made to the phrase close to the hearts of the left which pledged the party to aim for a 'classless society'. This is an important symbol for those like Josef Hindels, a veteran Austro-Marxist, and the youth leader Josef Cap. The leadership is quite content to retain a mainly rhetorical phrase which serves to consolidate Party unity. Bruno Kreisky considers a classless society to be a Utopian goal, but a noble one worthy of pursuit by social democrats. It was this kind of flexible approach to controversial issues which held the Party together and avoided the open conflict prevalent in the German SPD. A Bad Godesberg for the SPÖ would not have been acceptable because of its bald rejection of the Marxist legacy; the SPÖ had always contrived to find a third way which incorporated diverse elements, and Kreisky's leadership encouraged this preference.

The 1978 programme referred to the crises and contradictions of capitalism but refrained from any onslaught on social partnership or an attack on the economic pillars of the system which the SPÖ

158 *Melanie Ann Sully*

government is obliged to accept. The reorganization of Austria's economic structure has not been the chief priority of the SPÖ in power and instead it has concentrated on implementing social and educational reforms and preserving jobs. The programme emphasized the need for democratic control rather than an increase in state ownership. It envisaged an increase in political information and participation throughout the community, hoping in this way to reduce the influence of powerful élites. This outlook was in accordance with Kreisky's view of the SPÖ as a 'freedom movement' concerned with the democratization of all aspects of society.

After so long in office some leftists in the party felt that this was insufficient and that a fundamental and more radical reorganization of the economic system should be put in operation. The leadership seemed reluctant to experiment with such ideas at a time of recession and preferred to defend gains already made. The SPÖ has not wished to provoke unnecessary conflict and its efforts have been directed towards maintaining harmony both within the Party and in the country. An example of this has been the SPÖ's positive attitude to the Catholic church and Christians, expressed in this way in the 1978 programme:

We socialists recognize the change within the Christian churches. This is not only evident from official statements but above all from the social involvement of Christians. We welcome this development with deepest sincerity. Many involved Christians are active in our socialist movement. Every Christian can become a colleague in the fight for a more just social order and an ally in the struggle to implement our common ideals.

This emphasis on reconciliation instead of conflict was a departure from the pre-war fighting *Lager* mentality. The SPÖ showed that it could accept former foes of the labour movement from other political, economic or religious groups as partners in building a new future. The Party aimed to bring liberal and middle-class elements of society into its fold. The electoral performance of the SPÖ demonstrated that this was largely successful, although dissatisfaction on the left gradually became more articulate (Gerlich, 1983).

The Nuclear Controversy

The 1978 programme recognized the importance of the energy crisis and accepted the need for nuclear energy if maximum safety precautions were adopted. This proviso has delayed the implementation of a nuclear power programme, although there is a completed reactor sited at Zwentendorf near Vienna. Towards the end of 1978, tensions in the SPÖ on the question of commissioning the plant became acute. Kreisky, sensitive to the discontent especially among the youth, hesitated to proceed. The leader of the powerful trade unions (ÖGB), Anton Benya, made no secret of his support for nuclear energy and the Party found itself in an uncomfortable dilemma. In these circumstances Chancellor Kreisky decided to call a referendum on the subject for November 1978. The result was a narrow victory for the anti-nuclear lobby with 50.5 per cent against and 49.5 per cent in favour of Zwentendorf. This was a blow to the government which had declared its support for the plant and to Kreisky who had given strong personal backing to this line. After the surprise result, the SPÖ moved cautiously, aware of the delicate nature of the topic and concerned to avoid alienating young voters. The Party is still officially in favour of nuclear energy but maintains that Zwentendorf will not go on-stream without the consent of the population and only when full safety precautions are met.

The entire exercise resulted in the proliferation of initiative groups and organizations outside of the established parties, ranging from Maoists to Neo-Nazis. Many activists identified with the growing 'green' movement and felt it necessary to remain vigilant so long as Zwentendorf was not physically dismantled. The SPÖ has respected this strong feeling, yet at the same time is under pressure from industry to put the plant on-stream. The SPÖ considers that caution and compromise is the best strategy for party cohesion. The nuclear referendum boosted the 'alternative-green' movement and all the main parties have in different ways responded to this new challenge. The SPÖ has tried to maintain a dialogue with groups judged to be close to the Party. After a conference in 1979 a special department was established in the Party to liaise with the AL or 'alternative' groups. This followed an initiative of the central secretary Karl Blecha, a Catholic also regarded as being on the left, who appealed to all outside the party who criticized the capitalist system and its inhumanity. The department has become increasingly important for the SPÖ as the AL groups continue to flourish. Work in this area has been directed by Hildegard

Mauerhofer from a social-Catholic background and a member of ACUS, the socialist organization which seeks to build bridges with the Church (Sully, in Paterson and Thomas, 1977).

The Party's view is expressed through informal discussion groups and pamphlets and is aimed at those disillusioned with the established parties. The SPÖ hopes by patient persuasion to regain the confidence of these important voters who find the Alternatives more attractive. Many in the AL groups are sympathetic to the SPÖ although they believe that it has become stale in office and incapable of initiating further progress. Despite its efforts, the SPÖ does not always appear convincing on questions such as disarmament, the peace movement, ecology, and nuclear energy (Pilz, 1982). The weak points of the AL movement are its diversity and disunity; it lacks leaders who appear credible as practical politicians. The SPÖ stresses the importance of realism and argues that measures to curb industrial pollution and protect the environment can only evolve after a long process of discussion with those involved. The call for sober realism and patience has in the past found a response from the disciplined labour movement, although a new generation may not prove to be so compliant. In the election of 1983 an AL list won 1.36 per cent of the vote and failed to gain parliamentary representation. The ideas of the Alternatives have a greater following and the SPÖ will find it more difficult to integrate them as it embarks on a coalition with the right-wing Freedom Party (FPÖ).

Kreisky's Leadership

Under Bruno Kreisky the SPÖ developed the image of a Party sympathetic to 'alternative' ideas, yet possessing enough realism to act with moderation in government. Kreisky was a figure who embodied the old ideals of the Party and as leader sought to halt the drift to technocracy and opportunism which crept in during the late 1970s. Kreisky's own associations with the pre-war social democrats, his activities in the illegal movement during the corporate state and his admiration for the inter-war left socialist Otto Bauer, added to his mystique. For less ideologically-motivated voters, Kreisky became a symbol of conservative Austria and identified with security and international respectability. This wide-ranging appeal was an important electoral asset for the Party.

Kreisky was elected leader at the 1967 Party Conference on the basis of support from the provinces and largely against the Viennese party and the trade unions. Kreisky began to modernize the party, which had just suffered a heavy defeat at the polls, and encouraged organizational and programmatic changes. More representation for the provinces was introduced into the Party hierarchy and policy documents were formulated which became the SPÖ's electoral platform. The tone of this reform was moderation and the aim was to avoid too much disruption. From 1966–70 the Party's biggest desire was to regain power and Kreisky received the co-operation he needed from the rank and file. The new leader wished to avoid dogmatism and instead open the Party to the middle ground and liberal voters. In Kreisky's language, these voters could go part of the way in attaining the goals of the labour movement; they were also crucial for the SPÖ's absolute majority in the 1970s (Pelinka, 1983).

Election slogans such as 'Kreisky—who else?', 'the Austrian way', and 'for Austria' demonstrated the importance of the leader and the Party's loyalty to the country. In 1966 the SPÖ had won only 42.6 per cent of the vote but by 1979, at the peak of success, increased this to 51.0 per cent—an achievement largely attributed to the popular personality of Kreisky. Most were content to enjoy the electoral victories and the rewards that accompanied a *Regierungspartei*. The emphasis was on social welfare progress and the Party cautioned against too much internal criticism which could wreck this and pave the way for a conservative government. This deterred potential rebels and in the first phase of office the SPÖ introduced important reforms in education, the health service, and social policy which had been neglected. The penal code, the communications network, and working conditions were improved and, in accordance with the pledge to create a 'humane' society, the working week was reduced to forty hours and all workers were entitled to a minimum of four weeks' annual holiday. Inflation and unemployment were kept under control and incomes compared favourably with other European countries. The Party was still formally committed to create a 'classless' society and socialists on the left could feel that the SPÖ was the only effective political force worthy of support. A left conscience prevailed within the Party structure in the early 1970s, articulated by Karl Blecha, chairman of the 'Young Generation' and the parliamentarian Heinz Fischer.

Both became cabinet ministers in the coalition government with the FPÖ formed after the 1983 election. In the 1970s they cautioned the Party against becoming too preoccupied with daily governmental tasks and reminded the leadership that it should not neglect the rank and file nor abandon its socialist duty to transform society (Albers, 1982).

Kreisky was aware of these sentiments and argued the case for greater democratic controls on the power structure. Some activists became impatient with purely quantitative reforms which seemed to leave the capitalist order relatively intact. For them privilege and inequality under a socialist government were not receding but flourishing. Kreisky's paternal leadership served to channel potential frustration along positive channels through the encouragement of debate within the Party. The election victories of 1975 and 1979 boosted the morale of the Party but could not stop the disappointment of left-wing intellectuals, who felt that more use could have been made of the absolute majority for the cause of socialism. These feelings grew in the late 1970s when it was felt that the SPÖ had little new to offer and was stagnating in office. This unease met with little response from the majority of Party members and trade unionists who were grateful for full employment and an increase in the standard of living.

One major strain on the relations between the leadership and the minority on the left occurred over the 'Androsch affair'. The lucrative business activities of Hannes Androsch as Minister of Finance caused great embarrassment to the Party as the press daily claimed to have discovered more corruption in connection with Androsch and his 'clan'. Kreisky was irritated by the affair, which suggested that Androsch had unscrupulously used his position for personal advantage and profit-making. Provincial politicians and the trade unions supported Androsch who was regarded as a brilliant economic strategist. Kreisky became increasingly disturbed by allegations of the vast personal wealth of his Minister of Finance, who was also Vice-Chancellor. The left was outraged by the ostentatious life-style of Androsch which was considered to be inappropriate for a leading social democrat. At the end of 1980 the resignation of Androsch from the cabinet was announced and he moved on to become Director-General of Austria's largest bank with a handsome salary. For the left this was further evidence of the Party's integration with the Establishment and symbolic of the general abandonment of principle and justice. Kreisky personally retained integrity and popularity both in the country and in his Party and was respected as one of the few honest politicians.

The Chancellor's disagreements with Androsch continued and Kreisky publicly made clear his view that someone so closely involved with tax consultancy firms and business transactions would not make a suitable leader for a social-democratic party. Androsch seemed blissfully unperturbed by remarks of this kind and criticized the government's handling of the economy. In 1982 Androsch hinted that unemployment would rise alarmingly because of the government's reluctance to export arms and tanks. The left had frequently protested against these exports to South American dictatorships and the government had agreed not to pursue this trade where human rights could be violated. Kreisky was outraged by the insinuations of the former Minister of Finance, which he considered false and damaging. It was not considered ethical for a member of the Party to criticize official government policy in this way and even the trade-union leader Benya remarked that Androsch had been indiscreet. Androsch, once Kreisky's 'crown prince', had been disowned by his former protector although he retained popularity with the party in Carinthia and Burgenland. Fears of a come-back by Androsch still haunt the left although Kreisky was succeeded as *Kanzlerkandidat* in 1983 by Fred Sinowatz, who had replaced Androsch as Vice-Chancellor. Sinowatz, aged fifty-four when he became Chancellor, is amenable to advice from Kreisky and some continuity is likely to be maintained with the vanished era.

Electoral Position

The SPÖ, despite internal squabbles, did well in elections at all levels. The weakness of the opposition parties and their internal feuds helped. In the election for the federal presidency in 1980 the SPÖ nominee, Dr Kirchschläger, gained almost 80 per cent of the vote since the main opposition party, the ÖVP, decided not to put up a candidate. In elections to the provincial legislature of Styria in 1981 the SPÖ made gains in an area increasingly troubled by the recession in the steel industry. In this conservative, rural province the socialists increased their share of the vote from 40.3 per cent (1978) to 42.7 per cent and won an extra seat. The credibility of the ruling SPÖ at federal level was a crucial factor in this election. In the autumn of 1982 the SPÖ won 53.2 per cent in the provincial election in Burgenland, compared with 51.9 per cent in 1977. The SPÖ had capitalized on the misfortunes of the ÖVP in this province, reeling from corruption charges against the local politicians. A survey at the time discovered that 45 per cent of those questioned considered the ÖVP to be corrupt compared with 24 per cent who held this view of the SPÖ.

At the same time as the Burgenland result, elections in the city of Salzburg marked the appearance as a political force of a right-wing, 'green' Citizens' List which won seven seats on the council and 17.5 per cent of the vote. Its programme mainly centred around the idea of freedom for the individual from state interference and it tended to damage the middle-class parties such as the ÖVP and the FPÖ. It attracted affluent voters who had been disillusioned with the FPÖ's assistance in securing the banking post for the social democrat, Androsch. Following the Salzburg success a united green party (VGÖ) was formed to contest the 1983 election under the leadership of a professor of geology, Dr Alexander Tollmann. On the eve of the election the VGÖ was plagued by internal feuds, resignations, and expulsions which damaged its electoral chances. It gained 1.93 per cent of the vote and failed to win any seats in parliament.

A left-wing alternative list (ALÖ) also contested the 1983 election. This was a fragile alliance of different groups opposed to nuclear power. In January 1983 an AL list had scored well in the local elections in the city of Graz, winning 7 per cent of the vote but in the general election the ALÖ could only muster 1.4 per cent. There was still a feeling that the SPÖ could hold on to its absolute majority, and so there was a reluctance by left-wingers to sabotage this. The socialist youth movement during the campaign worked hard to stop the drift to the alternative/green camp and produced its own 'red-green' pamphlet dealing with environmental problems. The 1983 result was a setback for the SPÖ, even though it remained the largest party in parliament. By 1983 the SPÖ seemed an exhausted party led by the 72 year-old Chancellor Kreisky, not always in the best of health. The result confirmed the views of those on the left who had been arguing the case for more imagination and a regeneration of the party. The coalition with the FPÖ could not give these critics much hope that the party would find the courage to adopt a new course based on more explicit socialist principles.

Membership

At the party conference in 1982 the central secretary, Karl Blecha, argued that the party was a flexible organization open to different views. He considered that the network of associations in the SPÖ provided its members with a second 'home', and was a vital link with the rank and file. Activities such as rambling, music, stamp collecting, sport, and gymnastics are organized through the party for children and the elderly. Contact with members is further maintained through the *Vertrauenspersonen*, a trained group of party activists who regularly give talks to the local parties or

Table 6.2:　*Austrian Socialist Party membership, 1980–1*

Province	Year	Total	Men	Women
Burgenland	1980	29,543	23,103	6,440
	1981	29,886	23,237	6,649
Carinthia	1980	51,262	37,616	13,646
	1981	51,617	37,803	13,814
Lower Austria	1980	139,959	96,772	43,187
	1981	140,165	96,728	43,437
Upper Austria	1980	103,283	78,257	25,026
	1981	102,343	77,525	24,818
Salzburg	1980	26,615	19,092	7,523
	1981	26,314	18,811	7,503
Styria	1980	104,428	74,482	29,946
	1981	103,240	73,811	29,429
Tyrol	1980	15,498	11,562	3,936
	1981	15,006	11,233	3,773
Vorarlberg	1980	5,393	4,020	1,373
	1981	5,358	4,000	1,358
Vienna	1980	243,900	130,769	113,131
	1981	239,175	128,171	111,004
Austria	1980	719,881	475,673	244,208
	1981	713,104	471,319	241,785

Source: Jahrbuch, SPÖ, Vienna, 1982.

Sektionen, of which there are 3,370. These *Vertrauenspersonen*, making up 9.9 per cent of the membership, personally collect subscriptions, answer queries from members, listen to their grievances and pass them on to the leadership. They are vital in mobilizing supporters at election times, and their views cannot be ignored by the leadership. This method of maintaining contact with ordinary members has also assisted party cohesion.

The party suffered a slight loss of membership in 1980–1 except in the provinces of Burgenland, Carinthia and Lower Austria (see Table 6.2). Women traditionally constitute a low proportion of the total (33.9 per cent in 1981). The party has a high ratio of members to voters: 29.3 per cent of socialist voters were also party members in 1979. The SPÖ continues to be a mass-membership party, with 9.4 per cent of the total population as members. The tendency during the 1970s has been for the proportion of manual workers to decline, while white-collar workers and pensioners have increased, although not so rapidly, as can be seen from Table 6.3. Workers are also becoming less important for the Party at elections: in 1975, 58 per cent of the SPÖ came from workers and 35 per cent from salaried employees, compared with 68 per cent and 25 per cent respectively in 1969 (Raschke, 1978).

Table 6.3:   *Social background of members of the Austrian Socialist Party (%)*

	1955	1960	1970	1978
Manual workers	42.1	41.2	38.3	29.9
White-Collar	22.3	24.1	27.2	31.4
Professional/ self-employed	5.3	4.4	3.9	2.6
Pensioners	11.4	14.4	16.4	18.3
Housewives	17.3	14.6	12.2	9.7
Students	—	—	0.6	0.9
Unknown/others	1.6	1.3	1.4	7.2

Sources: compiled from *Berichte* and *Jahrbücher*, SPÖ, Vienna.

The Trade Unions

Party representation in the ÖGB in 1983 amounted to 75 per cent, and 60 per cent of the work force were organized in the trade unions. Membership of the ÖGB is voluntary, unlike the Chamber of Labour which is a public corporation with compulsory membership. Socialists predominate in the Chamber of Labour and in 1979 won 64.3 per cent of the vote in elections. The Chamber provides valuable legal advice and welfare services, and plays an important rôle in the economic decision-making process. The trade unions are more active on pay policy and negotiating collective agreements. One of their main priorities was to save and create jobs and the SPÖ's record in this area has assisted good relations between the party and the unions. Austria's unemployment rate compares favourably with most other European countries (see Table 2.1) but both the SPÖ and the ÖGB realize the need for constant vigilance on the labour front (Pelinka, 1981).

The head of the ÖGB's largest union of salaried employees, Alfred Dallinger, was in the cabinet as Minister of Social Affairs. He has advocated radical measures to cope with unemployment, including a 35-hour week and a minimum of five weeks' holiday for all workers. This has met with a mixed reaction from the SPÖ and the head of the ÖGB, Anton Benya, who would like to proceed cautiously. Plans were developed to give workers two days free each year from 1984 for three years. Benya has further agreed to a reduction in the working week if the arrangement can be applied in individual factories. A motion to introduce the 35-hour week by the end of the 1980s was passed at the SPÖ's conference in 1982. Dallinger was more critical than his colleagues of social partnership, which he considered to act as a brake on progressive legislation. This view, shared by the left, argues that the SPÖ in government is hampered in introducing fundamental societal changes because of its integration in the 'system'. A redistribution of wealth, it is felt, has not occurred under the SPÖ because of the social partnership mentality. The trade unions are closely identified with this which presumes consultations with employers' organizations and Dallinger has often been in a minority position in the ÖGB.

The trade-union movement in recent years has devoted much of its energy to maintaining jobs, but for the left and the youth movement the price paid has often been the sacrifice of socialist principles. The export of arms to Latin American dictatorships was a controversial way of saving jobs. Under pressure from the youth in the party and also Catholics and liberals, this has been curtailed. Demonstrations against the export of arms took place in 1981 in Graz where the SPÖ was holding its party conference. Other skirmishes occurred in Vienna in front of the factory where tanks were being produced for export to Argentina. Workers, whose jobs were threatened by halting production, clashed with the demonstrators. This highlighted the growing cleavage between social democratic and trade-unon functionaries and those active in the youth and peace movements. It showed clearly the dilemma of a party in power and committed to socialism being forced to work within the limitations imposed by the international capitalist environment. It further isolated the average worker and member in the party from the left intellectuals whose theoretical arguments had little impact on those concerned with keeping their jobs.

The government has encountered problems in maintaining a balance between safeguarding jobs and protecting the environment. In 1972 the SPÖ set up a Ministry for Health and the Environment with responsibility for reconciling the competing demands from industry and the ecological movement. Dr Kurt Steyrer, as minister of the department, was considered by the left to have insufficient power to implement a progressive policy which would include curbing industrial pollution, reducing noise levels, and putting the individual before the requirements of economic growth and profits. The trade unions oppose measures which shift the priorities of the government from safeguarding jobs, and Dr Steyrer has had to contend with this attitude.

The Youth Movement

Dr Steyrer came into the limelight during the Party Conference of 1982 when he was voted on to the Party executive to replace the youth leader, Josef Cap, who had failed to receive enough support. The Conference, staged in Vienna under the slogan 'For Austria and its people', was designed to demonstrate Party unity and eulogize the Kreisky era in the run-up for the 1983 election. Just before the climax of the Conference—the traditional speech of the party chairman Bruno Kreisky—came requests for comments on nominations to the party executive. This normally uncontroversial matter was surprisingly challenged by Cap who monopolized press and television coverage on the day intended to be devoted to Kreisky. Cap proceeded to the rostrum a little nervously and asked some pertinent and embarrassing questions concerning Theodor Kery, provincial governor of Burgenland, and a member of the SPÖ executive up for re-election. Cap wished to know if Kery earned more than the Chancellor and, if so, why? As chairman of the Burgenland electricity company, did he receive cheap electricity?

And, in his free time, did he practise target shooting? These blunt questions touched on issues of privileges and the conduct of party functionaries, which were important for rank and file members, as well as those in the peace and youth movements. A startled Conference waited for a reply, which came not from Kery but from the Minister of Education and Vice-Chancellor, Fred Sinowatz, also from Burgenland. He disputed that Kery was in receipt of such a vast salary, agreed that he was entitled to cheap electricity and implied that his shooting activities resulted from Kery's interest and ability in technical affairs. The youth section was not satisfied and discontent grew when Cap was voted off the executive by outraged delegates. The view was that Cap should have picked another place and time for his tactless comments. The storm in the party continued and it was apparent from letters to the party's newspaper, *Die AZ*, that Cap had considerable support. Some praised his honesty if not his methods, and pressed for more scrutiny and control on privilege in the party hierarchy. Kery, a close associate of Androsch, symbolized for the youth movement the type who had entered the Party for personal advancement rather than because of a socialist commitment (Marschalek, 1983).

Kreisky was irritated by what he regarded as Cap's childish behaviour but it was clear that the affair could not be dismissed. The vacancy on the Party executive was filled by Dr Steyrer as a way of placating those concerned with environmental issues. Cap was placed on the Party list for the 1983 general election and, although his chances were not rated very highly, it was an astute move. He worked energetically in the Party running a very personalized campaign. He mobilized for the SPÖ a reservoir of disgruntled voters who might otherwise have turned to the Alternative List. Cap consistently argued that it was better to work within the SPÖ and press for progressive reforms, such as the 35-hour week, more rights for women, and a redistribution of wealth, than waste a vote on minority parties and so allow a reactionary party to form a government. As an indication of the widespread sympathy for Cap's ideas, he received enough votes to become a member of parliament in the constituency of Vienna. This was a triumph for the youth movement and another jolt to the SPÖ, which sustained heavy losses in the election. Cap argued that the defeat would have been greater if a left-wing candidate such as himself had not campaigned on behalf of the Party. The SPÖ had to accept this, although the leadership warned Cap not to build a 'party within a party'. Kreisky's successor, Sinowatz, does not have the same integrationist capacity as his predecessor but is a solid, reliable figure who now has the task of holding the party together. Sinowatz has no pretensions as a theoretician, yet questions such as the role of social democracy in the modern world, its purpose in government, and its attitude to the peace and ecological movements still need clarification. After the loss of its absolute majority in 1983, the SPÖ formed a coalition with the right-wing Freedom Party (FPÖ). Cap had called for the Party to go into opposition for a period of self-examination and rejuvenation. The leadership seemed unwilling to relinquish office and preferred the prospect of a coalition with a small party. It remains to be seen whether this in the long run will promote the aims of social democracy or merely reinforce the lack of momentum and imagination in a party which, for some, has become firmly rooted in the Establishment.

Conclusion and Prospects

In 1983 the Kreisky era came to a close and an internal power struggle in the SPÖ began. Sinowatz had to consolidate his position in the Party and rely on the loyalty of his nearest rivals, Dr Heinz Fischer and Karl Blecha. Speculation persisted on the possible come-back of the former Minister of Finance, Hannes Androsch, as party leader. Androsch enjoyed popularity amongst trade unionists and the SPÖ in the provinces. Many identify him with a period of economic growth, stability, and commonsense financial management. Sympathy for him is likely to increase if the new government demonstrates incompetence in this field.

The coalition with the FPÖ does not look an impressive arrangement. The Freedom Party is seriously split between liberal and nationalist wings and its leaders are frequently attacked for weakness by members in Carinthia. This makes it a useful party to manipulate for the SPÖ but ultimately impairs the ability of the coalition to act decisively and with authority. A backlog of important problems looks like accumulating during these early days of the new coalition. These concern the budget deficit, rising unemployment, environmental protection, cut-backs on social welfare, an overall energy strategy, and limitations on the privileges enjoyed by those in public office. The question of subsidies for the nationalized industries and a possible tax on savings are also contentious points which, if not tackled resolutely, are likely to result in a loss of confidence and give the impression of immobilism in the coalition.

The election of 1983 left the SPÖ in power as the largest party in parliament but obliged it to accept a novel and unwelcome alliance with a small party struggling for survival and internally divided. The leadership of the SPÖ seeks to recapture an absolute majority at the polls, while the rank and file urges a re-examination of social-democratic principles to establish credibility. Both the party and the coalition face a critical and testing time in the 1980s and it is not yet clear if either possesses coherent and consistent policies which will be necessary if urgent, difficult decisions are to be made.

7

Social Democracy in Scandinavia: Can Dominance be Regained?

Alastair H. Thomas

SCANDINAVIA in 1972 was still pre-eminently the region of Europe most clearly conforming to a social democratic model of society. In Denmark the Social Democratic party had been in government for all but nine of the post-war years and its widely respected leader, Jens Otto Krag, had just successfully concluded negotiations to take his country into the European Communities. In Finland the Social Democrats had enjoyed six years of participation in broad government coalitions, following a decade of exclusion during 1957–66. In Norway, Trygve Bratteli had brought the Labour Party back into government after six years of bourgeois party coalition: his efforts to take his country into the European Community seemed, at least to the Party leadership, likely to succeed and to set the seal on the restoration of the Party to the natural governing position which it had enjoyed for the 35 years before 1965. In Sweden the Social Democratic Labour Party appeared un-challenged in the unbroken rule it had enjoyed since 1933.

Twelve years later, in 1984, the fortunes of social democracy in Scandinavia looked very different. Election results and the formation of governments in the Nordic countries are summarized in Tables 7.1 to 7.6, which show that the Danish Social Democratic party had continued in office for most of the period, and managed to regain much of the support which it lost in the 'earthquake' election of 1973. But the minority governments formed by Anker Jørgensen, the party leader who took over from Krag in 1972, had been dependent on hard-won support from the small parties of the centre-right, including the Radical Liberals, the Liberal Party *(Venstre)*, the Centre Democrats, the Christian People's Party and sometimes even the Conservatives. By 1982 this arrangement broke down and the latter four Parties, who had increasingly developed a concerted stance in opposition, came together in a minority coalition government led by the Conservative, Poul Schlüter. This was recognition of the Conservatives' growing domination of the non-socialist parties, a trend on which Schlüter was quick to capitalize when calling a parliamentary election in January 1984, almost two years before it was required constitutionally, although closely in line with the biennial cycle which had been established since 1971. His coalition emerged significantly strengthened, the first leader of a non-socialist government in Denmark since the ascendancy of the Social Democrats in 1929 to do so (Thomas, 1985), a fact which did not bode well for an early return to power for the Social Democrats.

Table 7.1:   *Election results in Scandinavia, 1975–85: Denmark*

	1975		1977		1979		1981		1984	
	votes	seats	votes	seats	votes	seats	votes	seats	votes	seats
RADICAL LEFT										
Communists (Moscow)	4.2	7	3.7	7	1.9	0	1.1	0	0.7	0
Danish Communist Party (Marxist-Leninist)					0.1	0	0.1	0	—	—
Socialist Workers' Party							0.1	0	0.1	0
Left Socialists	2.1	4	2.7	5	3.7	6	2.7	5	2.7	5
	6.3	11	6.4	12	5.7	6	4.0	5	3.5	5
MODERATE LEFT										
Socialist People's Party	5.0	9	3.9	7	5.9	11	11.3	21	11.5	21
Social Democrats	29.9	53	37.0	65	38.3	68	32.9	59	31.6	56
SOCIALIST PARTIES: TOTAL	41.2	73	47.3	84	49.9	85	48.2	85	46.6	82
NON-SOCIALIST CENTRE										
Justice Party	1.8	0	3.3	6	2.6	5	1.4	0	1.5	0
Radical Liberals	7.1	13	3.6	6	5.4	10	5.1	9	5.5	10
Centre Democrats	2.2	4	6.4	11	3.2	6	8.3	15	4.6	8
Christian People's Party	5.3	9	3.4	6	2.6	5	2.3	4	2.7	5
Pensioners' Party			0.9	0						
	16.4	26	17.6	29	13.8	26	17.1	28	14.3	23
BOURGEOIS RIGHT										
Liberals *(Venstre)*	23.3	42	12.0	21	12.5	22	11.3	20	12.1	22
Conservative People's Party	5.5	10	8.5	15	12.5	22	14.5	26	23.4	42
	45.2	78	38.1	65	38.8	70	42.9	74	49.8	87
EXTREME RIGHT										
Progress Party	13.6	24	14.6	26	11.0	20	8.9	16	3.6	6
NON-SOCIALIST PARTIES: TOTAL	58.8	102	52.7	91	49.8	90	51.8	90	53.4	93
TOTAL	100	175	100	175	99.7	175	100	175	100	175
Faroes		2		2		2		2		2
Greenland		2		2		2		2		2
		179		179		179		179		179

Source: Hvidt, Folketingets Håndbog, 1984: 298–301.

Table 7.2:   *Election results in Scandinavia, 1975–85: Finland*

	1975		1979		1983	
	votes	seats	votes	seats	votes	seats
People's Democratic League	19.0	40	17.9	35	14.0	27
Social Democrats	25.0	54	24.0	52	26.7	57
SOCIALIST PARTIES: TOTAL	44.0	94	41.9	87	40.7	84
Centre Party	17.7	39	17.4	36	17.8	38
Rural Party	3.6	2	4.6	7	9.7	17
Swedish People's Party and Åland Alliance	4.7	10	4.3	10	4.6	11
Liberal People's Party	4.4	9	3.7	4	[a]	
Christian Union	3.3	9	4.8	9	3.0	3
Coalition Party (conservatives)	18.4	35	21.7	47	22.2	44
Constitutional Right Party	1.6	1	—	0	0.4	1
	53.7	105	56.5	113	57.7	114
The Greens					1.5	2
TOTALS	97.7	199	98.4	200	99.9	200

[a] In 1983 the Liberal People's Party put up a joint list with the Centre Party

Table 7.3:   *Election results in Scandinavia, 1975–85: Iceland*

	1978		1979		1983	
	votes	seats	votes	seats	votes	seats
People's Alliance	22.9	14	19.7	11	17.3	10
Social Democratic Alliance					7.3	4
Social Democratic Party	22.0	14	17.4	10	11.7	6
Progressive Party	16.9	12	24.9	17	18.5	14
separate Progress Party list					0.5	0
Independence Party	32.7	20	37.9	22	38.7	23
separate Independence Party list					0.5	0
Women's List					5.5	3
Others	5.5					
TOTALS	100	60	99.9	60	100	60

Table 7.4:   *Election results in Scandinavia, 1975–85: Norway*

	1977		1981		1985	
	votes	seats	votes	seats	votes	seats
Communist Party	0.4	0	0.3	0	0.2	0
Socialist Left			4.9	4	5.4	6
Socialist Electoral Alliance	4.2	2			0.6	0
Labour Party	42.3	76	37.2	65	40.8	71
SOCIALIST PARTIES: TOTAL	46.9	78	42.4	69	47.0	77
Centre Party	8.6	12	6.7	11	6.6	12
Christian People's Party	12.4	22	9.4	15	8.3	16
Liberals	3.2	2	3.9	2	3.1	0
Conservatives	24.8	41	31.7	54	30.4	50
Progress Party (Lange's)	—		4.5	4	3.7	2
Others	4.1	0	1.3	0	0.9	0
NON-SOCIALIST PARTIES, TOTAL	53.1	77	57.6	86	53.0	80
TOTALS	100	155	100	155	100	157

Source: Heidar, 1983: table 4.2, *Politiken*, 11 September 1985, p. 2

Table 7.5:   *Election results in Scandinavia: 1975–85: Sweden*

	1976		1979		1982		1985	
	votes	seats	votes	seats	votes	seats	votes	seats
Communist Left Party	4.8	17	5.6	20	5.6	20	5.4	19
Social Democratic Labour Party	42.7	152	43.2	154	45.6	166	45.1	159
SOCIALIST PARTIES: TOTAL	47.5	169	48.8	174	51.2	186	50.5	178
Centre Party	24.1	86	18.1	64	15.5	56	12.5	44
Liberals (People's Party)	11.1	39	10.6	38	5.9	21	14.3	51
Conservatives (Moderate Alliance)	15.6	55	20.3	73	23.6	86	21.3	76
Christian democratic union	—	—	—	—	1.9	0	[a]	
Environment party	—	—	—	—	1.7	0	1.5	0
Others	1.8	0	2.2	0	0	0	0	
NON-SOCIALIST PARTIES: TOTAL	52.6	180	51.2	175	48.6	163	49.6	171
TOTALS	100.1	349	100	349	99.8	349	100.1	349

Source: Riksdagens forvaltningskontor, 1984. Riksdagen 1982–5: Biografiska uppgifer om ledarmoterna. *Dagens Nyheter*, 17 September 1985, p. 11.

Note [a] joint list with Centre Party

Table 7.6: *Government formation in Scandinavia, 1975–85*

Date formed	Prime Minister	Party	Support parties	Type of government
DENMARK				
13 Feb. 75	Anker Jørgensen	SD	Centre-right parties at parliamentary but not cabinet level	Minority, single-party
30 Aug. 78	Anker Jørgensen	SD	Liberals *(Venstre)*	Minority coalition
26 Oct. 79	Anker Jørgensen	SD	as 1975–8	Minority, single-party
10 Sept. 82	Poul Schlüter	Cons	Liberals Christian People's Centre Democrats in cabinet Radical Liberals in parliament	Minority four-party coalition
FINLAND				
13 June 75	Keijo Liinamaa	Non-party		Coalition
30 Nov. 75	Martti Miettunen	Centre	Liberals Swedish People's Social Democrats People's Democrats	Broad coalition
29 Sept. 76	Martti Miettunen	Centre	Liberals Swedish People's	Broad coalition
15 May 77	Kalevi Sorsa	SD	Liberals Swedish People's Centre People's Democrats	Broad coalition
25 May 79	Mauno Koivisto	SD	Swedish People's Centre People's Democrats	Broad coalition
19 Feb. 82	Kalevi Sorsa	SD	Swedish People's Centre People's Democrats	Broad coalition
30 Dec. 82	Kalevi Sorsa	SD	Liberals Swedish People's Centre	Broad coalition
6 May 83	Kalevi Sorsa	SD	Swedish People's Centre Rural	Broad coalition

Table 7.6: *Government formation in Scandinavia, 1975–85 (cont.)*

Date formed	Prime Minister	Party	Support parties	Type of government
NORWAY				
15 Jan. 76	Odvar Nordli	Labour		Minority single party
4 Feb. 81	Gro Harlem Brundtland	Labour		Minority single party
14 Oct. 81	Kåre Willoch	Cons	Centre Christian People's in parliament	Minority single party
8 June 83	Kåre Willoch	Cons	Centre Christian People's	Majority coalition
SWEDEN				
14 Oct. 69	Olof Palme	SD		
7 Oct. 76	Thorbjörn Fälldin	Centre	Conservatives Liberals	Majority coalition
18 Oct. 78	Ola Ullsten	Lib		Minority single party
12 Oct. 79	Thorbjörn Fälldin	Centre	Conservatives Liberals	Majority coalition
22 May 81	Thorbjörn Fälldin	Centre	Liberals	Minority coalition
8 Oct. 82	Olof Palme	SD	Communist Left in parliament	Minority single party

In Finland the decade to 1984 was one of growing stability based on a pattern of broad coalitions of which the centre of gravity comprised the Social Democrats and the Centre Party, with Liberals, Swedish People's Party, and the radical-left Finnish People's Democratic League for added weight. The continuing exclusion of the conservative National Coalition Party, which had not participated in government since 1966, was at issue in the 1983 election. In the event, however, the electoral gains were made instead by the populist Rural Party: having most successfully exploited the unemployment issue in the election campaign, it was accorded the cabinet mandate to develop solutions to the problem. At the presidential level the looming question of who was to follow Urho Kekkonen's period of office, unbroken since 1956, was solved when Mauno Koivisto took over at the beginning of 1982. A Social Democrat, his experience included office as Governor of the Bank of Finland as well as two periods as Prime Minister in 1968–70 and 1979–81.

The Labour Party in Norway has retained the status of largest party in the system throughout the 1970s and 1980s, although the débacle sustained in the 1972 referendum by those who advocated membership of the European Community was further reflected in the 1973 election, when the Party held a mere 62 of the 155 seats in the Storting, while the more radical Socialist People's Party gained 16. The Labour Party regained this ground in 1977 but the election that year also saw the Right (the Conservative Party) gathering strength within the non-socialist camp, a trend which saw them emerge in 1981 at the head of a bourgeois bloc which had the unusually large majority of 15 over its socialist opponents. The Labour Party had been in office continuously during 1973–81, heavily dependent until 1977 on Socialist People's Party support. The Conservative, Kåre Willoch, took over as Prime Minister, initially at the head of a minority government because his Party was unwilling to amend legislation so as to make access to abortion on social grounds more difficult. As the salience of this issue waned, however, it became possible in June 1983 to broaden the government's parliamentary base by including four ministers from the Christian People's Party and three from the Centre Party, thus converting the minority government into a bourgeois coalition with a secure majority of one and a composition similar to that of the 1982 Danish government. The September 1985 election wiped the Liberal Party from the parliamentary scene and reduced the strength of the Right, leaving Willoch with a nominal bourgeois majority which rested on the parliamentary support of the two Progress Party members.

The 1976 election in Sweden ended 44 years of continuous Social Democratic rule. The three non-socialist parties formed majority coalitions after both the 1976 and 1979 elections, but in each case their bonds of alliance were unable to withstand the strains of, first, the Centre Party's opposition to the country's nuclear power programme and then, in 1982, the conservative Moderate Party's demands for tax reductions. In the 1982 election the Social Democrats gained 12 seats and Olof Palme led them back into governmental office. The Moderates took the lead in the non-socialist bloc, a position which they shared with their conservative counterpart in Denmark and Norway. The September 1985 elections narrowed the lead of the socialist bloc but allowed Olof Palme to continue in office. At the same time Liberal gains and Moderate losses gave some basis to claims that the 'conservative wave' was losing its impact, in Sweden as in Norway.

The decade since the 1973 oil-price shock has thus seen decline and modest recovery for the social democratic parties of Scandinavia, but also a significant strengthening of the forces of conservatism within the region. At the beginning of 1985 there were conservative-led governments in Denmark and Norway while in Sweden, although the Social Democrats were in government, the conservatives were more strongly supported than at any time since 1932. In Finland the socialist group of parties was also weaker than at any time since 1945, although this was not exclusively to the benefit of the conservatives: the 19-year-long split within the Finnish Communist Party took a new turn in April 1985 when the nationalist majority moved to exclude the pro-Soviet minority by expelling branches that flouted Party rules. The majority faction wanted 'socialism with a Finnish face' but at the same time was very sensitive to any comments within Finland which were critical of the Soviet Union. The Communists hoped to resolve the split before the 1987 general election, since they had seen the vote for the Finnish People's Democratic League, the electoral list of which the communists were a major component, had fallen from 22 per cent in 1962 to 14 per cent in 1983, a decline which had been of some advantage to the Social Democrats.

The strength of the Conservative-led Danish government was severely tested in March 1985 when it faced the country's most extensive and severe industrial conflict since 1973. The Schlüter government's policies, including reduced welfare spending, increased taxes, and limits to the long-standing policy of index-linking incomes, had produced a 2 per cent fall in unemployment (the largest such fall in any EC country during the 1980s) to 9.5 per cent, well below the comparable figure of 13 per cent for Britain (*Sunday Times*, 31 March 1985) although higher than the figures for Finland—5.2 per cent; Iceland—1.1 per cent; Norway—3.4 per cent; or Sweden—2.7 per cent (*Yearbook of Nordic Statistics 1984*, figures for registered unemployment for November 1984). In its eagerness to prolong high rates of industrial investment and export growth, the Danish government sought a 2 per cent pay rise for 1985 followed by 1.5 per cent in 1986, with a reduction of the working week from 40 to 39 hours at the end of 1986 and compulsory savings of 8 per cent of pay from all Danes earning over £11,000, to be deposited for five years without interest, plus tight control of credit and mortgages. The labour movement argued that the 2 per cent offer compared with an inflation rate of 5.6 per cent, and made a claim for a five-hour cut in the working week, intended as a means of bringing down unemployment still further. Following a combined strike and lock-out lasting eight days and a very large demonstration by the labour movement outside the *Folketing*, the government obtained a parliamentary majority (with the assistance of the Radical Liberals) to impose its own terms by law, a decision which was accepted only very reluctantly by the 200,000 strikers from both public and private sectors of the economy. It also drew comment from bankers that the imposed settlement would not harm the government's political prospects. But the Danish trade-union federation (LO) described the imposed settlement as the biggest provocation to Danish workers since the 1920s, and directly contrary to the traditions of balance and stability in the labour-market, while even the Federation of Danish Industry expressed anxiety for its effect on the Danish tradition of calm working relations and few strikes. Such fears seemed amply justified as the protest strikes called by union shop-stewards in defiance both of the government and of their national union officials brought the arrest of pickets and mass demonstrations attended by an estimated half of all those affected by the legally binding collective agreements.

The significance of increased polarization between the previously predominant social democratic parties and the conservative-led governments or the conservative-dominated non-socialist party blocs becomes clearer when it is related to the five-party system which has prevailed in Scandinavia since the 1920s. This was characterized by a once-divided non-socialist bloc whose weakness relative to the social democrats was 'the condition which has permitted Social Democratic reformism—the politics of virtuous circles—to be practised successfully in Scandinavia.' (Castles, 1978: 131.) If the conservatives, increasingly dominating the non-socialist blocs, succeed in consolidating their allies and their hold on power, a resurgence of social democracy in Scandinavia will be problematic indeed.

The Scandinavian model of social democracy

Several constant features of a general model of social democracy can be identified (Kesselman, 1982: 402):

First, an acceptance of a capitalist economy is coupled with extensive state intervention to counteract uneven development. Second, Keynesian steering mechanisms are used to achieve economic growth, high wages, price stability, and full employment. Third, state policies redistribute the economic surplus in progressive ways, through welfare programs, social insurance, and tax laws. And finally, the working class is organized in a majority-bent social democratic party closely linked to a powerful, centralized, disciplined trade-union movement.

The Scandinavian version of this model was the result of developments in these directions over a century: the principle of governmental answerability to parliament was attained in the region first in Norway in 1884, and the labour movements of Scandinavia had their origins at about the same time. In the 1930s the Scandinavian social democratic parties attained the strength necessary to lead a period of slow, steady economic development along pragmatic lines which were increasingly independent of their German fraternal party, which with the advent of the Third Reich lost its influence and was destroyed. Finland suffered heavy destruction in the Winter War (1939–40) and its continuation to 1944; Denmark and Norway were occupied by German forces, and Iceland by British forces, during the war; but nevertheless the countries of Scandinavia came through the Second World War more lightly than others and were then better equipped to take advantage of the ensuing unique period of economic growth. They had the additional advantages of smallness, relative social homogeneity, and therefore of political stability. But they had also benefited greatly from 'the positive nature of their response to the crisis of the Great Depression. Instead of the fiscal orthodoxy and book-balancing exercises adopted, for example, by the Labour government of the time in Britain, the Social Democrats in Sweden put into practice the pre-Keynesian demand stimulation prescriptions of Wicksell and the Stockholm School of economists.' (Elder, 1982: 65.) This prescription was followed too in other parts of the region, establishing a well-extended infrastructure, both physical and social: for example, in Denmark bridges were built between Jutland and Fyn (1935) and between Sjælland and Falster (1937), while at the same time throughout the region effective education, health, and social services were set in train. When economic growth came in the 1950s and 1960s the foundations were already there on which to build. The growth of social security coverage from 1900 to 1970 is summarized in Table 7.7, which also indicates the extent of growth between 1930–60, a period chosen to illustrate the main impact of social-democratic policies in Scandinavia. The extension of various forms of social insurance gave the assurance of social security and may have encouraged social and geographical mobility during the years of economic growth of the 1950s and 1960s, but their cost in the period of relatively high unemployment and economic stagnation of the decade since 1973 has proved one of the contentious issues between social democrats and the bourgeois parties.

Table 7.7:　*Index of social security coverage, 1900–70, for selected countries*

	1900	1920	1930	1940	1950	1960	1970	Change, 1930–60
Denmark	10	30	38	87	87	88	90	50
Finland	0	4	5	40	49	63	107	58
Norway	2	27	15	90	95	130	125	115
Sweden	0	60	60	65	77	117	122	57
Austria	5	22	42	42	57	79	88	37
France	4	7	10	32	52	75	89	65
Germany[a]	40	45	60	60	70	80	84	20
Netherlands	0	25	38	42	45	105	108	67
United Kingdom	0	60	75	87	102	100	98	25

[a] West Germany after 1945

The Flora Index, used above, shows the cumulated and weighted percentage of the labour force covered by social security. Retirement pensions are weighted by 1.5, sickness and unemployment insurance by 1.0, occupational accident insurance by 0.5, and the percentage covered by subsidised voluntary systems is divided by 2.0.

Source: P. Flora, 1976: readings from Figure on p. 27

Speaking in Oslo in February 1981 on 'How the Scandinavian model was created', the prominent Danish Social Democrat, Ritt Bjerregaard (who had been Education Minister in 1973 and 1975–8, Social Affairs Minister in 1979–81, and Chairman of the parliamentary party from 1982) summarized its aim as being 'to make it possible to be old without ending in the poorhouse, to ensure that a whole family's situation was not wrecked by illness, and that poor people got the proper treatment when they were ill. This has largely succeeded.' To get so far it had been necessary that all should have a publicly provided old-age pension, everyone should have free treatment at the same public hospital, all should have the same medical attendance and the same medicines, whatever their social status. The labour movement's demand for equality, for equal opportunities in school regardless of whether one's father was a labourer or a factory owner, for equal chances of further education whatever the parental income, for equal access to cultural and artistic experience—all these followed and had been more or less achieved . . . In this light, the labour movement could be proud of its centenary. 'The old party programmes can be displayed: we can be proud to acknowledge them, whichever museum they are in.' (Bjerregaard and Lundegaard, 1982: 200–1.)

Bjerregaard's speech was significant for its ensuing analysis of the problems facing the labour movement in Scandinavia. To ask whether the Scandinavian model was dead (the general theme of the meeting at which she was speaking) would make sense only if the aim of social democracy had been to achieve social security and equality. With these aims largely achieved, and at a time when it seemed difficult to realize further goals, should the party abandon the struggle? If the purpose of the labour movement was to achieve specific political and union ideals, then the answer might be yes. Social Democracy, however, should be seen not as a party of ideals but as an interest party. What mattered was the relationship of workers to the means of production. Who should make what? Where was it to be made? How was it to be produced? Who was to organize and apportion the work? Who was to gain by it? Who would carry the risks?

Nationalization was never a central aim of Scandinavian social democracy: sometimes it merely increased the distance between workers and decision-makers, and state bureaucracy was even worse than private sector bureaucracy because at least in the latter case bankruptcy was one limiting factor; nor was it desirable to take over bankrupt firms just to save jobs. What was needed was to decrease the distinctions between workers and decision-makers: first, workers were well educated and now knew as much or more about production than the owners; and second, increasingly complex and automated production methods required a committed work-force. Microprocessors and other new technologies would allow many unhealthy and badly-paid jobs in the production, distribution, and office sectors to be done mechanically. This would not only eliminate tedious jobs, but also give employees as well as employers a say in allocating work, so the labour movement must join in developing the new technology, but must also demand its price in shorter working hours, healthier workplaces, influence, and co-responsibility.

The Scandinavian model must include work for all, not just because unemployment was expensive but because the labour movement was built on the principle that cultural identity was determined by 'how we earn our income'. Besides, the small but well-educated populations of the Nordic countries meant that neither women, nor foreign workers, nor people in peripheral communities could be left out.

Another element of the Scandinavian model was the social security system. Just as unemployment benefit was a second-best solution to full employment, so also pensions and institutions were not aims in themselves. While benefit levels should be raised for all whose sole income came from these sources, the main aim must be to integrate as many people as possible into work and society. Since the costs would be borne by ordinary working people, benefits could not be universal, but they must go only to the most needy, they must stop when no longer justified, and they must be used to further the interests of the working class. Since much the greater share of the cost of social change, whether by demonstrations, war, or revolution, was borne by ordinary working people, it was in their interests to find pragmatic solutions: package-deals, negotiations, the peaceful approach, rather than the iron fist or the revolution. It was in Scandinavia where working-class people had the best conditions, thanks to the pragmatically-oriented labour movement. 'And it had all been done so peacefully that it had even been able to keep the monarchy. Was the Scandinavian model dead? No, it was just stirring.'

For Ritt Bjerragaard, then, the main problems were how to retain equality and social security while defending and extending the real interests of the working class. In relation to the general model of social democracy which opened this discussion, her analysis lacks precision on how the state is to intervene in the economy, except in its rejection of centralized controls and its encouragement of workers' participation in production decisions. Nor, in a post-Keynesian era, are appropriate steering mechanisms for the economy specified, although there is an implicit ranking of full employment above high wages in the order of priorities. Both the Swedish and the Danish social democratic parties have, however, advocated 'employee funds' as the means of extending economic democracy and shifting control and ownership of investment capital into the hands of representatives of the workers: the progress of these proposals is examined below.

The legitimacy of the welfare state is not seriously in question in Scandinavia: even the Progress Party directed its fire primarily against taxation and administration, rather than against the provisions of the welfare state as such and, a decade after its spectacular appearance on the political scene in 1973, it was reduced by 1984 to a shadow of its former self (see Table 7.1 above). Moreover the welfare state is underpinned by very widespread support for the concepts of equality, the security of 'the safety net', and the high levels of employment which could only be achieved by a combination of political commitment and a highly adaptable work-force.

But there is a serious financial problem in deciding how to pay for the welfare state. It is convincingly argued by Bent Rold Andersen (1984: 136–8), a Social Democrat and prolific writer on problems of social policy who served briefly as Minister of Social Affairs in 1982, that this problem would not be solved simply by a return to full employment or by measures to secure technically more efficient administration of services. Since 'there will always be votes to garner by promising more and better services as long as there are no other brakes on the claims, and technical solutions will prove to be insufficient to break the dynamics', what was needed was some means of restoring 'a clear psychological connection between rights and duties, or the welfare state would break down'. This would require a much closer connection between contributions and eligibility—the insurance principle—or by confining the major responsibility of solidarity to smaller social units where neither the contributor nor the recipient is anonymous and where, consequently, a system of informal social controls can be established.

The latter option could be achieved in several ways. The whole system of delivery of social services could be decentralized to local authorities, with wide powers to determine priorities, standards, and the way that services are produced. This would give the local authorities full financial responsibility and the choice of employing professionals or of using private or voluntary organizations or families in mutual assistance arrangements, with the role of central government restricted primarily to establishing a system of grants to equalize local differences in need and resources. (It should be noted that local authorities in Scandinavia, since reforms in the early 1970s, have seen some delegation of responsibilities to them, but were also reorganized into somewhat larger sized units which were then much criticized for their remoteness from democratic influence, although still significantly smaller than their counterparts in Britain.)

Later sections of this chapter will examine the employee funds proposals and the relationship of these to strategic social democratic goals for economic development. A further theme will be the impact of heightened international tensions and concern for peace on the social democratic movement in Scandinavia. As we shall see, its effect has been marked on the two NATO members within the region (Denmark and Norway), but it has also been a significant factor in the politics and policy proposals of the neutral countries of the region.

But any significant advance of social democracy in the Nordic region presupposes the continuing unity and strength of the combined wings of the labour movement. How realistic such a presupposition is will be the subject of the following section.

Party membership, organization, and support

The role of party members, their influence on policy-making, and their relationships with the party leaders has been a central theme in the analysis of political parties. Ostrogorski (1902) focused on the defence of individualism against machine politics. Michels (1911) saw power within social democratic parties exercised according to an iron law of oligarchy which strengthened the hands of the party leaders against any influence which might be exerted by their members. Duverger, in 1951, argued that 'present-day parties are distinguished far less by their members than by the nature of their organization. . . . Modern parties are characterized primarily by their autonomy.' (Duverger, 1964: xv) (For a brief but helpful review of the literature on party power, see Heidar (1984).) After Duverger wrote, there was little comparative work done on the scale and fluctuations of party membership numbers until the Paterson and Thomas (1977) and Paterson and Schmitz (1979) volumes, which assembled extensive information on these themes. For the Scandinavian countries the picture presented by the party membership figures for the social democratic parties as a share of the total electorate varied quite sharply. In Denmark the ratio declined steeply from its peak in 1948: indeed, the rate of decline was greater in Denmark than in any of the dozen countries illustrated by Bartolini (1983: 188). In Finland there was a decline from 1948 until 1962 but then a slow and steady rise. In Norway the Labour Party's membership ratio peaked in 1945 but then declined fairly steadily and not nearly so rapidly as in Denmark. By contrast, party membership as a proportion of the electorate for the Swedish Social Democrats has been at a notably high rate ever since the 1940s and has maintained a largely upward trend throughout the

Table 7.8: *Recent trends in membership of Scandinavian social democratic parties*

Country	Party	Year	Membership	Source
Denmark	Social Democrats	1960	259,459	1
		1970	177,507	1
		1974	122,722	1
		1975	122,394	1
		1976	123,140	1
		1980	c.125,000	2
Finland	Social Democrats	1976	101,727	3
Norway	The Norwegian	1960	165,096	4
	Labour Party	1970	155,254	4
		1974	130,489	4
			(lowest)	
		1979	158,724	5
		1980	153,507	5
Sweden	Social	1960	801,000	6
	Democratic	1970	890,000	6
	Labour Party	1973	967,000	6
		1975–6	1,100,000	6

Sources
1. Thomas in Paterson and Schmitz, 1979: 98.
2. Thomas in Delury, 1983: 258.
3. Arter in Paterson and Schmitz: 36.
4. Heidar in Paterson and Thomas, 1977: 312.
5. Heidar, 1983: 112. Just less than one third of members (49,328 in 1980) were collectively affiliated.
6. Kuhn in Paterson and Schmitz, 1979: 22.

subsequent period. Recent trends in party membership numbers are summarized in Table 7.8. They show some recent growth in each instance: while the Danish Social Democrats have recovered some ground, they have by no means returned to the support they enjoyed before the 1973 'earthquake' election. This contrasts with the rather greater extent of the recovery in membership support for the Norwegian Labour Party.

These membership trends call in question the extent to which a sound and growing membership is essential to a successful claim by the social democratic parties to remain mass-based parties with real prospects of obtaining governing power. Originally the mass-parties sought to serve as sources of welfare for their members, providing evening classes, legal advice in disputes with employers, unemployment benefits, and even medical advice: all these functions have passed very largely to the welfare states which were the most tangible result of social democratic power and influence on governmental policy-making during, or even before the post-war era.

Other more directly political functions of party membership involve raising party finance, socializing voters, recruiting party activists and candidates, organizing the elctorate, getting across the party's policies, and, by no means least, mobilizing the vote at elections. The changing nature of party competition has reduced the need to rely on a corps of members for some, at least, of these functions. State subsidies have, in some countries, provided an additional source of finance. Voters are now better educated and may well have developed sophisticated political views in the course of their education. Moreover, political information and comment is now less likely to be received from a partisan provincial newspaper, and more likely to come from debate and current affairs programmes on the national television network. Given these functional changes, the continuing need for an extensively organized network of party members and branches may be questioned.

Bartolini (1983: 184–5) notes that there was an end of the steady growth of social democratic membership in most countries in the period since 1945; indeed the trend is one of decline. Only Belgium, Sweden, and West Germany experienced increases in membership, and even the Swedish case is ambiguous, given the high proportion of collective membership. If this is set aside, there has been a long-term decrease in the total of individual members since the 1950s (quoting G. Sjöblom, 1978). Bartolini (1983: 185) goes on to argue that, but for this factor, 'the Swedish trend would have been quite similar to the sharply declining trends in Denmark and Norway. Further, the particularly pronounced corporate model of Swedish society has possibly allowed the social democratic party to make up through institutional affiliation—going well beyond the traditional trade unions—what it was losing in individual membership.' The difficulty with this argument is that, while it may be true in relation to Denmark, in the Norwegian case almost one third of the membership of the Labour Party comes from collective trade-union affiliation (Heidar, 1983: 112), so that the success of the Swedish party in continuing to expand its membership requires some other explanation.

The relationship between organization membership and party membership or support is complex, especially in a region (Scandinavia) where levels of membership in organizations are high and where the corporate channel of policy-making is at least as important as the electoral-parliamentary channel. In his comparison of the sympathies of Danish citizens for parties and economic interest organizations, H. J. Nielsen (1982) has shown that people liked the party they voted for, and also (but to a rather lesser extent) the economic organizations, such as the Agricultural Council, the Teachers' Union, or the Trade Union Federation (LO) of which they were members. This contrasted with the view argued earlier by Dahlerup *et al.* (1975) that, in the protest elections of 1973 and subsequently in Denmark, voters had turned from parties (especially the old-established ones) to the organizations as the channels through which they could best further their interests. But while strong views were held about parties, respondents were much more likely to have neutral views, or no views at all, about the economic interest organizations. Part of the suggested explanation for this was that, if policy decisions are sectoralized (as is well demonstrated by Damgaard, 1977: 259–60 and *passim*), it will not be surprising if people lack strong views towards organizations which have little impact on their own sector. But there were also wide discrepancies between evaluations of 'own organization' and 'own party', particularly among trade-union members: 'among social democratic trade unionists only 3 per cent are without an affective orientation towards the Social Democratic Party but 21 per cent have no opinion on LO.' (H. J. Nielsen, 1982: 50.) While parties attracted strong partisan feelings, organizations attracted less affection or antagonism or, to go a step further, were seen as technical units. It was therefore open to doubt whether the rise of corporatism had caused a shift from parties to interest organizations as the perceived spokesmen for one's own interests. But LO constituted a special case. First, it had by far the largest membership of the economic organizations analysed by Nielsen. And second, LO is strongly involved in party politics: it is avowedly social democratic and there is reciprocal respresentation on the executive committees of LO and the SD party. But the two wings of the labour movement are far from unified: LO criticism of the governing coalition which brought together SD and the Liberals *(Venstre)* between August 1978 and October 1979 was loud, public, and probably the main factor bringing about the demise of its economic policy and of the coalition itself. In other circumstances LO acts as a significant faction within the Social Democratic Party.

Differences in strength of attitudes to parties and to economic organizations raise the question of whether it is parties or interest groups which citizens see as the better representatives of their interests. While the organizations are sectorally specific, citizens will also have interests in other sectors. In a two-party system, interest organizations may serve mainly to articulate interests, while the parties aggregate them. But in a multi-party system, where the organizations are partners in policy-making and where parties may seek to increase their support by articulating the claims of social sub-groups, the functions may to a significant extent be reversed: the interest organizations may modify their claims for the sake of co-operation in the policy-bargaining process and so as to enforce agreements, even against the will of their members. A further partial explanation for differences of attitude to parties and organizations may be that, while people may choose which party to support, they may have to be members of an interest organization (Nielsen 1982: 56). This may be because of closed-shop agreements, or because the union is in practice the sole supplier of material benefits. For example, trade-union membership rates are high and have increased in recent years because of the link with unemployment benefits (although organizations representing civil servants, foremen, and professionals show lower membership numbers for 1981 or 1982 than for 1976: see Table 7.9).

Table 7.9: *Membership of unions and organizations in Denmark, 1976, 1981, and 1982*

Organization	Membership numbers: 1976 [a]	1981 [b]	1982 [b]
LO	1,087,196	1,279,760	1,320,841
Other trade unions not in LO		36,990	37,154
FTF	268,936	286,075	297,140
CO:I	50,000	43,861	46,531
FR	26,858	23,900	23,723
AC	73,153	63,080	64,258
TOTALS	1,506,143	1,733,666	1,789,647

LO   Landsorganisationen i Danmark (The Danish confederation of trade unions)
FTF   Fællesråd for danske Tjenestemands- og Funktionærorganisationer (Federation of Danish Civil Servants' and Salaried Employees' Organizations)
CO:I   Statstjenestemændenes Centralorganisation I (The central organization of (senior) civil servants)
FR   Hovedorganisation for Arbejdsleder- og Tekniske Funktionærforeninger i Danmark (Federation of foremen and technicians' unions)
AC   Akademikernes Centralorganisation (Danish confederation of professional associations)

Sources
[a] Buksti, J. A. and Johansen, L. N., *Danske organisationers hvem-hvad-hvor* (Copenhagen: Politikens Forlag, 1977), figures for end-1976 or beginning of 1977.
[b] Statistisk Årbog 1983 (Copenhagen: Danmarks Statistik: 333).

The professed support for the Social Democratic Party by LO, and the cross membership of their élites, may well be a source of annoyance to those members of LO who vote for parties other than SD. When Nielsen was writing in 1982 this proportion was a near majority. By 1984 his analysis of that year's election showed (Table 7.10) that Social Democrats had declined to a mere 46 per cent of the membership of LO (H. J. Nielsen, 1984). But his 1982 study had also shown that, right across the party spectrum, the Social Democratic Party was rated significantly more positively than LO, so that the party's loss of support among '*its*' trade unionists did not necessarily betoken disaster for the party itself.

Have the links between social class and party choice weakened significantly during the 1970s? Andersen (1984a) takes as his starting point the large number of studies which use the conventional Alford Index—defined as the difference in percentage points between the proportion voting for the parties of the left in the

Table 7.10: *Political party support and membership of economic interest organizations (%), Denmark, 1984*

Party	Economic interest organizations		
	LO	Other trade unions	Employers' and trade organizations
Left-wing parties	21	28	11
Social Democrats	46	20	8
Non-socialist parties	33	52	80
N = 847	100	100	99

Source: Hans Jørgen Nielsen, *Valgundersøgelsen 1984* (Personal communication)

working class and the middle class—to show that the 'decline of class voting' is a typical trend both in Scandinavia (Worre, 1980) and, more widely, in Britain, West Germany, and the United States. He goes on to show that, at least in Denmark, hypotheses seeking to explain the 'decline of class voting' and presupposing an overall weakening of the relationship between social class and party choice are based on false premises. For Denmark, the Alford Index has certainly declined from above 50 in the 1960s to almost half that figure in 1977–9, when it reached a lowest point of 27 in the latter year. But this, it is argued, is because the association beween class and party choice has changed rather than weakened, in a way which is concealed by conventional measures of social class and class voting. The Alford Index is based on a simple middle-class/ working-class dichotomy. Andersen (1984) argues that it is essential to sub-divide the middle layers of the population between the publicly and privately employed, and that there are also important differences between public employees, performing different state functions, of which he distinguishes five: the 'repressive' (police and military), administrative, technical (nationalized industries, energy, transport), 'ideological' (education and culture), and 'reproductive' (health and care).

Andersen (1984) is able to show that 'nearly half of the apparent decline in class voting from 1966 to 1979 is spurious, due to the changed composition of the middle class and the entry of women into the labour force' (p. 249). Among wage-earners, the vote for socialist parties between 1971 and 1979 remained largely stable among working-class and among middle-layer private-sector voters, while higher-level private-sector wage-earners showed a decline in the percentage voting for the socialist parties. But there were sharp rises in socialist voting in the middle layers generally: this was most marked among higher-level public sector wage-earners. Narrowing it down still further, he finds that in the four and a half years between the 1977 and 1981 elections, the difference in socialist support between the public and private fractions of middle-layer wage-earners had increased from 9 per cent to almost 30 per cent: the change was mainly a dramatic increase in left-wing support among public employees. This is linked to the rapid deterioration of relative wage increases experienced by public employees since the mid-1970s, more than outweighing the advantages they gained in the 1960s. What has had serious consequences for the Social Democrats in Denmark, however, has been their loss of support among non-manual wage-earners over the 1977–81 period: private sector employees moved to the non-socialist parties while public sector employees moved to left-wing parties, both from the Social Democrats and from the non-socialist parties (Table 7.11). Furthermore, it was clear from analysis of party choice in 1979 that this pattern arose from the 'reproductive' (health and care), educational, and technical components of the public sector, while the political position of those employed within the police and military, or administrative components of the public sector are far less radical (although some of the sample numbers here are too small to carry great significance).

There have been important changes in party choice in Denmark, especially among educationists. Over the 1970s the total socialist vote among this group increased from 26 per cent to 66 per cent, distributed fairly evenly between the Social Democrats and the parties to their left. But the change of party choice went much wider, being clearly evident not only among teachers and lecturers but also among samples of respondents who had a longer education than average, whatever their occupation. (Specifically, the samples were of those with a 'gymnasium' education or above—the *gymnasium* provides a relatively theoretical secondary education on a three-year course leading to university matriculation. Until 1966 it produced relatively the smallest student body in the Nordic countries. Then an alternative, more flexible, two-year route was provided via the 'higher preparatory examination', HF (Sysiharju, 1981: 435–6). They showed that among the higher educated

Table 7.11:   *Party choice, Denmark, 1971–81 (percentages)*

(a)   Among non-manual wage-earners, 1977–81

	Left-wing parties	Social Democrats	Socialist parties: total	Non-socialist parties	N = 100 per cent
Private sector					
1977	9	31	40	60	258
1979	9	32	41	59	273
1981	11	20	31	69	110
Public sector					
1977	14	35	49	51	238
1979	20	38	58	42	281
1981	30	28	58	42	131

(b)   Among the middle layers of the public sector, 1979

	Left-wing parties	Social Democrats	Socialist parties: total	Non-socialist parties	N = 100 per cent
Military and police	(3)	(24)	(27)	(73)	28
Administrative	(6)	(44)	(50)	(50)	30
Health and care	18	49	67	33	114
Educational	29	34	63	37	115
Technical	(25)	(38)	(63)	(37)	23

(c)   Among the higher-educated by age, 1971 and 1979

	Left-wing parties	Social Democrats	Socialist parties: total	Non-socialist parties	N = 100 per cent
Totals					
1966	11	6	17	83	679
1971	24	7	31	69	53
1979	34	21	55	45	194
By age, 1966					
20–9 years	18	6	24	76	243
30–9 years	14	8	22	78	133
40+ years	5	4	9	91	303
By age, 1979					
20–9 years	54	18	72	28	88
30–9 years	27	26	53	47	48
40+ years	7	22	29	71	52

Source: Andersen, 1984: Tables V, VI, VII
Percentages in brackets relate to sample sizes of less than 50.

support for the socialist parties was strongest among the generation under 40. (Andersen, 1984: Table VII). While the Social Democrats made some gains between 1971 and 1979, the parties further to their left gained steadily and rapidly from 1966 onwards, from the time that the Socialist People's Party was founded and effectively replaced the Communist Party. (Logue, 1982, gives a detailed account of the SPP.) Among the cohort aged 20–9 of the higher educated, over half voted in 1979 for parties to the left of the Social Democrats, 'a veritable left-wing subculture . . . typical of the 1970s'. (Andersen, 1984: 254. See Table 7.11 for figures.) This sub-culture is thought not to be a life-cycle change, but is clearly attributed to the 1968 student rebellion, and the high Danish figures are contrasted with only 39 per cent of the youngest age cohort in Sweden voting Socialist in the 1976 election, and with the relatively even distribution of the corresponding age-group in Norway between the socialist and non-socialist blocs.

Summarizing the relationship between social class and party choice in Denmark in the 1970s, Andersen (1984b: 21) concludes that it is misleading to say that the links between class and *individual* parties are weakening. He argues, first, that in a multi-party system such as there is in Denmark, loyalty is directed not so much to a single party as to a group of closely-related parties. Second, it is meaningless to distinguish only between working class and 'middle class' in Denmark: the 'middle class' must be subdivided between those in independent occupations and employees, and the latter must, from the beginning of the 1970s, be subdivided between those employed in the public and private sectors. Once these distinctions are made there is little need to talk of the decline of class voting, and the following changes can be detected: first, the working class and employees in the private sector have moved to the right. In the case of the working class, however, this is partly an effect of a general move to the right which, in the middle layers and the petit bourgeoisie is countered by the increased employment of women and the more 'working-class' interest which this brings into the family: the picture of the relationship between class and party changes somewhat if the unit of analysis is the family rather than the individual. Second, employees in the public sector have moved to the left. Third, the young generation of intellectuals turned about in 1968 and, since then, have given their support to the left, markedly differing in this from the age-group over 40. Finally, there is a weak tendency for women to be further to the left than men (Andersen, 1984b: 21–3).

The electoral defeat of the Swedish Social Democrats in 1976 provoked heated debate (summarized by Stephens, 1981) between those (including Walter Korpi) who argued that the cause of defeat was the party's policies and those who attributed defeat to long-term changes in Swedish social structure. Looking back, Korpi (1983: 142) concludes that:

The setbacks for the Social Democrats during the spring of 1976 must be seen in the context of the prolonged and intensive treatment in the mass media of a series of incidents or 'affairs'. These incidents created an image of the Social Democrats as secretive, autocratic, and growing more distant from the people. . . . There is little indication that the electorate had grown weary of welfare policies and deserted the Social Democrats on this count. On the other hand, the debate on the wage-earners' funds during the spring and summer of 1976 led to some popular opinion losses for the Social Democrats . . . Various studies indicate that, at the finish of the election race, the Social Democratic government fell on the issue of nuclear power.

As in Denmark, there have been extensive changes in Swedish social structure. Stephens (1981) lists the occupational structure, where the rural sector has declined and non-manual occupations have expanded; reduction of the working-class electorate as a result of immigration of foreign workers; economic growth and an increased standard of living; some increase in social mobility; reduced segregation by class among urban residents; expansion of the public sector and the trade-union wage policy have substantially equalized standards of living, depopulation of the north and growth of large cities and suburbs; and decline in religiosity and status-consciousness. But the problem is to determine which of these were significant for political behaviour.

One conclusion is that the effect of education on party preference, as indicated by age cohort differences, is declining dramatically (Stephens, 1981: 170), a picture which differs sharply from the one presented above of Denmark in the 1970s. Secondly, changes in occupational structure tended to help the socialist parties until 1965, but thereafter were not so favourable.

Despite these factors, Stephens (1981) finds that class voting in Sweden has declined substantially in the post-war period, on the basis of the Alford Index. This is traced to an unambiguous increase in socialist preference among non-manuals: the pattern among manual workers is less clear, especially if the 1976 election is ignored. While in the Danish analysis Andersen (1984) uses more refined occupational categories to explain this phenomenon, in the Swedish case Stephens (1981) looks to changes in the class structure itself for explanations. Following Janson (1959), he links this with the effects of long-term trends in Swedish housing policy: housing subsidies; rapid growth of the urban middle class resulting in a decrease in the heavily working-class character of urban neighbourhoods; the short supply of housing, due to industrialization and urban growth, which meant that allocations when a new housing project was finished were generally to people of the same age-group, regardless of occupation or class; and, finally, that new suburbs were developed intentionally to result in a class mix. In other words, the decline in class voting in Sweden is linked by Stephens to class desegregation of residence patterns as a significant part of the explanation; and much of this, of course, was the intended outcome of much Social Democratic policy. But other causes are traced by Stephens to increased social mobility, changes in strata composition, decline in status consciousness, rising union organization particularly among white-collar workers, and a consequent leftward move on the part of the bourgeois parties.

Korpi, however, denied that structural changes were to the disadvantage of the Social Democrats, and Stephens (1981: 198) supports this as follows:

The potential base for socialist reform, the wage-earning population, is growing as is the power-base, labor organisation. And all this has been reflected in the constant move leftward in the electorate. The problems of Social Democracy were in the *content* of their policy, problems which, in part, were generated from the contradictory aspects of the compromise between labor and capital which paved the way for the very success of their equalization policy via growth, public sector redistribution and labor-market policy. The reliance on growth generated by the private sector, which controlled technological change, and the need for a high degree of centralization in the labor market to carry out labor market policy and wage equilization policy according to the Rehn–Meidner prescription are some of the contradictory aspects which led to the dehumanization of work, unplanned regional change and an ambitious nuclear energy program.

On these issues the Centre Party made gains from the Social Democrats in 1976, but there was no reason to be unduly pessimistic about the Social Democrats' long-term future, as the 1982 and 1985 election results showed. 'While the direction of change can be explained by policy, as Korpi argues, the growing intensity of the fluctuations is, in fact, explained by long-term structural changes.' (Stephens, 1981.)

The analysis of party decline and the relative weight of structural hypotheses which postulate that societal change is the source of party decline, as against functional hypotheses which relate party decay to the diminished capacity of parties to perform their characteristic functions, is applied by Sainsbury (1982) to a review of sources covering the Norwegian as well as the Danish and Swedish social democratic parties. All three parties have in common an erosion or stagnation in electoral support and greater problems than previously in attracting the votes of young people in the 1970s, together with a decline in their working-class vote during the 1960s and 1970s.

One of the structural hypotheses considered is an em-bourgeoisement thesis, predicting that affluent workers will join the ranks of middle-class voters and desert socialist parties. While it was true that in Denmark large numbers of working-class voters supported the newly-formed Centre Democrats and Progress Party after the 1973 'earthquake' election, by the end of the 1970s working-class support for the Danish Social Democrats had largely recovered, large numbers of middle- and higher-income workers had transferred their allegiance to other socialist parties, as we saw above. The social democratic parties have always attracted significant middle-class support, so this transfer is potentially serious. But further analysis (Sainsbury, 1982: 8) shows that middle-class social democratic voters were: (i) more often in lower-level jobs and lower-income groups; (ii) more likely to be raised in working-class than in middle-class homes; and (iii) more likely to be union members. The evidence from Andersen (1984) quoted above, by contrast, indicated that the other parties of the left were more likely than the social democrats to attract the young and the highly educated. Sainsbury concludes that indicators of affluence have inadequacies in explaining non-socialist partisanship among workers. 'Although exceptions exist, the affluent worker in Scandinavia has generally been more prone to vote socialist than less prosperous workers.' (Sainsbury, 1982: 22.)

The second range of structurally related explanations examined by Sainsbury are those of post-industrial theorists, which focus on white-collar employees. One feature common to both Sweden and Denmark is that, compared to other countries, unionization of salaried employees is extremely high, at about 70 per cent. In Norway it is lower, and weakest in the private sector. But, as was noted above in the Danish context, while this may betoken support for the socialist bloc in total, it does not necessarily imply strength for social democratic parties: they must beware of the need to guard their flank against their socialist rivals, both in the union movement and in competition for votes.

A further problem for the social democratic parties is the decreasing homogeneity of their electoral support, so that the parties' policies and appeals will have to cater for a greater variety of actual or potential support groups. The danger of failing to do so was illustrated by the formation of the Centre Democrats in 1973, when pressures from the left for higher taxes on owner-occupied housing produced a backlash, with the right-wing of the Social Democrats breaking away on that issue and in opposition to pervasive Social Democratic influence on radio and television programmes. But the 1973 Danish election was one of the exceptions (the other being the elections of 1965 and 1977 in Norway, and 1979 in Sweden) to the generalization that the social democratic parties have been the most successful of the parties in all three countries to attract white-collar votes (Sainsbury 1982: 12). Once again we are able to conclude that changes in the social structure in the post-war period have not all been detrimental to the social democratic parties, a fact that leads Sainsbury to conclude (p. 14) that 'one should be quite wary in accepting the claims of the post-industrial theorists. . . . At most structural factors set broad parameters, they do not singly determine outcomes.'

In discussing functional hypotheses, Sainsbury takes party membership as a significant indicator of the ability of parties to fulfil their functions in the political system. As we have already seen, the pattern differs quite distinctly in the three Nordic countries. In Denmark, Social Democratic party membership has been in sharp and continuous decline. The Norwegian Labour Party's membership fell and then remained level, while the Swedish Social Democratic Labour Party's membership has risen steadily. Sainsbury (1982: 17) rejects hypotheses based on the effects of television campaigning, state finance for parties, or whether membership is individual only, or also collective through union membership. A more fruitful line of speculation is the party's historical and current role in electoral mobilization and inter-party competition for voters. The option of a mobilizing strategy has a mass membership organization as its pre-requisite, and its success in turn helps to justify the membership's role. Sainsbury concludes that 'patterns of electoral mobilization and the option of a mobilizing strategy appear to be an essential part of the explanation' in relation to the Swedish Social Democrats.

Employee Funds and Strategic Economic Aims

The one issue which had greatest impact in Swedish politics during the past decade, and to which the Swedish Social Democrats have attached their greatest hopes, is the issue of 'economic democracy': how to secure social control of investment decisions and a broader spread of capital ownership. The Swedish answer has been the novel, controversial, and simple one of *löntagarfonder*, wage-earner funds or employee funds.

The employee fund debate in Sweden has dual origins. In part it concerns technical aspects of the form of pension funding to be adopted in Sweden. More controversially, it was realized that if a scheme was set up, not on the pay-as-you-go principle (as used in Britain), but on a fully funded insurance basis, a large reserve fund would accumulate initially. Investment policy for this fund could have extensive economic and social consequences. The inherent possibilities for using the funds to achieve politico-economic goals were examined by Dr Rudolf Meidner, the chief economist for LO (the Swedish peak organization for industrial workers' unions), in a report published in 1975 which suggested that the funds could be used to influence the distribution of wealth, to widen industrial democracy and to mitigate some of the side-effects of the wage policy of solidarity (based on the principle of equal pay for equal work) which the unions had long been pursuing (Meidner, 1975). The further objective of exerting an influence on investment capital formation soon became involved in the extensive debate which has ranged over the nine years since Meidner's ideas were published.

The Meidner plan was skilfully built upon the foundation provided by the Swedish system of funding state retirement pensions, which has a three-tier structure. There is a basic tier, the National Basic Pension Scheme (AFP): this provides a universal flat-rate pension which may be supplemented by an income-tested allowance in cases where a pensioner has little or no entitlement to an earnings-related pension, and is financed out of current revenue on the pay-as-you-go basis. The second tier, the National Supplementary Pension Scheme (ATP) is a compulsory scheme for all employees. It relates to earnings between base and ceiling levels which are periodically adjusted to keep pace with inflation. The third tier is one of complementary occupational plans, one for salaried employees (ITP) and the other for manual workers (STP), both of them centrally administered, a feature which facilitates transfer of pension rights and mobility of labour.

When the ATP was set up, a 1959 parliamentary committee recommended that contributions should be structured to build up considerable initial funds: with such a reserve fund, pension contributions would be spread more evenly across generations and so not be directly dependent on the age structure of the population at any given time. The contribution rate as a percentage of earnings has therefore been raised progressively from 3 per cent at the start in 1960 to 12 per cent in 1980. At the same time the retirement benefit level has grown from 6 per cent in 1962 to 60 per cent in 1980. To avoid the possibility that so large a fund might come to dominate the capital market, it was subdivided into three separate funds, each governed by representatives from the sector from which it received contributions: local and national employees for the First Fund, firms with at least twenty employees for the Second Fund, and smaller firms or the self-employed for the Third Fund.

Initially it was envisaged by the Pension Committee that the Funds would be invested in a variety of ways, but strong objections from business and the non-socialist parties prevented investments in such specific purposes as housing construction or power supply or in equity shares, on the argument that this might permit 'back-door' nationalization. Deposits in banking institutions were also rejected as likely to strain the credit system severely and concentrate credit undesirably in the hands of the large banks. These funds are therefore confined to investing in securities issued by and through financial institutions, mortgage institutions, or in government or local authority or similar promissory note loans. But within these confines the Fund has been free to decide its portfolio allocation.

In considering its economic effects, Daly (1981: 264–5) concludes that:

The establishment of the AP Fund *per se* cannot be said to imply a transfer of scarce capital resources from the private to the government sector. Instead, the rapid growth of the Fund should perhaps be seen as a limitation of the savings allocation process of the household sector . . . Only to the extent that these intermediaries have a portfolio allocation pattern more biased towards business loans and corporate bonds than that of the AP Fund can the business sector be said to have fared badly due to the existence of the Fund. This does not appear to be the case. What has changed is the supply of long-term capital. Whereas the AP Fund lends mainly on the long-term credit market, firms and households contribute to a large extent to the supply of short-term credit via banks and other institutions, so that the AP Fund can be expected to have increased the supply of long-term capital.' (Daly, quoting Lindbeck, 1975.)

Beyond this, the Fund could not be said to have served as an instrument of planning and government intervention, and the various restrictions on investment policy emphasized social democratic acceptance of the capitalist economy at the expense of possible state intervention to counteract uneven economic development. In the late 1960s, therefore, a debate began about expanding the investment scope of the AP Fund to include the supply of more risk capital to firms. The outcome in 1974 was a Fourth Fund within the AP structure, to invest money provided by the other three boards in Swedish shares. Initially the fund was limited in size to 500 million kronor, but with parliamentary approval this was extended in 1976 and 1978 to a total of 1,250 million kronor, a scale equivalent to some of the major Swedish investment companies, but smaller than the largest insurance companies. Even so, some fears were expressed that the AP Fund could be used to exercise a near monopoly in the capital market. While the non-socialist parties were in government during 1976–82, these fears were largely in abeyance. But they clearly underlay some of the initial hostile reactions to the Meidner Plan and to subsequent variations on the Employee Fund theme.

Towards the end of the 1970s the Swedish economy was in increasing difficulties. Production was growing much less fast, business profit levels fell, and so did the level of industrial investment. At the same time deficits in the government's budget and the current balance of payments were accelerating, and there was growing inflation. The remedies for these trends were broadly agreed: limitations on consumption in both private and public sectors together with a sharp increase in investment. The discussion centred on how to achieve these remedies.

The Swedish Social Democratic Party, in its 1978 congress, saw that a ready solution to the country's problem of finding increased investment lay in using their proposed Employee Funds as a way of increasing collective savings and channelling them towards productive industrial investments. This would supplement the initial aims of redistributing the ownership of wealth, influence, and income in Swedish society.

The distribution of wealth in Sweden, even after the 44 years of Social Democratic government up to 1976, was still heavily skewed: a 1981 survey showed that 89 per cent of households owned no shares, while less than 0.3 per cent of households owned half of all the shares held by individuals (as distinct from corporations) (Sonning, 1983: 2). This distribution had changed little because the bulk of business and industrial investment since 1945 was largely financed by the companies themselves. There was quite general support for more widespread share ownership, Conservatives arguing for voluntary methods and Social Democrats advocating Employee Funds as the means of achieving this aim of wealth redistribution.

Similarly, the Employee Funds were expected to improve industrial democracy. Legislative steps in this direction were tried in 1977 with the Act on Employee Participation in Decision-Making, but initially high trade-union hopes were disappointed. Instead, by becoming part-owners of corporations through the Employee Funds, employee representatives would gain ownership influence in their work-places.

The Employee Funds were also intended to advance the 'wage policy of solidarity' pursued by the Swedish trade-union movement. This policy is intended to achieve equal pay for equal work, regardless of how profitable a particular company may be. While intended to increase equality of individual incomes, in good times such a policy also increases the profitability of the more successful companies by keeping their wage costs lower than they might otherwise be. Conversely, in bad times the less profitable companies might be jeopardized by such a wage policy. Trade union proponents of the Employee Funds see an answer to this problem through basing contributions to the Funds in part on a levy on the 'excess profits' of companies.

While the Social Democrats were in opposition during 1976–82 the detailed form of the Employee Funds was much debated. When they returned to power the issue was given a higher priority in the legislative programme, not only for its potential contribution to solving the country's problems of a stagnant economy, low levels of investment, and (by Swedish standards) a relatively high level of unemployment. When enacted the policy would also show supporters and opponents of the party alike that it had used its return to office to renew the momentum of progress towards social democratic goals of increased equality of economic influence.

The Employee Funds Bill presented to the Riksdag late in 1983 was based on proposals drafted by Per-Olof Edin, previously an economist with LO. Its main feature was that there were to be five Funds established during 1984 for an initial experimental period ending in 1990. Each Fund would be regionally-based, and the nine board members appointed by the government to run it would include at least five chosen to represent 'employee interests'. Revenue would come from two sources: a proportion of the existing employer-financed supplementary pension contributions and, secondly, from a new profit-sharing scheme under which each company would contribute 20 per cent of its inflation-adjusted profit, after first deducting an annual 'exempted amount' of 6 per cent of the payroll or 500,000 Swedish kronor (about £50,000), whichever is the greater. The purpose of the Funds was stated as improving the supply of risk capital for the benefit of Swedish production and employment.

Preliminary calculations indicated that about one in ten of the country's businesses would be involved in making contributions to the Funds, which would yield 1–3 thousand million kronor during 1985, the first full year of operation. By 1990 the Funds channelled to the stock market would total 14–17 thousand million kronor, equivalent to about 8 per cent of the 1983 aggregate value of all listed shares—so the scheme was on a fairly modest scale. Investment would be primarily in Swedish shares and a rate of return of 3 per cent over the rate of inflation would be expected: this would be paid to the first three AP Funds. A ceiling was set on the annual level of investment of each Fund. In 1984 this was 400 million kronor, with the aggregate for the five Funds of 2,000 million kronor. The voting power controlled by the Fourth AP Fund and the five Employee Funds together must not exceed 49.9

per cent for any single company. Up to half the voting power controlled by the Employee Funds may be transferred, on its request, to the local trade union organization at the company concerned. So the Employee Funds are specifically debarred from 'backdoor nationalization'. Even as a means of locally accountable economic democracy they are fairly limited in scope.

The final draft Bill in October 1983 contained two significant changes from the Edin plan. The proportion of the voting rights owned by each Fund in any one company would be limited to 8 per cent. A special Fund was also created, linked to the investment bank and with a capital limit of 100 million kronor, to invest in small businesses.

The Bill was passed, including these changes, by the 164 votes of the Social Democrats, with 158 votes against from the three non-socialist parties. The Communist Left Party abstained, having not secured the amendment it wanted, to give the task of appointing members of the Fund boards to parliament rather than to the government. They also wanted to amend the aim of the Funds, to 'further the interests of the workers'.

Opposition from the three non-socialist parties to the whole idea was as firm as it had always been. Indeed, the Commission which had been established to examine the issue was wound up after seven years of deliberation (1974–81) when, perhaps predictably, it showed no sign of producing a set of united recommendations: in the end it produced no report at all (Arter, 1985: 61).

After the 1982 election the newly-returned Social Democratic government had delayed introducing its proposals so as to try to ensure that at least the whole socialist and labour movement supported them. But as late as May 1983 Olof Palme still could not say that he was ready to proceed: 'The Social Democrats won the (1982) election on a programme which contained some form of Employee Fund, and we still expect that we can discuss the matter objectively and in context.' (*Nordisk Kontakt* 1983: 674.) But pressures were mounting within both the political and the trade union wings of the labour movement: in a May Day speech, Stig Malm spoke for LO when he said: 'We cannot continue to delay our proposals to satisfy groups which will never be satisfied'.

Non-socialist opposition culminated, using tactics borrowed from the Labour movement, in a mass march to the Riksdag to present a petition organized by the Swedish Employers' Confederation

(SAF). Opinion polls also showed only about one Swede in five in support of the idea behind the Funds, especially if there was no parliamentary consensus in its favour. The Conservative leader, Ulf Adelsohn, argued that 'when economic power grows with political and trade union power, we will have a new economic system, a corporative socialism', and there were threats that private investors would transfer their funds and activities out of the country, following the well publicized example of the move to the USA by Datatronic.

The main opposition argument was that the trade-union majority on the board of each Fund would exert an influence on the capital-market out of all proportion to their small number. This suspicion was strengthened when the composition of the first four boards was announced in June 1984. Of the Chairmen, each appointed for a one-year term, two were provincial prefects (*landshövding*), one a television director, and one a former defence minister. The board members all came from 'socially-owned enterprises, institutions, and organizations connected with the popular movements, with a markedly strong contribution from the trade unions'. (*Nordisk Kontakt*, 1984: 776.) Only seven of the 52 were women. There was one Conservative, the chairman of the SIF union branch in the Saab-Scania works in Linköping, who said that he had agreed to serve 'to see that the money that is taken out of the company is used as sensibly as possible' (Loc. cit.). But, to the disappointment of the authors of the scheme, no representatives of the upper levels of private industry had accepted the offer to take part. This added weight to the threat by the opposition that the Funds would have a life of no more than two years, since they intended to repeal them if they won the 1985 election.

The Employee Funds scheme, as finally enacted, is a mere shadow of the original intentions. With members of the Fund boards appointed by the government, little is added to industrial democracy, and it remains to be seen whether the transfer of such a small proportion of shareholders' voting rights to union branches makes much impact on management decisions. Wealth redistribution is likely to be in the direction of pensioners. But the contribution to available investment capital, especially for small businesses, is perhaps the most imaginative aspect of the scheme and may prove to be its salvation.

As an illustration of the interchange of ideas among the social democratic parties of Scandinavia, and the different obstacles which these may encounter, the Swedish case can be compared with Danish attempts to implement a similar scheme of 'economic democracy'. The Danish proposals have even earlier origins than the Swedish Meidner plan but have met with less success in implementation. As early as 1969 Viggo Kampmann, who was Finance Minister in 1953–60 and then Prime Minister until 1962, obtained the endorsement of the Union of Metal Workers for his plan for a profits tax on larger firms, half to be retained for investment within the firm under the control of union representatives and the other half to be paid into a central fund for investment in the general economy. The firm could pay dividends to its employees by way of profit-sharing, but the plan did not provide for individual rights to own or sell shares. The idea was later developed within both the Danish LO and the Social Democratic Party, but met with critical opposition from the employers' organizations and the non-socialist parties for its bureacratic features and its tendency to centralize economic power. These criticisms were given added weight both by the electoral support which went to the Progress Party after 1973 for policies opposed to bureaucracy and taxation, and also by the sharp recession in the Danish economy from early 1974.

The idea was dropped in Denmark until December 1979, when it was included as one of the 18 components in a complex of legislation proposed by the Social Democratic government and intended to provide a comprehensive solution to the country's economic problems. This had been in preparation since the previous spring, and included a price freeze, substantial limits on increases in incomes, extensive changes in taxation law and the law on investments, rents, investment allowances, etc. and the introduction of profit-sharing schemes. (A full account of the development and final breakdown of these and previous negotiations is given by Due and Madsen, 1980.) The profit-sharing schemes were the guise in which the 'economic democracy' proposals were introduced, initially with a broader title which included 'rights of joint ownership and joint decision-making'. It was formulated as a resolution which invited the government to bring forward legislation during the coming year to increase the representation of workers on company boards, to increase public supervision of the ownership and finance of companies and to increase worker influence in public employment. The resolution was passed with the 75 votes of the Social Democrats, the Socialist People's Party, and the Radical Liberals (*Folketingsårbog* 1979–80: 399), but there was clearly insufficient support in the *Folketing* to carry the principle further: 90 votes would be required for a bare majority, and a larger margin than that would be desirable for so controversial a measure.

A fundamental problem with proposals for economic democracy in both Sweden and Denmark is that they appeal in a cross-cutting manner to conflicting notions of class powers and participatory opportunity, with the result that the support of employees for such measures is fragmented (H. J. Madsen, 1980). Appeals to class power rely on perceptions of collective class identity and do not necessarily involve extensive participation: capital-sharing provides a means of enhancing specific class interests. An alternative idea, of participatory equality, depends on participation in an individual capacity. 'From a class position, the invesment fund scheme embodies the idea of wage-earner control of the economy. From a participatory perspective of centralized versus decentralized control this class power is largely bought at the expense of direct participatory involvement' (ibid.). The Edin scheme in Sweden sought to meet this problem by setting up regional funds, but this was not enough to win over a clear majority, even among SD and LO supporters.

The Social Democratic government in Denmark, on the other hand, made a firm commitment to a centralized fund as a quid pro quo for wage restraint in its economic crisis package. The principle issues of Economic Democracy, therefore, became heavily entangled in the specific and necessarily brief debate on the impending crisis measures. The context of shorter-run concern, and perhaps specific personalities, diffused the Economic Democracy debate and was simply not fit for a longer-term educative mobilization of wage-earners . . . At present, no scheme contains a formula that accommodates simultaneously the demand for popular, effective investment control and individual participatory claims. (H. J. Madsen, 1980.)

The Danish trade unions tackled the investment problem in 1983 (by which time the Social Democrats were no longer in government) by proposing a 'reconstruction company' to avoid the adverse consequences for employment as many firms closed during the recession. This would put to use the capital from the various funds already under the control of the trade unions to increase the flow of risk capital so as to encourage employment, production, and exports. Investments by means of shares or other profit-related assets would be made in existing and newly-established industrial limited companies, co-operatives, etc. The capital to do so would come from such sources as employees' pension funds (some 41.8 milliard kroner), the workers' supplementary pension fund (ATP: 22.9 milliard kroner) and the inflation protection fund (*dyrtidsfonden*, 13.7 milliard kroner), as well as smaller amounts from union strike funds and the labour movement's co-operative finance fund. This was not economic democracy as it had previously been defined by the trade unions, however, and several problems were anticipated in implementing the scheme. How could union members ensure that they had direction and control over the use of their money? How would further trade union careerism (*pamperisering*) be avoided? How would the objectives be attained at a time when share prices were at a peak and shares in short supply?

Such an investment programme might buy some financial influence, but it could not be expected to shift the balance of power significantly in Danish industry and commerce. That, of course, was the underlying aim, both of the more ambitious Danish plans for economic democracy, as they were originally envisaged, and of the Swedish Employee Funds.

Reappraisals of defence and security policy

Social democratic parties in most of Western Europe distinguish themselves from the socialist parties further to their left by their acceptance of NATO membership and of the division between NATO and Warsaw Pact territory. In Scandinavia this acceptance did not come easily: the strong tradition of neutrality in the region, which is still the stance of Finland and Sweden, encouraged Sweden first to join with Denmark and Norway in seeking a regional solution to their post-1945 security problems. Only when this proved impractical did Denmark and Norway join NATO, and then only with significant reservations which exclude the permanent stationing of foreign troops on their territory, or the stationing of nuclear weapons in Denmark or Norway during peacetime. These and other reservations helped to make NATO membership more palatable to its domestic opponents. They also contribute an important component of 'the Nordic balance', the system of interlocking defence and security policies pursued by the four countries of the Scandinavian region by which they each, in their distinctive ways, seek to ensure their own security and reassure their neighbours of their non-aggressive intentions.

This pattern of balanced relationships has been threatened in recent times by several factors which have, in turn, had their domestic reverberations in each of the countries of the region. In Denmark and Norway concern at the implications of stationing cruise and Pershing-II missiles in other European NATO countries was widely expressed and, in the Danish case, led to the passage by the *Folketing* of resolutions which imposed significant limitations on the government's ability to support this policy within NATO council or with financial contributions. In Finland heightened international tensions led to proposals, later also taken up and extended in Norway, for a Nordic nuclear-weapons-free zone. In Sweden, too, concern at the vulnerability of the country's sea-space to persistent incursions by the USSR's submarines, and of its air-space to potential over-flying by cruise missiles, led to significant attempts to improve the country's military preparedness, although not to any modification of its long-standing stance of neutrality. In all these issues the social democratic parties in their respective countries played a leading role.

NATO's 'two-track' decision—to seek to negotiate with the USSR to limit installation of SS-20 missiles in Eastern Europe while planning and installing its own cruise and Pershing-II missiles in Western Europe, with a deadline of autumn 1983 if such negotiations did not achieve their aim by then—was the source of widespread concern in both Denmark and Norway, as also in other member-countries of NATO. The Social Democrats and the Labour Party had been in power when the original decision on NATO membership was taken in 1949 and had supported it both then and subsequently. They were therefore in some difficulty initially in accommodating to the widespread opposition to the new NATO missiles which was expressed both within their own parties and, even more vigorously, by the parties further to their left. Indeed, this problem of boundary maintenance on the left wing of the social democratic parties is one which they all share, but in

Scandinavia it has been of marked significance as the radical left has increased in diversity and support since the mid-1960s.

The serious division of opinion on the missiles issue was very evident when the defence budget was debated in the Norwegian *Storting* in November 1982. The Socialist Left Party's spokesman in the debate expressed the view that the weapons would probably be installed whether or not the Geneva negotiations were concluded or reached any result, and was dissatisfied with the assurance from the Defence Minister, Anders Sjaastad, that the *Storting* Foreign Affairs Committee would be kept informed. The Labour Party had already decided not to give its support to the NATO two-track decision, so when the matter was debated the *Storting* stood divided right down the middle, the first time since 1949 that defence policy had had this effect. The issue was raised in the context of the component of the defence budget which related to the Norwegian financial share of the common NATO installations for the new missiles: there was, of course, no intention that the installations themselves should be on Danish or Norwegian territory. The Labour Party was internally divided between supporters and opponents of the two-track negotiating strategy, but it was able to unite the opposition parties as well as its own members behind its proposal to postpone the financial contribution until the issue had been debated in Belgium, the Netherlands, and Denmark, and until the results of the Geneva negotiations were available in the following autumn. At the same time the Labour Party made it very clear that it continued to support NATO membership in all other respects, and it vehemently denied the Conservative allegation that Labour could not be relied on in defence matters. The Labour Party proposal was lost in the end by only the narrowest possible margin, of 76 votes to 77: Labour's own 66 members were joined by the Socialist Left Party, the Liberal Party, and the Progress Party's representatives. A further Labour Party motion of no-confidence in the Defence Minister for his failure to keep the *Storting* accurately informed was lost by a wider margin, but was additional evidence of the mistrust raised by the issue.

Within the Norwegian Labour Party defence policy was subjected to thorough review. A working group of the party's international committee was established which included former Foreign Minister Knut Frydenlund and former Defence Minister Thorvald Stoltenberg among its members. In February 1984 it reported with the following policy recommendations among others: first, the INF (Intermediate-range Nuclear Forces) and START (Strategic Arms Reduction Talks) negotiations should be combined, so that over the longer term the nuclear weapon arsenals of the superpowers could be seen as a whole, the better to bring pressures for reduction; second, all nuclear weapons should be frozen at current force levels; third, such a freeze should be used as the starting point for continued negotiations between the USA and the USSR on both strategic and intermediate nuclear weapons; fourth, and at the same time, preliminary agreement in the INF negotiations was needed to clarify the main question, which was how to find a way to reduce the number of the USSR's intermediate-range missiles and to prevent the installation of the new US missiles in the same category. In this context it was felt that British and French nuclear forces must be included in the totals on the western side of the calculation. Finally, NATO must then be able to halt all preparations for installing new nuclear weapons in Europe (*Nordisk Kontakt*, 1983: 113).

In both Denmark and Norway the development of this clear alternative to the simple acceptance of the US-initiated two-track negotiating strategy was seen as fully consistent with the two countries' continued and loyal membership of NATO. Later in 1983, for example, the Norwegian government was able to obtain broad support for a new defence expenditure plan for 1984–8 which involved real growth of current costs at the rate of 1 per cent per annum and an annual growth in the budget of 3.5 per cent. These figures allowed for expensive equipment procurement, some of it home-produced, such as the Penguin Mark 3 missiles for the F.16 aircraft for the Air Force. The Labour Party would have preferred a slightly lower level of growth (3 per cent rather than 3.5 per cent) for the defence budget, but were persuaded to agree with the government's projections of costs, and with the limits on current expenditure so as to favour capital investment on defence equipment.

High policy-making was accompanied by activity at the level of the grass roots. A broadly-based '*Nei til atomvåpen*' (no to atomic weapons) movement was well under way at the beginning of 1983, with its main initial aims being to work for an unconditional rejection by the *Storting* of support for the installation of new nuclear missiles in Europe, or else a referendum on the issue. Half-a-million copies of its aims were distributed in schools, organizations and work-places and the missiles issue was the main one at the Labour Party's national congress in April 1983. The Party resolved to continue to exert pressure in the Geneva negotiations to secure reductions in the number of nuclear weapons stationed in the East and prevent the addition of such weapons in the West. Together with other socialist parties, pressure would be exerted on both superpowers: if necessary the negotiations should be prolonged and the installation of the new weapons postponed. But a *Storting* vote on these lines had only the support of the Labour Party itself and was rejected by 66 votes to 44.

In Denmark the Social Democrats were in office until September 1982 in a minority government which relied on the parliamentary support of the non-socialist centre for most issues. But on legislation reorganizing the defence command structure, on defence personnel, and on the home defence force the opposition comprised the Left Socialists, the Socialist People's Party, and the Radical Liberals—the latter party, although not socialist, has a long tradition of pacifism. Jørgensen's government fell when it was unable to obtain the necessary support for a package of economic policies comprising expenditure reductions, guidelines for incomes policy, a comprehensive profits tax and the obligatory profit-sharing scheme which it had long sought to introduce. It was succeeded by Schlüter's four-party minority coalition. On many issues the new Conservative-led government had to rely for support on the Radical Liberals in the non-socialist centre and on the Progress Party (until the 1984 election) on the far right.

As the main party now opposed to the Schlüter government, the Social Democrats were able to achieve considerable success in building a coalition of opposition on the missiles issue and on the NATO two-track decision, to the government's great embarrassment. When the decision was originally taken by NATO in December 1979, it had originally been supported by the Social Democrat government. But by February 1983, strongly influenced by their Norwegian sister-party, the Social Democrat spokesman and floor-leader, Kjeld Olesen (who had previously been Defence Minister and was Foreign Minister from October 1979 to September 1982) argued that if the USA and the USSR did not reach negotiated agreement, the implementation of the missiles decision should be postponed until 1984. The Schlüter government was quick to condemn this as a volte-face and to threaten to call an election. But with the support of the Radical Liberals, as well as of the Socialist People's Party, and the Left Socialists, the Social Democrats had a majority in the *Folketing* when it came to a vote. Initially the government found it very difficult to accept this situation: the Liberal Foreign Minister, Uffe Elemann-Jensen, then announced that the government no longer saw the US government's 'zero-solution' stance in Geneva as essential to its own position.

The Social Democrats advanced the argument further in May 1983 when they succeeded by a vote of 83 to 70, in obtaining a *Folketing* resolution requiring the government to argue at forth-coming NATO meetings for the USA–USSR negotiations on European intermediate-range missiles to be extended in time, and that no new missiles should be installed while the negotiations continued. In addition, the *Folketing* majority wanted the British and French nuclear forces to be included and the INF and START talks amalgamated. Furthermore, while the talks continued neither preparation nor installation of the intermediate-range missiles should take place. But the first aim must be to obtain sufficient reductions of the USSR's SS-20 missiles to avoid the need for the Western missiles.

In favour of the resolution, the Social Democrat defence spokesman and long-standing chairman of the party's foreign and defence policy committee, Lasse Budtz, argued that to seek an extension of the negotiations and to postpone installing the missiles while the negotiations continued was not in conflict with the NATO two-track decision—it was essential to concentrate on the negotiations. The Socialist People's Party leader, Gert Petersen, supported the resolution. He saw the new missiles as inherently 'first strike' rather than deterrent, and detected an American determination to install them which would wreck the negotiations. At the same time he was critical of the Soviet Union for its invasion of Afghanistan and for the Swedish submarine affair.

The Foreign Minister was clearly reluctant to have to speak for this position in NATO, stating that the government 'could not emphasize strongly enough its will' to do all in its power to check and halt the arms race and to seek to realize 'the disarmament which we all want' but also strongly arguing the case for loyalty to NATO decisions. 'So we should avoid putting obstacles in the way of our allies to achieve negotiated results, and this included not expressing ourselves in a way which could damage the negotiations. Otherwise we would lose our credibility and our influence in the alliance, which would weaken the alliance and thereby the security of ourselves and our allies.' (*Nordisk Kontakt*, 1983: 772.)

While there was some misgiving within the Social Democratic Party about the breach which its policies entailed in the 34 years of unity on Danish foreign and security policy, at least among the parties which had formed or supported successive governments, it was on a very limited scale. In the *Folketing* one Social Democrat, Robert Pedersen, did not vote with his party—he was the author of a book entitled *From neutrality to involvement: Social Democracy and defence for 110 years* (1982), and a member of the Atlantic Pact Association's committee. But such views received very little support at the Social Democratic Annual Conference in October 1983, despite the arguments put forward in June in *Kristeligt Dagblad* (a paper inclined to support the government) in its comments on the Gallup finding that 69 per cent of the Danish population supported Danish membership of NATO: the paper argued that the new stance of the Social Democratic Party, although strongly supported in the party organization and the parliamentary group, was not widely held among voters. But when this judgement was put to the test at the 1984 election, losses by the socialist bloc were modest and, with the continuing support of the Radical Liberals, there was still a parliamentary majority for the critical stance adopted by the opposition parties.

The Social Democrats were able to add further victories over the government's viewpoint in November 1983. A parliamentary resolution was carried which required the government to make an active Danish contribution towards halting the build-up of armaments in the East, and immediately to initiate a re-evaluation by NATO countries of the course of the East-West negotiations before the missiles were installed in Western Europe. The Social Democrats further sought to ensure that the long-standing Danish reservation which had excluded the stationing of nuclear weapons on Danish territory ever since 1953 would apply in *all* circumstances. Hitherto the formula used by successive Danish governments was that they would not receive nuclear weapons (or foreign forces) on their territory 'under existing circumstances', although Kjeld Olesen, then Foreign Minister, used the phrase in October 1980: 'under present circumstances, that is to say, in peacetime' (quoted by Archer, 1984: 11). It was argued that this would be best achieved within a Nordic nuclear-weapons-free zone, and the Social Democrats had a resolution passed on 10 November 1983 which invited the government to work actively to ensure that Denmark remained free of nuclear weapons through the establishment of such a zone. The Radical Liberals supported the Social Democrats in this, and the only opposition comprised the 13 votes of the Progress Party and the Left Socialists, at opposing ends of the political spectrum. The government parties and the Socialist People's Party all abstained, for their own reasons: the latter wanted to use the occasion to commit the Social Democrats to the position outlined by Anker Jørgensen, their leader, which states unequivocally that the party would not accept nuclear weapons on Danish territory in either peacetime or war. The government parties were forced into abstention because they did not wish to change the country's previous policy position but did wish to distance themselves from the Social Democrats.

The Nordic nuclear-weapons-free zone (NNFZ) idea dates from a letter written in 1958 by Marshall Bulganin of the USSR to the Danish and Norwegian Prime Ministers, pointing out that the rejection of nuclear weapons by their countries, together with the absence of such weapons in Finland and Sweden, could be the starting point for a nuclear-weapon-free zone in all of Northern Europe; in turn this would guarantee peace and freedom in the area. The two governments replied by pointing to the Soviet border areas as part of Northern Europe. This and subsequent developments are recounted by Archer (1984).

The NNFZ idea was later taken up and extended successively by President Kekkonen of Finland. In 1963–5 its components comprised the proposals that Nordic states would neither procure nuclear weapons nor permit their stationing, while existing security policies would be maintained. In 1972–5 these three points were linked to general proposals for arms control and disarmament in Central Europe, with guarantees to be offered by the USA and the USSR to respect the zone. Two further points were added to the plan in 1978: consequent negotiations with the superpowers were proposed, and there were to be negotiations on security and non-nuclear weapons as well. By this stage SS-20 missiles were being deployed in the USSR, the threat of US cruise missiles in Europe was being pressed, and the Nordic countries were becoming aware that their neutrality or non-nuclear status could easily be compromised by missiles overflying their territory: this added urgency to their long-standing efforts to distance themselves from superpower tensions in Europe.

At first the Kekkonen proposals drew a non-committal response from the Scandinavian countries and the USA. In 1972–5 this took on a rather more negative tinge except in Sweden, where interest was shown but with the qualification that the Baltic and adjoining Soviet territory should also be discussed. When the 1978 proposals were made, similar reactions were expressed except that Norway now insisted that the proposed zone should be seen in a wider European context.

In 1980–2 the package was taken a stage further by Jens Evensen, a Norwegian former cabinet minister with senior Foreign Ministry experience. He proposed a NNFZ backed by a treaty and 'standing on four main pillars': NNFZ states would undertake to remain free of nuclear weapons in wartime as well as peacetime (hence the significance of the Danish *Folketing* resolution of November 1983); the nuclear powers would guarantee not to use or threaten use of nuclear weapons against zone countries; observance of the treaty would be supervised by an inspection or control body; and creation of the zone would help to lower tension and so preserve peace. The significant advance was that Evensen's ideas were followed by a proposed treaty. The Danish, Norwegian, and Swedish governments wanted the proposals to include a second zone which would extend 'thinning-out' arrangements more widely in Europe and include specific provisions for the Baltic. While there was extensive popular support for such proposals in both Denmark and Norway, the conservative-led governments in both countries took an increasingly reserved view of the idea. But in Sweden the plan was taken up by Olof Palme, back in power as Social Democratic Prime Minister, who argued in addition that NNFZ negotiations should be pursued in parallel with the discussions relating more broadly to other parts of Europe, and that the proposals should also be backed by negative security guarantees from the USA and the USSR.

The significance of the NNFZ issue, and the associated debates in the Danish and Norwegian parliaments about financial contributions from each country to the infrastructure of cruise and Pershing-II bases, lies in the way in which it was possible for the Social Democratic or Labour parties to put themselves at the head

of constructive opposition movements which united both parliamentary and popular feeling against their respective governments'
willingness to accept the US Government's unilaterally determined
negotiating stance. This in turn reflected a widespread perception
that the Geneva negotiations were a facade to cloak the intentions
of both superpowers to deploy weapons systems which they had
long had in preparation and which would be installed regardless of
the feelings of their European allies.

The Danish Social Democrats were able to point to considerable
tactical successes in consolidating opposition to the government's
tame acceptance of the NATO policy line. In this they effectively
exploited the parliamentary principle of ministerial responsibility
by mandating members of the minority coalition to advocate a
policy-line with which they were far from happy.

Danish analysis of proposals for the NNFZ rested on the work of
a committee established in October 1980 and comprising
representatives of the foreign and defence ministries, the economic
secretariat, university researchers, the media, and each of the
parties represented in the *Folketing*. After usefully summarizing the
successive proposals, the report reiterates the need for a reversal in
the current expansionary trends, not only through new arms control
measures but through actual steps toward disarmament as well.
This need is seen to arise for several reasons: the incalculable
destructiveness of nuclear weapons, their continuous growth in
both numbers and technological sophistication, the strategy which
makes their use highly probable in the event of war between East
and West, and the incalculable risk that, once used, their control or
limitation might not be possible. The debate on the NNFZ is seen as
the Nordic variant of the widespread alarm felt in Europe, 'the
primary area of confrontation between the world's greatest military
alliances and nuclear powers' (SNU, 1982: 188). The report sees the
NNFZ proposals in part as confidence-building measures, requiring
as a precondition that they enjoyed a mutual understanding in the
West and that the East would perceive them as a move towards
détente calling for some reciprocity. These preconditions were seen
to preclude Denmark (or Norway) from making 'major moves in
the field of nuclear weapons policy without active co-operation of
countries with an essential role in the security of the Nordic area'
(SNU, 1982: 189).

The cumulative efforts made by the Norwegian Labour Party and the Social Democrats in Denmark, chronicled above, were significant for their intention to secure such active co-operation, especially (but not only) within NATO. It was always the intention in both parties that their countries' membership of NATO would remain the cornerstones of their security policy. But the achievement of the Danish Social Democrats was to have forced a parliamentary re-alignment, so that the Conservative-led Schlüter government, while it could rely on the Radical Liberals to make up a majority on economic issues, found itself in a minority on the nuclear weapons issue, and compelled to advocate the viewpoint of the majority opposition, which on this issue comprised the socialist bloc plus the Radical Liberals. One result of this opposition was to push the Nordic conservative parties into taking the issue sufficiently seriously to plan a meeting of Nordic parliamentarians, thus seeking to upstage the one planned for November 1985 by the Danish Social Democratic leader Anker Jørgensen (*Nordisk Kontakt* 1985: 301–2), even though this would risk bringing out the different views taken by the various conservative parties: the Finnish National Coalition Party were clearly in favour and the Swedish Moderates also viewed the proposals positively, while the Danish Conservatives and the Norwegian Right specifically rejected a Nordic nuclear-weapons-free zone which was not part of a larger international agreement involving NATO approval and guarantees from both the USA and the USSR.

In addition to their response to superpower armaments policy, the Nordic countries have also had to generate a realistic response to potential or actual incursions into their airspace or territorial waters by both superpowers. That these had to be taken seriously was emphasized by such incidents as the publication of a map illustrating the possible trajectory of British-based cruise missiles over Swedish and Finnish territory on their way to Leningrad, the repeated incursions by Soviet submarines into Swedish waters off Karlskrona in 1983 and 1984, and the accidental flight and crash of a Soviet missile over Norwegian and Swedish territory in January 1985. The two NATO countries have looked in that direction for support while Sweden has set in train a programme to greatly improve facilities for detecting and intercepting missile incursions, and the Finns have relied on their close diplomatic links with the Soviet Union to make known their deep concern.

On defence and security issues the Scandinavian social

democratic parties have been able to make a distinctive contribution, even while in opposition, which has caught the mood of mounting public concern and has therefore attracted electoral support. But to a significant extent the pace has been set by the left wing of the socialist bloc, and the social democrats have varied in the extent to which they have been able to build support for a policy strategy which combines credible security with disengagement from superpower involvement.

Can dominance be regained?

Whether Scandinavian social democracy can come once again to dominate policy making in the countries of the region must depend in part on the ability of the parties to revive and extend their electoral base, and in part on their success in offering policy proposals which meet the perceived problems of voters.

Organizationally the parties have lost ground everywhere in Scandinavia except Sweden. Even there the secular trend which once favoured the SAP may not continue to do so. Party membership numbers have been continuing upward, but Olof Palme's pre-eminent leadership style has lent support on several issues to charges of autocracy by the opposition parties. In Norway party membership numbers have made a modest revival over the decade since 1974 (when they fell to a nadir) and there has recently been a similar modest growth in Denmark, but in neither case has this been enough to restore the strength of the 1960s or earlier. Nor is there the former compensating strength to be found in the trade-union wings of the Norwegian and Danish parties. As party leader, Gro Harlem Brundtland has to attain predominance over the Norwegian bourgeois parties, while in Denmark Anker Jørgensen, having led his party for over twelve years, faces the prospect of retirement from the leadership within the current decade: already successors are jockeying for position, with Svend Auken (the party's leading parliamentary spokesman and a former Employment Minister) tipped as a likely winner.

From the right, the challenge to Scandinavian social democracy in the 1970s came from the populist appeals of Mogens Glistrup in Denmark, and Anders Lange (less successfully) in Norway, to sweep away taxation and 'paper-shufflers'. Glistrup's Progress Party drew support from an enlarged petit bourgeoisie comprising not only small businessmen themselves but also their wives, first-generation descendants, and employees (Hansen, 1982). But his followers were too incoherent both in their policy claims and their parliamentary behaviour to be more than disruptive, and this challenge finally faded with his conviction for tax fraud. In the 1980s a more serious challenge came in Denmark, Norway, and Sweden (and to a lesser extent in Finland too) from conservative parties which have been able, increasingly, to consolidate and dominate the other parties of the 'bourgeois' or non-socialist bloc, overcoming as they have done so the rivalries or enmities of a previous era. But whether the attractions of the slimmed-down welfare state and an end to the apparently insatiable demands for tax revenue to pay for it will be sufficient to keep the conservatives in power must be doubtful. Extensive and bitter industrial protest action in the spring of 1985 was the response to the income-restraint measures introduced both by the conservative-led government in Copenhagen and the SAP government in Stockholm. Alternative conservative policies were based far less than those of Thatcher or Reagan on the alleged evils of the welfare state than on the search for solutions to the undoubted problems for the national economy of high balance of payments deficits, high levels of national debt interest, and low levels of economic growth.

From the left, the most telling challenges to Scandinavian social democracy were two: the sincerity of commitment to goals of international peace and security, and the demand to maintain momentum towards equality and welfare. On the former, the Danish and Norwegian parties acquitted themselves well, both successfully pressing their respective governments to question NATO acceptance of the US-driven twin-track strategy of negotiation with the USSR, both contributing to the alternative strategy of a Nordic nuclear-weapons-free zone and, in the case of the Danish Social Democrats, using the opportunities of parliamentary opposition to impel the Danish Foreign Minister, however unwillingly, to advocate their views on the international stage.

The commitment of the Scandinavian social democratic parties to equality and welfare is central to the aim of counteracting uneven development. The achievement and continuation of high levels of employment (even more than welfare and unemployment benefits) has always been seen as essential to the attainment of this goal, but here the countries of the region have varied considerably in their success: Iceland, Norway, and Sweden have kept unemployment to levels very little above those of the 1960s; the average level in Finland has been around 5 per cent, but this has concealed lower levels in the south and much higher ones in the northern periphery; while unemployment in Denmark has been seasonally higher than 12 per cent (February 1984: *Yearbook of Nordic Statistics*). These differences reflect both variations in the terms of each country's trade and in the proportions of gross national product each spends on welfare and transfer payments.

At the heart of the conservative critique of social democratic policies lies the view that they concentrate overmuch on demand management and fail to pay sufficient attention to the supply-side of the economy. An important lesson which the Scandinavian social democratic parties can offer to their brother parties elsewhere may be that nationalization of industry and commerce is unnecessary to the achievement of social democratic goals: there are other, often more effective, ways of ensuring the attainment of desirable redistribution of investment and control of work-place decision-making. Another lesson may be that employee funds can offer a means of attaining several medium-term economic objectives, including a shift of domestic investment capital from existing large and well-established enterprises towards new firms at the leading edge of innovation. A third lesson, especially from Swedish experience, is the value of high levels of access to and participation in education and training as the means of switching workers from declining to developing sectors of the economy. For those in search of future economic strategies for social democracy, these, or variants on them, may prove to be the signposts they need.

8

The French Socialist Party
Byron Criddle

DESPITE the Left's dramatic victory in 1981, (see Table 8.1) social democracy has traditionally been a weak plant in France. No party of significant size has ever borne the title and that party—the Socialist Party—affiliated to the social democratic Socialist International was, until the 1970s, a relatively small force stranded perennially on the margins of French political life, or, when locked in coalition governments with non-socialist allies, equally stranded at the centre.

Table 8.1:   *Election results in France, 1981*

PRESIDENTIAL ELECTIONS (April/May)

	First ballot %	Second ballot %
Giscard d'Estaing	28.3	48.2
Mitterrand	25.8	51.8
Chirac	18.0	
Marchais	15.3	

LEGISLATIVE ELECTIONS (June)

	First ballot votes %	Second ballot seats
Parti socialiste (PS)	37.8	287
Parti communiste français (PCF)	16.6	44
Union pour la démocratie Française (UDF)	19.2	62
Rassemblement pour la République (RPR)	20.9	88

In defining social democratic parties in the French context it is useful to employ the definition ventured by the French writer Hughes Portelli (1980) who sees such parties as distinguished by three essential characteristics: firstly, the possession of a strong working-class base sustained by direct links with the trade-union movement; secondly, organizational strength resting upon a mass membership, strong finance, and an effective machine; and thirdly, a commitment to the constitutional status quo and a consequent readiness to seek—and commonly to have experience of—government office in the liberal democratic state. In France these characteristics exist but are, critically, distributed across two quite separate and competing parties, thus preventing the emergence of a single large social democratic party: since the 1930s the first two features have been possessed by the Communist Party, and only the third feature by the Socialist Party. The Socialists have suffered, especially since the War, from an absence of significant trade-union support, after the leading confederation of unions, the CGT, fell under Communist control in 1946; and this was more than a mere private embarrassment for the Socialist Party, for it seriously affected its credibility and strength. Denied links with the labour movement, it has been prevented from acquiring a mass membership of the sort associated with, for example, the large northern European social democratic and labour parties; equally, and in consequence, it has been denied an effective organization, financial support and, more important, an industrial working-class clientele without which it has no serious representational function and consequently little clout. It has meant the party was powerless to influence events at crucial moments in French history—the Popular Front of 1936, the Liberation, and the Events of 1968. The great upsurge of union pressure in 1936, and again in 1968, were movements over which the party could exercise no control. In 1936 the Socialist prime minister, Léon Blum, was able to extract concessions from the employers only after factory occupations and strikes organized by others. In the post-war period, whilst the party served in most of the coalition governments before General de Gaulle's return to power in 1958, the division of union strength and the balance of forces created by this division never permitted the party to appear as the chief political expression of the labour movement (Martinet, 1979: 68). Denied the classic role of the large social democratic parties—that of organized working class representation—the Socialist party in fact became dominated by white collar professionals, especially teachers and other minor civil servants. By the 1980s moreover, Socialist trade unionists were scattered across a number of rival federations of *syndicats*, rather than being concentrated, as in the Communist case, in one federation, thus diluting whatever force the party might have. Furthermore, and significantly, that federation in which Socialist members have predominated has been the school teachers' union, the FEN. In 1981 FEN members accounted for 26 per cent of all Socialist trade unionists.

Only one characteristic of social-democratic parties—the propensity to govern in the liberal-democratic state—has been reflected in the party. After coming to office at the head of the Popular Front in 1936, the party participated in coalition governments more or less continuously with the exception of the Vichy period and a few years in the early 1950s, until the return in 1958 of de Gaulle, a return which was to consign the party to two decades of opposition until the defeat of the Right in 1981. The characteristic readiness of social democratic parties to govern in 'bourgeois' polities has however exposed such parties to the Communist charge of 'class treachery' and of an eagerness to 'manage capitalism'. The social democratic willingness to govern is certainly evidence of a firmly reformist orientation and it is this which has distinguished parties like the French Socialists from their Communist competitors and made it hard for social democracy to flourish in countries where large Communist parties prevail.

It is because of the presence of a Communist party with traditionally superior electoral support and industrial power that the French Socialist Party has failed to qualify as a social democratic party in Portelli's terms and failed, consequently, to make a substantial impact on French political life. The problem was twofold. First, the working-class roots needed by the party were in the possession of a Communist Party obsessed by the need to retain its hegemonic position within that class. Secondly, the Socialists' desire to observe the liberal-democratic rules of the game, and indeed to rally to the defence of an unstable regime in the period before 1958, and to take part in governments within which the party lacked the weight to extract the ameliorative reforms it favoured, was exploited by the Communists as a weapon in the wholly uneven struggle for the ear of the working class. The term 'social democracy' itself became in the mouths of Communists an all-purpose term of abuse, a euphemism for class collaboration, opportunism and chauvinism. As a result few Socialists in France have sought to use the term, and fewer still applied it to themselves. Some indeed have argued that, because of the Communist Party, social democracy is not on offer in France (Motchane, 1978: 41), and even Lionel Jospin, who was to succeed François Mitterrand as party leader in 1981, came to such a pessimistic conclusion after the Left's defeat in 1978 (Jospin, 1978: 55).

Communist dominance, and the Socialist attempt to counter it, served to colour the whole character of political debate within the Left by perpetuating a tradition of 'revolutionary verbalism'. This tradition predates, and indeed partially explains, the presence of a large Communist party and the absence of an organic relationship between *syndicats* and any political parties in the accepted sense; in the early 1900s, at a time when the British unions were forming their own political party precisely for the purpose of gaining parliamentary representation of their interests, the French unions, meeting at Amiens, set out their hostility to political organization *per se*, turned their backs on the bourgeois parliamentary regime and retreated into a revolutionary rhetoric which was thereafter never to be discarded. Thus, in place of German social democracy's Bad Godesberg programme is the French Left's *damnosa hereditas* of revolutionary rhetoric simultaneously sustained by and in turn sustaining a party honouring the Russian Revolution and Leninist organizational principles. The perennial need to compete with such a party has perpetuated in the Socialist Party a tradition of linguistic radicalism reflected in the use of a vocabulary and concepts largely eschewed by social democrats in northern Europe. Thus as recently as 1980, the *Projet socialiste*, the programme on which the Socialists officially campaigned in 1981, contained chapter headings redolent of a Marxist seminar (e.g. *la deuxième grande crise du capitalisme au XXe siècle*, and *la restructuration idéologique du capitalisme*). Employed too, in the same document, were such explicitly Marxist concepts as 'the dominant ideology (is) that of the dominant class', and statements affirming that the Party 'seeks not to manage the capitalist system, but to replace it'. Since the early 1970s the Socialists have also been pledged, somewhat boldly, to 'break with capitalism'. They have also set much store by the concept, sounding Marxist but in fact not found in Marx, of the '*front de classe*', and embracing the idea of a coalition of blue- and white-collar workers and farmers and others of the self-employed against the forces of monopoly capital. The party's image, and more important its self-image, is thus, to social democrats, uncharacteristically left-wing and radical (Garraud, 1978); and yet the radicalism is essentially verbal and figurative, a largely liturgical necessity to honour a long tradition in French political discourse and to counter the threat posed by the Communist Party.

Many of the social trends that sustained the growth of social democratic parties in north western Europe in the post-war period have certainly been evident in France. Thus, secularized Catholics have turned towards a Socialist Party attracting many Catholic activists where once only anti-clericals were to be found. Equally the growth of 'post-bourgeois' qualitative demands, such as the call for *autogestion*, of which the Socialists made much under Mitterrand's new leadership in the 1970s, became a major recruiting theme with appeal to the *soixante huitards* and their younger heirs. The belated interest of the Communists in this area was wholly unconvincing given the incompatibility between the concept of 'self-management' and the principles of democratic centralism practised inside the PCF and all its satellite organizations. Regionalism, too, was a cause articulated by Socialists with more conviction than was likely from the statists and centralists of the Communist Party. The Communists, in fact, saw many of the new issues as mere bourgeois diversions from the age-old class struggle. Such explanations of the growth in support for the Socialist Party and its eventual victory in 1981 do not sufficiently explain that success, however. Victory would have been impossible without the electoral marginalization of the Communist Party, a marginalization which was not to be explained solely in terms of European-wide social trends, but also by important institutional changes. Notably, these were: the introduction of a directly elected Presidency; an electoral system necessitating alliances between parties in order to convert votes into seats; a subsequent bipolarization of political competition and an associated need for aggregative, catch-all electoral strategies. All these changes threatened to consign a party as 'extreme' as the PCF to the outer darkness unless it drew appropriate conclusions and accommodated itself to the inevitable emergence of a Socialist Party as the leader of the Left.

But the enduring problem for the French Left in office after 1981 was that the newly-established Socialist dominance necessary for electoral credibility and exercise of the governing role was not a dominance that a Communist party of essentially unreconstructed type could accept as anything more than temporary. The 'italianization' of the PCF in the 1970s, although prompted by the new structural constraints in which it had to work, was no more than a tactical expedient. For compelling reasons, in fact, the changes could not be permitted to go too far: to preserve its identity, the party could not afford to sacrifice its two most distinguishing hallmarks, namely its international links (or, what one writer (Kriegel, 1979) has called its *'double appartenance'*), and its Leninist model of organization. Such a move towards the 'social democratization' of a Communist party could only be risked where, as in Italy, no threat existed from a strong Socialist party of the sort emerging in France in the 1970s. Where, as in France, the Socialist and Communist parties were vying for supremacy, Communist brand-identity had to be maintained. Moreover, dilution of the PCF's democratic centralism could well threaten its possession of the two 'social democratic' credentials sought by the Socialists, namely its hold over the working class through union strength and its equally important organizational power which in turn guaranteed factory floor influence and electoral force.

The context in which the social democratic 'problem' has to be set in France is thus complex. On the one hand the situation is familiar, and common to other countries: the Left took office in 1981 on the back of the unpopularity, during an economic recession, of a government of the Right whose tenure in office had lasted twenty-three years. Thus, to the rather circumstantial social trends and the entirely fortuitous institutional forces, had to be added the cliché that 'governments lose elections', especially after two decades and when the government's supporters are as divided as Giscard's were by 1981. The Socialist Party was thus both 'in the right place at the right time'—a credible, available alternative, and a party 'whose time had come'—and the beneficiary of social and institutional changes. But in addition to this widely applicable analysis of governmental change, there were the problems specific to socialist parties of southern Europe, namely, the Communist Party and the fragility of a temporarily dominant Socialist party. The task for a Socialist-led government (37 Socialist ministers, 4 Communists and 3 others) in such circumstances was not only to survive the 'management of capitalism' at a time of recession, but to square its stewardship both with a broadly conservative electorate and its own radical activists, and yet also satisfy hostile Communist 'allies' who possessed a certain extra-parliamentary veto power over the government, and whose long-term interests certainly required that the Socialists should fail.

Yet despite these peculiar constraints the Socialist-led administration took power more securely in 1981 than on any previous occasion. The institutional supports for the new government were substantial and there was certainly no risk of the same fate befalling Mitterrand as befell Blum in 1937, when his government succumbed to an adverse parliamentary vote. The Socialist-led government of 1981 rested on a clear Socialist majority in the National Assembly; even the 44 Communist deputies could be discounted. The support of the 287 Socialist deputies, though crucial for Mitterrand, was in fact assured by their realization of their dependence (for election) on Mitterrand's recently-acquired presidential stature and by the unwritten convention of the Fifth Republic that in a system of presidential dominance the role of parliament is essentially to ensure a majority for the President. The parliamentary majority was now less the guarantor of the President's power: rather the President had become the arbiter of the deputies' collective fates. Such institutional supports for incumbency were not available to Léon Blum in 1937, or to Guy Mollet in 1957, and even if the government appointed by Mitterrand in 1981 were to *fail* it was difficult to see how it could *fall*. In that sense, social democracy *à la française* was secure at least until the parliamentary elections due in 1986, and on that occasion, as in 1981, the electorate would be enjoined by President Mitterrand to 'give me the means' with which to govern until the end of his presidential term in 1988. It had taken the Right twenty-three years to lose power in 1981.

Though formally deficient in social democratic credentials, the French Socialists approached their task in government with a characteristically social democratic programme designed to reduce unemployment by reflating out of recession, and to decentralize power to reformed local government units (see Bell and Criddle, 1984: Ch. 8 and Hall, 1985). The government was thus one that would seek neither to abolish the free market, nor reverse the country's traditional alliances. Although substantial elements of the party's rank and file certainly took seriously the commitment, enunciated in the party's declaration of principles, to be in some ill-defined way a party pledged to 'break with capitalism', in the hands of François Mitterrand and the moderate figures prevailing in the government of Pierre Mauroy (1981–4), such expressions were purely declaratory, and served to supply the sort of ideological ballast provided in the British Labour Party by Clause Four of that party's constitution. The intention was firmly reformist: to introduce a moderately Keynesian programme with additional redistributive aspects. In this the government seemed to conform with popular desire as reflected in a post-election survey showing more than half the voters believing the government was elected to apply the programme of reforms put to the country by Mitterrand in his presidential campaign. Equally the poll showed that two thirds of the sample saw the victory of the Socialist party in the general election as a victory over both the outgoing government *and* the Communist Party (SOFRES, 1981). Thus, for all its four Communist ministers (all of them in minor ministries), the government was seen as representing a rejection both of Right and 'extreme' Left. These findings suggest that a 'victory of the Left' in 1981 was neither a victory for a radical version of socialism, nor even for an especially radical policy. The unpopularity of unemployment under the rule of Giscard and Raymond Barre was certainly a contributory factor in their defeat. But more important in securing the Socialists' success was the deradicalization of the Left's image, achieved through the substantial defeat of the Communist Party's leader, Georges Marchais, in the first round of the presidential election, and the wide gap opened up between his share of the poll (15 per cent) and Mitterrand's (26 per cent). This clear reversal of the traditional balance of strengths within the Left was then followed by the Socialist Party overhauling the Communists in all but 60 of the 473 metropolitan constituencies. Such a marginalization of the PCF was essential to the necessary reassurance of an electorate which, though disillusioned after two decades of conservative rule, was still apprehensive of the Communist Party. Doubts about the strength of a radical commitment to change among the electorate in 1981 were also fed by the absence of any significant increase in membership either in the Socialist Party or in the unions; certainly nothing to compare with the upsurge of affiliations at the time of the pre-War Popular Front when party membership had doubled.

As in the cases of social democratic governments elsewhere

succeeding to office in the depths of a recession, the French Socialists were soon to be deflected from their reflationary course. By the spring of 1983 the franc had been devalued three times and, significantly, the only senior ministers to be drawn from the left-wing CERES faction of the party, Madame Nicole Questiaux and Jean-Pierre Chevènement, had left their important new 'super ministries' of National Solidarity (Health and Welfare) and Industry, Research, and Technology as the government slammed on the brakes under pressure from the orthodox Finance Minister, Jacques Delors.

Having made much of the rise in unemployment under Giscard d'Estaing, the new policy was designed to reduce unemployment through reflation. Although the problem was contained through deficit financing, a reflationary dash for growth, at a time when France's trading partners were deflating, sucked in imports and seriously damaged the trade balance, which by the beginning of 1983 had reached 90 billion francs and was still rising. Equally inflation, the control of which had been the central objective of the Giscard administration, moved upwards whilst inflation rates elsewhere were falling: most notably in West Germany where by the end of 1982 the rate, at 5 per cent, was only half the French rate. Blaming the rest of the industrial countries for failing to reflate, and the United States for high interest rates and an over-valued dollar, the government was obliged in mid-1982 to move away from reflation in order to address the problem of inflation. A prices and incomes freeze was introduced, and public spending was cut instead of being increased as during the first year of the government. The cuts specifically hit the ambitious welfare spending plans and provoked the resignation of the minister, Mme Questiaux; she had set her face against such 'realities', and was replaced by a trusted protégé of the President, Pierre Bérégovoy, whose task was to rein in the deficit in the social-security budget. From 1981 through 1982 to March 1983 the lights changed from green to amber to red with the final lurch being dictated by France's EMS partners who made loans available in return for a heavily deflationary package designed to reverse the trade deficit. By 1983, austerity disguised as 'rigour' was the order of the day with tax increases on all but the lowest paid, increases on tobacco and drink, and foreign currency restrictions introduced. Thus, somewhat predictably, under pressure from European partners whom the new government had sought to encourage to reflate with France in 1981, the Keynesian dash for growth was dropped. The Socialists' voyage of discovery in the first two years of office was reminiscent of the British Labour government between 1964 and 1966, with Mitterrand, like Wilson, coming to regret the failure to devalue the franc immediately on assuming office.

The '*virage à droite*' of the Socialist government ought, it might be supposed, to have provoked trouble with the party's rank and file and with the Communists. That no serious disputes arose inside the party was due in some degree to the government having honoured a number of its promises on the minimum wage, family allowances, and unemployment; but there were other reasons too for the relative quiescence of the rank and file—reasons most easily discerned from an examination of the nature of factionalism in the party.

Factionalism is an important—indeed integral—feature of the life of the French Socialist party, with places on two of its leading bodies (the *Bureau Exécutif* and *Comité Directeur*) being awarded only to signatories of rival motions that manage to secure the backing of at least five per cent of the votes before biennial party congresses (Bell and Criddle, 1984: Chapter 10). Thus at the last (1979) congress before the victory of 1981, votes were distributed across five rival motions in the ratio of 40:21:17:15:6, and at the 1983 congress across three motions in the proportions of 77, 18 and 5. Such a biennial resort to the measurement of faction strengths has notably served to record the changing fortunes of the party's left-wing faction, CERES, (from 25 per cent in the mid-1970s, to 15 per cent in 1979, and 18 per cent in 1983), this being the section of the party least likely to accept the compromises of office. Factional rivalries, however, have always been conducted within certain limits.

First, there are the familiar arguments adduced by Michels for leadership domination even within supposedly pluralistic social democratic parties, where the 'perennial incompetence' of the mass and the infinitely greater skills of the leadership serve to ensure the latter's predominance (Michels, 1962 edition). Certain developments since Michels wrote have rendered some of his arguments for oligarchy insubstantial, not least the replacement of the 'perennially incompetent' and ill-educated party members by the articulate and disputatious white-collar professionals who have come to swell the ranks of contemporary social democratic parties. At the same time, however, certain other changes have served to strengthen immeasurably the position of the party leader. Thus, in France, the process of presidentialization of politics has worked greatly to the benefit of the leaders of those parties capable of mounting a serious bid for the Presidency. Presidential politics, and the nature of the electoral laws sustaining it, has promoted the growth of catch-all parties seeking to aggregate some 14 million votes to ensure victory, and to this end necessarily elevating the position of the leader, downgrading the role of the party member in policy formulation, and discarding where necessary any contentious ideological baggage. In adapting to such requirements the French Socialists have been aided, somewhat paradoxically, by the absence of a policy-oriented approach to politics on the French Left, where theatricality, theory, and abstraction have traditionally taken precedence over the formulation of detailed policy blue-prints (Cayrol, 1982: 32–41). Such a tradition of generalized discursive debate fits well with the requirement of presidential politics where candidates require, in their quest for millions of votes, as few precise and constraining policy commitments as possible.

In addition to the encouragement of leadership domination offered by presidentialization there has been the incessantly electoral character of French politics since the institution of presidential—in addition to parliamentary—elections in 1962. The perennial shadow of the ballot box has put a premium on party unity, particularly as the Socialist Party's persistently improving performance in the 1970s appeared to lend credence to the 'one last heave' view of politics—a final push before the Party could come into what political scientists saw as its inevitable inheritance. Thus despite all the strains traditionally endemic in socialist politics, not least where half the potential electorate of the Left was in the hands of the Communist party, the claims to unity behind the chief were compelling. Moreover the chief himself possessed qualities that induced respect, having rebuilt the Socialist Party, grasped the nettle of an alliance with the Communists, and performed well in two previous presidential elections. The case for Mitterrand's indispensibility seemed unanswerable before 1981 and constitutionally irrelevant thereafter. In Mitterrand's ten years as party leader (1971–81) only once, in 1978, after defeat in an election the Left was supposed at one time to win, did factional conflict break out in a form serious enough to pose a threat to his leadership.

Following the *rupture* of the Left alliance in 1977—when the Communists sought to dismantle the instrument which appeared to be creating a dominant Socialist Party—and its defeat in 1978, Michel Rocard launched a bid both to replace the Left alliance with a more 'autonomous' strategy and to secure his own nomination as Socialist presidential candidate in 1981. He received the backing of Pierre Mauroy, seigneur of the party's powerful Nord federation, and together the two men—to each of whom the label 'social democrat' may most appropriately be affixed—proceeded to commit both *lèse majesté* and, notably in Rocard's case, *lèse orthodoxie*. Their challenge amounted to the first serious questioning of the party's hallowed *ligne d'Epinay*, the strategic commitment to the Union of the Left which had been adopted at the Epinay Congress of 1971 and formed the basis for Mitterrand's political career in the Fifth Republic. Rocard's apparent belief was that the alliance be neglected at leadership level in favour of the pursuit of Communist voters, regardless of the demands of Communist leaders whose intentions could not be trusted. The fences broken by this clash were not mended after 1981. Rocard was dispatched by Mitterrand to the internal exile of the Planning Ministry, in a country where planning had become more fiction than reality; and in 1983, having found in the rather small planning job too much time, from Mitterrand's point of view, to make speeches critical of the government's austerity programme ('too little, too slowly'), he was moved to the exposed and difficult Ministry of Agriculture. The marginalization of Rocard after 1981 extended to his two supporters who had been given junior ministerial posts; by 1983 both had left office. The campaign to marginalize Rocard was left to 'Marxist' Mitterrandists such as the parliamentary group leader Pierre Joxe and the Finance Committee Chairman, Christian Goux, who sought to isolate the President's only serious rival in public opinion (polls having for some years shown Rocard to be the most popular Socialist politician in the country), and one moreover, constantly fêted by the media. To the left wing of the party, Rocard represented the '*gauche américaine*' and the '*gauche maso*'—keen to point the government down the road of realism, retrenchment, and austerity.

And yet the policy and strategy implications in what was essentially the rivalry of two men were proved in the event to be slight. Rocard's advocacy of an autonomous strategy was roundly rejected by Mitterrand only to be employed by him in the elections of 1981 when he was projected as a reassuringly bland *force tranquille* untainted by any dealings with the Communist Party. Likewise, in office the Rocardian call for austerity was by 1983 the centre-piece of the government's economic strategy. Moreover, although side-lined into Agriculture in 1983, Rocard was still in the Cabinet, whilst the most high-ranking left-winger, Chevènement, was dropped. The government reshuffle in 1983 in fact saw the elevation of the belt-tighteners as Finance Minister Delors moved up to second ranking behind the Prime Minister. Chevènement meanwhile left office with a reputation as an ineffective would-be interventionist Industry Minister. The CERES case for intervention was made in a book *Le Socialisme et la France* (Mandrin, 1983) and a CERES motion was put to the party congress in October 1983, but significantly was not pressed to the point of a break with Mitterrand.

After 1981 the prospects for factionalists of both Right and Left— Rocard and Chevènement—were poor. The Presidency, Rocard's objective in his clash with Mitterrand after 1978, was out of bounds until 1988, or at least until the party had successfully, or otherwise, negotiated the parliamentary election of 1986 and Mitterrand had announced his intentions for 1988. Even after the dropping of CERES leaders from the government in 1982/3, factional balance within the government, carefully established by the President in 1981 (with the exception of the under-represented Rocardians whose leader himself left office in 1985) was maintained. Chevènement was restored to office in 1984, albeit to a bed of nails (Education). Amongst activitists, moreover, there was a strong desire to sustain the first government of the Left for a generation. Just as in Britain, where it took two periods of 'compromised' Labour government and sixteen years (after 1964) before serious fractricidal strife erupted in 1980, so in France low activist morale— reflected by 1983 in a declining party membership—was unlikely to be provided with effective rebel leadership before an election had actually been lost. Equally, there were grounds for activist loyalty in the face of the periodic attacks on the government from its internal enemy, the PCF, the conventional rectitude of whose four ministers was matched by the increasingly critical observations of its political (Marchais), parliamentary (Lajoinie), and union (Krasucki) leadership, culminating in the ending of ministerial participation in 1984.

Finally, such evidence as existed of the social and ideological characteristics of the various currents in the party as its leaders embarked on government in 1981 suggested that they lack sufficiently clear boundaries to pose a significant threat to the Government. Thus whilst CERES, as its non-personalized title implies, is a more self-consciously ideological faction than the more personalized, or in part regionally-based, currents formed around Mitterrand, Mauroy, and Rocard, its activists were little different in their perceptions of issues. At the 1981 congress they were shown to be at one with those of other currents in ranking unemployment, inflation, and the reduction of wage differentials as the most important issues, even if their interest in inflation was perceptibly slighter than that of other activists. CERES and Mitterrand activists did however evince greater interest in controlling multinational companies, whilst the more 'social democratic' Mauroy and Rocard activists reflected a significantly greater commitment to 'pragmatism' (cited by two thirds of Rocardians and half of the Mauroy supporters but a mere third of the rest) and in the 'new' issues of regionalism and (in the Rocardian case) sex-equality (Cayrol and Ignazi, 1983). In occupational terms differences were somewhat slighter (Cayrol and Ysmal, 1982). In an activist base, 90 per cent of which is drawn from white collar and professional groups, with the largest single component from teaching, there was in 1981 little to choose between the currents. Only CERES backers were drawn slightly more heavily from the ranks of clerical and manual workers, and then only one in six. Rocardians were moreover somewhat more likely to be Catholic (40 per cent as compared to nearer a third of other currents) and equally less likely to have been reared in a Left-voting family—again 40 per cent, but this comparatively low figure was also shared by CERES activists. Equally, 'social democratic' Rocardians and 'Marxist' CERES supporters belonged in similar proportions to CFDT unions—a reflection of the recruitment of both currents in the Catholic West (Rocardian) and East (CERES) (Cayrol and Ysmal, 1982). Whilst the distribution of variables (occupation, religion, union affiliation, etc.) could not be said to be entirely randomly distributed across the four main currents, neither was there any significant clustering to demarcate one grouping clearly from another (see Hanley, 1983).

Thus was party–government cohesion after 1981 well-maintained. From January 1981 the party leader was Lionel Jospin, a man owing everything politically to François Mitterrand and who would not have become the party secretary had Mitterrand not so decided. Jospin was put there as guarantor of the party's loyalty to the chief. Immediately after assuming office Mitterrand instituted weekly meetings at the Elysée attended by Jospin, Mauroy, and himself, with the purpose of ensuring that everyone kept in step. This was not always easy. The large Socialist group in the National Assembly, containing 170 new deputies who had been elevated suddenly—in many cases to their great surprise—from ordinary party activists to parliamentarians, pressed the government on some issues, such as broadcasting policy, and obtained concessions. Joint government–party policy formulation groups covering taxation and social policy, were also set up following a major meeting between the government and senior party workers in mid-1982.

Whilst critical spirits were thus not overridden, the call by the party's number three, Paul Quilès at the 1981 Congress for 'rolling heads' in the higher reaches of the civil service to prevent sabotage of socialist proposals, was little more than an extravagant flattery of the activists. In fact in important ministries such as Finance, Interior, and Defence, relatively few senior heads rolled. Moreover when dealing with recalcitrant elements in parliament, whether in its own or other ranks, the Government had at its disposal the vast arsenal of executive powers with which parliament can be cowed in the Fifth Republic, and, for all the Socialist Party's long-expressed opposition to such 'Gaullist' devices, they were resorted to with some frequency. Socialist backbench opposition to aspects of the government's energy policy and an amnesty for army officers who had acted seditiously during the Algerian crisis were overridden by application of such devices. Equally, Communist resistance to the prices and incomes freeze in 1982 was squashed by use of Article 49, which enables bills to go through on the nod; and further PCF hostility to more austerity in 1983 was evaded by a device enabling legislation by ordinance.

What the government was doing was to give priority to meeting the nervousness of the electorate rather than the Party, and after the first year in power it was clear than many of the new deputies were also beginning to consider how best to secure re-election in

1986. An equally essential loyalty to the government from the parliamentary group was ensured by the perceived need to defend it from a Communist Party down in 1981 but still not out.

Communist behaviour in government from 1981 to 1984 was essentially uncontentious, with the Party having been enjoined by the senior of its four ministers and deputy leader, Charles Fiterman, to present a 'positive image'—to build, manage, and govern'. Initially stunned by the scale of its defeat in 1981 (the loss of one fifth of its support), the Communist Party gratefully accepted the ministerial crumbs brushed into its lap by Mitterrand, and little was heard of the four ministers thereafter. Essentially, with some exceptions when the Communist ministers put down critical markers for future reference, the requirements of 'collective responsibility' were observed, notably by Fiterman who presented very much the acceptable governing face of the Party.

But the Communist tactic appeared to be that of a traditional waiting game; making the most of its new foothold in government to deepen its penetration of the public authorities—in the Communist-run ministries a higher proportion of heads did roll. This was already considerable at municipal level where PCF kept closely in step in the run-up to the March 1983 local elections, where Socialist votes would be indispensible for the survival of Communist mayors. On the other hand the CGT, under the new and harder leadership of Henri Krasucki, probed the factory floors for discontent and presented the critical view of the government's performance, involving essentially the view that the workers should not have to pay for the crisis. More problematic, however, than domestic policy differences (where distributive reforms had sugared the pill), was foreign and defence policy where a largely Atlanticist stance by Mitterrand made life hard for the PCF. The President's staunch defence of the siting of new US missiles to counter the Soviet SS-20s was opposed by the Communist Party; and on Poland the PCF also retained a broadly pro-Soviet line.

It was, however, bad national and local election results in 1983–4 and working class disgruntlement at rising job losses that led the Communists to take the opportunity provided by a change of Socialist Prime Minister, from Mauroy to Fabius, in July 1984, to leave office. The PCF was to seek, by detaching itself from Mitterrand and the Socialist Government, what it had equally sought in joining them in 1981, namely a revival of its electoral strength. In 1981, for the first time since the Liberation, the Communist Party had registered a significant decline in its working class heartlands of the Paris red belt and the northern industrial areas. Communist deputies were ousted from their proletarian redoubts as the Socialist Party outran the PCF by a margin of 2:1 (PS 44 per cent, PCF 24 per cent) among working class voters nationally; less than one in four workers were heeding the call of the self-proclaimed vanguard party. Moreover, the malaise was also being reflected in a parallel decline of the CGT.

For the Socialists, the movement of industrial workers toward them in 1981 appeared to offer hope of remedying the traditional deficiencies of the party in this important area, but it was essentially an electoral movement that could easily be reversed. The motives underlying the movement of working class votes in 1981 were to a degree ephemeral. There was, first, the desire for a change of government in response to the declining appeal of the Right, to which end a vote for Mitterrand was the only plausible course; secondly there were clearly negative judgements made of the PCF's behaviour in recent years, notably its pro-Soviet stance on Poland and Afghanistan. Neither implied a necessarily permanent movement of support to the Socialists. Nor did the electoral demise of the PCF in the early 1980s (down from 20 per cent to 16 per cent in 1981, and to 11 per cent in the European Assembly election in 1984) augur well for the Socialists, themselves down from 37 per cent in 1981 to 21 per cent in 1984. By 1984 both parties were declining simultaneously as their supporters abstained or deserted to the Right in protest against an austerity programme defended by the PS and condemned by the PCF. The very low Left aggregate vote, of some 35 per cent, in 1984, confirmed that Communist decline was good for the Socialists only if accompanied by a commensurate Socialist growth as in 1981.

It was the sharp electoral decline of the Left as a whole, and its ideological fragmentation as an unbridgeable gulf widened between the un-socialist policies of the Socialist Government and the radical dogmas of the Communist Party, that led President Mitterrand in 1985 to initiate the reintroduction of proportional representation for the 1986 legislative election. Proportional representation, in direct contrast to the electoral system in place since 1958, carried great potential for disaggregating the two electoral alliances of Left and Right. It offered Mitterrand some hope of producing a fragmented parliament from which by wheeling and dealing the President would seek to cobble together a majority to see him through to the end of his term in 1988. To this end, in order to appeal to centre and centre-right leaders to reach some sort of *modus vivendi*, or *cohabitation*, with a minority Socialist President and Party, Mitterrand would more than ever invoke the vision of a moderate *rassemblement républicain*, thus detaching his Party even more starkly than had the practices of the Mauroy and Fabius governments from the traditional dogmas of French socialism. Moreover, whatever the outcome of the parliamentary election of 1986, arguments for Socialist Party discipline remained compelling as the more important contest for the presidency itself loomed. Short of a clearly decisive victory for the Right in 1986, social democracy, at least in the somewhat ambiguous sense of mildly reformist aspirations laced with monetarist rectitude, seemed assured under the subtle and supple guidance of François Mitterrand. If, on the other hand, the Socialist Party sustained a significant defeat in 1986, followed by the departure by or before 1988 of President Mitterrand, the great federater of contemporary French socialism, it would face a period of destabilization involving a possible war of chiefs, a messy inquest, and a prolonged debate around the party's perennial strategic dilemma of having to fight its wars on two fronts.

Meanwhile, the Socialist Party retained all the problems of a workers' party without many workers. Advancing more on the votes of the expanding white collar class than on those of an eroding working class, and internally dominated by the new professionals in teaching and administration, the Party is unapologetically the party of the tertiary (largely public) sector, credentialled middle class. It is a party which assembled an unpredictable electorate in 1981. Popular within the working class, it lacks roots in that class, however. Capable of taking protest votes from the parties of the Right, it can certainly not rely on that support. Nor can it effectively rely on its own support, for unlike the Right, which rests on the traditional bourgeoisie and the farming vote, and the Communists, who continue to rest on the albeit declining industrial working class, the Socialist Party is essentially the expression of a politically volatile new class, which in 1981 voted for change rather than radicalism, but which has a certain vested interest in the public sector. Although numerically expanding, it is a class of too recent origin to make prediction of its future political orientation easy.

Catch-all parties, of the type that the Socialist Party became in opposition in the 1970s, rely on many factors for their health and well-being: close attachment to a single, well-defined social class is not essential. But certainly all successful parties of this type on the European Left have rested on a rock of working class support. The Socialist Party's drift away from its already slight attachment to such a class at activist and leadership level is admittedly mirrored in other socialist parties, and the slow decline of the political identity of the working class is evident elsewhere. But the Socialist Party's lack of an organizationally-based entrée into the working class makes it more vulnerable than similar parties elsewhere to the fickleness of its 'new middle class' constituency, most notably when its leaders seek to govern through a major economic recession.

9

Socialist Parties and European Integration: Variations on a Common Theme

Kevin Featherstone

> Democratic Socialism is international because it recognizes that *no* nation can solve all its economic and social problems in isolation. Absolute national sovereignty must be transcended.
>
> From '*The Aims and Tasks of Democratic Socialism*', adopted by the Socialist International at its Frankfurt Conference of 1951.

THE process of integration experienced in post-war Western Europe has provoked a series of major debates within the socialist parties of the political systems concerned. Indeed, since 1945 few other policy issues arising initially in the sphere of foreign affairs have impinged so deeply upon the domestic domain and have prompted such a thoroughgoing debate amongst left-wing political parties.

At a comparative level, the development of the various parties' policies can be clarified and analysed in a number of different ways. Historically, the trends of party support can be charted and the degree of consensus existing amongst the parties assessed. Ideologically, party differences can be discussed on a Left–Right basis, so as to determine the strength of correlation existing between support for supranational integration and Left–Right identification. Similarly, changes of party policy can be related to the government and opposition rôles adopted by particular parties. At a deeper level, an explanation can be developed of party differences according to the various national factors that seem relevant to the distinctive policies. At the same time, such an approach can highlight the extent to which all socialist parties have been affected by common factors independent of particular national circumstances, or how far party policies are the result of a 'nationalized' response. Explanations such as these would also require careful attention being paid to the differing policy rationales presented by the parties, so as to determine what factors have shaped their conclusions. Various themes might well underlie such policy justifications: the differing conceptions of the 'national interest', of national sovereignty, and, indeed, of 'socialism' itself. Moreover, in contrast to some of the earlier neo-functionalist literature on European integration, a considered analysis of party policies ought also to distinguish between attitudes towards the existing operation of the European Community (EC) and those concerned with alternative conceptions of European integration.

Against this background, seeking to compare the differing responses exhibited by socialist parties during the history of European integration is a daunting and complex task. However, the aim of this chapter is less ambitious. Rather, it is to try to discern how fruitful the alternative approaches referred to above might be to a more substantial, and as yet undeveloped, body of literature seeking to explain this process. In the present context, nothing more than a preliminary illumination of a number of themes relevant to a future comprehensive explanation can be sought. Yet, such a first step towards a more substantial explanation seems appropriate, given the limited literature existing on the subject.

Historical trends in the policies of socialist parties

The development of support for European integration amongst socialist parties is summarized and illustrated in Table 9.1. Perhaps the most notable long-term trend discernible from the table is of the gradual increase in support amongst socialist parties for the principle of supranational integration within the European Community. The development of this consensus indicates that in 1983 only the Labour Party in Britain was committed to withdrawal from the EC, as a result of its 1980 party conference decision.[1] The only other socialist party which has a policy approximate to that is the Pan-Hellenic Socialist Movement (PASOK) in Greece, which opposed Greek accession to the Community but, now it is in government, is pursuing a much more ambiguous approach (Featherstone, 1983).

Since 1977, PASOK has been committed to a policy of seeking a special relationship for Greece within the Community and of putting EC membership to a referendum. However, under the Greek Constitution [art. 44 (23)] only the President can call a

Table 9.1: *The development of support amongst Socialist Parties for European integration*

Socialist/Labour Parties of:	Party attitude towards: General Objective of European Unity in 1920s [a]	ECSC	EDC	Euratom	EEC 1957	1961	1967	1971	1975	1980	1983
Belgium	In favour	–	–	–	–	–	–	–	–	–	–
Netherlands	n.a. No official statement	In favour	–	–	–	–	–	–	–	–	–
Luxembourg	n.a.	In favour	–	–	–	–	–	–	–	–	–
France	In favour	In favour	Party split	In favour	–	–	–	–	–	–	–
Germany/ W. Germany	In favour, no comment on Briand	Against German reunification first priority	Against	In favour	–	–	–	–	–	–	–
Italy	n.a. Party in exile	PSI: Against/Social Democrats: In favour	Against	In favour	Abstained in Parliament	Acceptance of membership	~				
Denmark	Limited support	Against	Against	In favour of a looser, wider European economic entity		In favour	–	–	–	–	–
Ireland	n.a.	n.a.		No clear stance			Affected by Britain	Against	Acceptance of Membership	–	–
UK	Against Briand	Against	Against	Against	Against	Against unless terms were very favourable	Negotiating for favourable terms	Against terms of accession	Gvt. in favour/ Party against	Against	Ambiguous
Greece	X	X	X	X	X	X	X	PASOK founded in 1974; Against	Against	Against; seeks referendum	Renegotiation
Spain	n.a.	Clandestine organization under Franco dictatorship: Policy commitments not applicable							In favour	–	–
Portugal	X	X	X	X	X	X	X	PSP founded in 1972	In favour	–	–

Notes: [a]. This period has been specified so as to cover the Briand initiative at the League of Nations in 1929.
n.a.: information not ascertained. It should also be noted that the Norwegian Labour Party recommended its voters to support E.C. accession in 1972, but the referendum defeated the proposal.
ECSC: European Coal and Steel Community.
EDC: European Defence Community.
Euratom: European Atomic Energy Community.
EEC: European Economic Community (European Community).

referendum, and the incumbent until 1985, Karamanlis, was strongly committed to continued EC membership. Despite PASOK taking office in 1981, he consistently resisted demands for any such referendum. In contrast to PASOK's earlier desire for a 'special relationship' and its past references to the cases of Norway and Yugoslavia, the new Papandreou Government opted for a modification of the terms of entry, which it outlined in a memorandum to the Council of Ministers in March 1982. The memorandum called for 'special arrangements' on the part of the Community to meet Greece's need for economic development. It sought increased agricultural and regional aid, and it also wished to establish the provision that individual member-states could, temporarily, derogate themselves from particular Community regulations. Such 'special arrangements', the Government said, would 'constitute the minimum possible' basis on which membership would not be 'in conflict with basic Greek national interests'. In February 1983 the EC Commission allowed Greece a special derogation, provided for under the Treaty of Rome, which authorizes it to block imports of eight groups of products from other member-states. Later, the Commission's response to the Greek memorandum was regarded in Athens as a suitable basis for compromise, and negotiations took place to resolve minor problems. The Papandreou Government indicated that it expected Greece to remain in the EC and its change of policy was finally exhibited by the enthusiasm with which Andreas Papandreou began his term as President of the EC Council in the second half of 1983. PASOK now apparently wishes to change the EC from within, though domestically it continues to portray itself as the sole protector of Greek interests. Moreover, given Karamanlis' unwillingness to hold a referendum, there is perhaps little else that the Papandreou Government could have done in practice.

Moreover, as Table 9.1 indicates, the socialist parties of the two applicant countries, Portugal and Spain, also favour EC membership. Both Mario Soares for the PSP and Felipe González for the PSOE have sought to persuade government leaders and fellow socialists to allow their respective countries to enter the EC as quickly as possible. Following its sweeping election victory in October 1982, the González Government made special overtures to a cautious Mitterrand administration in Paris, which had been forced to be sensitive to the interests of French farmers in the south.

Domestically within Spain, however, virtually all parties and pressure groups support EC accession, and socialists in both Spain and Portugal see it as an important basis on which to consolidate their democratic institutions and modernize their economies. Both countries look set to have a prolonged transitional period before they are allowed to become full EC members, but when they eventually do so it will constitute a major re-orientation of the EC towards the Mediterranean and may provide a bloc of member-states where concerted left-wing action is especially feasible.

At the time of writing, therefore, only the Labour Party in Britain stands aside from the consensus of socialist parties supporting EC membership. Yet, after its disastrous election performance in June 1983, the Labour Party looks set to re-examine many of its policy commitments, including that of EC withdrawal. In the near future the situation could thus arise where all socialist parties in the EC either support or accept EC membership. If so, it would be the first time in at least a decade that this consensus existed.

The development of support amongst socialist parties can be broken down into several distinct phases. During the first period of integration, up to 1957, support was strongest amongst the socialist parties of France, Belgium, the Netherlands, and Luxembourg. Indeed, for at least some of these parties their support for European unity dates back to the 1920s and their reactions to the Briand initiative at the League of Nations, in September 1929. By contrast, though the SPD in Germany in the 1920s had expressed some support for the idea of European unity, in the immediate post-war period the West German SPD opposed their country's participation in the developing integration process, largely because of their fear that it would prevent the re-unification of Germany which was their first priority (Paterson, 1974). Amongst the six nations participating in the early schemes of European integration, the West German SPD therefore joined the Italian PSI as the only two socialist parties opposing the process, though the SFIO in France were divided in their reactions to the European Defence Community proposals. The Italian PSI strongly opposed Italy's participation in the European Coal and Steel Community, seeing it as another manifestation of the USA's growing hegemony in Europe and fearing that the tiny Italian coal and steel industry would be destroyed by foreign competition (Willis, 1971). Later, the PSI supported Euratom and gave a limited welcome to the EEC, though they abstained on the latter in Parliament.

By the start of the second period of European integration, after 1958, therefore, the socialist parties of the Six shared a consensus of view which supported the process, and in most cases, wished to set it more ambitious objectives. In contrast, the social democratic and labour parties of Britain, Denmark, and Ireland were much less enthusiastic and preferred more limited forms of European co-operation. The British Labour Party had received repeated calls from socialist parties on the continent urging them to support the post-war initiatives on European integration, but it opposed British participation in the ECSC, the EDC, Euratom, and the EEC, fearing that they would undermine British national sovereignty, hinder the prospects for socialism, and weaken the links with the Commonwealth. The Danish Social Democrats were also wary of supranational controls, and preferred to see a more limited form of economic co-operation including a larger number of nations and, preferably, Britain, West Germany, and Sweden, for trading reasons (Miljan, 1977). So the British, Danish, and Irish parties supported the proposals for a European Free Trade Area, but later differed in their reactions to the prospect of EEC accession in 1961. In 1962, the British Labour Party enunciated five rather stringent conditions which it believed had to be met before Britain should join the EEC. These were concerned with protection for the Commonwealth, a fulfilment of obligations to Britain's EFTA partners, the freedom to pursue an independent foreign policy, the right to plan the economy, and safeguards for British agriculture.[2] By contrast, the Danish Social Democrats, who were in power at the time in a coalition government, supported the policy of trying to follow Britain into the EEC. The party maintained that policy until Danish accession in 1973.

Continental socialists were shocked and outraged by de Gaulle's veto on British accession in January 1963, and again by his actions in support of national independence which prompted the 1965–6 crisis in the EEC's decision-making process. The British Labour Party, having meanwhile entered government in 1964, adopted a more positive approach towards the EEC, and in 1967 lodged Britain's second application for membership, which was again vetoed by de Gaulle (Kitzinger, 1968). When Britain did finally join the EEC in 1973 under the Heath Government, the Wilson policy to maintain party unity was to oppose the terms of entry. On returning to power in March 1974, the party was committed to re-negotiation and either a referendum or an election on continued membership. At the June 1975 referendum, the Wilson Cabinet recommended support for the re-negotiated terms, but a majority of Labour MPs and a special party conference opposed them (King, 1977). After the referendum supported continued membership, the policy of the Labour Party was to seek a wider, looser European Community, with added safeguards on national sovereignty.[3] At its 1980 Party Conference, however, the Labour Party voted firmly in favour of withdrawal from the EC so that a future Labour government should 'disengage Britain from the EEC institutions and in place of (Britain's) EEC membership work for peaceful and equitable relations between Britain and all nations in Europe and the rest of the world.'[4]

The evolution of the British Labour Party's policy after the referendum towards being one of EEC withdrawal is in marked contrast to that of the Irish Labour Party which, having opposed membership at the time of the 1972 Irish referendum, later came to accept membership after a decisive vote in favour by the electorate. Yet, despite the gradual development of support for EEC membership amongst Europe's socialist parties, it would be incorrect to suggest that the EC policies of other socialist parties have not changed over the years, nor that they are uncritical of the existing operation of the EC.

Indeed, whilst the Danish and Irish parties are cautious and seek to protect national independence, the socialist parties of the original Six EEC member-states have adopted, to varying degrees, radical objectives for the future development of the EC. Most of them have adopted the practice of calling for 'a Europe of the Workers' which entails fundamental reforms of the existing EC, with added emphasis on social and regional inequalities (Bound and Featherstone, 1982). As a notable exponent of this approach, shortly after his election in 1981, François Mitterrand urged his colleagues at a European Council meeting to establish a new social dimension to existing EC policies, in order to combat the recession and relate integration more directly to the circumstances of workers throughout Europe (Bound and Featherstone, 1982).

As is examined in the preceding chapter, the Mitterrand administration since 1981 has experienced severe difficulties in implementing its election policies, which at times has strained party unity. Despite its early attempts to maintain a loyal public posture, CERES (a left-wing group established in the 1960s and now a tendency within the *Parti socialiste*) had by 1983 begun to express its serious misgivings at the increasing moderation of the socialist government. At first this appeared not to affect debate on the EC: CERES' leading minister, Jean-Pierre Chevènement, seemed prepared not to provoke controversy by repeating his long-held criticisms of the EC. By spring 1983, however, Chevènement had resigned from the government and had reiterated his belief that France should pursue a more independent economic policy which would include withdrawal from the European Monetary System.

The CERES tendency has developed a wide-ranging left-wing critique of the way in which the EC operates. CERES has said that it is not against the principle of supranationality, rather it is its possession by EC institutions which appease multinational capitalism that it opposes. It has seen the existing EC as serving the bourgeois internationalism of grand capital, which supports the EC because it breaks down the sovereignty of individual nation-states and fosters the development of multinational markets. In the present situation, the EC is thus not a means by which democratic control can be exercised over transnational capitalism. Rather, national sovereignty must be maintained and developments such as EC enlargement to include Portugal and Spain opposed, as they are likely to threaten the interests of those working in French agriculture. Left-wing criticism of the EC within the PS looks set to continue, therefore.

Nevertheless, with the policy of compromise followed by PASOK in Greece and the prospect of a retreat from withdrawal by the British Labour Party, socialist parties in the EC look set to enter the latter half of the 1980s sharing a consensus of view over the basic question of EC membership. However, as will be shown throughout this discussion, major differences still remain between the parties over the type of integration to be pursued.

Interpreting the development of the socialist parties' policies

Having briefly charted the course of policy adopted by each of the EC's socialist parties, their development can now be examined according to a number of different themes, which might help to provide a deeper understanding of their evolution and character.

The discussion that follows can only cover illustrative examples rather than the details of each case, but the historical overview presented above has suggested something of the necessary background.

Analysing the diverse responses to European integration made by socialist parties prompts the observer to consider how far these policy differences are the result of Left/Right distinctions existing between the parties. Indeed, there does seem to be some evidence available to support the view that left-wing socialists have been more critical of the existing European integration process than have their more moderate, right-wing counterparts. In Britain and Greece, in particular, the Left–Right dimension seems to closely overlap that of support or hostility towards the existing EC. To a lesser extent, a similar correlation has existed in both Denmark and Ireland. Amongst the six original EEC states, however, the relationship is more complex and less easily defined, given that EC membership is not in question. Within the French Socialist Party, the hostility of the CERES tendency can be highlighted, with its concern to protect national sovereignty in an era of multinational capitalism, and those most opposed to CERES are also more supportive of schemes for further European integration. But classifying the differences between the various *tendences* in the French Socialist Party solely on the basis of a Left–Right dimension appears much more problematic than for other parties, partly because the leading protagonists often strongly resist such an indentification (Featherstone, 1982). Moreover, in both the British Labour Party and the French Socialist Party a move to the left was experienced in the 1970s, but whilst one sought national independence, the other did not. The change in direction within the West German SPD and the Italian PSI during the latter half of the 1950s in favour of European integration does, though, seem to have been accompanied by a more general shift of policy which was regarded at the time as representing a rightward move, aimed to attract more electoral support (Paterson, 1974; Willis, 1971). More generally, amongst continental socialists in the 1980s, Left–Right differences of attitude towards European integration often appear to be more a matter of qualitative distinctions involving the form of integration to be pursued in social and economic affairs, largely reflecting the contrasts existing in domestic policy debates. That is, the debate has been internalized so as to reflect wider ideological differences and emphases.

At the comparative level, however, it would seem more rewarding to relate distinctive attitudes to differences over the principle of safeguarding national sovereignty or support for supranational action. At that level, one could contrast the diverse attitudes towards supranational integration held by those on the left of their respective parties. A clear contrast exists, for example, between those on the left in the Netherlands and Belgium, and the CERES tendency in France, let alone the Labour Left in Britain. This theme will be further taken up later in the discussion. The relevance of Left-Right distinctions to an explanation of differing policy attitudes on the EC does, however, seem difficult to resolve. Highlighting the incompatibilities between left-wing factions in different parties does not, of course, necessarily compare like with like: a left-winger in one party may be more pro-integrationist simply because he/she is more moderate than a left-winger in another party. Whilst such an explanation may seem simplistic, it cannot be dismissed without a clear objective criterion being developed on which to define ideological distances on a cross-national basis.

An alternative interpretation of changes and differences in the policies of socialist parties is attained by relating them to whether a party was in or out of power. Closely allied with this question is the apparent impact of public opinion on party policies and the quest for electoral support. At one level, many examples seem to have arisen to support the view that socialist parties in government have been more favourably disposed towards the EC than have socialists in opposition, and that the strongest criticism has only come from those out of power. Perhaps the most obvious case is that of the Labour Party in Britain and the various approaches it has adopted since the 1961 Macmillan application. Out of power in 1961, the party saw entry as being feasible on the basis of five rather tough conditions; in power, the Wilson Government applied for entry in 1967. Out of power after 1970, the party opposed the Heath terms of entry; in power, the Wilson Government kept Britain in the EC after the 1975 referendum. Out of power, the Party Conference of 1980 voted in favour of withdrawal. Each approach closely reflected the changing climate of public opinion on the issue, and they may have enhanced the party's short-term electoral position (Jowell and Hoinville, 1976).

Other cases of antagonism towards the integration process also stem from periods of opposition: PASOK in Greece from 1974 to 1981 was noticeably more antagonistic than the subsequent Papandreou Government; both the West German SPD and the Italian PSI opposed integration whilst in opposition in the early 1950s; and out of power the Irish Labour Party opposed entry in 1972. Even amongst parties like the Belgian Socialists, changes in policy can be distinguished: the PSB/BSP was strongly critical of the pro-ECSC policy of the Catholic Government in 1952–4, whilst it adopted a much more positive approach when in power with the Liberals from 1954–8 (Featherstone, 1982). The same general rule also seems applicable in France. The SFIO had frequent experience of power in the 1950s—indeed, it was a crucial component of any successful coalition—and it displayed less ambiguous support for the ECSC and EEC than did the PS in the 1970s (Bound and Featherstone, 1982). Again, the Mitterrand administration has seemed less radical in its European policy than is suggested by the debates it held whilst in opposition.

Perhaps the most prominent cases which run counter to this interpretation were to be found in the two applicant countries of Portugal and Spain. Both the PSP and the PSOE have consistently supported and pursued EC accession, partly as a result of their believing that it was a means of maintaining liberal democratic institutions within the domestic polity. Their concern with the issue has, though, covered a relatively short period.

The degree of association existing between government–opposition roles and changes in support for European integration does, therefore, seem very close and worthy of careful attention. Yet, it would seem simplistic to ignore other considerations. In political systems with frequent experience of coalition governments—like those of the Benelux countries—the consociational party systems have created different government–opposition rôles from those found in systems such as Britain. Each individual party having shared power also shares responsibility for the foreign policy established over the long-term. The scope for clear policy contrasts is thus reduced. In addition, in the Benelux systems public opinion has been favourable to European integration for many years: it is difficult to establish whether that is a result of a policy consensus existing between the parties or whether it is itself the cause of the consensus. Again, the West

German and Italian socialists adopted a more favourable policy towards European integration some time before they came to power. At a comparative level, it is thus difficult to determine how far the responsibilities of government and opposition roles have actually shaped party policies, and how far they are merely superficial historical correlations. Nevertheless, it is an interpretation that cannot be dismissed.

More substantive explanations of the way in which individual parties have developed their European policies would have to consider the impact of uniquely national factors, covering historical, geographical, and economic concerns. Moreover, a comparison of their impact would suggest how far the politics of socialist parties have been 'nationalized' by such questions or how far the common ideoloogy has provoked a common response. Certainly, a number of examples can be cited to emphasize the importance of uniquely domestic circumstances.

With respect to distinctive historical legacies affecting policies on Europe, perhaps the three most obvious examples are those of the British Labour Party, the West German SPD, and PASOK in Greece. The strength of commitment to the Commonwealth held by a generation of leaders within the Labour Party helped to prevent them fully embracing a solely European venture. Labour Party policy statements in the immediate post-war period emphasized this concern, and it was further explained by Hugh Dalton at the 1952 Party Conference, when he declared that 'we as socialists and as members of the Commonwealth hold ourselves responsible for making our contribution towards bridging the gap between the living standards of the developed and of the under-developed countries'.[5] Similarly, Kurt Schumacher, the first post-war leader of the SPD in West Germany argued that 'any European solution which rested on German division was essentially anti-European' (Paterson, 1974: 10). More recently, PASOK in Greece has adopted a strongly anti-Western orientation, which has covered both the EC and NATO. The party's 1977 election manifesto stated that 'following the US-sponsored seven year dictatorship, the partition of Cyprus, NATO's support to Turkey, and the threats against our territorial integrity, it has become evident that our foreign policy orientation is wrong' (Featherstone, 1982). These three cases are each instances of opposition to the integration process, but other historical legacies promoting a pro-EC stance could also be cited, of course.

In terms of geographical circumstance, socialists in countries such as Belgium and Luxembourg are quick to emphasize this as a factor making support for supranational integration almost inevitable. A leading Belgian socialist explained this point to the present author thus:

Belgium being a tiny country, having no nationalistic tradition, no grandeur, no imperial tradition (in spite of the Congo), it is natural—in national, psychological and political terms—for the Belgians to consider that the EEC is the best way out, and to recognize that we are too small to have any influence in the world, so the way forward is with the Community. (Featherstone, 1982.)

A combination of geography and economics has led some in the French Socialist Party to uphold the importance of agriculture within the EC and to be wary also of Spanish and Portuguese accession, given the fact that farmers in the south of France—an area with a long tradition of socialist support—would be in direct competition with the low-cost farmers of the Iberian peninsula. As has already been noted, the CERES tendency opposes any such enlargement of the EC. One leading CERES spokesman commented to the author in an interview in 1981 that, 'we do not want to worsen the pre-existing drawbacks of the Community, rather we want to protect ourselves against them.' Sharing a similar concern, the French Socialist Parlty has adopted a policy containing a number of stringent safeguards for the Community to take before it would consider enlargement practicable.

As has already been noted, the domestic circumstances of the Spanish and Portuguese socialists have provoked a more basic political factor in favour of EC accession: that of the need to support domestic democratic institutions by integrating them into the Community framework. In both countries, attempts at *coups d'état* have reiterated the importance of this factor. This willingness to accept supranational support on the grounds of promoting democracy is in sharp contrast to the attitude of those in socialist parties of established member-states who fear the Community's intrusion upon national sovereignty. This latter concern is one that has affected the attitudes of socialists in the four most recent members of the EC: Britain, Ireland, Denmark and Greece.

Within the British Labour Party, the restoration of sovereign rights lost to the European Community institutions when Britain acceded in 1972, is typically seen as being crucial to the ability of the party to implement its domestic economic policies. As a party document in 1981 explained, 'the restoration of full sovereignty to the British Parliament will mean that we will be freer to pursue our socialist alternative without being restricted by the strait-jacket of the EEC.'[6] At the 1980 Labour Party conference, Peter Shore, who was then the party's Foreign Affairs spokesman, declared that Community membership had meant 'a rape of the British people and of their rights and constitution.'[7]

Shortly afterwards in a television interview, Peter Shore elaborated other reasons which supported British withdrawal from the EC, and which returned to the legacy of British history. He commented:

Well, you know, we've been an off-shore island for some two thousand years of recorded history, and we have been, I suppose, the most successful nation-state of all nation-states for the past 500 years. And I do not take this view at all, that we should be cataclysmically damaged. I do not believe that we would be damaged at all, if we handle the future of our relationships with the EEC sensibly.[8]

Few comments perhaps better illustrate the importance of national considerations, rather than non-national ideological factors, to the character of a socialist party's policy. Other Labour Party spokesmen have referred, though, to a contrast of experiences existing between Britain and continental socialists. Tony Benn, for example, has expressed the belief that:

Britain has the most powerful domestic democracy and strongest labour movement of any in Europe. For the French, German and Italian Socialists the Common Market represented an aspiration towards solidarity and peace after years of Nazi occupation and fascist regimes. For them, the Treaty (of Rome), with all its defects, is a step forward; for us it was a step back. Britain is, to that extent, a century ahead of them in democratic experience. (Benn, 1980: 169.)

Whilst continental socialists would dismiss this as being a rather insular and patronizing view, the implication here is clearly that, given their different historical experiences, there is little need for Britain to join with European Socialists in a common approach on the European Community.

Underlying the examples cited above has been the clear conclusion that the policies socialist parties have adopted on European integration have been shaped more by domestic circumstances than by common ideological concerns. The extent of these 'nationalized' responses suggests that to speak of a 'European Socialism' in the contemporary era, in the sense of anything like a single conception, is misleading. This is not to suggest, however, that these responses have not exhibited a concern for common ideals amongst various parties at various times—the protection of workers' interests and of democratic accountability have been oft-repeated themes, for example—but whether or not a party has seen the same logical conclusion from these ideals has been primarily determined by national circumstances. Given the context of seeking national electoral support this is perhaps not surprising, but the extent to which socialists have differed over questions of national sovereignty and supranational action suggests that a fundamental dilemma exists for the ideology and its adherents. Indeed, in a wider sense, the reconciliation of 'socialism' and 'nationalism' has been the subject of prolonged debate amongst left-wing political activists since the middle of the nineteenth century (Wright, 1981).

As has already been indicated, in recent years there have been three main sources of opposition to integration within the EC: that of the British Labour Party, PASOK in Greece, and the CERES tendency within the French *Parti socialiste*. However, their opposition has been distinct from that of the West German SPD and the Italian PSI in the 1950s, in that neither of the latter directed their opposition towards the principle of supranationality. Similarly, the opposition of the Irish Labour Party and of part of the Danish Social Democratic Party in 1972 abated after the outcome of the referendums held in each country, and both now seek reform from within. The British Labour Party, PASOK, and CERES thus display some important similarites of attitude: each has sought to safeguard national sovereignty in order to loosen themselves from the 'strait-jacket' of the EC and to pursue socialist policies at home. At root, each sees a socialist advance as coming from a national initiative (or 'breakthrough') armed with national independence, and setting an example for workers' movements in other countries to follow. As one CERES spokesman told the present author in 1981 'the first aim of socialists should consist of making a reality of national sovereignty—therefore, we are national and not nationalist, that's quite different' (Featherstone, 1982).

Their policies and rhetoric are not uniform, however. CERES has not advocated French withdrawal from the Community, PASOK now seems content to 're-negotiate' the terms on which Greece entered the EC, and the Labour Party looks set to re-examine its policy of withdrawal. PASOK has criticized the EC's impact on economies of the 'periphery', and it has sought to develop alternative orientations for Greek foreign policy. CERES also sees the EC as serving the interests of multinational capitalism and it criticizes the view that the EC can be used as a vehicle for socialism. By contrast, the British Labour Party places less emphasis on an anti-multinational capitalist campaign, and dwells instead on how British parliamentary institutions have been undermined and how individual Community policies are inferior to those existing before UK accession.

The analysis of these critical attitudes typically assigns to them the label of being 'anti-European', though proponents in each party strongly resist the charge. It would seem much more accurate to describe them as being anti-integrationist, as they do not oppose the EC by proposing alternative forms of European integration or co-operation in the short-term. By contrast, as has been noted, the official policy statements of the French Socialist Party since the early 1970s have called for an alternative conception of European integration—a 'Europe of the Workers' with a supranational form—distinct from the form of the existing EC. Other continental socialist parties have followed their lead. They have thus indicated that it is possible to be anti-EC, for a number of reasons, whilst still being pro-integrationist. This is not the framework adopted by neo-functionalist students of the European integration process in the past, however. Ernst Haas, for example, appeared to assume that being against the existing integration process was necessarily equated with a 'nationalist' stance (Haas, 1968). His analysis considered attitudes towards the existing integration process, not alternative conceptions of the form of integration. Neither did he discuss any distinction existing between a party's strategy and its long-term objectives, in the context of its European policy. In the 1980s at least, however, comparing socialist party policies requires a wider framework of analysis.

258   *Kevin Featherstone*

Conclusions

The foregoing discussion has sought to illuminate possible lines of explanation for the history of socialist party policies towards the European integration process. It has charted the degree of consensus existing in the trends of socialist party support, and has considered alternative interpretations for the type of policies adopted. It found Left/Right differences in relation to support for integration difficult to assess without a basis on which to draw ideological distinctions on a cross-national basis. Explaining policy differences by reference to whether a party was in or out of power prompted a number of cases to be cited relevant to the notion that socialist parties in government are more favourably disposed to the integration process. But such a general explanation could not apply in the same manner in all cases: for example, the frequent participation of Belgian parties in coalition governments and the strong consensual support of the electorate blurred such distinctions. The consideration of how far party policies had been influenced by uniquely national factors rather than by cross-national ideological principles, suggested the conclusion that parties have responded to national circumstances more than to a common socialist imperative. In that sense, the responses of socialist parties have been far more 'national' than 'ideological'.

Fundamental to the policies of socialist parties have been two subjective choices: whether or not the party favours supranational integration or co-operation, and whether or not the party considers that working within the European Community is the best strategy for attaining its objectives. In practice, both questions have become closely inter-connected, blurring both principle and strategy. This has compounded the difficulties facing the analyst as a result of the apparently differing conceptions, existing between the parties, of socialism itself.

The writings of Tom Nairn have suggested the importance of the concepts of class and nation to understanding the policies of different parties (Nairn, 1972). To some degree, they do help to clarify the analysis. Whether or not a British or Belgian socialist holds different views as to the rôle of class and of how socialists ought to protect class interests, it has already been noted above that one is likely to consider the domestic nation-state as being too small to countenance independent action, whilst the other may consider it to be the best strategy for attaining socialist policies. The essential difference is in the perception of the role of the nation-state, not of socialism. It is a difference of view over the national interest and of dependence between nations.

In the past, differences between socialist parties have revolved around the question of EC membership. The European policy debates amongst socialist parties in the future are likely to be concerned with the question of more or less supranational integration and the type of integration, if any, to be pursued. At a time of world recession, it is unlikely that the response of socialist parties will be uniform. Some attempts to establish a European-wide response to the economic crisis are being made by socialists without reference to the framework of the European Community.[9] These moves may open up new forms of European co-operation, if not integration, and may be a more accurate basis on which to judge the validity of referring to a 'European Socialism' than has so far been provided by the differing responses to the European Community. Indeed, by such moves, socialist parties could be responsible for creating a very different future for the European Community from that suggested by its past history.

With continued debate over the financing of EC policies and on their limited success in reducing economic and social inequalities between member-states, the socialist parties of the EC will indeed be forced to consider what sort of Community they want to see in the future. Some are certain to have more ambitious objectives for the EC than are others. If the British Labour Party reconciles itself to membership, it is likely to prefer not to expand the EC's budget or its policy responsibilities, thereby hoping to limit its domestic impact.

Moreover, the French and German Socialists could well settle for a similar course, given the domestic controversies they might face if they were to adopt a more adventurous policy. By contrast, the Benelux and Mediterranean socialists are more likely to want to use the EC as a means of overcoming national constraints in both the economic and social spheres. The issue is a familiar one: the EC has been established as a vehicle, and most European socialists have come to accept their rôle as passengers within it, but the vehicle's destination still remains to be determined. Despite owing their allegiance to a common set of ideological principles, it continues to appear unlikely that European socialists will be able to come to one answer which is held across national boundaries. The search for European unity will continue to be met by a disunited response.

Notes

An earlier version of this chapter was presented to the 1983 PSA Conference, University of Newcastle. It takes account of developments up to mid-1983.

1. See *Report of the Annual Conference of the Labour Party, 1980* (London, 1980).
2. See *Report of the 62nd Annual Conference of the Labour Party* (London, 1962).
3. See *The Labour Way is the Better Way* (London, 1979), election manifesto.
4. *Report of the Annual Conference, 1980:* 126.
5. *Report of the 51st Annual Conference of the Labour Party*, (London, 1952: 113).
6. *Socialism in the '80s: A Socialist Foreign Policy*, (London, 1981: 6).
7. *Report of the Annual Conference, 1980*, 130.
8. *Newsweek*, BBC TV, 21 November 1980. Quoted from transcript.
9. See article by S. Holland, M.P. in *New Socialist*, Nov.–Dec., 1982.

10

Leaders and Followers: Democracy and Manageability in the Social Democratic Parties of Western Europe

David Hine

Who Decides?

THE changing fortunes of social democracy in the last decade—in particular the difficulties faced by social democratic parties in northern Europe, and the new governing role of their Latin counterparts—have not left untouched the internal lives, and especially the distribution of power, in such parties. In facing new issues, coming to terms with new rôles in the political system, and absorbing shifts in the composition of party membership, several parties have experienced significant changes in their cohesiveness and 'manageability', and in the relationship between leaders and followers. This chapter attempts to chart these changes, outline some possible explanations for them, and assess their implications for the future of social democratic parties.

The question 'who decides?' in political parties has, in the past, frequently been a controversial one, especially for those parties nominally committed to a democratic and participatory ethos. From Ostrogorski through Michels to Duverger, the distribution of power and the existence and indeed desirability of intra-party democracy have been widely debated (Ostrogorski, 1902; Michels, 1962; Duverger, 1964). Unfortunately, to measure accurately the distribution of power inside a party, and even more to compare that distribution between parties, is exceedingly difficult, even when the parties in question are similar in type. Formal procedures and informal practices vary greatly, as does the type of decision with which parties are predominantly concerned. There can also be variations in the importance of the very wide range of protagonists involved in party affairs: ordinary party members, committed activists, trade unionists, paid officials, elected members of local councils or national parliaments, cabinet ministers, and ultimately the party leader.

Systematic analysis of the relationships between all these actors across several parties would require resources and treatment beyond the scope available here. It is possible to concentrate only on the most fundamental and generalized relationships—those between professional leaders such as members of parliament, national leaders, and paid party officials, on the one hand, and, on the other, the ordinary unpaid, and mostly locally-based, party members, and activists. Other divisions, between party leaders and trade union leaders, or between rival sets of politicians (for example parliamentarians and paid party officials) are sometimes important, but are less fundamental, and are certainly not common to all social democratic parties of western Europe. Only in Britain, and in less marked form in Norway and Sweden, is there an organic link between social democracy and the trade unions, giving trade unionists an institutionalized role in party life. And while elsewhere there are frequently disputes between party groups in parliament and the party executive outside parliament, these disputes rarely centre on the rival claims of paid party officials and members of parliament, since even in continental Europe the distinction between these rôles has become blurred.

The fundamental relationship considered here is therefore that between leadership and base. This relationship is not, of course, solely a matter of *democracy*, but also one of *manageability*. Few party leaderships which set out simply to respond to the demands of the rank and file would enjoy much success, for on many issues the rank and file has no clear demands to express until the agenda is set by the party leadership or its component parts. In any case, it would be rare for there to be a systematic division of opinion across a wide range of issues separating a cohesive leadership from ordinary party members. Divisions tend to be between groups or factions, each of which exists at various levels in the party, and the composition of these groups may vary from issue to issue.[1] The role of leadership is thus not just to respond, but also to manage. In so doing, party leaders are likely to believe—whether to enhance their own chances of being elected to office, or through a commitment to governability in the world outside the party itself—that they have a responsibility to reflect not just the opinion of the rank and file, but also that of the electorate which, often irrespective of the policies it pursues, has already voted, or is likely to vote, for their party.

The Traditional Context

If there has been a conventional wisdom about the relationship between leadership and base in post-war Europe's social democratic parties, it has fallen, until recently, into two parts. On the one hand, social democracy has been seen as providing more difficult terrain for leadership than other parties. This is because, while leadership battles in centrist or right-wing parties may temporarily be intense, they tend to be fought out within a restricted party élite. Such parties put little stress on the democratic ethos, and have evolved around a consensus that the parliamentary leadership is the focus of decision-taking, and that any extra-parliamentary network should play a secondary and supportive role. In social democratic parties, in contrast, the strong formal commitment to internal democracy has generated an expectation that the rank and file will play a major role in determining party policy, and this has placed parliamentary leaders under different, more complex constraints.

Despite this, the literature is studded with observations on the extent to which the professional party leadership has nearly always been able to come out on top in most party disputes, certainly in relation to what the party does in office, and frequently in relation to statements of official party policy. At least until the late 1960s the British and Dutch Labour Parties, the SPD, and Scandinavian social democratic parties were all seen as *manageable* parties. By and large they were led from the centre-right of the social-democratic spectrum, by a reasonably cohesive parliamentary leadership, which rarely had difficulty from the leftist minorities which each of these parties undeniably harboured. Leaders were almost never overthrown, MPs were rarely repudiated by their local party organization, and policies unacceptable to the party leadership were rarely adopted as party policy.

A major factor in the alleged manageability of the social democratic parties was their close link with the trade-union movement. In Britain, the block vote of the major unions was a source of fairly constant support for the moderate leadership of the Labour Party until the conflicts over trade-union reform and incomes policies in the late 1960s. In Scandinavia, the trade-union movement enjoyed a close and co-operative relationship with the social democratic parties throughout the 1950s and 1960s. In Germany, and even more in the Netherlands, the relationship was a looser one, consisting of overlapping memberships, but here too, the centralized and disciplined nature of the unions and the moderation of their leaders combined to give the parliamentary leadership a solid and dependable basis of support.[2]

A second but more intermittent factor, and in the long run one which rebounded against them, was the governing vocation acquired by most of the north European social democratic parties during the post-war era. This insulated the parliamentary leaders from the rank and file to some extent by giving them a special status—not simply party leaders, but also members of governments and even prime ministers. Such leaders were normally prime electoral assets to their parties, and hence possessed an authority lacking in those who held only party office. Moreover, once in office, the day-to-day decisions of government, with which leaders were henceforth preoccupied, were less susceptible to rank and file control than policy formulation inside the party, and naturally had to be negotiated with a wide range of interests beyond the party.

In the Latin versions of post-war social democracy the position was generally rather different. The professional leadership (largely drawn from the parliamentary ranks) still dominated, but it was often more divided, and partly because of this it was subject to greater control by the party outside parliament. At least until the start of the 1970s, these parties retained a strongly Marxist ideological charge in their rhetoric. They were normally also parties of opposition, or parties which played only a minor role in government coalitions, and they had to operate in complex multi-party systems, alongside powerful communist parties. Their political agendas were thus dominated by questions of alliance strategy and broad political philosophy. These questions were inevitably more controversial and more clear-cut than the incremental issues of policy formulation and implementation with which a party with major governmental responsibilities is normally concerned. At least formally, the actions of the parliamentary leadership were closely bounded by the extra-parliamentary decision-making structure, because questions of alliance strategy or philosophy could more easily be referred to arbitration by the members than could incremental issues. In addition, the constitutions of the Latin parties often laid down some form of direct power structure which, through custom and practice, had based competition for party office around competing groups. These groups normally staked their claims around rather abstract statements of party strategy which dominated debate at, and leading up to, party congresses. If combined with internal proportional representation, this provided a guarantee of factional divisions running from top to bottom of the party (Hine, 1982: 41–7).

Only where central discipline was imposed administratively from above, as under Guy Mollet's leadership of the SFIO, could the inherently divisive nature of Latin social democracy be curbed. Even under Mollet, the SFIO was hardly a model of cohesive solidarity or purposive parliamentary leadership and in 1971, its successor party made a virtue out of necessity and institutionalized factional divisions into party life (Criddle, 1977: 35–41). The same was true, with a brief exception after 1948, of the Italian Socialist Party, where uncertainty of purpose, rivalry over patronage, and lingering ideological divisions, culminated in the bitter factional divisions which racked the party in the 1960s and 1970s (Hine, 1977: 75–7). In Spain, the picture was complicated by the long period the party spent in clandestinity, but from the start of the 1970s, as it emerged into the daylight once more, it too was the scene of a number of confrontations between the 'exiled' leaders and those from the interior, between different generations, between different regional interests, and in two dramatic congresses in 1979, between traditional Marxists and moderate secular modernizers (Nash, 1983: 147). Finally, in Greece, where, before the military dictatorship, orthodox social democracy hardly existed, the first years of PASOK's existence were characterized by fierce infighting which extended from the leadership to a large part of the rank and file, and which eventually culminated in the mass explusion of more than five hundred of the middle- and upper-level party leaders (Lyrintzis, 1983: 147).

Pressures for Change

The distinction between north European and Latin social democracy, always something of an over-simplification, has in recent years been significantly altered by important changes in the domestic political environments of both types of party. Some of these changes have worked, or may eventually work, in the same direction. Others are at least for the present working in contrasting directions. As a result, there are now good grounds for reworking the conventional wisdom about the relationship between leaders and followers in social democratic parties. The present section examines the factors working to alter that relationship; the following one considers their consequences.

(i) *The Policy Agenda*

The first change is linked to changing perceptions of the policy agenda of social democratic parties amongst activists and leaders. It is evident that almost everywhere the way in which that agenda is perceived by activists (which is not necessarily the same thing as the agenda in some 'objective' sense) has been greatly modified in the last decade. The fiscal crisis of the state, combined with the electoral rebellion of social democratic voters facing high marginal rates of taxation, has placed contrasting pressures on social democratic leaders. On the one hand, they face the imperative to restrain public-sector borrowing, or tax rates, or both, coming from national treasuries, private industries, and indirectly from private-sector workers.[3] On the other, they face pressure, coming from their own rank and file activists, to maintain existing standards of public-service provision, if not actively to improve them—pressures which are particularly strong where these activists are themselves in the public sector, and thus have a personal as well as an ideological interest in the issue.

Behind this dilemma, there is the outline of an even more fundamental policy problem: that of whether, in an era of low, or even occasionally negative economic growth, and rising structural unemployment, the market mechanism itself is any longer adequate in modern industrial societies. It would be premature to argue that post-war social democratic ideology has abandoned one of its fundamental tenets—namely that the essentials of free-market capitalism are to be maintained. The solutions which have been advanced which depart from this framework cannot, as yet, be said to have a particularly strong intellectual base to them, and often seem to arise as much from frustration and impatience as from any real theoretical foundation.[4] Nevertheless, in so far as they are genuine attempts to break out of the present policy straight-jacket, these solutions, whether they involve old-fashioned nationalization, large-scale state-investment funds derived from so-called 'excess' profits, or major expansions of redistributive labour-market policies, begin to look as if they are differing in kind as well as in degree from simple Keynesian reflation. As long as labour-shedding productivity growth continues to outstrip new employment generated through output growth, the pressure to resort to these solutions, however alien to social democratic leaders bred on Keynesian demand management, may grow stronger. From the leadership point of view, as the British Labour Party's recent experience suggests, the fact that the rank and file is attracted to such solutions is as significant as the question of their intellectual coherence.

Even assuming, however, as seems most realistic, that social democratic parties do not abandon the market framework, they still face the dilemma that has become increasingly acute in the last ten to fifteen years: that of reconciling full employment, or its modern equivalent, with free or relatively free collective bargaining on the one hand, and with price stability and external equilibrum on the other. In so doing, they confront the problem of persuading trade unions of the need to deliver self-restraint—a problem which, from the end of the 1960s, became increasingly intractable.[5] There may now be a 'new realism' amongst trade unionists in Western Europe, but there is no certainty that it is a permanent one unless demand and output are restrained at artificially low levels for very long periods, and perhaps not even then. The decentralization of union power so widely noted a decade ago may yet return if workers perceive that new growth- or employment-oriented policies are being pursued with less than complete vigour by social democratic governments.

In any case, if the problems of obtaining wage restraint have declined, they are being replaced by those of poor labour mobility. One of Western Europe's major competitive disadvantages, compared to the United States and the East Asian economies, stems from low labour mobility and rigid labour practices. These problems are themselves to an important degree the product of a particular set of 'social democratic' assumptions about social security and welfare provision, and the legal framework of labour protection. Resolving problems of labour mobility, without challenging these assumptions and running into direct conflict with the trade-union movement, is likely to prove one of the most difficult challenges social democratic governments will face in the coming decade.

In addition to these distributive, material issues, there are also challenges to social democracy posed by what may loosely be identified as 'moral' or 'qualitative' questions. The increasing tensions in the Atlantic Alliance between Europe and the United States, the product of a multiplicity of factors (trade, the Reagan administration's evangelistic anti-communism, technological changes in weapons systems, etc.) have slowly undermined the old social democratic confidence in the Atlantic Alliance. In the Federal Republic there has even been talk of a new 'neutralism' in SPD ranks. On these matters, and even more on environmental issues, the parties confront an increasingly difficult task in reconciling the views of their traditional blue-collar voters and members with those of newer recruits to social democracy, in particular the so-called 'post-materialist' generation. Quite how serious these tensions will become is unclear, but on such issues the traditional class-based ideological patrimony of social democracy provides even less of a guide to the 'correct' policy solution than it does for policies to promote growth or employment.[6]

Clearly, such policy dilemmas are present throughout western Europe, but they have provided far more acute problems for those parties which spent long periods in office in the 1960s and 1970s, than for parties which, like those in France, Spain, or Greece, have arrived in office only recently. The very fact of having occupied power during an era when tensions were accumulating—especially in the fields of economic policy and the distribution of public expenditure—concentrated attention on the policy dilemmas thus presented, and the inadequacies of the parties in coming to terms with them. The sense of 'failure' in office, and the demands for change—both in policies and leadership—which experience of office generates, are likely to be far more intense in those parties where there exists only a vague and easily-ignored discomfort about the difficulties which might be faced in office.

The contrast between northern and Latin social democracy is striking. Greece, Spain, Portugal, and even France, were, in the latter half of the 1970s, societies which had experienced a long period of highly conservative rule; their social democratic parties had borne no responsibility for the administration of the economic crisis. In three cases where the mid-1970s saw a return to democracy, moreover, the social democratic parties had the added advantage of young and attractive leaders, and of operating in fluid social conditions where party allegiances were only loosely formed, and where new alliances could be forged. The demand for 'change'—political liberalization, wider social justice, greater openness and honesty in government—was thus arguably more generic and imprecise, and less subject to widespread differentiation, than in countries further north, where such demands were more precisely articulated, and could have contradictory implications for voting behaviour. Against a background of declining religious barriers to leftist progress, the possibility of building an eclectic social alliance gave Mitterrand, González, and Papandreou victories hitherto denied to the Left in their societies, at the very moment when the Left was in decline in those parts of Europe where it had hitherto been strongest.[7]

The one exception to this trend in Latin Europe is the Italian Socialist Party, but it is the exception which proves the rule. The PSI had for so long in the 1960s and 1970s been on the fringes of government, forming a small but essential part of the centre-left coalition, that it had little prospect of emulating the successes of its sister parties. Its public image was so compromised by its long alliance with the Christian Democrats, and by a series of unfortunate scandals, that it could not hope to be the focus of demands for political liberalization, reform, or wider social justice. In 1976 there was a once-for-all shift to the left, but the beneficiary was the Communist Party not the Socialists.[8]

(ii) *The Composition of Party Membership*

Changing perceptions of the policy agenda may be the most obvious factor influencing party cohesion, but it is not necessarily the most significant. Of the others, probably the most important have been the changes in the sociological and sectoral composition of party members, and in the attitude of those members to leadership, party discipline, and participation in decision-making. Middle-class party members generally have skills and resources enabling them to participate more fully in internal party life than do working-class members, and they may also obtain different rewards from party membership. Its meaning for them is perhaps less likely to be limited to the mere acts of joining, dues paying, and carrying out simple tasks at election time. They may obtain substantial psychological rewards from participating in party decision-taking and affirming publicly their commitment to a particular set of values. If so, to the extent that this satisfaction is independent of that obtained from their party's electoral success, they are likely to prove more troublesome to the party leadership.

It is, of course, difficult to prove conclusively that the middle-class contains a greater proportion of members who join for ideological or expressive reasons than does the working class, or that the latter form a manageable, dependable group, joining for solidaristic reasons alone. Nor, if this is so, is there conclusive longitudinal evidence that the composition of social democratic party memberships has changed substantially over the post-war period. However, there are reasons—rooted in the changing nature of the middle class itself—for thinking that this may have been occurring. One such change has been the relative decline of the entrepreneurial and service-sector independents and the growth of a white-collar, clerical/technical/managerial, and frequently unionized group of workers.[9] Much of the latter group has developed in the public sector, and assumes a particular importance in this context because of the increasing prominence as a political issue of the size of the public sector, and the proportion of GNP which it absorbs. Recently there has been much academic discussion of the electoral consequences of a sectoral cleavage between public and private realms of the economy, transcending traditional social cleavages; it is suggested that this cleavage stems from the growth of a state-dependent sector of welfare beneficiaries and employees, and, at least in Britain, from the increasing visibility of industrial action by public-sector workers (Dunleavy, 1980). It is unlikely that such developments provide the key to an understanding of class dealignment, in so far as it has occurred, in the broader world of European *electorates*, but in the more rarified and restricted world of party *memberships*, their influence may well have been very much greater. Social democratic parties are uniquely seen by their adherents as the defenders of public-sector employees and welfare-beneficiaries, and as the debate over the size of the public sector proceeds, social democracy might be expected to draw a greater part of its members from public-sector dependents than in the past. This in turn may increase the pressure to defend, or even expand, the public sector at the very time when, for broader electoral reasons, or as a result of the constraints of economic policy, the party leadership might not wish to do so.

Moreover, with the rising number of white-collar and professional groups in the public sector—teachers, social workers, local and central government officials, etc.—social democratic parties may contain a more educated, articulate and also a more ideologically-oriented membership than in the past. If so, then it is equally likely that these groups will, because of their educational advantages, play a more prominent role in the grass-roots activities of the party, and ultimately in the decision-making bodies higher up, than their absolute numbers would suggest. It is certainly not necessary for all, or even a majority of those in the white-collar and professional groups in the public sector to share the same political outlook. In most social democratic parties, even those with a nominally large membership, the level of participation is fairly low, and the number of activists who actually run the party organization at grass-roots level is very small; a few thousand such activists might be enough to substantially affect relationships between par-liamentary leadership and the rank and file.

In the northern half of Europe, and especially in Britain and West Germany, there is at least some evidence that these types of changes in the composition of social democratic party membership have been occurring. In recent years, evidence has emerged that grass-roots activists in the British Labour Party have become increasingly middle-class in nature, and that they have been increasingly drawn from the public sector. A recent study of Sheffield City Labour Party found not only a high proportion (62 per cent) of middle class members, but also that this group was largely from the public sector. The study also concluded, contrary to the argument put forward by Forrester to the effect that Labour has always had a sizeable middle-class membership, that in Sheffield at least the phenomenon was a recent one (Chandler, Morris and Baker, 1982). Similarly, a survey of London Labour councillors, although not distinguishing clearly between classes, showed a very high level of public-sector extraction. In 1982, 55 per cent of Labour councillors with identifiable jobs in Lewisham were teachers, local government officials, or were employed by other organizations dependent on public funds. In Camden the figure was 48 per cent (*The Times*,

1982; Webster, 1981). Whiteley's survey of Constituency Labour Party Conference delegates found that 70 per cent were in white-collar occupations, with a high proportion of 'caring' professionals, and that 60 per cent were employed in the public sector (Whiteley, 1981). Using the same data in a more extensive study of party membership, Whiteley examined the relationship between social class and the motivation both to join, and to leave, the Labour Party. He concluded that there was evidence that middle-class members joined in greater numbers than working-class members for 'expressive' (i.e. ideological) motives, and conversely that working-class members joined in greater numbers for 'instrumental' (i.e. class-solidarity) motives. He also suggested that in so far as the Labour Party in power failed to satisfy those instrumental aspirations, it led to a decline in working-class political activism, thus helping to make grass-roots activists 'increasingly more middle-class, more ideological in their approach to politics, and less concerned with pragmatic instrumental questions' (Whiteley, 1983: 42–3). It should be added that when the apparently 'expressive' middle-class is in the public sector, its real motivation for Labour Party membership may in fact be instrumental (i.e. *public-sector*, as opposed to *class* solidarity) but this is not incompatible with the possibility that working-class activists in the private sector have a greater propensity to leave the party then *either* white- *or* blue-collar activists in the public sector.

In Germany, the middle-class nature of party membership in the SPD has also increased over the post-war period. From the essentially working-class party of the Weimar era (60 per cent of members were working-class in 1930, and indeed 45 per cent were working-class in 1952) the proportion declined to just under 30 per cent in the 1970s. By 1980, members from white-collar, civil-service, professional, and student categories outnumbered the working class by 45 per cent to 30 per cent (the remainder were mostly from 'inactive' categories such as housewives or pensioners). A majority of the membership retains working-class family *origins*, but the current occupations of SPD members betray a substantial shift in the direction of the middle-class (Braunthal, 1983). In line with this change, and with the expansion of opportunities for higher education, the entry of large numbers of young members since 1969 has greatly enhanced the educational qualifications of party members. Those who had received some form of higher education rose from 23 per cent to 37 per cent between 1968 and 1977, and in terms of both education and income, the SPD membership ranks well above both the SPD electorate and the electorate as a whole (Braunthal, 1983: 46–7). Evidence suggests that in terms of self-identification on the Left–Right scale, SPD members see themselves as substantially further to the Left than does the SPD electorate, and it is significant that there is a clear link between Leftist attitudes and both age and education (younger and better educated members are both progressively further to the Left). Shifts of this type have clearly given rise to important cleavages within the party between the value-systems of different sub-groups of members: between younger and older members, between radicals and moderates, and between 'participatory' and 'hierarchical' attitudes to party life (Braunthal, 1983: 47–50).

How important the role of the public-sector group may be in these tensions is uncertain. Some have suggested that the clear over-representation of public officials, especially among activists and public office holders, increases the potential for opposition to the parliamentary leadership (Johnson 1982: 160–3). Others have suggested not only that public officials in Germany may have a hostility to party democracy, but also that the patronage motivation for their membership, and the imperative from a career point of view that their party stays in office, may lead such members to support a moderate (and thus electorally popular) policy stance (Paterson, 1981). Whether officials really do make this association, or whether they may in fact be unaware of, or indeed ignore, the contradiction (if there is one) between their party's policy position and their personal career prospects, is a matter for conjecture. The likely answer is that those at the highest levels tend to make the association, while those at more modest levels are less prone to do so.

The evidence of shifts in the social composition of other social democratic parties of northern Europe is unfortunately more impressionistic. The Dutch Labour Party, however, seems to have experienced developments very similar to those described above. The substantial changes which occurred in the party after 1966 led to the influx of a large group of new members. By 1978, 40 per cent of the membership had joined within the previous five years and more than two-thirds had joined since 1966 (Wolinetz, 1983: 135–8). Wolinetz's study of the New Left group which engineered this change underlines the common culture of a highly educated, service-sector group, and research on both party activists (as represented by congress delegates) and party members, suggests a group very different from the PvdA electorate as a whole (see also Wolinetz, 1977). At the 1978 congress, nine out of every ten delegates were of middle or upper-middle class extraction, and nearly half (47 per cent) worked in the public sector, compared with only 27 per cent in the private sector (the remainder coming from 'non-active' groups). 58 per cent of delegates had some form of higher education or professional training, compared with 30 per cent of ordinary party members, and only 10 per cent of (1977) PvdA voters (Middel and van Schuur, 1981).

The social composition of the membership of the Latin social democratic parties has of course always been very different from that of north European social democracy. In both France and Italy the natural working-class and trade-union base has to a large extent been captured by the communist parties, and for much of the post-war period the membership has been a composite mixture in which the blue-collar sector has represented a minority of the membership. Moreover, while through involvement in clientele politics at national and local levels both parties have for long had a substantial public-sector base to party membership, it is rather different in both type and significance from that which seems to have emerged more recently in the social democratic parties considered above. In both the SFIO/PS, and the PSI, however, there is evidence of a long-term decline in the working-class element of party membership (the limit case of the Paris federation—70 working-class recruits out of a total membership of 4,700 in 1974—is well known) (Hardouin, 1978: 243). At the level of party activists the middle-class domination is striking, with research showing that no less that 60 per cent of delegates to the PS's 1981 congress were graduates, and that in terms of income and education delegates to that congress ranked higher than those to the congresses of either the Gaullist Party or the UDF (Niedermayer and Schmitt, 1983; Cayrol and Jaffre, 1980). Nevertheless, the divided nature of the Left in France and Italy, and the roles the socialist parties have played, have ensured that party membership has always been of a rather different type from that in social democratic parties further north, with a more dominant position in the party system and a closer link with the union world.

The same applies, albeit for slightly different reasons, to the Spanish socialists. The longer period of clandestinity gave the PSOE peculiar characteristics and an extremely restricted social base. Membership only reached the 100,000 mark at the end of the 1970s, and stood in 1984 at around 150,000. In terms of the characteristics discussed above, it has a mixed profile. It has a larger blue-collar group within its membership than that in parties for which comparative data is available, and the average age, at 48, seems strikingly high, as the party officially acknowledges. In contrast, the activists rather than the ordinary members, are, to judge from the the characteristics of congress delegates, younger, and largely white-collar and professional (63 per cent came from these categories at the 1979 extraordinary congress).[10] However, until recently, the public sector hardly seems to have been represented at all in the PSOE membership, as indeed might be expected given that, until the 1979 local elections, the party had no power of political appointment at any level, and the overwhelming majority of those in the public sector were the appointees of an authoritarian regime. The PSOE's role in government, at local and, after 1982, national level may now be changing that situation, of course, as may the many new administrative jobs created by the recent devolution measures.

The Consequences: Changing Patterns of Party Democracy

It is not the thesis of this chapter that differences between the two types of social democratic party outlined at the outset have disappeared altogether, still less that it is now Latin social democracy which is characterized by united and purposive leadership, and north European social democracy which is being torn apart by grass-roots pressures and ideological factionalism. The factors discussed in the previous section—the changing policy agenda, the changing composition and outlook of party activists, and the influence of the public-sector lobby—are probably at work to some degree in most social democratic parties. The crucial point is that parties which have been in power for long periods during the post-war era, and which, with the current exception of the Swedish Social Democrats, seem to have been facing a declining trend of electoral support, and are now out of office, are more likely to develop internal tensions between the party leadership and the rank and file than are parties which were for a long time excluded from office, and which only in the last two to three years have come to power. This can be seen by considering some of the main changes in party life which have occurred in the parties under discussion.

(i) *Northern Europe*

Least probably needs to be said of the British Labour Party. The shift to the left in the party in the last decade, and the attempts to devolve power to the party's extra-parliamentary decision-making centres, are well-documented.[11] The two processes are of course closely linked. The various elements which compose the Labour Left gradually evolved a conscious strategy to undermine the long-standing dominance of the Parliamentary Labour Party (PLP) by ending its traditional insulation from the remainder of the party. But the strategy was more than a cynical attempt to manipulate party rules to favour the candidacies and policies of a particular group within the party. The changes in attitude to leadership and authority in the Labour Party in the last decade have been too far-reaching to be easily reversed if and when the 'Left' comes to dominate the PLP—not least because the 'Left' itself is anything but a homogenous group.

Moreover, the change in formal procedure—mandatory reselection of MPs before each election, and the selection of the party leader by an elected college of the 'whole party' rather than simply the parliamentary party—are possibly less important than the changes in climate produced by the campaign for their implementation. It was always possible, if difficult, for Constituency Labour Parties (CLPs) to get rid of their sitting MPs at a fresh election, but by drawing attention to the issue, and focusing the attention of grass-roots activists on the process of candidate selection, an atmosphere has been created the primary effect of which is to force sitting MPs to take far more account of their constituency party's sensibilities. The eventuality that the sanction of deselection will actually be used is probably of only secondary importance. To date, in fact, the number of 'deselections' has been limited (see A. Young, 1983). If there has been a shift to the left in the composition of Labour's prospective parliamentary candidates, it has come more from selection contests following the retirement or death of sitting MPs. Indeed, the shift to the left had already begun significantly before the debate over reselection reached its height. As Berrington has shown, there was a slow drift to the left in the PLP throughout the 1970s, a factor which generated the election of a 'centrist' if not 'left-of-centre' leader of the party even before the new electoral-college procedure was adopted (Berrington, 1982).

Naturally, the changes described above could not have occurred, in a party with over five million members affiliated to the Party through the trade-union movement, and a conference procedure dominated by the union 'block vote', without changes at union level as well. Until the late 1960s, the unions displayed an almost completely consistent record of support for the party leadership— the one great exception being at the 1960 Conference. Thereafter, in parallel with the politicization of industrial relations and incomes policies, and with somewhat arbitrary shifts in the political positions of the leaders of the largest unions, the position has become at best less predictable, and at worst, as in the head-on conflict between the parliamentary leadership and the Conference over wage restraint at the 1978 Party Conference, completely destructive of the authority of that leadership. In this process the growing importance of white-collar and public-sector unions within the Labour movement as a whole has probably played a significant role.[12]

Not unexpectedly, then, and quite independently of the qualities of the three individuals who have led the party over the last decade, the Labour Party has become a far more difficult party than previously to lead and to manage. Factional divisions have become more clear-cut, and the number of identifiable groups has increased substantially as the right has been forced to organize in response to the challenge of the left. The decay of the grass roots organization has exacerbated this problem, as CLPs can easily be infiltrated and taken over by particular groups. In short, a major shift has occurred in the balance of power inside the party, not just between left and right, but between leadership and base.

Very similar events took place in the Dutch Labour Party in the late 1960s and early 1970s. During these years the consensual basis of the political system was profoundly modified as the solidly corporatist and hierarchical ties of Dutch society were loosened. The PvdA, formerly a moderate, disciplined example of post-war social democracy, underwent a major transformation under the challenge of the so-called 'New Left'. This group, unlike its ephemeral predecessors, proved hard to neutralize by the bureaucratic measures previously used by the parliamentary leadership. On the contrary, its rejection of centralized control, and of the PvdA's compromising predisposition in coalition politics, found ready sympathy at grass-roots level. The group called for a more open, decentralized, and democratic party in which representatives in parliament, and central and local government would be closely supervised by local party activists. It also sought changes in the process of candidate selection, and limitations on the power of the party leadership to compromise on declared programmatic intentions. Within the space of three years, New Left scored a remarkable success. It infiltrated the party from the grass roots upwards, meeting only limited opposition. By 1971 it had a majority on the party executive, and nearly one quarter of the parliamentary group of the PvdA was drawn from its ranks. At local level, party officials, municipal councillors, and mayors were increasingly replaced by younger New Left activists.[13] Accompanying the change came a substantial revision of party policy both domestically and internationally. The PvdA henceforth adopted a shrill anti-Americanism in stark contrast to its pro-NATO anti-Communism of the 1950s, and supported almost every radical cause in the Third World; the culmination of this process has been the lead taken by the PvdA in rallying social democratic parties against the siting of the new generation of intermediate-range nuclear weapons in Western Europe—a role which has had a paralysing effect on internal Dutch politics.

As a result of these changes, PvdA leaders have in recent years found their hands severely tied in negotiations with potential coalition allies. Compromises can no longer be imposed on the party rank and file, and it is no coincidence that even when the party has done relatively well in elections, it has been unable to use this strength to maintain the regular place it occupied in government before 1966. This is so even though the New Left as an organized group has disappeared, and many of its leading figures have been incorporated into the party's parliamentary leadership. For that leadership's relationship with the rank and file has profoundly changed. New regulations concerning the number of par-liamentarians in the party executive have ensured that it no longer dominates the parliamentary leadership; indeed, disputes between the two are frequent. The procedure for nominating parliamentary candidates has been devolved to regional level, and local government councillors are subject to recall by their local party organizations. Finally, changes in the formal rules of, and the attitudes of rank and file members to the party congress and the party council have increased the importance of both these bodies (Wolinetz, 1983: 134–5). As one commentator has recently observed:

Internal democracy has reduced the control of the leadership and made relationships inside the party more fluid than before. Although the leadership continues to lead the party, it must do so by facing up to, persuading (and occasionally threatening) the party congress and the council. The process is far more public than in the past. The character of the party leadership has also changed. (Wolinetz, 1983: 135.)

The situation of the SPD presents a rather less drastic variant on the same theme. Since the late-1960s the SPD has experienced two distinct waves of leftist radicalism seeking to challenge the post-Godesberg orthodoxy. The first came in the period from 1969 to 1974, the second has emerged since the 1980 general election. In neither period has the challenge made a significant impact on the policy of the parliamentary leadership in office and the radicals who have presented the challenge have remained until now in a containable minority. Nevertheless, the left in the SPD has, since the late-1960s, been far stronger at rank-and-file level than at the top levels of the party, and in this sense the party's internal conflict has made leadership a more difficult art even in the SPD.

As in the British and Dutch cases, the terms of the conflict have frequently been linked to organizational issues, and to the debate over the role and responsibility of elected SPD leaders in party and public office. In the early-1970s, the Young Socialists united around the banner of the 'imperative mandate', the doctrine that 'delegates to any of the higher party bodies and to parliament would be controlled by those who elected them. If they wanted to diverge from a position . . . they had to get a new mandate from "the basis"' (Paterson, 1977: 188). The weakness of this in a party with a long tradition of centralized bureaucratic control was that it was simply too drastic and wide-ranging to conjure up sympathy. The issues on which the CLPD alighted in Britain (which envisaged changes long-accepted as normal in most European social democratic parties, including the SPD) were extremely difficult to refute by most standards of democracy. In contrast, the imperative mandate served largely to discredit the cause of intra-party democracy in whose name it was raised—not least because of the difficulty of implementing it in a political system where coalitions are the norm. It was further discredited by the evident millenarianism of the so-called 'dual strategy': the idea that socialists could work within the SPD, and at the same time work alongside leftists of other persuasions in a variety of rank-and-file protest movements and citizens' action groups whose purposes were frequently at odds with the SPD in power (Paterson, 1977: 188). However attractive this 'broad left' strategy might be to the *Jusos*, it was unlikely to find favour in a society where the obsessive fear of extremism led even the social democratic party to support the *Berufsverbot*.

Eventually, the pressures which arose in the early-1970s were unsuccessful. Although the SPD is a 'direct' party, with no union block vote to protect the leadership once the grass-roots organizations have fallen to the left, the left itself was not able to capture either the conference and party executive or the grass roots. The organizational framework and bureaucratic apparatus of the SPD were sufficiently vigorous and sufficiently alienated from the activities of the *Jusos* to provide a loyal majority behind the parliamentary leadership. Even if it had captured the party organization, the left would still, in the short term at least, have faced the problem of how to force its policies on the leadership. Brandt and Schmidt proclaimed their responsibilities to the wider audience of coalition and electorate, and both made short shrift of the 'imperative mandate'. The threat posed by the radical left was defused, and if anything the relationship between leaders and rank and file under the Schmidt chancellorship tilted in favour of the former.

Nevertheless, the spectre of radicalism never entirely disappeared, and as events since 1980 have shown, it has returned in even more virulent form to haunt the party leadership. An emotive combination of environmental and defence issues provided the spark which rekindled the SPD left, and as the recession deepened the leadership found it ever more difficult to reconcile the demands of its coalition partners with the aspirations of the rank and file. The confidence of the left grew as the 1969 generation, incorporated into the party apparatus, rose to inherit control in several parts of the country, including Hamburg, Berlin, the Saarland, and Bavaria (Braunthal, 1983: 72–7; Braunthal, 1984). Meanwhile the need to respond to the new challenge of the Greens forced the party leadership into a reappraisal of its position in a wide range of policy areas. The results have been far-reaching: the collapse of the coalition, the departure of Schmidt, and the party's unequivocal rejection of INF deployment in the Federal Republic at the 1983 Special Conference. Beyond this, against a background of a new and brittle relationship between Europe and the United States, potentially awkward questions loom on the horizon concerning issues long-since buried in party history: the relationship with the East, and the Federal Republic's integration in the western alliance. Shorn of the benefits of the so-called 'Chancellor effect', it looks improbable that Rau will be able to deal with these challenges with the ease and authority of his two predecessors.

A partial exception to the trend of declining cohesion and manageability in north European social democracy is Scandinavia, and especially Sweden. Social democracy in Norway and Denmark has in fact experienced similar, if less marked, problems to those in Britain, the Netherlands, and Germany—declining electoral support and major challenges from the Left, most notably on defence. These challenges have forced the parties into more radical policy stances, but in neither country has control slipped away from the parliamentary leadership in a decisive sense, and in Sweden cohesion and centralized control remain impressive.

A part of the explanation in Sweden's case is doubtless rooted in the legendary discipline of the labour movement as a whole—no social democratic party in Europe wins a higher proportion of either the total vote or the working-class vote: as various writers have remarked, the social democratic cultural consensus is probably more strongly entrenched in Sweden than anywhere else on the continent. (Scase, 1977a and 1977b; Castles, 1975). However, several other factors have also played a part in the relative absence of tensions between leadership and base. One of these is the high absolute level of affluence and the absence, until very recently, of major distributive conflicts over public spending, transfers, and employment levels. A second factor is the intimate relationship between the trade unions and the party; in return for a highly progressive labour-market policy, the unions are willing and almost always able to deliver wage restraint (see Chapter 2). A third element is the absence until 1985 of contentious issues of nuclear defence. Thanks to Sweden's neutral status, Palme can lead from the left rather than the right on international questions, unlike many of his social democrat colleagues in other countries. Finally, there is an organizational feature: the infrequency of SAP conferences. They occur only once every three (formerly four) years, preceding general elections. Quite apart from the infrequency of opportunities to challenge policy or manifest dissent, there is clearly great pressure on potential dissidents to come to heel, given the proximity of elections and the need to project an image of party unity. In any case, the policy-making process in Sweden is a complex one, and few social democrats believe, despite the increasing importance of congresses in recent years, that policy can be made by glib congress motions rather than by the long process of inter-party, interest group, and parliamentary consultation customary in Sweden.

It should also be remembered that on many scores the SAP leadership has spent a great part of the last fifteen years anticipating and defusing rank-and-file dissatisfaction by a process of policy revision which by most standards has been extremely wide-ranging. This process culminated in the commitment to what the party in its 1975 programme called 'the democratization of economic life', the most important element of which is the so-called Meidner Plan for the creation of employee investment funds (Meidner, 1978. See also Chapter 7). It is impossible to demonstrate with certainty that these policy departures have contributed to the SAP's relative manageability over the last decade, and indeed the employee investment funds issue has caused some considerable internal dissension. However, resistance has come more from the party's economic advisers than from parliamentary leaders, and there have been few strains between the latter and the party's rank and file. It should be added, of course, that the SAP enjoyed the luxury—if such it be—of exclusion from power between 1976 and 1982, and this enabled it to make a series of radical statements on labour-market policy and public expenditure, as well as on the investment funds issue, which doubtless kept its followers content.[14] In office once more, party unity is facing a sterner test as party leaders begin to doubt the wisdom of the party's policy commitments; the announcement early in 1984 that the massive funds allocated by successive Swedish governments to support ailing industry are to be cut by over two-thirds is symptomatic of this, and suggests a rather tougher future for party leaders.

(ii) *Southern Europe*

What is most striking about southern Europe in recent years is the importance of personal leadership in the social democratic parties, and the absence of challenge to the authority of incumbent leaders. Mitterrand, Gonzáles, Papandreou, and even Craxi, have succeeded in imposing a stamp of personal authority on their parties which has made them indispensable electoral assets. The prospect, and subsequently the reality, of the governing role has in turn endorsed that authority, and has submerged the former, sterile debates about strategy and ideological purity beneath more concrete policy questions. The prospect of power has also greatly increased the incentive to unite behind a single leader, and as a result has reduced the tendency for rival leaders to form factions vying with one another for the support of the membership. Since authority in a party is often closely linked to personal electoral popularity, there may well be a limit to this cohesion, set by the length of time each party can maintain its electoral popularity. Certainly, given the restrictive economic policies pursued by Mitterrand and González from 1982 and 1983 respectively, it is to be expected that rank-and-file tolerance of these leaders will eventually wear thin, but as yet it cannot be said that this has occurred.

Thus in France, where in any case personal leadership is institutionalized in competition for the presidency, Mitterrand's personal position in the party was only really in doubt during the period 1978–80, when there was a question mark over not just the common-programme alliance, but also his own intentions of running again for the presidency. His standing, at and for a short while after the Metz Congress of 1979, was temporarily eroded by the challenge from Rocard and by the need to rely on the left-inclined CERES group to maintain control of the party. But having dealt with that challenge, he (or, at least formally, his lieutenant, Jospin—once he had become President) enjoyed two further congresses (Valence and Bourg-et-Bresse) at which real opposition dwindled to an insignificant level.[15] Rocard remains as at least a potential heir to the leadership, but as long as Mitterrand is President (and if he serves his full term to 1988 he will have been effective leader of the party for seventeen years) Rocard and other claimants are likely to feel it prudent to maintain a low profile in party affairs. Given that the Mitterrand entourage is a fairly heterogenous one, united mainly by loyalty to Mitterrand himself, it may be that his eventual departure will return power at least briefly to the rank and file, who will become the arbiter of party life for the duration of the struggle for the succession. Should that successor fail to win the presidency, his position will doubtless be more fragile than that of Mitterrand, but for the immediate future the President's men remain firmly in control of the party machine, and the President himself retains a position of solid authority over his own party.[16]

González' fortunes in the PSOE, especially his remarkable and comprehensive defeat of the party's left wing, reveal a very similar story. Elected secretary in 1974, and confirmed in 1976 at the first post-Franco congress, he was determined to build on the partial electoral successes of 1977 and 1979 by shedding the party's Marxist inheritance, and creating a new moderate image to reassure voters and the Spanish military. This design naturally ran up against resistance from the orthodox Marxists at grass-roots level, but in defeating the symbolic proposal to remove the word 'Marxist' from the party constitution at the 1979 congress, González' detractors had not calculated that this rejection would provoke his resignation. Indeed, the prospect that the party would lose its prime electoral asset led to a rapid reappraisal within the party, and showed how far González had established a personal ascendancy over the PSOE. At the extraordinary congress of 1979 he was returned to the leadership in triumph, and since that time his hold on the leadership has become firmer (see Tezanos, 1983; Nash, 1983; Pollack, 1983). At the 1981 Congress, he was re-elected secretary unanimously, the so-called '*sector critico*' of Castellano and Gómez Llorente being reduced to a tiny fringe minority. Indeed the victory was so complete that press critics dubbed it the 'Moscow Congress', and to meet such criticism the leadership felt constrained to introduce special rules to guarantee the opposition a presence on the party's decision-making bodies. The apotheosis of González' personal charisma came, of course, in late 1982, with the party's overwhelming electoral success, and demonstrated that he had established for himself a position comparable in every way to that of Mitterrand.

However, in many ways the most remarkable case of personal ascendancy is that of Papandreou in Greece. Although PASOK, the party he founded in 1974, was not the direct heir of a particular social democratic party of pre-1967 Greek politics, it nevertheless acquired, on paper, a structure very similar to that of continental social democracy. The party was to be built upon a 'direct' organization, with authority resting in a national congress, and a central committee and president both elected from it. The parliamentary party was to be responsible to the president's executive office, and in reality it has proved to be decidedly subordinate to it. Only a small minority of the members of the central committee are drawn from parliamentary ranks, and the executive has found no difficulty, where it chooses, in preventing members of parliament from presenting themselves for re-election; the clientele power base which traditionally gave Greek MPs a substantial independence from their party organization has in fact played little part in PASOK (Lyrintzis, 1984). Nevertheless, the control exercised by the party organization has been almost exclusively bureaucratic and personal, rather than democratic, and the most eloquent testimony to this is the fact that the Party Congress met for the first time only in 1984, no less than a decade after the party was first formed. Until the 1984 Congress, the only legitimation of the power exercised by the party executive had been the 1977 Panhellenic Conference, which elected the central committee and the executive office. Of these two bodies the latter, closely controlled by Papandreou, kept a tight rein on party affairs, while the former met only infrequently, and did little more than ratify decisions taken further up the hierarchy. It is therefore no exaggeration to suggest that, after the conflicts of the first three years of PASOK's existence, the rank and file played a minor role in party decision-taking (Lyrintzis, 1983: 147–8). Certainly, the personal ascendancy exercised by Papandreou over the membership was reaffirmed at the 1983 Congress, and despite the wider economic difficulties faced by his government, he was able to maintain his authority over the party at a fairly minimal price in terms of lip-service to radical ideals, and to maintain a decidedly moderate course in both the domestic and international policies of his government.

Conclusion

The issues discussed in this chapter are closely related to those which arise in wider debates about the nature of party government, and about the alleged problems of 'governability' in advanced industrial societies.[17] These debates have admittely not always been very conclusive, and it has yet to be demonstrated clearly that there ever was a golden age of party government from which Europe has declined. Party government, and indeed 'governability' might, under analysis based upon sufficient breadth of historical vision, prove to be subject to something like cyclical variation. Nevertheless, whether Europe is moving towards a 'post-party era', or whether it is simply passing through a phase of readjustment, in the role of, and support bases for, political parties, the variables which underlie these changes are very similar to those considered earlier in this chapter. In this sense, the problem of social democratic leadership is a part, albeit an important part, of wider changes taking place in the role of parties in European society. Private organized interests, including those in the 'public' sector, are becoming more effectively organized, more numerous, and more influenced by instrumental considerations about limited aspects of government policy specifically touching themselves. The classes or other groups around which parties are formed are becoming more internally diversified. In this neo-corporatist environment, as a consequence of such changes parties may become less obviously relevant to the building of government programmes and to the linking of society and state. Under the impact of such changes, where new forms of political behaviour challenge the predominance of parties, the concept of party government may need to be modified, and associated more with the filling of public offices, with management and response, than with programmatic leadership. If these developments are occurring, even on a temporary basis, it is not surprising that social democratic parties, more than most types of party, are influenced by them. They are expressly programmatic, and rely traditionally on the solidarity of a particular social class.

It would be tempting to conclude that, Sweden excepted, the Mediterranean version of social democracy has adapted better to these problems than the traditionally more successful north European parties. Indeed, it has even been suggested recently that in Mediterranean Europe the social democratic parties have led a trend towards something akin to 'plebiscitary democracy', characterized by a decisive concentration of power in a single role (prime minister or president) and by a direct link between the 'masses' and personal leadership—a link based upon the almost 'charismatic' qualities of the individual involved (Cavalli, 1984). This is partly explained in terms of the 'newness' of these parties; even if, PASOK excepted, they have historical roots in the social democratic tradition, they have been substantially regenerated. They are alleged to have new followers and activists, derived from newly-emerging classes or social groupings, and hence, unlike their counterparts in northern Europe, are not the prisoners of past commitments and present realities. As a result, they can take advantage of the increasing fluidity of contemporary European society (declining class and religious solidarity) and of new means of communication which transcend the old face-to-face relationships of the labour movement and party organization. In so doing, epecially through their highly personalized style, men like Mitterrand, González, and Papandreou can establish a direct and quasi-charismatic link with public opinion, giving them unassailable resources of leadership against potential detractors at the base of their parties.[18]

The information assembled above on recent developments in these parties provides support for such an interpretation, and it is one of the main purposes of this chapter to elucidate the difference between northern and southern Europe as it has developed in recent years. But it would probably be wrong to conclude that what has happened in southern Europe is a permanent phenomenon. It is unlikely to be, because plebiscitary democracy, if such a thing exists, may prove extremely brittle in the face of perceived policy shortcomings and failures over extended periods in office. It is of course possible that González or Papandreou might eventually achieve the same sort of leadership status in public opinion as Adenauer or de Gaulle achieved, stimulating a realignment in which the moderate left became the 'natural' majority in Spain and Greece. But given the economic and social conditions under which they have to operate, such a permanent realignment of electoral attitudes looks improbable. The ability of the moderate left to come to power in these countries depended on conditions of social and electoral fluidity which made it possible to construct broadly-based, but rather imprecise, coalitions for change and reform. Whether these coalitions can face the test of a structural environment of more articulated corporatism in which social demands are more precisely formed and differentiated, is unclear.

Mediterranean social democratic parties have benefited from a combination of a long period out of office, followed by a period of social fluidity in which they have succeeded in projecting their leaders as the embodiment of change and reform. This fortuitous situation has enabled their leaders to control their respective parties; without it, their control, or that of their successors, may look a great deal more tenuous. Indeed, they are likely to face the same combination of circumstances which seem to have made leadership so much more difficult an art in social democratic parties in northern Europe: a more diverse and demanding participatory membership base, albeit a numerically more limited one; a set of policy problems not easily satisfied by broadly redistributive welfare measures—indeed frequently quite unrelated to such measures: and a society in which highly organized and mobilized interests greatly limit party choices in office.

The industrial societies of the 1980s are very different from those of 25 years ago. Both social deference and educational inequalities have declined, political legitimacy has at times been called into question, and direct action has become widespread. In the face of such changes, it would indeed be surprising if the authority structure inside parties—especially social democratic parties—remained unaltered. Discipline has frequently given way to dispute and dissent, and the tasks of leadership—uniting the party, winning elections, and, having done so, implementing a programme—have become more complex.

All this is not necessarily to imply that large democratic, programmatic mass party organizations are unwieldly instruments for governing the open industrial societies that have emerged in Europe in the last 25 years. As instruments for the generation of those societies, they were highly effective; as instruments for management they look less so, but this is not to imply that there are necessarily any better instruments available. What is clear is that electorates, and party members and activists, will have to adapt their ideas of what these parties can do. And in the process they may have to revise radically their ideas of the type of leadership and authority structure which such parties may reasonably be expected to display.

The nature and role of party leadership are thus changing. Understanding these changes, and how they are affected by the many local contextual variables which it has been impossible to examine here, is an important task. Much more information is required on who joins social democratic parties today, who participates in local decision-taking, how this is translated into pressures on party leaders, and how both leaders and followers perceive their respective roles. Comparative data of this type are at present very thin on the ground, and the ideas presented in this chapter are, in consequence, very unevenly supported, but enough has been said to demonstrate that issues of party democracy and manageability are as important today as they were in academic debates about social democracy several decades ago, even if they now appear in a somewhat different guise.

Notes

1. These issues are discussed in D. Hine, 1982.
2. For resumés of the nature of this relationship, as it applies to the various parties listed in the paragraph, see the relevant chapters in Paterson and Thomas, 1977.
3. For an excellent statement of these issues see D. Heald, 1983. See also the series of articles under the general heading 'Critique et autocritique d'un modele' in *Le Monde diplomatique* (September 1981: 10–14) where some of the philosophical dilemmas posed by the social democratic model are analysed.
4. There have, of course, been some very serious efforts to provide this base, of which one of the best known is that by the Swedish economist, Meidner. See his defence of the employee-investment funds approach in Meidner, 1978. In Britain it is rather harder to point to such a central documentary source, but for a lively if critical account of how new policy approaches were developed in the Labour Party in the first half of the 1970s see Hatfield, 1978.
5. For a recent study of European experience of incomes policies over the last two decades see Flanagan, Soskice, and Ulman, 1983.
6. The literature on these issues is extensive. See Inglehart, 1977 and 1981. For an examination of these ideas as applied to German political culture see Baker, Dalton, and Hildebrandt, 1981.
7. On the social democratic victories in these three countries see Lyrintzis, 1983; Nash, 1983; B. Young, 1983; Wright and Machin, 1982; and Giner, 1984.
8. It is true that, after 1976, the PSI came under the control of a leader, Bettino Craxi, who styled himself very much in the image of his counterparts in other southern European social democratic parties, but despite this, in elections in 1983 and 1984 the party vote remained at

only around 11 per cent of the total, far below its sister parties. On the weight of the past as a factor preventing the PSI's electoral take-off see Pasquino, 1983.

9. For a brief discussion of these changes in Britain, in relation to the Labour Party, see Kavanagh, 1982B: 103–7.

10. Data in this paragraph are drawn from an unpublished study by the Gruppo Federal de Estudios Sociologicos, Pefil Sociologico del Militiante Socialista, summaries of which can be found in *Boletin PSOE* nos. 4 and 5, 1980 and no. 9, 1981; and also from J.F. Tezanos, 1983.

11. See, *inter alia*, D. Kogan and M. Kogan, 1981; Williams, 1983; and the chapters by Williams, Berrington, McKenzie, and Kavanagh in Kavanagh, 1982B.

12. Events summarized here are discussed in greater detail in Drucker, 1981.

13. For an account of the developments described in this paragraph see Wolinetz, 1977.

14. An interesting piece of research by Berglund, designed to test rational-actor models of political behaviour, which compared the attitudes of political leaders and party members in the SAP (and in the Moderate Party) produces evidence of a substantial identity of view between leaders and followers over a wide range of issues (Berglund 1980). Unfortunately there are no comparable data on other social democratic parties which would make it possible to tell whether the SAP really is different on this score.

15. The Valence congress was the first since the formation of the party which recorded complete unity, and that at Bourg-et-Bresse saw significant opposition only from the CERES group. For a brief account of the factional divisions in the party see Bell and Shaw, 1983: 26–32 and 45–62. See also Cayrol and Ignazi, 1983.

16. As Mitterrand's second Prime Minister, Laurent Fabius acknowledged in his declaration on taking office that there was not even 'the width of a cigarette paper' between the President's views and his own (*The Times*, 1984).

17. The literature in this area is extensive. See in particular the writings of Philip Schmitter, especially in S. Berger, 1979, and Schmitter and Lehmbruch, 1979. See also Flanagan and Dalton, 1984.

18. These issues are discussed in Pasquino, 1983: 29–33 and also in Cavalli, 1983.

BIBLIOGRAPHY AND INDEX OF AUTHORS CITED

Numbers in italics at the end of an entry refer to pages in this book on which the work in question is cited.

Albers, D. (1982). *Kapitalistische Krise und Strategien der Eurolinken* (Berlin: SPW Verlag). *162*

Alf, Sophie G. (1982). 'Die französiche Beschäftigungspolitik seit dem 11. Mai 1981', in *WSI-Mitteilungen*, no. 2 (February). *54 n. 9*

Allardt, Erik *et al.* (1981). *Nordic Democracy: Ideas, Issues, and Institutions in Politics, Economy, Education, Social and Cultural Affairs of Denmark, Finland, Iceland, Norway, and Sweden* (Copenhagen: Det Danske Selskab).

Andersen, Bent Rold (1984). 'Rationality and irrationality of the Nordic welfare state', *Dædalus* 113 (1): 109–39. *185*

Andersen, Jørgen Goul (1984a). 'Decline of class voting or change in class voting? Social classes and party choice in Denmark in the 1970s', *European Journal of Political Research* 12, 243–59. *191–2, 195, 197*

Andersen, Jørgen Goul (1984b). 'Aspekter af den politiske kultur i Danmark efter 1970', in Damgaard (1984b). *195*

Arblaster, Anthony (1977). 'Anthony Crosland: Labour's last "Revisionist"?', *Political Quarterly* 48 (4): 416–28. *104 n. 8*

Archer, Clive (1984). 'Deterrence and Reassurance in Northern Europe' (Aberdeen, Centre for Defence Studies: *Centrepiece* 6, Winter 1984).

Arter, David (1979). 'Die finnische sozialdemokratische Partei', in Paterson and Schmitz (1979). *187*

Arter, David (1985). 'The Nordic Parliaments: Patterns of Legislative Influence', *West European Politics* 8 (1), 55–70. *205*

Baker, K., R. Dalton, and K. Hildebrandt (1981). *Germany Transformed: Political Culture and the New Politics* (Cambridge). *141, 289*

Barry, R. (1982). 'Review', *Political Quarterly* 53 (3: July–September), 351–7. *108*

Bartolini, Stefano (1983). 'The Membership of Mass Parties; the Social Democratic Experience 1889–1978', in Daalder and Mair (1983). *188–9*

Baxter, R. (1972). 'The Working Class and Labour Politics', *Political Studies* 20 (1): 97–107. *107 n. 47*

Becker, Horst and Bodo Hombach (1983). *Die SPD von Innen.* *136*

Bell, D. S. (ed.) (1982). *Contemporary French Political Parties* (London: Croom Helm).

Bell, D. S. (ed.) (1983). *Democratic Politics in Spain* (London: Frances Pinter).

Bell, D. S. and B. Criddle (1984). *The French Socialist Party: Resurgence and Victory* (Oxford: Oxford University Press). *229, 232*

Bell, D. S. and E. Shaw (1983). *The Left in France* (Nottingham: Spokesman).

Benn, T. (1980). *Arguments for Socialism* (Harmondsworth: Penguin).

Berger, S. (ed.) (1979). *Organising Interests in Western Europe* (New York: Cambridge University Press). *290*

Berglund, Sten (1980). *Paradoxes of Political Parties: Rational Choice and Beyond* (Umeå: UPSA, Umeå Studies in Politics and Administration). *290*

Berrington, Hugh (1980). 'The Common Market and the British Parliamentary Parties, 1971: Tendencies, Issue Groups . . . and Factionalism' (Florence: ECPR Workshop paper). *277*

Berrington, Hugh (1982). 'The Labour Left in Parliament: Maintenance, Erosion and Renewal', in Kavanagh (1982b).

Bielka, E. (1983). *Die Ära Kreisky* (Vienna: Europaverlag).

Bilski, Raphaella (1977). 'The Common Market and the Growing Strength of Labour's Left Wing', *Government and Opposition* 12 (3): 306–31.

Bish, G. (1979). 'Drafting the Manifesto' in K. Coates (1979).

Bjerregaard, Ritt and Lars Lundegaard (1982). *Til Venner og Fjender af Dansk Socialpolitik* (Copenhagen: Gyldendal). *183*

Blecha, Karl (1979). *Die Nationalratswahl 1979: Strategie und Analysen* (Vienna: Karl Renner Institut). *57 n. 29*

Bochel, J. M. and D. T. Denver (1983). *The Scotsman*, 15 March.

Bochel, J. M. and D. T. Denver (1984). 'The SDP and the left–right Dimension', *British Journal of Political Science* 14 (3): 387–93. *114–15*

Boelling, K. (1982). *Die Letzten 30 Tage des Kanzlers Helmut Schmidt— Ein Tagebuch* (Hamburg). *149*

Bosanquet, Nick (1980). 'Labour and Public Expenditure: an Overall View', in Bosanquet and Townsend (1980). *54 n. 7*

Bosanquet, Nick and Peter Townsend (eds.) (1980). *Labour and Equality: A Fabian Study of Labour in Power, 1974–79* (London: Heinemann Educational).

Bound, J. and K. Featherstone (1982). 'The French Left and the European Community' in Bell (1982). *248, 252*

Boyce, R. W. D. (1980). 'Britain's first "No" to Europe: Britain and the Briand Plan 1929–30', *European Studies Review* 10 (1980): 17–45.

Braunthal, G. (1983). *The West German Social Democrats, 1969–82: Profile of a Party in Power* (Boulder, Colorado: Westview Press). *272–3, 281*

Braunthal, G. (1984). 'The West German Social Democrats: Factionalism at the Local Level', *West European Politics* 7 (1), 47–64. *137, 280*

Bremer, Hans-Hagen (1982). 'Paris schmeichelt den Patrons—aber "der Esel hat keinen Durst" ', *Frankfurter Rundschau*, 13 November 1982. *33*

Bremer, Hans-Hagen (1983). 'Paris entdeckt die Patrons', *Die Zeit* (18), 29 April 1983.

Brittan, Samuel (1975). 'The Economic Contradictions of Democracy', *British Journal of Political Science* 5 (2): 129–59. *8, 104 n. 8*

Bundesministerium der Finanzen (Federal Ministry of Finance) (1980). *Finanzbericht 1981* (Bonn).

Bundesministerium der Finanzen (Federal Ministry of Finance) (1981). 'Personalentwicklung bei Bund, Ländern und Gemeinden 1960–1980', *BMF-Finanznachrichten*, 14 October 1981.

Bundesministerium der Finanzen (Federal Ministry of Finance) (1982). *Finanzbericht 1983* (Bonn).

Bundesministerium für Arbeit und Sozialordnung (Federal Ministry of Labour and Social Affairs) (1978). 'Infratest-Studie über das Verhalten von Arbeitsuchenden und Arbeitgebern', *Sozialpolitische Informationen* (12), 10 July 1978.

Butler, David and Donald Stokes (1969). *Political Change in Britain: Forces Shaping Electoral Choice* (London: Macmillan). *6*

Butler, David and David Marquand (1981). *European Elections and British Politics* (London: Longman). *104 n. 11*

Byrd, Peter (1975). 'The Labour Party and the European Community, 1970–75', *Journal of Common Market Studies* 13 (4): 469–83.

Byrd, Peter (1978). 'The Labour Party and the Trade Unions', in Kolinsky (1978). *62, 104 n. 4, n. 9*

Castles, Francis G. (1975). 'Swedish Social Democracy: The Conditions of Success', *Political Quarterly* 46 (2), 171–85. *281*

Castles, Francis G. (1978). *The Social Democratic Image of Society: A Study of the Achievements and Origins of Scandinavian Social Democracy in Comparative Perspective* (London: Routledge and Kegan Paul). *180*

Cavalli, L. (1983). 'Nuovi leaders per un'Europa nuova', *Città e regione* 9 (3: June) 5–21. *290*

Cavalli, L. (1984). Plebiscitary Democracy in the West: The Socialist Case in Italy (Florence: Working Papers de Centro di Sociologica Politica, Facoltà di Scienze Politiche 'C. Alfieri', Universita degli Studi di Firenze, No. 1).

Cayrol, R. (1982). 'Le godillot et le commissaire politique: six contradictions à propos du Parti socialiste', *Projet* 161 (January): 32–41. *233*

Cayrol, R. and P. Ignazi (1983). 'Cousins ou frères? Attitudes politiques et conceptions du parti chez les militantes socialistes français et italiens', *Revue française de science politique* 33 (4), 629–50. *236, 290*

Cayrol, R. and J. Jaffre (1980). 'Party Linkages in France: Socialist Leaders, Followers and Voters', in K. Lawson (1980). *274*

Cayrol, R. and C. Ysmal (1982). 'Les militants du PS: originalité et diversités, *Projet* 165 (May), 572–86. *236*

Cerny, Karl H. (ed.) (1977). *Scandinavia at the Polls: Recent Political Trends in Denmark, Norway and Sweden* (Washington DC: American Enterprise Institute).

Cerny, Karl H. (ed.) (1978). *Germany at the Polls: The Bundestag Election of 1976* (Washington, DC: American Enterprise Institute).

Cerny, P. and M. Schain (eds.) (1985). *Socialism, the State and Public Policy in France* (London: Methuen).

Chaloupek, Günter (1979). 'Vollbeschäftigung im Alleingang? Gewerkschaftspolitik in Österreich seit der Rezession 1975', *WSI-Mitteilungen* (4: April 1979). *30*

Chandler, J., D. S. Morris, and M. J. Barker, (1982). 'The Ascent of Middle Class Politics: The Middle Class Membership of the Labour Party' (Unpublished paper presented to the Political Studies Association of the United Kingdom, Annual Conference, University of Kent). *97, 271*

Charlot, Jean (1982a). 'La gauche à la hausse', *Le Point* (507), 7 June 1982, 62–4. *57 n. 33 and n. 34*

Charlot, Jean (1982b). 'Sondage: le pouvoir en baisse', *Le Point* (532), 29 November 1982, 65–8. *57 n. 33 and n. 34*

Coates, David (1980). *Labour in Power? A Study of the Labour Government* (London: Longman). *62, 104 n. 3*

Coates, K. (ed.) (1979). *What Went Wrong?* (Nottingham: Spokesman).

Cox, Andrew (ed.) (1982). *Politics, Policy and the European Recession* (London: The Macmillan Press Ltd).

Crewe, Ivor, Bo Särlvik, and James Alt (1977). 'Partisan de-alignment in Britain 1964–74', *British Journal of Political Science* 7 (2), 129–90. *104 n. 7*

Crewe, Ivor (1982). 'The Labour Party and the Electorate', in Kavanagh (1982b). *52, 104 n. 7*

Crewe, Ivor (1983). 'Post Mortem: The disturbing truth behind Labour's rout', *The Guardian*, 13 June. *39, 55 n. 17, 60, 103 n. 1, 104 n. 7*

Criddle, B. (1969). *Socialists and European Integration: A Study of the French Socialist Party* (London: Routledge and Kegan Paul).

Criddle, B. (1977). 'The French Parti Socialiste', in Paterson and Thomas (1977). *265*

Cripps, Francis, *et al.* (1981). *Manifesto: A Radical Strategy for Britain's Future* (London: Pan). *105 n. 18*

Crosland, C. A. R. (1964). *The Future of Socialism* (London. Revised edition; originally published 1956). *3, 19, 72, 109*

Crouch, Colin (1979). *State and Economy in Contemporary Capitalism* (London: Croom Helm).

Daalder, Hans and Peter Mair (eds.) (1983). *Western European Party Systems: Continuity and Change* (London: Sage Publications). *v*

Dagens Nyheter (1982). 'Sysselsätningen vigtigast' (results of IMU opinion survey), 3 August 1982.

Dahlerup, Drude *et al.* (1975). 'Korporatisme-begrebet i studiet af samspillet mellem politiske institutioner', *Økonomi og Politik* 49 (4), 317–44. *189*

Dahlstrom, Edmund (ed.) (1959). *Svensk Samhällstruktur i Sociologisk Belysning* (Stockholm: Svenska Bokförlaget).

Dahrendorf, Ralf (1980). *Life Chances: approaches to social and political theory* (London: Weidenfeld and Nicolson). Ch. 5: 'The end of the Social Democratic Consensus?' *7*

Daly, Michael J. (1981). 'The Swedish approach to investing public pension funds: some lessons for Canada?', *Canadian Public Administration* 24 (2), 257–71. *201–2*

Damgaard, Erik (1977). *Folketinget Under Forandring.* (Copenhagen: Samfundsvidenskabeligt Forlag).

Damgaard, Erik *et al.* (eds.) (1984). *Dansk Demokrati Under Forandring* (Copenhagen: Gyldendal). *189*

Delors, Jacques (1981). 'Frankreich hat einen Rückstand aufzuholen' (interview), *Der Spiegel* (29), 13 July 1981, 86–8. *36*

Delors, Jacques (1982). 'Jedem sein Doktrin' (interview), *Wirtschaftswoche* (32), 6 August 1982, 63–7.

Delury, George E. (ed.) (1983). *World Encyclopedia of Political Systems* (New York: Facts on File and London: Longman).

Der Spiegel (1982). 'Opposition würde der SPD guttun' (results of Emnid opinion survey) (15), 12 April 1982, 43–51.

Der Spiegel (1983a). 'Zweifeln zu viele SPD-Wähler an der SPD?' (Results of Emnid opinion survey) (7), 14 February 1983, 34–7.

Der Spiegel (1983b). 'Ich muss jetzt nach Hause' (13), 28 March 1983, 135–7.

Döring, H. and G. Smith (eds.) (1982). *Party Government and Political Culture in Western Germany* (London: Macmillan).

Drucker, H. M. (1981). 'Changes in the Labour Party Leadership', *Parliamentary Affairs* 34 (4), 369–92. *290*

Due, Jesper, and Jørgen Steen Madsen (1980). *Overenskomstsystemets sammenbrud* (Copenhagen: Akademisk Forlag). *207*

Dunleavy, P. (1980). 'The Political Implications of Sectoral Cleavages and the Growth of State Employment. Part I: The Analysis of Production Cleavages'. *Political Studies* 28 (3), 364–83; and 'Part II: Cleavage Structures and Political Alignment', *Political Studies* 28 (4), 527–49. *270*

Dünsch, J. (1975). 'Party Elites and European Integration: The British Labour Party and Entry into the EEC 1970–74' (London: ECPR workshop paper).

Duverger, M. (1964). *Political Parties. Their Organisation and Activity in the Modern State* (London: Methuen, 3rd ed.). *89, 186, 261*

Ebsworth, P. (ed.) (1979). *Europe: A Socialist Strategy* (Edinburgh: Edinburgh University Student Publications Board).

Elder, Neil (1982). 'Continuity and innovation in Sweden in the 1970s', in Cox (1982). *181*

Ellis, Adrian and Krishan Kumar (eds.) (1983). *Dilemmas of Liberal Democracies: Studies in Fred Hirsch's Social Limits to Growth* (London: Tavistock). *9*

Emnid-Institut (1982). 'Regierungswechsel in Bonn im Meinungsbild der Bundesbürger' (survey), October (Bielefeld).

Esping-Andersen, Gosta (1978). 'Social Class, Social Democracy and the State: Party Policy and Party Decomposition in Denmark and Sweden', *Comparative Politics* 11 (1), 42–58. *11*

Fay, Stephen, and Hugo Young (1978). *The Day the Pound Nearly Died* (London: The Sunday Times). *62*

Featherstone, Kevin (1979). 'Labour in Europe: the work of a national party delegation to the European Parliament', in Herman and van Schendelen (1979).

Featherstone, Kevin (1981). Socialists and European Integration: the Attitudes of British Labour Members of Parliament', *European Journal of Political Research* 9:407–19.

Featherstone, Kevin (1982). 'Socialists and European Integration: A Comparison of the Attitudes held within the British Labour Party, the French Socialist Party and the Belgian Socialist Parties' (Manchester University, Ph.D. thesis). *250, 252*

Featherstone, Kevin (1983). 'The Greek Socialists in Power', *West European Politics* 6 (3: July): 237–50.

Flanagan, R. J., D. W. Soskice and L. Ulman (1983). *Unionism, Economic Stabilisation and Incomes Policies: European Experience* (Washington DC: The Brookings Institution). *289*

Flanagan, S. C., and R. J. Dalton (1984). 'Parties under Stress: Realignment and Dealignment in Advanced Industrial Societies', *West European Politics* 7 (1), 7–23. *290*

Flora, Peter, with Jens Alber and Jürgen Kohl (1976). 'On the development of the Western European Welfare States' (Edinburgh:

IPSA Conference Paper). *182*

Folketingsårbog 1979–80 (1980), comp. Arne Marquard (Copenhagen: J. H. Schultz Forlag).

Forester, Tom (1975). 'Labour's Local Parties', *New Society*, 25 September. *96*

Forester, Tom (1976). *The Labour Party and the Working Class* (London: Heinemann). *96*

Forester, Tom (1980). 'The Labour Party's Militant Moles', *New Society*, 10 January.

Frankfurter Rundschau (1981). 'Staatsbetriebe sollen Frankreichs Wirtschaft anheizen', 15 September 1981.

Frankfurter Rundschau (1983). 'Kleine Koalition in Wien?', 26 April 1983.

Gallup Political Index, 1975–82, various issues. *43, 55 n. 20, 57 n. 30*

Gamble, Andrew (1981). *Britain in Decline: Economic policy, political strategy and the British State* (London: Macmillan). *104 n. 8*

Gamble, Andrew (1983). 'Economic growth and political dilemmas: post-war policies in Britain', in Ellis and Kumar (1983). *14*

Garraud, P. (1978). 'Discours pratique et idéologie dans l'evolution du Parti Socialiste', *Revue française de science politique* (April), 273. *227*

Gaus, C. (1966). *Staatserhaltende Opposition oder Hat die SPD Kapituliert?* (Reinbech: Ro-Ro Verlag). *143*

George, Bruce, and Curt Pawlisch (1983). 'Defence and the 1983 British Election', *Armament and Disarmament Information Unit 5*, (July/August).

Gerlich, P. (1983). *Zwischen Koalition and Konkurrenz* (Vienna: Braumueller). *158*

Giner, S. (1984). 'Southern European Socialism in Transition', *West European Politics* 7 (2), 138–57. *289*

Glotz, P. (1984). *Die Arbeit der Zuspitzung* (Berlin: Siedler Verlag). *151*

Goodman, D. and David Hine (1982). 'The SDP in Newcastle-upon-Tyne: a survey-based analysis'. Unpublished paper for Political Studies Association of the United Kingdom Annual Conference, University of Kent. *114, 123*

Gruppe Politikinformationen am Internationalen Institut für Management und Verwaltung (1981a). 'Ausländerbeschäftigung und Arbeitsmarktpolitik', *Internationale Chronik zur Arbeitsmarktpolitik* (4: April), 1–4.

Gruppe Politikinformationen am Internationalen Institut für Management und Verwaltung (1981b). 'Frühverrentung im internationalen Vergleich', *Internationale Chronik zur Arbeitsmarktpolitik* (5: July), 1–4.

Gruppe Politikinformation am Internationalen Institut für Management und Verwaltung (1981c). 'Förderung der Beschäftigung durch Arbeitsumverteilung', *Internationale Chronik zur Arbeitsmarktpolitik* (6: October), 7–8.

Gruppe Politikinformationen am Internationalen Institut für Management und Verwaltung (1982). 'Die neue französische Beschäftigungspolitik', *Internationale Chronik zur Arbeitsmarktpolitik* (7: January), 1–4.

Gruppo Federal de Estudios Sociologicos, 'Perfil Sociologico del Militante Socialista' (1980 and 1981), *Boletin PSOE*, Nos. 4, 5 and 9.

Güllner, Manfred (1983). 'Zwischen Stabilität und Wandel: Das politische System nach dem 6 März 1983', *Aus Politik und Zeitgeschichte* (14), 9 April 1983. *51*

Haas, E. B. (1968). *The Uniting of Europe* (Stanford: Stanford University Press). *257*

Hall, P. (1985). 'Socialism in one country: Mitterrand and the struggle to define a new economic policy for France', in Cerny and Schain (1985). *229*

Hanley D. (1983). 'Thoughts on Steering the French Economy', in S. Williams (ed.) (1983). *236*

Hansen, Erik Jørgen (1982). 'The Progress Party in Denmark is a Class Party—But Which Class?', *Acta Sociologica* 25 (2) (1982): 167–76. *221*

Hardouin, P. (1978). 'Les caracteristiques sociologiques du Parti Socialiste', *Revue française de science politique* 28 (2: April), 220–56. *274*

Harenberg, Werner (1982). 'Sicherer Platz links von der SPD?', in Mettke (1982). *57 n. 32*

Hatfield, M. (1978). *The House the Left Built: Inside Labour Policy Making, 1970–75* (London: Victor Gollancz). *289*

Heald, D. (1983). *Public Expenditure* (Oxford: Martin Robertson). *289*

Heffer, Eric (1982). 'Socialist Europe', *New Socialist* (3), 26–9. *104 n. 12*

Heidar, Knut (1977). 'The Norwegian Labour Party: Social Democracy in a Periphery of Europe', in Paterson and Thomas (1977). *187*

Heidar, Knut (1983). *Norske politiske facta, 1884–1982 (Oslo: Universitetsforlaget)*. *187, 189*

Heidar, Knut (1984). 'Party Power: Approaches in a Field of Unfilled Classics', *Scandinavian Political Studies* 7 (1): 1–16. *186*

Henning, Roger (1981). 'Swedish Employment Policy' (Paper presented to workshop on selective labour market policies at joint sessions of the European Consortium for Political Research, Lancaster).

Herman, V. and M. P. C. M. van Schendelen (eds.) (1979). *The European Parliament and the National Parliaments* (Farnborough: Saxon House).

Hindess, Barry (1971). *The Decline of Working Class Politics* (London: MacGibbon and Kee). *107 n. 47*

Hine, D. (1977). 'Social Democracy in Italy', in Paterson and Thomas (1977). *265*

Hine, D. (1982). 'Factionalism in West European Parties: A Framework for Analysis', *West European Politics* 5 (1) 36–53. *265, 289*

Hirsch, Fred (1977). *Social Limits to Growth* (London: Routledge and Kegan Paul). *9*

Holland, Stuart (ed.) (1983). *Out of Crisis: a Project for European Recovery* (London: Spokesman). *107 n. 49*

Howell, David (1979). *British Social Democracy: A Study in Development and Decay* (2nd ed., London: Croom Helm). *104 n. 8*

Hughes, John (1979). 'Public Expenditure: The Retreat from Keynes', in Ken Coates (1979). *48*

Hvidt, Kristian (ed.) (1984). Folketingets Håndbog efter valget 10 januar 1984 (Copenhagen: A/S J. H. Schultz Bogtrykkeri). *173*

Infas (Institut für angewandte Sozialforschung) (1981). 'Gewerkschaftliche und Politische Orientierung in der Bundesrepublik: Bericht und Tabellen' (survey) (Bonn).

Inglehart, R. (1977). *The Silent Revolution* (Princeton: Princeton University Press). *132, 289*

Inglehart, R. (1981). 'Postmaterialism in an Era of Insecurity', *American Political Science Review* 75 (4), 880–90.

Institut für Demoskopie: various opinion surveys, 1975–82.

Institut der deutschen Wirtschaft (Institute for the German Economy) (1984). *International Economic Indicators 1984* (Cologne).

Ionescu, G. (ed.), (1972). *The New Politics of European Integration* (Basingstoke: Macmillan).

Jackson, Robert J. (1968). *Rebels and Whips: an analysis of dissension, discipline and cohesion in British Political Parties* (London: Macmillan). *77*

James, Janet (1983). 'An investigation into the relationship between the SDP and the Liberal Party: A Case Study of Bristol' (Bristol: Bristol Polytechnic, mimeo). *123*

Janson, C. G. (1959). 'Stadens Struktur', in Dahlstrom (1959). *197*

Johnson, N. (1982). 'Parties and Conditions of Political Leadership', in Döring and Smith (1982). *273*

Jospin, L. (1978). 'Des mots et des choses', *Nouvel Observateur*, 2 October: 55. *226*

Jowell, R. and G. Hoinville (eds.) (1976). *Britain into Europe: Public Opinion and the EEC 1961–75* (London: Croom Helm). *251*

Just, Dieter and Peter Röhrig (eds.) (1978). *Entscheidung ohne Klarheit: Anmerkungen und Materialien zur Bundestagswahl 1976* (Bonn).

Kaase, Max (1978). 'Public Opinion Polling in the Federal Republic of Germany', in Cerny (1978). *56 n. 22*

Kaldor, Mary *at al.* (1980). *The Report and Papers of the Labour Party Defence Study Group: Democratic Socialism and the Cost of Defence* (London: Croom Helm). *105 n. 22*

Kaltefleiter, Werner (1977). *Vorspiel zum Wechsel: Eine Analyse der Bundestagswahl 1976* (Berlin: Duncker and Humblot). *56 n. 23*

Kaufman, Gerald (ed.) (1983). *Renewal: Labour's Britain in the 1980s* (Harmondsworth: Penguin).

Kaur, Prunella (1983). *Go Forth and Multiply* (Bristol: Dialogue of the Death). *106 n. 39*

Kavanagh, D. (1982a). 'Still the Workers' Party? Changing social trends in Elite Recruitment and Electoral Support', in Kavanagh (1982b).

Kavanagh, D. (ed.) (1982b). *The Politics of the Labour Party* (London: George Allen and Unwin). *289, 290*

Keegan, William and R. Pennant-Rae (1979). *Who runs the Economy? Control and Influence in British Economic Policy* (London: Maurice Temple Smith). *62*

Kellner, Peter (1983). 'Anatomy of a landslide', *New Statesman*, 17 June (MORI Poll). *60, 103 n. 1*

Kerschgens, K. (1985). 'Gratwanderungen Zwischen Zwei Verlockungen—Tolerierung Einer SPD Minderheitsregierung', in W. Bickerich (ed.): *SPD und Grüne—Das Neue Buendnis* (Hamburg: Spiegel Verlag). *150*

Kesselman, Mark (1982). 'Prospects for democratic socialism in advanced capitalism: class struggle and compromise in Sweden and France', *Politics and Society* 11 (4), 397–438. *3, 180–1*

King, A. (1977). *Britain Says Yes* (Washington: American Enterprise Institute). *248*

Kirchheimer, O. (1966). 'The Transformation of the Western European Party Systems', in La Palombara and Weiner (1966). *128*

Kirchner, E. J. (forthcoming). *Liberal Parties in Western Europe* (Cambridge: Cambridge University Press). *v*

Kitzinger, U. (1968). *The Second Try: the Labour Party and the EEC* (London: Pergamon). *247*

Knapp, V. (1980). *Austrian Social Democracy 1889–1914* (Washington DC: University Press of America). *155*

Kogan, D. and M. Kogan (1981). *The Battle for the Labour Party* (London: Fontana). 2nd edition (1983). *105 n. 28, 106 n. 34 and n. 36, 290*

Kolinsky, Eva (1984). *Parties, Opposition and Society in West Germany* (Beckenham: Croom Helm). *134, 135, 136*

Kolinsky, Martin (ed.) (1978). *Divided Loyalties: British Regional Assertion and European Integration* (Manchester: Manchester

University Press).

Korpi, Walter (1983). *The Democratic Class Struggle* (London: Routledge and Kegan Paul). *196–7, 198*

Kreisky, Bruno (1983). ' "Bei uns gehen die Uhren anders" ' (interview), *Der Spiegel* (14), 4 April 1983, 126–35. *46, 53 n. 6*

Kriegel, A. (1979), in O. Duhamel and H. Weber (eds.), *Changer le PC?* (Paris: PUF), 178–95.

Kühlewind, Gerhard (1982). 'Die Beschäftigungspolitik Frankreichs', *Mitteilungen aus der Arbeitsmarkt und Berufsforschung* (3: October). *54 n.9*

Kühn, Karl (1979). 'Die Sozialdemokratie Schwedens,' in Paterson and Schmitz (1979). *187*

Labour Party (1982). *Labour's Programme 1982* (London). *53*

Labour Party Defence Study Group (1977). *Sense about Defence* (London: Quartet).

Lafay, Jean-Dominique (1982). 'Chômage et comportements politiques: bilan des analyses économétriques', *Revue Française de Science Politique* (4–5: August–October). *44, 56 n. 27*

La Palombara, J. and M. Weiner (eds.) (1966). *Political Parties and Political Development* (Princeton: Princeton University Press).

Lawson, K. (ed.) (1980). *Political Parties and Linkage* (New Haven and London: Yale University Press).

Layton-Henry, Zig (1983). *Conservative Parties in Western Europe* (London: Macmillan). *v*

Le Figaro-Magazine (1982): various SOFRES surveys in the issues of 9 January 1982, 8 May 1982, 8 July 1982, 4 September 1982, and 4 December 1982.

Le Monde (1983), 29 March.

Le Monde Diplomatique (1981) September, pp. 10–14: 'Critique et autocritique d'un modèle'.

Lever, Harold and George T. Edwards (1980). 'Why Germany beats Britain', *The Sunday Times*, 2 November 1980, 16–18. *34*

Lindbeck, Assar (1975). *Swedish Economic Policy* (London: Macmillan Press). *202*

Lipset, Seymour Martin (1959). *Political Man* (London, Heinemann). *5*

Logue, John (1982). *Socialism and Abundance: Radical Socialism in the Danish Welfare State* (Minneapolis: University of Minnesota Press). *195*

Löwenthal, R. (1981). 'Identität und Zukunft der SPD', *Neue Gesellschaft*, 1085–90. *144*

Lyrintzis, C. (1983). 'Il PASOK: leadership carismatica e "personale" politico emergente', *Città e Regione* 9 (3), 147. *285, 289*

Lyrintzis, C. (1984). 'Political Parties in Post-Junta Greece: A Case of

"Bureaucratic Clientelism" ', *West European Politics* 7, (2), 109–14. *285*

Machin, Howard and Vincent Wright (1982). 'Why Mitterrand won: The French Presidential Elections of April–May 1981', *West European Politics*, 5 (1), 5–35. *44*

Mackintosh, John P. (1978). 'Has social democracy failed in Britain?', *Political Quarterly* 49 (3), 259–70. *104 n. 8*

Madeley, John T. S. (1983). 'Norway', in Delury (1983).

Madsen, Henrik Jess (1980). 'Class Power and Participatory Equality: Attitudes towards Economic Democracy in Denmark and Sweden', *Scandinavian Political Studies* 3 (n.s.) (4): 277–98.

Mandrin, J. (pseud) (1983). *Le Socialisme et la France* (Paris: Eds. le Sycomore). *235*

Maraval, J. (1980). *The Transition to Democracy in Spain* (London: Croom Helm).

Marschalek, R. (1983). *Rot-Grüner Anstoss* (Vienna: Jugend und Volk). *169*

Martinet, G. (1979) in Rocard, M. (1979). *Qu'est-ce que la social-démocratie?* (Paris: Seuil). *224*

Mauroy, Pierre (1982). ' "Wir gehen unseren Weg weiter" ' (interview), *Der Spiegel*, (40), 4 October 1982, 158–65.

Meadows, D., D. Meadows, J. Randers and W. W. Behrens (1972). *The Limits to Growth: A Report from the Club of Rome's Project on the Predicament of Mankind* (London: Pan). *9*

Meidner, Rudolf (1975). *Löntagarfonder* (Stockholm). *200*

Meidner, Rudolf (1978). *Employee Investment Funds* (London: George Allen and Unwin). *282, 289*

Merkl, Peter H. (ed.) (1980). *Western European Party Systems: Trends and Prospects* (New York: The Free Press). *v*

Mettke, Jörg R. (ed.) (1982). *Die Grünen: Regierungspartner von morgen?* (Hamburg: Spiegel Verlag).

Michels, Roberto (1962). *Political Parties: A Sociological Study of the Oligarchical Tendencies of Modern Democracies* (New York: Collier Books. First published 1911). *134, 186, 232, 261*

Michie, Alistair and Simon Hoggart (1978). *The Pact: The Inside Story of the Lib–Lab Government, 1977–78* (London: Quartet).

Middel, B. P. and W. H. van Schurr (1981). 'Dutch Party Delegates', *Acta Politica* 16, April, 241–63. *274*

Miljan, T. (1977). *The Reluctant Europeans: the Attitudes of the Nordic Countries towards European Integration* (London: C. Hurst and Co.). *247*

Mintzel, A. (1975). *Die CSU: Anatomie Einer konservativen Partei* (Opladen: Westdeutscher Verlag).

Mishra, Ramesh (1984). *The Welfare State in Crisis: Social Thought and Social Change* (Brighton: Wheatsheaf Books Ltd.). *11–12*

Mitchell, Austin (1983a). 'Go for growth, not bureaucracy', *New Socialist* (10), 22–5. *105 n. 19*

Mitchell, Austin (1983b). *The Case for Labour* (London: Longman). *105 n. 19*

Mitterrand, François (1983). ' "Sans faiblesse et sans complaisance, soyez mobilisés au service de la France" ' (text of television address), *Le Monde*, 25 March 1983. *54 n. 11*

Morris, Max (1983). 'The Other Way that Labour is Not Working', *The Guardian*, 28 February. *97*

Morris, Nick (1982). 'To work or not to work', *New Statesman*, 26 November, p. 10. *56 n. 25*

Motchane, D. (1978). 'Les trois causes de l'échec de la gauche', *Nouvel Observateur*, 3 April, 41. *226*

Müller, Wolfgang C. (1981). 'Zur Genese des Verhältnisses von Politik und verstaatlichter Industrie in Österreich (1946–1981)', *Österreichische Zeitschrift fur Politikwissenschaft* (4). *30*

Nairn, T. (1972). *The Left against Europe?* (Harmondsworth: Penguin). *258*

Narr, W. D., H. Scheer, and D. Spöri (1976). *SPD—Staatspartei oder Reform Partei?* (Munich: Piper Verlag). *129*

Nash, E. (1983). 'The Spanish Socialist Party since Franco' in Bell, D. (1983). *265, 284, 289*

Nenning, Günther (1981). 'Eichler-Symposion. Diskussion', *Die Neue Gesellschaft*, 12 December, 1073–5. *49*

Neuwirth, Erich (1983). 'Analyse der Nationalratswahl 1983 aus statistischer Sicht', *Österreichische Zeitschrift fur Politikwissenschaft* (3). *56 n. 28*

Niedermayer, O. and H. Schmitt (1983). 'Social Structure and Party Organization' (Freiburg: unpublished paper for the workshop on party organizations, ECPR Joint Sessions of Workshops). *274*

Nielsen, Hans Jørgen (1982). 'Electoral politics and the corporate system: the question of support', *Scandinavian Political Studies* 5 (1): 43–65. *189–90*

Nielsen, Hans Jørgen (1984). *Valgundersøgelsen 1984*, (personal communication, 21 June 1984). *191, 192*

Nordisk Kontakt (political news summary issued by the Nordic Council), various issues.

O'Connor, James (1973). *The Fiscal Crisis of the State* (New York: St Martin's Press). *12*

OECD (1982). *Employment in the Public Sector* (Paris).

OECD (1983). *Main Economic Indicators* (May) (Paris).

Ormerod, Paul (1980). 'The Economic Record', in Bosanquet and Townsend (1980). *30*

Ostrogorski, Moisei (1902). *Democracy and the Organization of Political Parties* (London: Macmillan, 2 vols.). *186, 261*

Palme, Olof (1983). 'Wie Schweden die Krise bekämpfen will', (interview), *Zukunft* (theoretical magazine of the SPÖ), (1: January), 11–14. *25*

Palmer, John (1982). 'Britain and the EEC: the Withdrawal Option', *International Affairs* (London) 58 (4): 638–47. *107 n. 49*

Pasquino, G. (1983). 'La Strategia del PSI: tra vecchie e nuove forme di rappresentanza politica', *Critica Marxista* 1, 29–50. *289, 290*

Paterson, W. E. (1974). *The SPD and European Integration* (Farnborough, Saxon House). *246, 250, 253*

Paterson, W. E. (1975). 'The SPD after Brandt's Full-Change on Continuity', *Government and Opposition:* 165–86. *130*

Paterson, W. E. (1977). 'The German Social Democratic Party', in Paterson and Thomas (1977). *279, 280*

Paterson, W. E. and Kurt Th. Schmitz (eds.) (1979). *Sozialdemokratische Parteien in Europa* (Bonn: Verlag Neue Gesellschaft). *186*

Paterson, W. E. (1981). 'The Chancellor and his Party: Political Leadership in the Federal Republic', *West European Politics* 4 (2), 3–17. *135, 140, 273*

Paterson, W. E. and A. H. Thomas (eds.) (1977). *Social Democratic Parties in Western Europe* (London: Croom Helm). *v, 96, 160, 186, 289*

Paterson, W. E. (1985). 'The Union Parties', in Romoser and Wallach (1985).

Pedersen, Robert (1982). *Fra neutralitet til engagement: Socialdemoktratiet og forsvar gennem 110 år*. (Copenhagen: Chr. Erichsen).

Pelinka, A. (1981). *Modellfall Österreich?* (Vienna: Braumueller).

Pelinka, A. (1983). *Social Democratic Parties in Europe* (New York: Praeger). *1, 161, 167*

Pilz, P. (1982). *Die Panzermacher* (Vienna: Verlag für Gesellschaftskritik). *160*

Plant, R. (1983). 'Hirsch, Hayek and Habermas: Dilemmas of Distribution', in Ellis and Kumar (1983): 45–64. *9*

Plasser, Fritz and Peter A. Ulram (1983). 'Wahlkampf und Wählerentscheidung 1983: Die analyse einer kritischen Wahl', *Österreichische Zeitschrift für Politikwissenschaft* (3). *46*

Pollack, Benny (1983). 'The 1982 Spanish General Election and Beyond', *Parliamentary Affairs* 36 (2), 201–17. *284*

Portelli, Hughes (1980). *Le Socialisme française tel qu'il est* (Paris: PUF). *223, 225*

Projet Socialiste (1980) (The programme of the French Socialists) (Paris).

Rabinbach, A. (1983). *The Crisis of Austrian Socialism 1927–34* (London:

University of Chicago Press). *153*

Radice, Giles (1983). *The Guardian*, 8 July. *60*

Raschke, J. (1978). *Die politischen Parteien in Westeuropa* (Reinbeck: Rowohlt TB).

Rattinger, Hans (1979). 'Auswirkungen der Arbeitsmarktlage auf das Ergebnis der Bundeswahl 1976', *Politische Vierteljahresschrift* (1: May). *39*

Reif, Karlheinz (1981). 'Keine Angst, Marianne! Die fränzosische Präsidentschaftswahl 1981', *Aus Politik und Zeitgeschichte* (29–30), 18 July 1981. *44, 56 n. 27*

Renger, A. M. (1981). 'Kampf der Atomtod, Friedensbewegung, SPD—ein Lehrstuck', *Neue Gesellschaft:* 704–9. *143*

Richardson, J. J. and Roger Henning (eds.) (1984). *Policy Responses to Unemployment in the Western Democracies* (London and Beverly Hills: Sage).

Robins, L. J. (1979). *The Reluctant Party: Labour and the EEC, 1961–75* (Ormskirk: Hesketh). *104 n. 4*

Romoser, G. and K. Wallach (1985). *West German Politics in the mid-80s* (New York: Praeger).

Rose, Richard, and G. Peters (1977). *The Political Consequences of economic Overload* (Glasgow: University of Strathclyde, Occasional Papers). *8*

Rose, Richard (1979). 'Ungovernability: is there fire behind the smoke?' *Political Studies* 27: 351–70. *104 n. 8*

Sainsbury, Diane (1982). *Structural and functional hypotheses of party decline: how much do they explain in the case of the Scandinavian Social Democratic Parties?* (Aarhus: ECPR workshop on Problems of Party Government). *198–200*

Sales, Claude (1981). 'Sondage: le vote des demandeurs d'emploi', *Le Point* (437), 2 February 1981, 33–4. *39, 55 n. 18*

Särlvik, Bo (1977). 'Recent Electoral Trends in Sweden', in Cerny (1977). *56 n. 28*

Särlvik, Bo and Ivor Crewe (1983). *Decade of De-alignment: the Conservative Victory of 1979 and Electoral Trends in the 1970s* (London: Cambridge University Press). *104 n. 7*

Scase, R. (1977a). 'Social Democracy in Sweden', in Paterson and Thomas (1977). *281*

Scase, R. (1977b). *Social Democracy in Capitalist Society* (London: Croom Helm).

Scharpf, Fritz W. (1982). 'Massenarbeitslösigkeit und politischer Quietismus: Das Modell Deutschland', *Wirtschaftsdienst* (2: February). *37*

Schmidt, Helmut (1983). 'The inevitable need for American leadership', *The Economist*, 26 February 1983, 21–32.

Schmidt, Manfred G. (1981). 'Economic crisis, Politics and Rates of Unemployment in Capitalist Democracies in the Seventies', in Lehmbruch and Schmitter (1981). *54 n. 12*

Schmitter, Philippe C. (1979). 'Interest Intermediation and Regime Governability', pp. 287–317 in S. Berger (1979).

Schmitter, P. C., and G. Lehmbruch (eds.) (1979). *Trends towards Corporatist Intermediation* (Beverly Hills: Sage Publications). *290*

Selbourne, David (1983). *The Guardian*, 20 June. *60*

Seyd, Patrick and Louis Minkin (1979). 'The Labour Party and its Members', *New Society*, 20 September. *107 n. 46*

Seymour-Ure, C. (1982). 'The SDP and the Media', *The Political Quarterly* 153 (4: October–December): 433–42.

Shell, K. L. (1962). *The Transformation of Austrian Socialism* (New York: State University of New York Press). *153*

Shore, Peter (1983). 'The Purpose of Labour's Economic Programme', in Kaufman (1983). *105 n. 19*

SI (Federation of Swedish Industries) (1983). *The debate on collective wage-earner funds in Sweden* (Stockholm).

Sjöblom, G. (1978). 'The Swedish Party System in the Post-War Period' (paper presented to the colloquium on Recent Changes in Western European Party Systems, Florence, 15–19 December).

Skidelsky, R. (1979). 'The Decline of Keynesian Politics', in Crouch (1979). *8, 12*

Smith, Dan (1980). *The Defence of the Realm in the 1980s* (London: Croom Helm). *105 n. 22*

SNU: Det sikkerheds- og nedrustningspolitiske udvalg (1982). *Dansk sikkerheds politik og forslagene om Norden som kernevåbenfri zone* (Copenhagen: Forlaget Europa).

SOFRES (1981). Survey, *Nouvel Observateur*, 4 July, 37–40. *230*

Sonning, Steffan (1983). 'The employee fund issue moves toward a decision', *Current Sweden* (No. 309, October). *203*

SPD (Sozialdemokratische Partei Deutschlands) (1983). *Das Regierungs-programm der SPD 1983–7* (Bonn).

Stadler, K. R. (1982). *Adolf Schärf* (Vienna: Europaverlag). *153*

Stephens, John D. (1981). 'The Changing Swedish Electorate: class voting, contextual effects and voter volatility', *Comparative Political Studies* 14 (2), 163–204. *196–7, 198*

Sully, M. A. (1981a). *Political Parties and Elections in Austria* (London: Hurst). *153*

Sully, M. A. (1981b). 'Austria', *Tribune*, 24 July. *156*

Sully, M. A. (1982). *Continuity and Change in Austrian Socialism* (New York: Columbia University Press). *153, 155*

Swedish International Press Bureau (1982). 'Newsletter from Sweden'

(39), 15 October 1982, p. 5.

Sysiharju, Anna-Liisa (1981). 'Primary Education and Secondary Schools', in Allardt *et al.* (1981). *193*

Tezanos, J. F. (1983). 'Il rinnovamento della classe dirigente PSOE', *Città e Regione* 9 (3: June), 107–24. *284, 289*

The Economist Intelligence Unit (1982). *Coping with Unemployment: The Effects on the Unemployed Themselves* (London).

The Times, 3 September 1981. 'French Nationalization meant to aid economy'.

The Times, 27 August 1982. 'London Labour Councillors' Public Sector Ties'.

Thomas, Alastair H. (1979). 'Die Sozialdemokratische partei Dänemarks: Vorherrschaft, Niedergang und Wiederaufstieg', in Paterson and Schmitz (1979).

Thomas, Alastair H. (1983). 'Denmark', in Delury (1983). *187*

Thomas, Alastair H. (1985). 'The Danish Folketing Election of 1984', *West European Politics* 8 (1), 113–15. *173*

Tivey, L. (ed.) (1981). *The Nation-State* (Oxford: Martin Robertson).

Tschirner, Wolfgang (1978). 'Die Entwicklung der politischen Stimmung der Bevölkerung und ihre Bedeutung für die Bundestagswahl 1976', in Just and Röhrig (1978). *56 n. 22*

Turner, John E. (1981). 'The Labour Party: Riding the Two Horses', *International Studies Quarterly* 25 (3): 385–437. *105 n. 28*

Von Beyme, Klaus (1985). *Political Parties in Western Democracies* (Aldershot: Gower). *v*

Von Manikowsky, Arnim (1983). 'Wie die Arbeitslosen wählen wollen', *Der Stern* (9), 24 February 1983, 176–8. *39, 55 n. 17*

Von Rosenbladt, Bernhard (ed.) (1981). *Arbeitslose—ein Jahr später* (Research report of the Federal Ministry of Labour and Social Affairs) (Bonn). *37*

Warde, Alan (1981). *Consensus and Beyond: The Development of Labour Party Strategy since the Second World War* (Manchester: Manchester University Press). *104 n. 2, 110*

Webb, Norman and Robert Wybrow (eds.) (1981). *The Gallup Report* (London: Sphere). *55 n. 19*

Webber, Douglas (1982). 'Zwischen programmatischem Anspruch und politischer Praxis: Die Entwicklung der Arbeitsmarktpolitik in der Bundesrepublik Deutschland von 1974 bis 1982', *Mitteilungen aus der Arbeitsmarkt- und Berufsforschung*, 3 (October). *26, 50*

Webber, Douglas (1983a). 'The Crisis and Renewal of the Labour Party in Western European Perspective', unpublished paper, Centre of European Governmental Studies, University of Edinburgh.

Webber, Douglas (1983b). 'Combating and Acquiescing in

Unemployment? Crisis Management in Sweden and West Germany', *West European Politics* 6, (January).

Webber, Douglas and Gabriele Nass (1984). 'Employment Policy in West Germany', in Richardson and Henning (1984). *26, 48, 53 n. 5, 54 n. 15*

Webster, D. (1981). *The Labour Party and the New Left* (London: Fabian Tract No. 477). *272*

Wheaton, M. A. (1972). 'The Labour Party and Europe, 1950–71', in Ionescu (1972).

Whiteley, P. (1981). 'Who are the Labour Activists?', *Political Quarterly* 52 (2), 160–70. *107 n. 47, 272*

Whiteley, Paul (1982). 'The Decline of Labour's Local Party Membership and Electoral Base', in Kavanagh (1982b). *107 n. 46*

Whiteley, Paul (1983). *The Labour Party in Crisis* (London: Methuen). *104 n. 8, 106 n. 32, 107 n. 46*

Willis, F. R. (1971). *Italy Chooses Europe* (New York: Oxford University Press). *246, 250*

Williams, P. (1983). 'The Labour Party and the Rise of the Left', *West European Politics* 6 (4), 26–55.

Williams, S. (ed.) (1983). *Socialism in France* (London: Frances Pinter).

Wolf, A. (1978). 'Has social democracy a future?', *Comparative Politics* 11 (1: October): 100–25. *13*

Wolinetz, S. B. (1977). 'The Dutch Labour Party: A Social Democratic Party in Transition', in Paterson and Thomas (1977). *274, 290*

Wolinetz, S. B. (1983). 'La leadership e il potere nel Partito Socialista olandese', *Città e Regione* 9 (3: June) 135–8. *273–4, 279*

Worcester, R. (1981). 'Disillusioned from Warrington vote SDP', *New Statesman*, 11 November: 3.

Worre, Torben (1980). 'Class Parties and Class Voting in the Scandinavian Countries', *Scandinavian Political Studies* 3 (4), 299–320. *192*

Wösendörfer, Johann (1980). *Beurteilungskriterien für das Arbeits-marktförderungsgesetz* (Linz). *30*

Wright, A. W. (1981). 'Socialism and Nationalism', in Tivey (1981). *256*

Wright, V. and H. Machin (1982). 'Why Mitterrand won: The French Presidential Elections of April–May 1981', *West European Politics* 5 (1), 5–35. *289*

Wright, William E. (1971). 'Comparative Party Models: Rational-Efficient and Party Democracy', in Wright (ed.), *A Comparative Study of Party Organisation* (Columbus, Ohio: Charles E. Merrill). *89*

Yearbook of Nordic Statistics 1984, vol. 23 (Copenhagen: Nordic Council and Nordic Statistical Secretariat).

Young, A. (1983). *The Reselection of MPs* (London: Heinemann). *276*

Young, B. (1983). 'The 1982 Elections and the Democratic Transition in Spain', pp. 132–46 in Bell, D. (1983). *289*

INDEX

European policy (*cont.*):
 conditions for joining EEC (1962),
  247; EC membership opposed, 246;
  in government, 247, 251; national
  sovereignty and, 248, 254–7
 government by, 181
 House of Lords abolition vetoed, 80
 incomes policy, lacked, 52–3
 Labour Co-ordinating Committee, 68
 leadership, 103
 leadership, election (1976), 64
 leftward move, 14, 250
 Lib–Lab pact (1977–8), 65
 local government, 102
 manageability, 263, 277
 manifesto (1983), 74, 99
 membership: composition, change
  in, 271–2; decline, 96; middle-class,
  96–7; trade unions and, 95;
  working-class members, loss of, 112
 'party democracy' model, 86, 88–9
 party structure, 89
 Peace, Jobs and Freedom, 74
 policies not popular, 66
 recovery, basis for, 101–3
 reform of party constitution, 67–8,
  77–90; democracy and, 276–7;
  effects, summarized, 86–8;
  electoral college, 80, 81–5;
  extra-parliamentary activity and,
  86–7, 99, 100; manifesto, control
  of, 79–80; parliamentary and party
  democracy, 89, 96; 'party
  democracy model', 77, 96; party
  leadership, 80–6, 89; reselection of
  MPs, 77–9, 86–7, 101; social
  democrats and, 113; trade unions
  and, 89–90, 99
 St. Ermin Group, 94
 Social Democratic Party, v, 52, 101
 social democratic wing of, 65, 67
 trade unions links, 61, 63, 64, 89, 101,
  102, 262, 263; 'white-collar' and
  public-sector unions, 277
 'ultra-left': Anti-Nazi League and, 90;
  'entryism', 91–3; ex-Communists
  (1956 and 1968) and, 90; Militant
  issue, 90–4; 'proscribed list'
  abolished (1973), 92
Labour Party (Ireland), European
 integration and, 248, 252, 254
Labour Party (PvdA) (Netherlands):
 anti-Americanism, 278

 factionalism, 278
 manageability, 263
 membership composition, 273–4
 'New Left' and, 277–8
Labour Party (DNA) (Norway), 2,
 Ch. 7 *passim*
 decline of, 198–200, 281
 defence policy review, 211–12
 dominance and, 177–8, 220
 European Communities and, 178
 membership, 187–9, 199, 220
 NATO and, 210–13
 trade union links, 262, 264
 young voters and, 195
Labour Solidarity, 94
Lafontaine, Oskar, 142, 150–1
Lahnstein, Manfred, 131
Lajoinie (PCF parliamentary leader),
 235–6
Lambsdorff, Count, 132
Lassalle, Ferdinand, 1
Leber, Georg, 145
Left Socialists (Denmark), 213–14, 216
Leinen, Jo, 151
Leninist principles, 1
Lestor, Joan, 63, 84
Leverküsener Kreis, 138
liberal parties:
 coalition with SPÖ (Austria), 50
 electoral support for, 44
 Liberalism 'outmoded', 6
 Liberal Party (Denmark) (*Venstre*),
  172, 190
 Liberal Party (Sweden), 21
 Liberal Party (United Kingdom):
  alliance with SDP, 52, 53, 59,
  122–3; Bermondsey by-election
  success, 98; devolution and, 65;
  differences from SDP, 123;
  Lib–Lab pact (1977–8), 65
 Liberal People's Party (Finland), 177
 Liberals in Belgium, and ECSC, 252
 Liberals (Norway) and 1985 election,
  178
Liebknecht, Karl, 127
Limehouse Declaration (SDP), 93,
 113–14, 124–5
Liverpool City Council, 102–3
Livingstone, Ken, 91, 102
Lloyd George, David, 10
London Labour Briefing, 91
Luxemburg, Rosa, 127